# TRUE TO MY GOD AND COUNTRY

STUDIES IN ANTISEMITISM
Alvin H. Rosenfeld, *editor*

FRANÇOISE S. OUZAN

# TRUE to MY GOD and COUNTRY

How Jewish Americans
Fought in World War II

INDIANA UNIVERSITY PRESS

This book is a publication of

Indiana University Press
Office of Scholarly Publishing
Herman B Wells Library 350
1320 East 10th Street
Bloomington, Indiana 47405 USA

iupress.org

© 2024 by Françoise S. Ouzan

All rights reserved
No part of this book may be reproduced or utilized in any form or by any means, electronic or mechanical, including photocopying and recording, or by any information storage and retrieval system, without permission in writing from the publisher. The paper used in this publication meets the minimum requirements of the American National Standard for Information Sciences—Permanence of Paper for Printed Library Materials, ANSI Z39.48–1992.

Manufactured in the United States of America

First printing 2024

Cataloging information is available from the Library of Congress.
ISBN 978-0-253-06826-2 (hardback)
ISBN 978-0-253-06827-9 (paperback)
ISBN 978-0-253-06828-6 (ebook)

In memory of Lieutenant Hadar Goldin, who fought bravely and gave his life for his country.

# CONTENTS

*Acknowledgments* ix

*List of Abbreviations* xiii

Introduction: Unexpected Encounters  1

1. "True to My God, True to My Country"  16

2. Invisibility of Jews in the Military?  32

3. Heroines Took to the Skies  51

4. Confronting Biased Attitudes  69

5. Operation Torch and Local Jews  95

6. Religiosity in the Pacific and India  115

7. Prisoners of War of the Japanese  138

8. Camaraderie beyond Prejudice  159

Conclusion: Bridging Worlds Apart  183

*Notes*  197

*Bibliography*  227

*Index*  239

# ACKNOWLEDGMENTS

This book is part of a series of volumes in the timely Studies in Antisemitism collection. Its conception partly originates in colorful accounts related by my relatives in North Africa about American service members. American and British GIs landed on French soil with the daring amphibious invasion of Algeria and Morocco during Operation Torch on November 8, 1942. Their epic story of tenacity and courage ignited my fascination with World War II. I imagined the weary and homesick young men and valiant women (from the Women's Army Corps) sharing their Friday night meals or Jewish holiday celebrations with local Sephardic Jews, feeling a renewed sense of family warmth. Thanks to these servicemen and servicewomen, a generation of North African youth—harshly discriminated against by antisemitic Vichy laws—discovered the delight of Hershey's chocolate bars and Wrigley's chewing gum. In turn, GIs were surprised by culinary novelties such as wheat-grain couscous, a staple dish of their time in North Africa.

During my research, I interviewed French people from North Africa who clearly remembered their encounters with American military personnel in the years 1942–43. Emile Moatti, Max Benhamou, and Denise Zerah spontaneously related to me their gripping memories. They emphasized that the landing of American and British troops in Algeria raised the morale of local Jews, who had been stripped of French citizenship by drastic Vichy laws. I was surprised to find references to seeing violent anti-Jewish slogans on the walls of public buildings in the written testimonies of American service members; housed at the YIVO Institute for Jewish Research in New York, these writings captured this memory of infamy that shaped their American Jewish identity. This is an opportunity to thank the YIVO team, in particular archivist Gunnar Berg, for helping me delve into the World War II memoirs collected in 1946.

I am also grateful to various archival institutions for making their archives available online, including the Library of Congress and its Veterans History Project; the United States Holocaust Memorial Museum; the Museum of Jewish Heritage-A Living Memorial to the Holocaust, in New York, in particular Treva Walsh, who made available interviews of women in the military; the Museum of Jewish Military History in Washington, DC, especially Pamela Elbe; as well as Gail Pietrzyck at the Delaware Jewish Archives, and the staff at the William Breman Jewish Heritage and Holocaust Museum in Atlanta, Georgia. My visit to the immense National World War II Museum in New Orleans was literally an immersion into a war that was fought on many fronts.

This book examines the fascinating transformations of women and men in the military resulting from interactions both within the military and with Jews and their communities abroad. In this research, I benefited from the guidance of noted scholars, including Jonathan Sarna, who helped me locate precious sources and shared with me his insights into American Jewish history. Inspiring conversations with Atina Grossman at Cooper Union in New York convinced me that the topic of American Jewish military personnel could benefit from more research. Alvin Rosenfeld, founding director of the Institute for the Study of Contemporary Antisemitism at Indiana University, encouraged my analysis of anti-Jewish attitudes in the military and made invaluable suggestions. I am glad that Gary Dunham, the director of Indiana University Press, displayed enthusiasm for this book. I am most grateful to the three anonymous reviewers who generously offered constructive remarks. I also appreciate the manner in which Derek Penslar challenged my views on the subject of American Jewish soldiers in World War II during a webinar on the subject.

Help in finding maps to locate various countries and cities visited by American military personnel was offered by Michael Neiberg. Jeff Goldberg, the West Point cartographer at the United States Military Academy Department of History, was prompt in giving permission and assistance to reprint maps in this volume.

I am happy to thank those who generously shared the scrapbooks of their fathers, diaries, memories, precious military documents, and Jewish community newspapers published during World War II. This list includes Howard Rosen, Noam Tzion, Ruth Tomases Joffe, Faith Tomases, Arthur Tomases, and Frieda Macarov, as well as Jonathan and Deena Parmet and David Dichon. Even if I did not use all the firsthand testimonies kindly provided to me, they greatly shaped my understanding of the uniqueness of GI war experiences, expressions of patriotism, and sense of self-sacrifice. I am indebted to Dr. David Geffen, a military chaplain during the Vietnam War, for sharing the testimonies of his father, an officer and judge advocate in the United States Army, of the war crimes trials in Japan in 1945. He made available his own research on World War II, and we have a rich ongoing dialogue. I am particularly grateful to him for sharing his correspondence with the two Fenichel children, whose father (Captain Benjamin Fenichel) volunteered as a doctor in the American army and served on the Solomon Islands. I want to thank his daughter, Sandy Asher, for allowing the publication of rare documents and photos. Artistic reproductions of the World War II illustrations by "soldier in art" Arthur Szyk were kindly permitted by Irvin Ungar, the expert on this artist. Szyk fought with passion for the recognition of the Jewish people and for human rights and dignity. Unexpectedly, USO venues that welcomed soldiers and their families during World War II exhibited his works throughout the United States.

Above all, I express my heartfelt gratitude to my academic home, Tel Aviv University's Goldstein-Goren Diaspora Research Center for its generous support, and its director, Professor Roni Stauber. His dedicated staff, in particular Sara Appel and Adi Moscowitz, kindly offered expertise to prepare my manuscript and secure permissions. Shimrit Hadad and Anat Shimoni were always quick to respond to my various inquiries, as was the former head of the Mehlmann Library, Sofia Tel-Abramov, who tirelessly provided dusty books from the basement holdings. My deep thanks also go to Professor Simha Goldin, who initiated a project on Jewish soldiers in 2014. My colleagues Lylya Belenkaya, Galit Haddad, and Dror Segev deserve a special word of thanks for keeping my morale up while dealing with the heartrending memoirs of American soldiers. For this book, my faithful language editor, Yochai Goell, went above and beyond the call of duty and located references for me. I am also grateful to Elissa Rosenberg, who edited two chapters. As the reader can imagine, this volume required the support of an army of good-natured people, and I extend my thanks to all of them and particularly to my publisher.

I gratefully acknowledge the support of the entire team of Indiana University Press for their unflinching commitment to moving this project forward from beginning to end. This applies in particular to Anna Francis, assistant acquisitions editor, who enthusiastically worked on my book with her colleagues in other departments to ensure that this volume would engage a broad range of readers and spark inspiring discussions.

I am appreciative of the guidance of Lesley Bolton, project manager, and Stephen Williams, marketing manager at Indiana University Press. I extend my gratitude to Vinodini Kumarasamy at Amnet systems for her editorial assistance in reviewing the manuscript.

As always, my special thanks go to Elisha and our children for asking relevant questions.

In appreciation to the Conference on Jewish Material Claims Against Germany (Claims Conference) for supporting this research project and publication.

# LIST OF ABBREVIATIONS

| | | | |
|---|---|---|---|
| AJC | American Jewish Committee | POW | prisoner of war |
| ATS | Auxiliary Territorial Service (women's branch of the British army) | USO | United Service Organizations |
| | | WAAF | Women's Auxiliary Air Force (British) |
| CANRA | Committee on Army and Navy Religious Activities (of the National Jewish Welfare Board) | WAC | Women's Army Corps |
| | | WAFS | Women's Air Force Ferry Service |
| JAVA | Japanese American Veterans Association | WASP | Women Air Force Service Pilots |
| JDC | American Joint Distribution Committee | WAVES | Women Accepted for Volunteer Emergency Service (US Navy Corps) |
| JWB | National Jewish Welfare Board | WJC | World Jewish Congress |
| JWV | Jewish War Veterans | | |

# TRUE TO MY GOD AND COUNTRY

# INTRODUCTION
## Unexpected Encounters

Norman Mailer wrote his best-selling war novel *The Naked and the Dead* after serving in the Philippines during World War II. Published three years after the end of the war, his fiction paints a vivid portrait of anti-Jewish prejudice in the army. Mailer compassionately portrays the pain of Private Goldstein, one of his Jewish characters, on hearing a truck driver "with a round red face" curse "the goddam Jewboys." The young author describes how the character "felt an awful depression: that kind of face was behind all the pogroms against Jews."[1]

Along with the fear, discomfort, and longing for home that all American soldiers experienced during the war, Jewish service members often confronted prejudice in the American military both on the home front and overseas. One of the aims of this book, however, is to challenge the notion that being Jewish was mainly a burden for servicemen and servicewomen. The rich testimonies that veterans provided in the immediate aftermath of the war, or some years later, form the basis of this study. Through their accounts, this volume explores how Jewishness was a significant asset for soldiers adjusting to army life overseas.[2]

Of the sixteen million American men and women who served in the military in World War II, more than half a million were Jews. They served in every branch of the military and every theater of the war, from Europe to the South Pacific to North Africa and the China-Burma-India theater. Encounters with Jewish communities and Jews overseas played a central role in strengthening American Jewish identities during World War II.[3]

Drawing on personal narratives, interviews, and memoirs, the book offers an intimate account of the soul-searching of young men and women leaving home—and their Jewish neighborhoods—for the first time. Jewish GIs' encounters encouraged them to fight antisemitism both among fellow members of the armed forces and in the war against Nazi Germany and its allies. While some branches of the American military forbade keeping a diary for security reasons, most soldiers remembered signs of anti-Jewish hostility of varying degrees. In his memoir *Leaving Home*, famous American humorist Art Buchwald, who served in the Marines in the Pacific, recalled: "I often found myself in fistfights over my Jewish persuasion. A few of the men in our squadron had problems with Jews, either because they had never met any or because there were not many Jews in the Marine Corps. Once you were called a dirty Jew, or even just a Jew, you had no choice but to fight or risk being considered a Jewish coward."[4]

Buchwald clearly described the additional mental pressure felt by Jewish service members in World War II. This emotional aspect was crucial to the social behavior of Jews in the military. Their stress was even more pronounced when they were estranged from Jewish observance: "I wasn't big and I wasn't strong, and I wasn't even *bar mitzvahed*, but when someone challenged me for being Jewish, adrenaline surged through my body, and I just kept swinging with tears in my eyes."[5]

The columnist analyzed various manifestations of anti-Jewish prejudice, including accusations of being a Christ killer, not being good at anything, or not being "military material." While denouncing the constant psychological stress that antisemitism generated for Jewish soldiers, he also noted that some Jewish soldiers were inclined to interpret any negative remark as antisemitic: "Like most Jews, I always assumed that the only reason anyone picked on me was that they were antisemitic."[6] That remark helps explain why mental stress might have been pervasive for Jewish soldiers. When they saw that fighting antisemitism led nowhere and could even be detrimental, some soldiers gave up on constantly defending their self-respect. Such an attitude may have been wrongly interpreted as passivity. Yet humor and derision apparently helped Buchwald overcome the stings and slurs of anti-Jewish hostility: "I can't tell you how exhausting it is to continually defend all the Chosen People. The antisemitism I experienced was mild, if you don't include the time Fedlock broke my thumb because he said I had killed Christ."[7]

Such confrontations consumed energy needed to survive everyday fighting in hostile environments. Buchwald's witty remarks point to another consequence of anti-Jewish attitudes: creating solidarity. Many Jews felt responsible for fighting in the name of Jewish peoplehood. The humorist offered two main conclusions from his wartime experiences. First, he fought for "the honor of a being a Jew in the Pacific," and second, he succeeded in becoming integrated into the Marine Corps through a fistfight.

Antisemitism is a leitmotif in most of the GI memoirs collected by the YIVO Institute for Jewish Research in 1946. This theme raises a number of questions: Did the expression of anti-Jewish feelings or stereotypes in the armed forces foster anxiety, anger, fear, passivity, or aggressiveness in Jewish soldiers? If so, how did these emotions weaken or perhaps reinforce the soldiers' Jewish identities, whether religious or secular? To what extent did encounters with welcoming Jewish communities in French North Africa and India strengthen Jewish identities and empower these young men and women? An analysis of the concept of feeling at home in distant countries is crucial here. This phenomenon occurred in Jewish communities in the arid landscape of North Africa whose customs, both familiar and different, instilled a sense of belonging to a larger Jewish diaspora.

This book builds on the research of previous scholars in the field. Deborah Dash Moore argues, based on rich vignettes of fifteen Jewish soldiers, that the war was a transformative period for servicemen who had to cope with antisemitism.[8] Military service empowered these soldiers as Jewish men and as Americans. My volume adds the stories of women to this narrative through documentation of the adventurous and sometimes tragic experiences of Jewish servicewomen in different theaters of the war. Hasia Diner and Beryl Lieff Bendersky offer a historical panorama of Jewish women who played important roles in shaping American culture.[9] I adopt a similar perspective here by detailing the wartime involvement of many intrepid young women serving their country.

Approximately ten thousand Jewish women enlisted in the US Armed Forces during World War II. For the first time in American history, thousands of women volunteered to take administrative or technical jobs in the military to "free the men" to fight in the infantry. Women also brought Jewish values to their patriotic enlistment, serving in the Women's Army Corps (WAC), the Women Accepted for Volunteer Emergency Service (WAVES) of the American Navy Corps, and as nurses overseas. Countless Jewish women served courageously both stateside and overseas. As members of the armed services in the war effort, they also joined the SPARS (Semper Paratus—Always Ready), an arm of the US Coast Guard established by the United States Congress and signed into law by President Roosevelt in November 1942.[10]

Many of the women who volunteered in various branches of the military did not reveal their Jewish background until much later in their lives.

This was the case for Juliette Jenner Stege, a former Broadway dancer and member of the Ziegfield Follies cast who enlisted and became an aircraft pilot in the Women Air Force Service Pilots (WASP) program.

Women risked their lives in dangerous assignments. In the South Pacific, First Lieutenant Yetta Moskowitz wore a thirty-eight-caliber revolver in case her plane was shot down and the crew had to bail out in enemy territory. Servicewomen, like their male counterparts, faced challenges such as surviving in difficult jungle terrain. After rigorous basic training, many underwent a significant transformation, acquiring courage and mental and physical strength. Their war experiences in the American military empowered them as Americans, as Jews, and as women. In turn, these daring servicewomen inspired and emboldened generations of American women—Jews and gentiles alike.

Selma Kantor Cronan was among the striking women who challenged the social order of the 1940s. Cronan participated in various postwar flying competitions, including the three high-ranking All Women's Transcontinental Air Races held across the United States, known as the Powder Puff Derbies. The WASP pilots' relentless efforts to obtain recognition as World War II veterans only bore fruit in 1977. Bernice Falk Haydu led the struggle, backed by other women pilots whose war experiences had toughened them. Jewish servicewomen had firsthand knowledge and experience with Jews not being welcome in the workplace—even if they had broken the glass ceiling as women fliers during and after the war. Like Haydu and other WASP pilots, Betty Haas Pfister received the Congressional Gold Medal in the Oval Office in 2009. Like the more than one thousand women who had qualified for employment as noncombat pilots of aircraft in the US Army Air Forces during the war, these women pilots had ferried military planes and tested them after repairs. Why did recognition come so late? Perhaps one reason for the long delay is these women's defiance of the social and symbolic order of the 1940s. Unlike the flying nurses, who symbolized tenderness, pilots may have been viewed as a threat as they competed for jobs toward the end of the war.

This volume offers new archival materials that shed light on the servicewomen and servicemen's diverse and sometimes colorful personalities and their evolving Jewish identities. This broad examination of Jewish service in the European and Pacific theaters documents little-known interactions with local Jewish populations in French North Africa and analyzes their long-lasting impact. It includes unpublished sources and personal interviews with French Jews residing in French North Africa during World

War II. Focusing on the encounters between service members and Jewish communities or Jewish families fills a gap in the historiography. These interactions not only strengthened GIs' Jewish identities but also bridged a cultural gap. Ashkenazi American Jews who had never been exposed to Sephardic traditions became aware of the similarities and differences between the cultures. They understood that being Jewish does not only mean belonging to an all-Jewish American neighborhood. For the first time, they identified with the Jewish diaspora abroad despite varying community traditions.

These interactions instilled in them a sense of Jewish peoplehood, which helped them face antisemitic slurs within the military. Being the "adopted GI" of a North African Jewish family brought comforting feelings of home. The archival material also reveals the impact that Jew-hatred had on American soldiers in North Africa; young Jewish soldiers who fought heroically in Oran (Algeria) were impacted by witnessing anti-Jewish insults inscribed in French in the streets. They learned that discriminatory measures were applied more severely there than in France. This experience reinforced their determination to defeat the Nazis. It shaped their understanding of what it means to be an American, at home and abroad: to safeguard freedom and democracy and fight discrimination wherever it rears its ugly head. In that respect, my approach provides a Jewish perspective to Atkinson's book *An Army at Dawn: The War in North Africa, 1942–1943*, the narrative of which begins in November 1942, on the eve of Operation Torch. Jewish GIs also discovered, to their amazement, that Jews who fled Nazism and found refuge in Tunisia ran the risk of being arrested. A few refugees from Germany and Austria who worked as interpreters in Tunisia were deported by the SS when their identities were discovered—a lesser-known historical point.

While historian Martin Sugarman has admirably detailed the ordeal of Jewish prisoners of war (POWs) and internees from Commonwealth and Dutch forces in the Far East, the experiences of American Jewish POWs of the Japanese have not been fully documented.[11] Diaries and testimonies from soldiers in Germany, sent to me by the GIs' families, enrich and broaden the discussion of issues often raised in memoirs. Based on archival material, I examine the ordeal of captivity at the hands of the Japanese and compare the fate of Jewish POWs when captured by the Nazis. In particular, I analyze how American Jewish prisoners' use of improvised religious rites to express their Jewish identity sustained their morale in the Pacific. These intimate accounts provide a new lens to view religious observance and challenge the widespread perception of a singular form of Jewish identification in the military. My discussion of what it meant to be an American citizen and a Jew in the military during World War II expands on Jessica Cooperman's analysis of Jewish engagement in the American armed forces during World War I.[12]

My volume also builds on Derek Penslar's deconstruction of the myth of Jewish draft dodging. *Jews and the Military* evinces that Jews have frequently been willing to do military service.[13] In World War II, Penslar emphasizes, Jews sought to prove themselves as soldiers and to fight *Amalek*, or evil.[14] My analysis of the letters and testimonies of American servicemen and servicewomen in WWII provides the basis for an emotional history that charts their responses to antisemitic slurs. Through first-person accounts, this book deepens understanding of the Jewish military experience from the perspective of service members themselves, complementing Joseph Bendersky's analysis of anti-Jewish hostility in the US Army's higher ranks.[15]

More specifically, servicemen and servicewomen's encounters with anti-Jewish prejudice changed their perceptions of what it meant to be American citizens and Jews. Jewish service members translated the words "fighting for democracy" into fighting Hitler. In this way, many reclaimed their Jewish identity and place in American society. Their selflessness and excellence in combat would help them gain acceptance—or so they thought.

Finally, this work adds to the larger cultural history of twentieth-century American Jewish life. It chronicles the experiences of American Jewish service members during a period when Jewish culture was beginning to take its place within the cultural mainstream. Tracing the effects of Judaism on society in the postwar era, Jonathan Sarna has pointed out that books by Jewish authors, including those by Jewish veterans, "broke into the mainstream book market, bringing fame to their authors and introducing the American reading public to Jewish themes and characters."[16] Irwin Shaw's *The Young Lions* and Norman Mailer's *The Naked and the Dead* were both published in 1948. A year earlier, the film *Gentleman's Agreement*, based on Laura Z. Hobson's best-selling novel of the same name, courageously gave voice to the pervasiveness of anti-Jewish discrimination in the United States. The film won an Academy Award for best picture. Sarna observes that "in different ways, all of these works condemned antisemitism as Un-American, presented Jews in a new and more sympathetic light and promoted intergroup understanding and tolerance."[17]

After finishing their basic training at other camps, a group of recent immigrant soldiers completed intensive training at Camp Ritchie, Maryland, and became known as "Ritchie Boys." They made significant contributions to the intelligence services—during and after the war—with their knowledge of languages, specifically the German language and culture. These GIs could deftly extract crucial tactical information from German POWs. The Jewish refugees' fierce motivation to fight the Nazis who persecuted their families made them the best soldiers in every frontline unit. Their paths, however, were strewn with hurdles. Alexander Breuer, for example, was born in Austria in 1926 and fled Nazism, crossing the Atlantic in 1938. Called "Fritz" by his schoolmates because of his heavy accent, he found it difficult to be associated with the Germans as a Jewish refugee. When he tried to enlist at the beginning of the war, he was automatically rejected on the grounds that he was an "enemy alien." Mistrusted refugees suffered humiliating rebuffs. The US Army eventually drafted Breuer at the age of eighteen and sent him overseas as an infantry replacement.[18] Veteran testimonies bring these poignant stories to light.

Harrowing personal narratives describe how service members' attitudes toward Jewish issues and their identification as Jews shaped their experiences. David Macarov's wartime encounters were especially formative. Eager to fight Hitler, Macarov volunteered to serve after the attack on Pearl Harbor. He was sent to the Pacific front and spent two years as a weather forecaster observer in the China-Burma-India theater, often "mortared and bombed." There he met members of the Jewish community in Calcutta. The relationships he developed with them strengthened Macarov's Jewish identity and influenced his Zionist views.[19]

Who is a Jew? That question has always been difficult to answer—and even more so during World War II. On December 29, 1942, the US Army ruled that every soldier was to wear identification tags (so-called dog tags) when on the battlefield or garrison duty. GIs could decide to wear a dog tag that bore the letter H for "Hebrew," revealing their identity as Jews and allowing them to be identified for Jewish burial. However, that decision could be life-threatening if captured by the Nazis. They could be tortured, sent to a concentration camp, or put to death immediately. Adding the H made the dog tag doubly emotional, confronting the soldier with his own potentially imminent death. The Committee on Army and Navy Religious Activities (CANRA) of the National Jewish Welfare Board (JWB) notes that chaplains made every effort to inform bereaved families whether their loved ones had received a Jewish burial. Yet a report indicates that "a large percentage of the Jewish casualties were not buried under the Star of David."[20]

Along with their Christian counterparts, Jewish chaplains dodged bombs and shared soldiers' cramped conditions and canned rations. More than half of the rabbis in the United States volunteered for the chaplaincy; only 311 were accepted to serve in all branches of the armed forces, a small number often deplored in letters by military personnel in North Africa and even more so in the Pacific Islands.[21]

One of the numerous tasks of rabbis in uniform was to raise troop morale—for Jews and non-Jews alike, as chaplains performed interdenominational services for all faiths. Chaplain Earl Stone, who served in the early days of the North African campaign, remained in a trench under constant fire for some fifty days until the unit whose fate he shared was relieved. Chaplain Irving Tepper boosted the morale of an infantry unit that was the first to enter Bizerte, Tunisia. He was later killed in action in France by a Nazi fragmentation bomb. These rabbis in uniform were the first representatives of American Jewry to make contact with local Jewish communities. In Morocco and Algeria, Jewish soldiers could not all be put up with well-to-do French-speaking members of the Jewish community for the Sabbath and Jewish holidays. Some were sent to the narrow streets of the Kasbah, the poor Jewish quarter, which GIs referred to as "ghettos" in their personal accounts. They often experienced a joyous, colorful, warm welcome as men, women, and children kissed their sleeves. Some locals would shout "me Jew too," seeking a shared empathy to which many soldiers responded with a "spontaneous understanding," movingly expressed in their written testimonies. Other locals would venture the well-known Hebrew phrase "Shalom Aleichem!" In a letter, Chaplain Earl Stone wrote that he rejoiced to find in Oran a "very fine Jewish community with a most gorgeous synagogue." Most Jewish soldiers were deeply moved by the warmth of encounters with local Jews.[22] In turn, they impressed a generation of Jews from French North Africa, eventually recognized as Holocaust survivors by the Conference on Jewish Material Claims against Germany. The author vividly remembers hearing her parents, then young teenagers, elaborate tales describing the meaningful interactions they had with American soldiers.

The landing of American and British troops in Casablanca, Oran, and Algiers on November 8, 1942—known as Operation Torch—thwarted the Vichy Regime's plan for the deportation of Jews from French North Africa and uplifted the mood of the local Jewish population. As a chaplain,

Louis Werfel observed that "it was an inspiring sight to watch those French-speaking, Sephardic-familied youngsters, about 200 of them, singing the same Palestinian songs that our youngsters sing back in the US." On a foggy day in December 1943, Werfel was killed in an airplane crash as he was flying to conduct a service in a remote place.[23]

My examination of chaplains' multifaceted role demonstrates how these rabbis at war rekindled the flame of Judaism and helped the American military understand the unique needs of Jewish service members.[24] Organizing Jewish holiday observance was easier in Europe, North Africa, or India, where Jewish communities existed, than in the Pacific. The JWB planned Passover observance for most places overseas where Jews were serving. General Eisenhower himself oversaw the delivery of one thousand packages of kosher Passover food to bedridden patients in the European theater of operations. As we will discover, the Pacific Islands' hot climate and hostile environment did not deter service members from celebrating the Jewish New Year and Passover in 1943.

This picture would not be complete without "the story the figures tell," as Isidore Kaufman, a distinguished war reporter aptly put it. Interpreting the findings of the National Jewish Welfare Board's War Records Bureau, he emphasized the contributions of the Jewish men and women in the American armed forces during World War II. Overall, the Jewish casualties among American forces—the dead, wounded, captured, and missing in action—authenticated up to July 1, 1946, amounted to more than 35,000. Of the 10,500 Jews who died in service, 8,000 fell in combat. As with their non-Jewish fellow GIs, the loss was cruelly felt within the family unit. More than fifty Jewish families lost two sons—and one family lost three. Medals awarded posthumously were of little comfort. Patriotism was so intense in some Jewish families that four families contributed eight members each to the military, while nineteen numbered six members in the armed forces. Some 36,000 Jews in uniform received awards for valor and merit. These figures somehow indicate their love for their country and willingness to sacrifice for the United States.[25]

Throughout history and in various countries, Jews have fulfilled their obligations to serve in the military—whether in times of peace or war. Both in France and French North Africa, Jews defended French soil. In the British Empire and the Soviet Union, a common enemy united Jewish servicemen and servicewomen: Nazi Germany, whose goal was to annihilate Jews worldwide. Derek Penslar points out an important difference between the two world wars. During World War I, Jews fought other Jews.

During World War II, over one and a half million Jews joined the Allied forces; a third fought in the US Armed Forces and another third served in the Russian army. The rest were mostly from Europe, the largest group of which comprised about one hundred thousand Polish Jewish soldiers. They fought (in vain) in defense of their country against the massive German invasion that began on September 1, 1939.[26]

One of the questions this study raises concerns Jewish self-identification and its implications. The book's thematic chapters variously address this question for Jewish service members based on letters and personal narratives. Scholars who have focused on Russian Jews in the military often emphasize that Russian servicemen and women considered themselves fervent patriots. The example of the twenty-one-year-old fighter pilot and heroine Lidiya Vladimirovna Litvyak is revealing. Litvyak was posthumously awarded the "Hero of the Soviet Union" decoration in 1990 by President Mikhail Gorbachev. Russian female fighter pilots were the only women who engaged in combat during World War II. The Germans nicknamed them "The Night Witches," as they dropped bombs on enemy territory through the veil of darkness. Born in Moscow to Russian Jewish parents, Litvyak seemed to have internalized from her school years the essence of "motherland." Russia became her allegorical mother, inherent in the perception of her identity. Yet her Jewishness may have strengthened her relentless determination to shoot down German planes.[27]

Letters from Soviet Jews serving in the military reveal that Jews felt compelled to prove their use to the motherland by being intrepid combatants. The state viewed them as Jews—even if they did not identify with Jewish culture and religion.[28] Since Jews like Lidiya Litvyak felt more vulnerable than other citizens, they were eager to prove that they were capable of heroic feats during World War II. Therefore, they volunteered for dangerous missions, as did Jewish soldiers in all the Allied armies. The significant participation of Jews in the Red Army and the great number of decorations and promotions they received confirm that stance. During World War II, 154 Jews received the award of Hero of the Soviet Union, the highest military honor.[29] Jews' patriotic duty to the Red Army was heightened by news of the Nazi annihilation of European Jewry, which gave rise to the formation of a Jewish division in February 1943, led by Abram Margolis, commissar of the Thirty-Second Infantry Division.[30]

Several testimonies show that assimilated French Jews in the Free French Forces volunteered first and foremost out of patriotism. This was the case of André Zirnheld, a Jew of Alsatian origin born in Paris in 1913 who served as a member of the Free French Air Force in the French Squadron, Special Air Service (SAS). At the outbreak of the war in 1939, Zirnheld, then working as a philosophy professor, was sent to Lebanon, where he joined an antiaircraft unit. After the French surrender, he joined the Free French Forces in British Mandatory Palestine. He was assigned to the First Colonial Infantry Battalion and served as a private in the battle of Sidi Barrani (December 10–11, 1940), the first British attack of the western desert campaign. Sent to the French Congo for officer training, he finished the course with the rank of lieutenant. After training as a paratrooper, he fought behind enemy lines with the Third French SAS. He died in combat in 1942 in Benghazi, Libya, during the North African campaign. On his last mission to destroy enemy planes, he and his team successfully planted explosives on six German bombers. He is remembered for his poem "The Prayer," which became known as "The Prayer of the Paratrooper." It was found in a notebook on his body, buried in a sand dune in the desert. In collective memory, Lieutenant Zirnheld remains the first French paratrooper officer killed in action. His Jewish identity (duly kept in the private sphere in secular France) has largely been ignored or rendered invisible. The prayer he addressed to God has been adopted by French paratroopers and the Foreign Legion. It is either recited or sung by heart. Other French Jewish paratroopers included Commanding Officer Maurice Rheims, born in 1910 and miraculously released from the French detention camp of Drancy, later known as the "antechamber of death" for Jews deported from France. The son of a French general in World War I, he distinguished himself as a member of the Free French Forces with the Allied troops in Algiers. Of the four hundred paratroopers serving there, about one hundred were Jews, including fifteen officers. French Jews accounted for 10 percent of the Allied Intelligence Service, whereas they only represented 1 percent of the French population. The highest military honors were accorded to these French patriots and heroes, such as the *Médaille Militaire*, *Croix de Guerre*, and *Médaille de la Résistance*.[31]

Conflicting feelings arose among British Jewish soldiers in the immediate postwar period. For instance, Woolf Marmot, a patriotic serviceman in the British army, refused to intercept a ship of Holocaust survivors bound for the Jewish homeland in Palestine. He commented on his dilemma with an understatement: "Being a Jewish British soldier sent to Palestine was not a pleasant job." Fortunately, his commanding officer was understanding and transferred him. He knew that Woolf had been among the first soldiers to fight at Anzio, Italy, in 1943, where he was wounded.[32] This brief comparison between countries helps understand how Jewish service members coped with issues linked with the hyphenation of American Jewish identity.

Chapter 1 concentrates on what motivated Jewish men and women to enlist. While fighting the Nazis was meaningful for most American Jews, service members also had to wage a battle against the negative portrayal of Jews as draft dodgers, cowards, and poor military material. Besides patriotism, some Jewish youth were motivated to enlist to suppress self-doubts about their capabilities as soldiers. This desire may be one reason why a significant number volunteered for frontline duty or dangerous missions. The refugees who fled Nazism displayed the greatest motivation to defeat Hitler. Their determination added to the patriotism they felt for their new country.

Chapter 2 focuses on servicemen and servicewomen's choice to be identified as Jews. This decision impacted whether they would be buried according to Jewish law. It also affected the accuracy of the registered number of Jewish casualties and Jewish participation in World War II. In October 1944, a group of fifty Jewish soldiers, GIs among them, expressed a vital urge to pray together—on German soil. The first broadcast of Jewish religious service from Nazi Germany, near Aachen and under enemy artillery fire, testifies to the need to affirm the Jewish faith, the essence of which lies in its perpetual reaffirmation.

Chapter 3 describes the experiences and hardships of Jewish servicewomen, who were among the nearly 350,000 American women serving in uniform in World War II. WACs were sent throughout North Africa, Europe, and the Philippines, serving on bases or close to the front. Although they were not sent overseas, WASP members were the first women in history to fly military aircraft. The chapter appraises the capabilities and selflessness of women pilots, mechanics, and flight nurses and the dangerous missions they undertook. Through letters, interviews, and narratives, Jewish servicewomen highlighted the nontraditional roles they played in these positions and the hurdles they had to overcome.

Chapter 4 discusses anti-Jewish attitudes in the military, shedding light on various ways in which soldiers responded to slurs they perceived as antisemitic and on the impact of this hostility on their Jewish identity. Instead of encouraging the suppression of identification as Jewish, anti-Jewish attitudes may have led to the reawakening or appearance of feelings of religiosity. The chapter also examines what the concept of heroism meant for American Jewish soldiers. Heroism as a response to prejudice appears throughout the artworks of celebrated artist Arthur Szyk, exhibited at over five hundred recreation centers intended for GIs.

Chapter 5 analyzes soldiers' diverse encounters with Jewish communities in North Africa during and after Operation Torch in November 1942. It articulates how meeting Jews abroad not only broadened soldiers' horizons but also helped them fight homesickness. Whether in the home of French Jews in Algeria for Sabbath meals and Jewish festivals or in Morocco or Tunisia, these encounters played an important role in encouraging soldiers to engage in the war.

The Pacific theater is the setting for chapter 6. Even in hostile territory, the Jewish New Year was observed and endowed with deep, cathartic meaning. A glimpse into the Jewish community of Manila in the Philippines is provided through three in-depth accounts of American soldiers, while testimonies of two former GIs transport us to India—Bombay and Calcutta—during the war in the Pacific. The chapter also unveils how, in 1946, the ceremony of the New Year of the Trees became part of the rehabilitation program for the devastated island of Okinawa. Chaplain Moshe Sachs and the American Jewish servicemen on the island took the unusual initiative to plant trees with the participation of local Japanese high school children.

What gave Jewish POWs of the Japanese the strength to survive in horrific conditions? Were their encounters with chaplains (both Jewish and non-Jewish) of any help? In what ways did Jewish POW experiences of captivity in the Pacific differ from those of POWs of Jewish origin in Germany? These questions are addressed in chapter 7, which details how Jewishness provided POWs with a form of spiritual resilience.

Chapter 8 examines how camaraderie helped service members overcome the stress of war, anguish, and hunger. Through various examples, I explore the bonds of GIs (among them infantrymen and flying crews) who shared the experience of battle and captivity. Jewish servicewomen, too, suffered the ordeal of internment under the Japanese. In these exceptional circumstances, wartime contacts among Jews and Christians broke through barriers of prejudice. In a significant case study, the postwar impact of camaraderie between Jews and non-Jews was found to extend even to the families of sympathetic Japanese guards in POW camps. This camaraderie also involved Japanese Americans—Nisei—who helped secure crucial intelligence and, like the Ritchie Boys, save American lives.

Fig. Intro.1 World War II Europe, 1943. Courtesy of The United States Military Academy Department of History. Public domain.

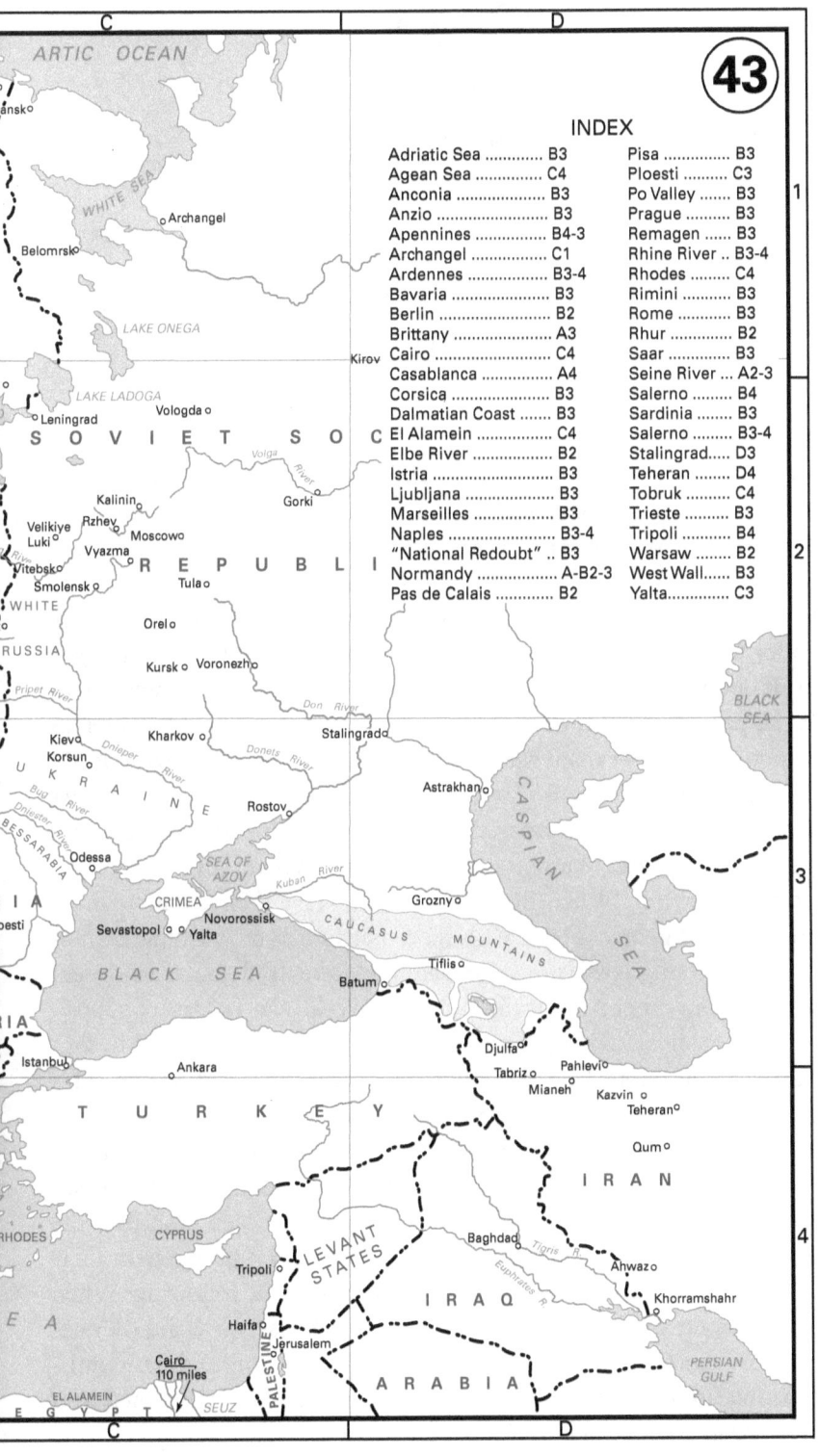

## INDEX

| | | | |
|---|---|---|---|
| Adriatic Sea | B3 | Pisa | B3 |
| Agean Sea | C4 | Ploesti | C3 |
| Anconia | B3 | Po Valley | B3 |
| Anzio | B3 | Prague | B3 |
| Apennines | B4-3 | Remagen | B3 |
| Archangel | C1 | Rhine River | B3-4 |
| Ardennes | B3-4 | Rhodes | C4 |
| Bavaria | B3 | Rimini | B3 |
| Berlin | B2 | Rome | B3 |
| Brittany | A3 | Rhur | B2 |
| Cairo | C4 | Saar | B3 |
| Casablanca | A4 | Seine River | A2-3 |
| Corsica | B3 | Salerno | B4 |
| Dalmatian Coast | B3 | Sardinia | B3 |
| El Alamein | C4 | Salerno | B3-4 |
| Elbe River | B2 | Stalingrad | D3 |
| Istria | B3 | Teheran | D4 |
| Ljubljana | B3 | Tobruk | C4 |
| Marseilles | B3 | Trieste | B3 |
| Naples | B3-4 | Tripoli | B4 |
| "National Redoubt" | B3 | Warsaw | B2 |
| Normandy | A-B2-3 | West Wall | B3 |
| Pas de Calais | B2 | Yalta | C3 |

# "TRUE TO MY GOD, TRUE TO MY COUNTRY"

Some observers contend that there would be little need to focus on Jewish servicemen and servicewomen's motivation to enlist if the subversive voices of anti-Jewish propaganda in American society had not sown seeds of suspicion regarding Jews and their patriotism. Thanks to the spontaneity of oral testimony and the diverse experiences of young men and women, the reader will discover to what extent the commonly held view of the Jew as a draft dodger is but a lasting stereotype. In addition, this chapter challenges the perception of the war experience of Jewish men and women as one of victimization—even if their last wartime encounter was with death.

Over the course of World War I, approximately 225,000 American Jews enlisted in the US military, prepared to sacrifice their lives for their country and national values out of a sense of moral duty. General John J. Pershing praised their service: "When the time came to serve their country under arms, no class of people served with more patriotism or with higher motives than the young Jews who volunteered or were drafted and who went overseas with our other Americans."[1] During World War II, fervent opposition to Hitler motivated over 550,000 servicemen and servicewomen to contribute to the war effort. Leaving home to discover the world was an extra incentive. Above all, patriotism often intersected with Jewish identity. Selma Cronan, a certified civilian pilot before the war, enlisted in the Women Airforce Service Pilots (WASP) to fight Hitler in hopes of being sent overseas.

It is interesting to explore how Jewish men and women described the impulse they felt when enlisting after Pearl Harbor, complying with their official call to duty. A few relevant questions include the following: When and in what contexts did they mention their Jewishness? How did they explain the influence of Jewish identity on their patriotism? Did basic military training fulfill the expectations of servicemen and servicewomen who had never been away from home?

Jewish men faced many challenges during their military service, but their motivation to answer the call of duty often made the experience worthwhile. Their perceived masculinity was enhanced in the process; they were empowered as men and American Jews from basic training through various war experiences.[2]

### Patriotism, Belonging, and Jewish Identity

Bernard Branson, whose family name was Abramson during his army service, was eager to fight for his country. Patriotism, a desire to fight Hitler, and a sense of adventure stirred him into action: "I graduated at sixteen, in 1941. There was a war on, so what you did was you waited to get old enough to go into the army.... I used to work at the Brooklyn Navy Yard delivering telegrams. I remember seeing the HMS *Barham* come in. It was a British battleship, which had been pretty shot up, and I would go down there and look at it and I couldn't wait to get into service."[3] Branson dreamed of the Army Air Corps, but the Marines wanted him. He recounted the story of his induction, when he received a stamped letter: "It said 'Army,' And I'm like Oy!, that's what I wanted. I'd always wanted the army ever since I was a kid.... And then my mother made me swear—and that was the only thing—on my father's grave that I would not fly as a pilot. I would not try to be a pilot. She had a thing with the military. She had a son in the military.... He was a radar man when it was still top secret." Among other motivations to join the army, finding a way to belong was important at a time when Jews were socially rejected, unwanted in certain jobs, and victims of quotas (as in some colleges).

Young Art Buchwald spent his childhood in an orphanage and several foster homes; shortly after his birth, his mother was admitted to a mental hospital, where she remained confined for the last thirty-five years of her life. His father, a curtain manufacturer, was unable to support the family during the Great Depression. The only son and youngest of four children, he fled his home to join the military at age seventeen. At the news of the war, he said, "I'm going to fight for my country."[4] Wearing the American uniform and serving in the Marines or air force was a dream for numerous young men, Jews included. Most of them had never been away from their neighborhoods.

Art Buchwald's motivation to leave home and join the military was so strong that he bribed a vagrant in the streets to sign as his legal guardian. "You have to be my father for an hour," exclaimed the young Art. The vagrant replied, "That's very patriotic." Was Art Buchwald eager to belong for the first time in his short life? Was he eager to embark on an adventure? In any case, years later, the famous humorist would say that his "father was the Marine Corps," not hesitating to reiterate this assertion in various ways.[5] He spent most of his two years in the Pacific on an atoll cleaning machine guns as an ordnance man. The future columnist also edited his squadron's newsletter, "The U-man Comedy," a two-to-four-page leaflet with squadron news and jokes to boost soldiers' morale.[6] Of the new recruits who relieved his squadron, whereby "guaranteeing his survival," he wrote: "The next stop for the squadron was Okinawa, where the new men saw far too much action from the kamikazes."[7] Discharged as a sergeant, Buchwald expressed gratitude to the army for having made him feel "at home" after "leaving home": "I owe the Corps a lot. When I meet another Marine, we share a bond. It's like belonging to the same lodge.... I can now say without hesitation the Marine Corps was the best foster home I ever had."[8]

Eager to belong and integrate, European refugees were thankful for their new country and keen to avenge themselves on Nazi Germany. That was the case for Maximilian Lerner, whose parents were emigrants from Vienna. They had first fled by going to France: "On September 4, 1942, when I was eighteen, I volunteered. I didn't want to wait to be drafted. I signed away my right as a foreigner. And I remember standing and getting it notarized.... And they didn't call me in for induction until I reported for duty the beginning of May 1943. I had anticipated they would get me sooner. Mysterious are the ways of the army.... This was my war and I wanted the opportunity to get my own back.... You know, at eighteen you're invulnerable."[9] Maximilian Lerner had only been in the United States for two and a half years when he joined the American military. Like many refugees fluent in German, Lerner was assigned to the Military Intelligence Training Center at Camp Ritchie, Maryland. He found there a group primarily made up of emigrants from Germany. Along with other Jewish refugees, he joined experts on Germany, Japan, and Italy—the enemy countries. Army life brought changes to his practices as an observant Jew, yet he was willing to adjust: "I stopped putting on tefillin [phylacteries], but I kept kosher to the extent that I could. It meant occasionally not having the main dish and filling up on potatoes or bread; it was not onerous."[10]

The refugee soldiers were stationed at Camp Ritchie for intensive instruction after completing basic training. Lerner became an American citizen in September 1943. He and his group (made of German and Austrian Jewish refugees) shipped out to Europe in March 1944. Once in Paris on

August 25, 1944, he interrogated German soldiers and prisoners brought by the Forces Françaises de L'Intérieur (FFI), "The Résistance." Some missions carried out by other "Ritchie Boys" involved considerable risks, such as going on patrol to capture prisoners when there were not enough prisoners for questioning. Guy Stern, a scholar of German and comparative literature, fled Nazi Germany and escaped to the United States in 1937. He became a "Ritchie Boy" while his whole family—deported to the Warsaw ghetto—perished. Young refugees in uniform played a pivotal role in highly classified missions. Most were eager to exact revenge on their former oppressors. Their determination and courage saved American lives: "Sergeant Sy Lewin was charged with inducing Germans to surrender. He approached the German front lines and, using a microphone, appealed directly to the enemy to capitulate. His sound truck was blown up several times. Sergeant Tom Angress jumped behind German lines during our initial paratroop attack just hours prior to D-Day without ever having jumped before."[11] A few days later, Werner Tom Angress was captured behind enemy lines; he was personally motivated to take revenge on Hitler and the Nazis who had humiliated him so much. A prisoner of war (POW), he managed to conceal his identity as a German-born Jew. Finally freed by advancing American forces, he rejoined the fight. He, too, became a shrewd battlefield interrogator. As a former victim of Nazi persecution, Angress was shocked at the liberation of the Wöbbelin concentration camp. So was Manfred Steinfeld, a Ritchie Boy who had fled Germany without his family, arrived in the United States in 1938, and joined the army in 1943. In the Military Intelligence Specialist Unit, he was attached to the Eighty-Second Airborne Division and took part in the entire Normandy invasion on June 6, 1944. He also participated in most of the central European campaigns.[12]

To better understand soldiers' desire to prove themselves in combat, it is rewarding to turn to archives kept from their basic training. For instance, the lines of the Rifle Creed might have made an impression on servicemen.

> This is my rifle. It is my best friend—without it, I am helpless. Without me, it is useless.
>
> I will master my rifle as I will master my life—I will know it as I know myself. I will know its strength and its weakness, its balance, its sights, its "feel."
>
> My rifle will be cleaned before I am cleaned, before I eat, before I rest. It will be ready always. I will be true to my rifle and guard it from weather

and dirt, from all harm or damage. As I guard my rifle, so it will guard me in time of danger, shoot straight and destroy the enemy that would destroy us both.

I am true to my God, true to my country and true to my rifle, we will conquer.

Right from basic training in Camp Pickett, these words were distributed and read aloud. Herman J. Obermayer went through basic training multiple times, including combat engineer basic training. They were "somber words" each time he heard them during basic training.[13] Others saw handling a rifle as an opportunity to prove that they were no coward. The courageous medics in the battlefields, who carried no rifle because the Geneva Convention forbade it, accounted for a high proportion of casualties among the Jews. As a medic, Hyman Epstein's motivation to remain his "brother's keeper"—a Jewish value—even on a bloody battlefield is worth recalling. Epstein, a young medical aide from Omaha, Nebraska, risked his life for others under heavy shell fire from Japanese troops in New Guinea. The last twelve hours of his altruistic dedication to his buddies were recounted thus by another soldier: "But the Japs knew we were all there and kept their fire in that spot. . . . But this little Jewish kid crawls right from the mud to the wounded man."[14]

A few paragraphs of a letter written "in the possibility of my not coming back," found on the body of a boy of eighteen, encapsulate Jewish Americans' motives for fighting. Corporal Harold Katz of the Bronx suffered serious wounds in an attack on the German town of Attweilnau on March 30, 1945. He received the Silver Star but was killed in action shortly after. The letter reads as follows.

Dear Mom,

Mom, I want you to know that I asked for combat assignments. I did so for several reasons. One is that I had certain ideals within my own mind, for which I have often argued verbally. I didn't feel right to sit safely far behind the lines while men were risking their lives for principles which I would fight for only with my lips. I felt that I also must be willing to risk my life in the fight for freedom of speech and thought I was using and hoped to use in the future. Another reason is the fact that I am Jewish. I felt again it wasn't right for me to be safe behind the lines while others were risking their lives with one of their goals the principles of no race prejudice. I knew this meant fighting for me because if Hitler won, my family, you, Rolly, and Pop would certainly suffer more than the families of other soldiers who died in the fight.

I hope you realize exactly what I am trying to tell you, Mom. I want you very much to be more proud than sorry. I don't want you to think of it as losing a son for no good reason, but rather as sacrificing a son so that all mankind could live in a peaceful and free world.[15]

Many more last letters found on servicemen show the eagerness of loyal Jews to serve the United States of America during World War II. Sergeant Irving Strobing, a radio operator, sent a last message before his capture by the Japanese "to tell Joe to give them hell for us."[16]

In numerous cases in World War I, "four or more members of a single family" enlisted.[17] Such instances also occurred during World War II, perhaps even more frequently, since "fighting Hitler" was not only a strong motive but also a leitmotif—all the more so as women, too, were encouraged to serve their country. A notable example of the patriotism of a whole family is the enlistment of Navy Aviation Machinist Mate Sidney Friedlander together with six of his siblings, one of whom died in combat. Several cases were recorded in which women enlisted after learning that a brother or husband had been killed in action, as if to pursue the mission he had been trying to accomplish when he met his death. Some instances were also recorded of World War I veterans reenlisting after the enlistment of a son.[18] Elizabeth (Betty) Haas Pfister from Great Neck, New York, enlisted as a WASP after her graduation. While she was in basic training, her brother, who had been flying torpedo bombers off an aircraft carrier, was shot down and killed in the Pacific. Betty Haas went home to comfort her family after the tragedy but returned to Avenger Field, Texas, to participate in the flight classes she needed to complete her training. In some families, patriotism was so strong that the moral duty of serving one's country was transmitted from one generation to another. This patriotism is exemplified in the case of Naval Lieutenant Jacques Rodney Eisner, born in 1918 in Red Bank, New Jersey, a veteran of Pearl Harbor who was killed in action aboard the *San Francisco* in the battle of Guadalcanal on November 12, 1942. A midshipman of the United States Naval Reserve in March 1941, Lieutenant Eisner participated in most of the battles in the Pacific over the course of his two and a half years of service. The words of his father J. Lester Eisner, a major in World War I and a colonel in the reserve, are most significant: "While I am grieved at the loss of my son, I am at the same time proud that he contributed his life to make this world a decent place in which to live for those of us who remain." At the time he spoke, he had two other sons in service: Lieutenant J. Lester Eisner Jr., Air

Corps, and Lieutenant Gerald Eisner in the field artillery.[19] Their World War I veteran father expressed that human history is shaped by numerous individual acts of courage.

### WOMEN: BEYOND PATRIOTISM AND JEWISH IDENTITY

Since the birth of the United States, women have been informally serving in the American army. In the Revolutionary and Civil Wars, they often fought disguised as men. While women primarily served as drivers, secretaries, or telephone operators during World War I, their participation was most needed by the army in World War II to replace men in the positions they left to serve in combat units.

In the USSR, Great Britain, France, Germany, and elsewhere, the military thus encouraged the participation of women. In the United States, massive publicity campaigns and attractive posters urged women to contribute to the war effort in both traditional and nontraditional roles, which they did. Motivated by patriotism, hundreds of thousands volunteered on the home front, on bases, and close to battlefields, in the case of nurses. The Army and Navy Nurse Corps recruited civilian nurses from every segment of American society, while millions of young people enlisted or were drafted into the American armed forces. Growing concern with manpower shortages led to the creation and development of the Women's Army Corps (WAC), with servicewomen sent throughout North Africa, Europe, and the Philippines, and the navy's Women Accepted for Voluntary Emergency Service (WAVES), mostly performing secretarial and clerical duties. The first women in history trained to fly American military aircraft were the WASP, whose narratives will be shared in chapter 3.

It is interesting to focus on what motivated Jeanne Zamaloff (Dworkin) of New York to volunteer when her boyfriend joined the army: fighting against Hitler, who symbolized evil and was a threat to European Jews, and escaping the boredom of everyday life following the Great Depression. Eager to join the WAC, she changed her birth certificate: "I had to be twenty, so I only changed it by about six months." Jeanne Zamaloff had graduated from high school at the age of sixteen and a half and taken a job "so the family could eat." Her family greatly objected to her decision to enlist, but the young woman's determination won them over. To her mother (originally from Poland), who did not want to let her go—especially as her brother was already in the navy—she replied: "All your relatives are in danger there." Zamaloff recorded what led her to volunteer for military service: "Not only did I want to get away from the home front, which was a little boring at the time, I really did want to participate in the war and I wanted to see the world. I knew there was a woman's division in the army, which was available to me to participate in. The politics of it was that Hitler was conquering the world and I'm not going to stand by and let him do it."[20] The desire to fight Hitler was omnipresent among Jewish men and women and strengthened their Jewish identity. In contradistinction, non-Jewish servicemen and women tended to express wanting revenge for the humiliation and death inflicted by the Japanese at Pearl Harbor.

First assigned to the Medical Corps in Fort Dix, New Jersey, to do secretarial work, Zamaloff "was totally disillusioned with the brutality of army life." She eventually managed to get sent overseas to one of General MacArthur's headquarters in Australia, New Guinea, Leyte, and Manila in the Philippines, as the famous general advanced through territories the Japanese had conquered.[21]

Patriotism among immigrants and their children appears to have been particularly strong. Beatrice (Bea) Hirshcovici Abrams Cohen, who was born in 1910 in Bucharest, Romania, and grew up in Los Angeles, confessed in a filmed interview that she enlisted in the American army out of gratitude for the generosity of the country that took her in. To "pay back for becoming an American," as she put it, she enlisted in the WAC in 1943. On D-Day (June 6, 1944), Beatrice Abrams, who had never been away from home, was stationed at Elveden Hall outside London, mimeographing top-secret documents in the Communications Department. A private first class, she was awarded a good conduct medal. She explained that her mother, who spoke mostly Yiddish and Romanian, was proud of the American flag and what it represented. For Beatrice, who had received a Jewish education, life consisted of doing *mitzvot*, performing good deeds. Immediately after the United States entered the war, she took a job with Douglas Aircraft in Santa Monica, California, before enlisting. Beatrice worked there for less than five cents an hour in the manner depicted by *Rosie the Riveter*, the iconic wartime poster of a female factory worker and the title of a movie released in 1944. It was a turning point for women in America; their contributions outside the home were most needed. As a private first class in communications, she, as a Jew, "got along beautifully" with the Irish girls.[22] On September 28, 1945, she was discharged and lived with her mother before meeting her husband, Ray E. Cohen, a Marine who had been captured at Corregidor in the Philippines and spent three and a half years in a Japanese POW camp. "He did not do much talking," she recalled, perhaps hinting at post-traumatic stress disorder (PTSD), while he remained in the army for twenty years. Beatrice Abrams Cohen's motivation to serve her country was so deeply entrenched and linked to her inclination to do good deeds that she continued good deeds in war veteran organizations after her service in uniform: "My life is dedicated to helping others." During an interview, she emphasized several times her Jewish-ingrained need to help the underdog. She spent more than seventy years supporting American military organizations and charities and helping children with palsy in the framework of the National Ladies Auxiliary of the Jewish War Veterans. "Makes me feel good to make a mitzvah," she stated, using again the Jewish word for "a good deed."[23] "Never forget our veterans," she repeated in front of the camera. "It is because of them that we are enjoying freedom." Her statements encapsulate how Jewish values reinforced and interacted with patriotism.

Selma Kantor Cronan, another strong-minded woman, knew how to fly before the Japanese forces bombed the American naval base at Pearl Harbor on December 7, 1941. The next day, the American Congress was asked to declare war on Japan. A few days later, Germany and Italy declared war on the United States. In an interview conducted in Florida in June 2000, Selma Cronan explained why she enlisted in the WASP as a pilot: "I wanted to fight Hitler." "I simply had to do it," she later added. While her family was not particularly observant, she "never had any doubts about my religious identity" and never sought to hide it. An outdoor person, she was a Girl Scout as a child and met other scouts at the synagogue. Her interest in aviation, which developed when she was about eight years old, was initiated by her mother's love of planes. When she left home to enlist in Washington, DC in 1944, she took with her an old *mezuzah*, a small parchment scroll inscribed with a biblical passage, that belonged to her mother.[24] Reflecting on her war experiences, Selma Cronan called the WASP "a peculiar organization." The twelve hundred pilots who enlisted in the WASP in 1944 "went in as civilians but with the promise that we would be militarized."[25] That promise materialized in the late 1970s through an Act of Congress obtained by the relentless lobbying of women pilots who had served in World War II, such as Bernice Falk Haydu, another Jewish American pilot. Selma Cronan made the point that she would not have enlisted as a WASP had she not been promised she would become military personnel. "Why wouldn't you have enlisted?" asked her interviewer. "I was much more interested in fighting that war, than anything else," she replied with a sad smile. She confessed that she had been considering joining the navy when she received a call from Jacqueline Cochran, a renowned American pilot who was promoting the WASP and with whom she was on friendly terms. After passing a test, she had to wait for a telegram from General Arnold to be admitted to a military base in Texas. She left her supportive husband, Walter Cronan, with whom she had been religiously married in 1935, and arrived by train near Sweetwater, a very small "ghost town," in her words.

Selma Kantor expressed her surprise that men were not permitted to land at the base, where about four hundred women pilots worked "twenty-four hours a day." There were a few male mechanics on the base, but most mechanics were women—"they were protecting the men from us," Selma noted with humor. Women underwent the same basic training as men, the final aim of which was to be able to fly a plane. Being a WASP meant taking part in an experiment: for the first time in history, women were being trained to fly American military aircraft.

A document prepared for an annual report to the secretary of war helps explain why the WASP program was limited in duration and in scope, leaving Selma Cronan somewhat frustrated at not being sent overseas or immediately recognized as military personnel in the Air Corps. Written and signed by Jacqueline Cochran, director of women pilots, and dated November 25, 1944, the document sums up the program in which Selma Kantor Cronan and Bernice Falk Haydu took part: "There was a two-fold purpose in the activation of the WASP program; (a) As an experiment to prove their capabilities in handling domestic flying missions in case of potential need in great numbers, (b) To release men pilots for higher types of duty including combat. This purpose has been accomplished. It has been established that women pilots can be relied on in great numbers to perform any domestic flying mission."[26] The abrupt ending of the WASP program was a shock for women pilots, who had performed their mission to the best of their abilities. With the return of sufficient male pilots to handle all American air force missions, the WASP program was inactivated on December 20, 1944.[27] However, the successful experiment involving highly motivated women pilots, Jews among them, did entail casualties. Thirty-eight young women lost their lives during approximately two years of the program.[28]

As for nurses, there was high motivation to enlist in the military. Born in New York in 1923, Ruth Gottlieb Cohen recalled the life-changing moment when ineluctable decisions were made that would affect many lives. The military strike by the Imperial Japanese Navy Air Service against the naval base at Pearl Harbor on Sunday, December 7, 1941, surprised and shocked all Americans. She remembered it as the moment when all the boys she knew exclaimed, "Well, this is it!" It was their elliptic way of expressing the basic necessity of enlisting without too much thought. Ruth Gottlieb's parents were "devastated," since both her brother, Milton, and her older sister, Yetta, enlisted too. The atmosphere of that ineffable period is best encapsulated in a sentence that notes the turning point: "Anxiety about the next paycheck gave way to anxiety about loved ones in uniform."[29]

As a WAC, Yetta Gottlieb was sent overseas, but Ruth was assigned to a hospital in the South as a nurse, together with a group of Jewish friends. Racial discrimination in the South came as a shock. Expanding on her motivation to enlist, Ruth insisted that "we were patriotic, we felt this was something we had to do." She also shed light on a positive element of her military service: "It was an opening instead of staying in a nursery home." Yet, she was "surprised" by the difficulty of basic training at Fort Dix: girls had to do everything men did except learn how to handle a weapon. Barracks life and basic training included scaling fences, climbing ropes, and even taking hikes with gas masks. Going through such a harsh physical challenge required strong motivation. Asked if she had felt the need to keep kosher, Ruth admitted that she had not and had only occasionally accepted invitations from Jewish families outside the base on Friday evenings. A Jewish chaplain was there to encourage observance and boost morale.

Yetta Moskowitz, from New York City, was just finishing nursing school when she enlisted in the Army Nurse Corps in June 1943: "Fever was running high for nurses to serve in the military."[30] She went through difficult training at the Air Force School of Air Evacuations in June 1944. It was not long before she was called on to evacuate combat casualties from battlefields in the South Pacific. There, she took care of the wounded GIs with whom she flew to the nearest regional area hospitals, becoming a pioneer in air evacuation medicine. The urge to enlist was shared by many young Jewish nurses like Ruth Karsevar from Atlantic City, New Jersey, who cared for troops under combat conditions before switching to the difficult medical treatment of inmates recently liberated from POW and concentration camps in Germany suffering from PTSD.[31] Lilian Krell enlisted in October 1943 after her graduation from Mount Sinai Hospital School of Nursing in New York City. After being stationed at Fort Dix, she was sent to England on the eve of the Normandy invasion as part of the 297th General Hospital Unit. Nothing could lessen her motivation to care for the wounded under the most difficult conditions in combat zones: "Nurses worked 12–15 hour shifts and round the clock whenever a new load of patients arrived."[32] If resilience was needed from servicemen, it was also required from the nurses who kept them alive and comforted them. Their altruism was noteworthy. Lilian Krell voiced the hope that their dedication would remain in the writing and rewriting of history: "In retrospect I would like to feel that I, and my fellow nurses in the U.S. Army Nurse Corps served our wounded men and our country well. I also would like to feel that as women we played an important and much needed role in the Armed Forces."[33]

A number of Jewish nurses received recognition from the army. They include Ellan Levitsky Orkin and her sister Dorothy, who grew up in Salem, New Jersey, and were children of immigrants. They enlisted together and treated numerous soldiers wounded at the Battle of the Bulge in France. In recognition of their selflessness and helpfulness, the two sisters received the American Theater Ribbon and the European-African-Middle Eastern Theater Campaign Ribbon, as well as the World War II Victory Medal. It is interesting to note that they both chose to have an H on their dog tags, as seen in the pictures of their World War II memorabilia.[34]

Jewish servicewomen, like all American women serving in the military, came from every segment of American society and were eager to comply with the call to duty. Serving in traditional or more unusual roles, their motivations to enlist included a spirit of adventure, an interest in a physical challenge, and a dream to make the world a better place. For Jewish servicewomen, many of whom had ancestors who had fled anti-Jewish hostility and violence in Europe, the idea of "repairing the world" (*Tikkun olam*) present in Judaism may have been in the back of their minds. The concept was congruent with the American ethos. Often appreciated by combat servicemen, Jewish servicewomen performed all sorts of necessary tasks behind the front lines, including decoding enemy messages, weather forecasting, and operating radios. They even developed artificial eyes for wounded GIs, as in the case of Jewish servicewoman Bernice Baumel, stationed at San Diego Naval Hospital. She became a pioneer in using a new technique that matched the existing eye. Her desire to help translated into a patient temperament that served her well when dealing with the emotions of young soldiers who had lost an eye in the war.[35] Servicewomen of all faiths repaired cars, checked planes, served as Link trainer (flight simulator) instructors, or operated control towers, while women pilots like Selma Cronan or Bee Falk Haydu were assigned flying duties so that more soldiers could fight on the front lines.

\*\*\*

Despite the strong resolve of Jews to enlist, as illustrated in this chapter, stereotypes persisted among officers or soldiers who clung to uninformed representations of Jews as draft dodgers, quartermasters, or clerks. The mass of oral and written testimonies and the list of war casualties will not suffice for those who, like Holocaust deniers, persist in denying the fact that Jews have been faithful patriots since 1654, when Jewish men and women, led by Asher Levy, took part in defending the walls of New Amsterdam. Jewish servicemen have fought in every branch of the US Armed Forces and in every war since the founding of the United States. During World War II, the military assigned different roles to women, and a departure from traditional models can be seen in the case of women pilots, a group that included some Jewish servicewomen. However, some instructors claimed that "Jewish women can't fly" and were intent to "wash them out" after their training period.[36] Although anti-Jewish hostility reflected the trends of civilian society in the 1930s and 1940s, as of June 30, 1945, the Bureau of War Records of the National Jewish Welfare Board (JWB) recorded 6,477 awards received by Jewish servicemen and servicewomen.[37]

It is impossible to generalize what motivated Jewish servicemen and women to enlist in the Allied armies. For instance, some left-wing Jews shared an involvement in politics that included a commitment to economic justice. Their participation in the war was prompted by an eagerness to save socialism after the invasion of the Soviet Union by German troops on June 22, 1941 (Operation Barbarossa). The letters of American serviceman Benedict Alper, written to his wife from Algiers, French North Africa, reveal that he identified more with communism than with Judaism. A letter dated December 12, 1943, relates an encounter with the local superintendent of education, who inquired whether he was "juif" (a Jew), to which Alper simply replied, "My parents were."[38] Still, servicemen and servicewomen whose parents or grandparents were immigrants from Europe were more intent on combating the Nazis and their allies, even if patriotism seemed like the first reason for enlistment.

Furthermore, testimonies vary depending on the audience and the questions asked. If a testimony is delivered in the presence of a Jewish audience or given to a Jewish museum, a veteran may feel obligated to shed light on the Jewish elements of his war experiences. Besides, the reasons to fight evolve among combatants in a unit. With the experience of comradeship as the war progressed, the reasons for Jewish GIs to go on waging war included the desire to save their comrades. An esprit de corps developed while on the battleground, aboard a ship, or on a plane. Motives may thus have become mixed: fighting for a cause, for glory or promotion, and—more often than not—to gain respect and acceptance. On what inner resources did Jewish servicemen and servicewomen draw to be good soldiers despite encountering prejudice? Each chapter of this book considers this question from a different perspective and focus.

For most Jewish Allied soldiers, the issue of motivation was complex. Jews in France defended their country out of patriotism. In 1939, when French Jews volunteered, the atrocities perpetrated by Hitler were not yet known. Their patriotism was as strong as during World War I. Though Jews endured discrimination and persecution, they enlisted in the Free French Forces and in Jewish resistance groups. Free France was the government in exile led by French army officer Charles de Gaulle in London after the Armistice of June 22, 1940. In early November 1942, a high percentage of the total Jewish population were members of the underground in French Algeria. They fought as French patriots against the Vichy regime—aligned with Germany—when they helped Anglo-American landings in Operation Torch and facilitated its success. More generally, for Jews and American Jews in particular, motivations to fight included different perceptions of Nazism.

Using a pen and colorful illustrations to motivate American soldiers, Arthur Szyk's work was noteworthy during the war years. A Jew and a Pole born in 1894, exiled from Lodz and living in Paris, Szyk (pronounced "shick") was interested in creating heroic Jewish models inspired by Jewish history. As an immigrant in the United States, he felt privileged to fight the Nazis through powerful cartoons on *Collier's* covers. Widely circulated, they appealed to a large public. He even used a magazine insert to emphasize his deeply personal involvement as "a soldier in art," a Polish exile, and a future American. The first of the artist's eight covers for *Collier's* magazine compares to the wide circulation of Norman Rockwell's covers for the *Saturday Evening Post*. Entitled *Historic Poker Game* and published in New York in 1941, it exposes the game being played. Hitler holds three jokers: Japan, Italy, and the Vichy regime in France. Ivan of Russia holds only two cards against Hitler's three jokers, but the expression on his face reveals how powerful his cards are. The symbols on the cards represent Great Britain and the United States.

The earlier works of the Polish immigrant—who had fought in World War I—had an impact on American Jews. A famous watercolor and gouache entitled *Trumpeldor's Defense of Tel Hai* (1936) was created in the context of the Arab revolt against the British Mandate in Palestine, which began in 1936. In response to this event, Arthur Szyk depicted the hero against the Arab riots in 1920: having lost an arm, Captain Joseph Trumpeldor defended the Jewish settlement of Tel Hai in Galilea. He was eventually

Fig. 1.1 *Collier's* magazine cover, November 1, 1941. Reproduced with the cooperation of Historicana, Burlingame, CA.

shot, and Tel Hai was burned by the Arab militia. But his dying words were: "It is good to die for our land."[39] In July 1942, an enlarged reproduction of the painting was significantly retitled *The Modern Maccabees*, aiming to inspire Jewish heroism and self-defense in Europe and America. Numerous issues addressed in Szyk's work still resonate today, including the fight against prejudice and bigotry. For Szyk, "the Jewish struggle for freedom," notes Michael Berenbaum, "was part of a universal freedom."[40] It is significant that one of the artist's final works was the illumination of *Thomas Jefferson's Oath, New Canaan* (1951), a pledge against tyranny, making Szyk, the immigrant, a prominent patriot.

Of the young Jewish American patriots who readily enlisted, some were disappointed about not taking part in the war in Europe. Gideon Lichtman, for instance, was an American Jewish pilot eager to fight a war that was both American and Jewish. He wanted to stand up against the Nazis. Stationed at Clark Field in the Philippines with the Third Air Commando, where he flew P-51 aircrafts, he was unable to do so. After the war, he saw British soldiers sending the survivors of the Nazi extermination scheme back to Germany, as they did with the ship *Exodus* in 1947. He transformed his deep frustration into steadfast involvement to "rescue my people." His self-imposed mission culminated in his heroic fight in the new Israeli Defense Forces in 1948. He appeared as Israel's first pilot and founders of its fledgling air force.[41] His response was shared by non-Jewish servicemen who had witnessed the liberation of concentration camps and were willing to fight for the survivors' rights to have a homeland.

During his service in the American military, Gideon Lichtman never hid his Jewishness. Yet it was not unusual for cadets to be discriminated against while in training: "My name is Gideon and [because] I was Jewish [they] called me 'A. B.' for Abe, so you can go from there."[42] Indeed, it was not unusual for Jewish GIs to be called Abe because many Christians gave that name to Jews automatically. The notion of visibility as a Jew is fathomed mostly through Jewish-sounding names. The issue of self-identification will be addressed in the next chapter.

# INVISIBILITY OF JEWS IN THE MILITARY?

When studying anti-Jewish attitudes, the issue of Jews' invisibility or visibility plays a role. Its dynamics often resemble a dialectical process. Jews may be accused both of being invisible, making them an object of suspicion, and of being too visible, of standing out instead of blending in. Faced with these contradictory accusations, Jewish servicemen and servicewomen behaved as American patriots, exemplifying zeal, boldness, and heroism.[1] It is not surprising that they felt compelled to do more than the average American to convey patriotism and debunk negative stereotypes.

### Visibility, Invisibility, and Anti-Jewish Attitudes

Antisemitism was on the rise during the war years. American Jews feared for their security and felt vulnerable as hostility toward Jews was clearly reflected in opinion surveys. In November 1942, a poll asked American high school students which of various ethnic groups would be their "last choice as a roommate." Their responses displayed animosity and distrust against Jews (45 percent) as well as an even higher rejection of African Americans, then called "Negroes" (78 percent), while Irish, Protestants, and Catholics respectively fared the best.[2] At a time when racism was a strong current in American society, the Marines and Army Air Corps refused to accept African American soldiers into their ranks at the beginning of the war. These soldiers were relegated to noncombat and menial tasks, serving in segregated units. As the war went on, they were allowed to become officers and engage in combat. The Army Air Corps formed its first black combat unit, the Tuskegee Airmen, often highly appreciated by Jewish pilots, who could identify with the rejection and hardships experienced by African Americans in society at large. It is significant to add that Black people were more visible color-wise and yet, socially speaking, more invisible, as illustrated by Ralph Ellison's aptly titled novel *Invisible Man* (1952).

No special unit was established for Jewish GIs, who were considered a religious minority, not a racial one. However, they could suddenly become ignored or rejected by others when their religious identity was revealed or discovered. Legendary movie actor Kirk Douglas provided an example. Before he became a GI, his name was Issur Demsky, later changed to Izzy Demsky. In his memoirs, he recalled his sadness and surprise when, on campus, he was abruptly rejected by a group of students with whom he was meant to have dinner: "I went to bed that night with no dinner, not that unusual for me, but completely perplexed. . . . When they found out I was Jewish, they just dropped me. No one even made an attempt to call to say that something had come up, maybe we'd make it some other time—to lie, even. They just ignored me, said nothing. They never made any reference to it. That rejection hurt. I had assumed that a university was above anti-Semitism."[3] Instead of facing social exclusion, was it best to remain incognito? He could pass as a Gentile to gain the social acceptance he wanted.

After graduation, the humiliated youth radically changed his name to Kirk Douglas. That move made it easier for him to join the navy and train as a naval officer at Notre Dame Midshipman School in South Bend, Indiana. However, not being labeled as Jewish the invisibility gained through this change of identity raised his awareness of the pervasive antisemitism of the war years:

"Now that I had a WASP [White Anglo-Saxon Protestant] name, I was introduced to another level of anti-Semitism. I'd find myself in a group of people who didn't know I was Jewish, listening to them say the things that are accepted in large sectors of the non-Jewish population, the things that in their nightmares Jews speculate non-Jews say, and that I found out, they do."[4]

Douglas also admitted that at the time, his response to anti-Jewish hostility corresponded to a strategy of assimilation: "Years back, I tried to forget I was a Jew. I remember saying, 'Oh no, I'm half Jewish,' to minimize the stigma of being a Jew, one hundred per cent."[5] Although chaplains were supposed to discourage intermarriage, Kirk Douglas was married as a GI to a Gentile woman by a Jewish chaplain, who made him promise he would bring up his children as Jews. While not denying his Jewish origin, Douglas managed to assimilate by eventually finding a role in the Gentile group he joined. The son of poor Russian Jewish immigrants, he made it clear that from a young age, wherever he was, Yom Kippur was the only time he did fully feel Jewish. "And I fast," he confessed. "Yes, I'm a Jew. And that feeling lasts me the rest of the year until the next Yom Kippur," he added wittily. He admitted that he had moved away from observance and ate the foods forbidden to Orthodox Jews.[6] This example helps understand the multiplicity of self-perception among Jews; Douglas confessed that "coming to grips with what it meant to be a Jew" was not only a theme of several of the films in which he participated but also, in his own words, "a theme of my own life."[7] For a number of Jewish youths in the military, the war experiences that transformed them from a civilian into a soldier entailed a desire for social acceptance by non-Jews.

Joining the armed forces provided servicemen and women with different perspectives on antisemitism. A recurring pattern can be illustrated by the case of a Jewish nurse who came across anti-Jewish attitudes. As she stood in a group with four other Jewish nurses, she saw a Gentile girl next to her point to a new doctor and disdainfully call him a "kike." Only when the Jewish nurses looked at each other did the blaspheming nurse exclaim: "I didn't know." Ruth Gottlieb Cohen sadly related that episode, which she bore in mind long after it happened.[8] Indeed, it sounded incongruous that doctors trained to treat all types of patients, including prisoners of war (POW), should still be looked down on. The four Jewish nurses apparently did not look Jewish; the invisibility of their Jewish identity enabled the free expression of antisemitic slurs, reminiscent of the discrimination faced by civilian physicians in medical schools or hospitals, where quotas limiting admission existed in the 1940s.

Ruth Cohen, who came from an Orthodox home and enlisted along with her elder sister, recalled that she was issued a dog tag stamped with an H for Hebrew. However, others were not supposed to know about that identification. Like all soldiers, whether Catholic or Protestant, Jewish men and women entering the American military could choose how to be identified, as they were asked to indicate their religion on their metal dog tags. They could choose to be discreet about their Jewishness if they were not identifiable through Jewish names. Pilot Selma Kantor Cronan, who confessed that she never hid her Jewish identity, felt ambivalent after experiencing rejection by her counterparts on the military base. She consequently wondered whether she should not have been more discreet about her origin and done like the other girls at the base who "were sensible enough not to open their mouths." In fact, she learned after her service that a bunch of girls were Jewish. In an interview in 2000, she admitted that only later had she understood why she had felt "excluded" from some activities on the base at Avenger Field, Sweetwater, Texas.[9] Asked if she experienced antisemitism in Texas, she replied that she did not feel it in town, where she rarely went, but did on the base. "At that time," she went on, "I had no idea that it was directed against me, though." Only later was she "able to put two and two together" and understand things "that were happening" to her. "Like what?" asked the interviewer. "Being excluded from some things, tending to push me off the base, particularly because I was not identifiable as Jewish." She analyzed the price she had paid for having carelessly revealed her Jewish identity further: "It came out as an insult to some people, when it did come out, and I was very open about it."[10] Selma Kantor Cronan did not remember exactly what she had said to trigger such a revelation, because she was by nature spontaneous and "open." Did she mention her mother, a Jewish immigrant from Russia? Could her sudden appearance as a Jew behind the mask of a woman pilot have caused alarm because of prejudiced misconceptions? What is unknown produces fear. Selma Kantor Cronan was obviously emotionally distressed throughout her service. As in the case of Kirk Douglas, rejection was not voiced by anyone, but the feeling of belonging to a group vanished. It was as if their previous invisibility as Jews became a threat to non-Jews. Selma Kantor Cronan felt the distrust of other servicewomen toward her when she was doing her best to adjust to strict discipline on the base and to various challenges of being a woman pilot. The frustration she expressed years later in her interview stemmed from her awareness of a gap between her being part of a Jewish subcommunity and belonging to the larger American community. It was as if being a member of one group excluded membership in the other. It was painful for the young woman, who had strived to gain the identity of pilot that now defined her. Her example evinces the complexity of the processes at work in self-image development for young Jewish servicewomen and men.

Unlike Kirk Douglas, the then-famous baseball star Hank Greenberg (born Hyman Greenberg) identified strongly as a Jew. His choice not to play on the solemn Jewish Day of Atonement (Yom Kippur) in September 1934 was welcomed by Jewish Americans. He was one of the most visible Americans of Jewish origin—a beacon of hope and social integration. Born in 1911 in the Bronx to Orthodox Romanian immigrant parents, the American champion recounted in his autobiography how he willingly interrupted his brilliant career to serve in the armed forces.

> I was inducted on May 7, 1941, the first outstanding ballplayer to go into the military service. I was stationed at Camp Custer. The All-Star game was held in Detroit that year, I didn't even get an invitation to come and watch the games or to be an honorary selection to the team since I was in the service. When I came back from the service, just before the All-Star break in 1945, I had no chance to participate in the game. And then, in 1946 I was

Fig. 2.1 Aircraft pilot and Women Air Force Service Pilots (WASP) Selma Kantor (Cronan) wearing bulky flight gear at Avenger Field, Sweetwater, Texas, 1944. Courtesy of the National Museum of American Jewish Military History, Washington, DC.

not invited to Boston to play. That was my whole record in the American League. I only played one full year in 1939. So I often wonder, looking back, why I wasn't selected more often and why I wasn't played more often."[11]

The veteran, whose monthly salary dropped from $55,000 to $21 when he joined the military, was not bitter because "I made up my mind to go when I was called. My country comes first."[12] However, the passage from his autobiography quoted above shows frustration at feeling excluded. In November 1941, Greenberg was serving as an antitank gunner and was promoted to sergeant. On December 5 of that year, the United States Congress exempted men aged twenty-eight years or older from the draft. Greenberg was honorably discharged two days before the attack against Pearl Harbor. While he could have served as an athletic instructor in the United States, he reenlisted as a sergeant on February 1, 1942, and volunteered for the Army Air Corps. In doing so, he became the first Major League player to enlist. Graduating from officer candidate school and commissioned as an officer, he was promoted to first lieutenant in the United States Army Air Corps, where he was assigned to the physical education program. Greenberg was sent to the US Army Special Services School in February 1944; he was promoted to captain and volunteered to go overseas later that year. Serving in the China-Burma-India theater for over six months, his assignment was to look for locations (location scouting) for bases for B-29 bombers, the Superfortress four-engine propeller heavy bombers designed by Boeing and flown by the United States during World War II. In China, he was a special services officer of the Twentieth Bomber Command, whose last assignment was with the Twentieth Air Force based in Okinawa. Greenberg was with that unit when it began fire-bombing Japan on June 15. He returned to New York and to Richmond, Virginia, at the end of 1944, thus accomplishing a term of military service of forty-seven months. No other Major League player served his country out of patriotism for such a long period.[13]

In his uncompleted autobiography, the professional baseball player recounted more occurrences of antisemitism in Major League baseball and in the postwar period than during his time in the military. A secular Jew, he noted that "I didn't have much contact with the Jewish religion except that I was Jewish."[14] In the military, he was an outstanding baseball player, excelling in a sport that was a badge of both American identity and masculinity. It helped his integration as a Jewish GI. However, he remained visible as a Jew in the labor market. As such, he felt discriminated against despite his heroic military service and the universal admiration he had earned: "After I came back from the war and worked as a general manager and was known among the owners and the most successful businessmen in the Cleveland community, I was in contact with anti-Semitism. I had the feeling that had I not been Jewish I could have been accepted but instead the door was shut to me."[15]

Greenberg maintained his dignity as a Jew, refusing to play the game of invisibility or "low profile," as antisemites call it. He recalled: "I've been invited to many clubs that were restricted. They let in a token Jew or two, and then think they are liberal. I realized I would be 'passing' in that environment, and I never joined any of those clubs."¹⁶ Reflecting on the effect of antisemitic slurs on his life, Greenberg—who was sometimes nicknamed "The Hebrew Hammer"—admitted that humiliating provocations such as "Come on, you big Jew, can't you do better than that?" had an impact on him. "It would always hit me like a cold shower," he confessed. But to him, these anti-Jewish slurs were not the "terrific burden" they were meant to be for Jews in the eyes of Gentiles. On the contrary, he observed: "I found it to be a great help."¹⁷ Humiliation can be a launching pad for those who have the resilience to rebound. Often, Jewish GIs took insults as a challenge and chose to behave like heroes, defying death in difficult battle assignments that tested both masculinity and courage.

Jews in the military faced a choice about whether to indicate their religion on their dog tags. Some did not want to face antisemitism in training or negative perceptions in the military and changed their names. This was the case with Sergeant Milton Fields, who was born Finkelstein and thought it wise to change his name in January 1942. Although he took this step to avoid anti-Jewish prejudice during training in the Air Corps, he volunteered as a lay leader (or parachaplain) to conduct Jewish services in the Persian Gulf Command, through which he was sent to Iran and Iraq. He joined a local synagogue along with a few GIs in Basra, Iraq. On one occasion, he asked the major for permission to take Jewish men to worship and was met with disapproval. It was not long before the major used the excuse that Fields had gone AWOL (absent from his post) to court-martial him. Fields, who did not intend to desert, was eventually cleared of the charges, while the major was transferred.¹⁸ This example evinces that changing one's name to be invisible as a Jew during training did not equate to abandoning Judaism or assimilating.

Gideon Lichtman deplored the fact that, as a cadet wishing to become a pilot, he repeatedly heard instructors state that Jews could not make good pilots. When interviewed years later, he said that his instructor had spent much less time instructing him than he had non-Jewish cadets. Lichtman had to solo after only eight hours of flight time, having never been shown required maneuvers such as loops, rolls, Immelmans, and Chandelles. He risked being "washed out" if he did not pass his solo flight. Fortunately, although he did not have the expertise of his fellow cadets, he had listened to them carefully when they spoke in detail about the new maneuvers they had performed with their instructors. He was put into "the washing machine," an expression meaning that he was put to test to be "washed out" for not meeting requirements.

So I was put into the washing machine. Luckily for me, you got a check by another instructor, and then another—all of whom were civilians, and then the final check before washout was by a second Lieutenant who was a commissioned pilot. The commissioned officer took me up and told me to do a loop. I said "I never learnt how to do a loop." So he did a loop and said, "Now you do it." So I did it. And then he [did] the same with the other maneuvers. . . . So he got furious and brought me back to the squadron and chewed the instructor out, and I got another instructor, and I breezed through. . . . Well, let me put it to you this way—I was the only Jew among the six. I'll put it to you better—they were a lot of Jews who were flying and didn't tell anybody they were Jewish. They had dog tags with "P" on them for Protestant, because they knew the situation. . . . I'm not saying this because I am bitter, but this was a fact. I had an "H" on my dog tag for Hebrew.[19]

Lichtman was bold enough to make his case to the second lieutenant. He knew that good Jewish pilots had been washed out.

In a dialogue with a woman pilot, Jean Hascall Cole, a Women Airforce Service Pilot (WASP), recorded the following remark: "I wonder about the Jewish prejudice thing. Because I can remember one instructor saying, those Jewish girls can't fly. And he was washing them out right and left."[20] WASP Juliette (Julie) Jenner Stege in the class 44-3 did not reveal her Jewish origins. In her memoir, Bernice Falk Haydu mentioned that Juliette Jenner was a Ziegfeld Follies girl and had stage experience before turning test pilot in World War II. Full of joyful energy, Bernice Falk helped Juliette Jenner organize a successful show to boost morale at Avenger Field. Bernice only discovered decades later that more WASP members were of Jewish descent.[21]

The dog tags issued to Jewish service members were stamped with an H for Hebrew (or, more rarely, J for Jewish) and contained useful personal information such as name, serial or service number, date of most recent tetanus shot, and blood type. Discarding dog tags for whatever reason could endanger a person during an emergency and deprive a soldier of being buried according to Jewish ritual. Being identified as a Jew was, of course, more dangerous for soldiers serving in the European theater, who could be taken prisoner, than for soldiers engaged in fighting the Japanese in the Pacific theater.

Private Harold Baumgarten behaved differently than Jewish GIs who obeyed the orders of their commanders and threw away their dog tags to avoid the possibility of being sent to slave labor camps or shot down by the Nazis. A soldier who tried to enlist at age seventeen, Baumgarten was rejected by the army but stayed in a military framework for two years before being drafted in June 1943. His attitude toward the Germans was one of defiance as soon as he landed on Omaha Beach in French Normandy. In the first-wave landing of the 116th Infantry Division on D-Day, June 6, 1944, young "Hal" did not wear the heavy, dark-green canvas jacket with six big pockets he had been issued by the army. An older buddy had warned him that he could drown with such weight on his back. Instead, he wore his field jacket, on the back of which he drew a big Star of David with an Eversharp pen. Underneath the Jewish Star, he wrote: "The Bronx, New York."[22] The nineteen-year-old became a Jewish American GI "fighting Amalek," a figure that embodies evil in the Hebrew Bible. He had to stand neck-deep in bloody water with his rifle over his head to make it to the beach. Baumgarten saw officers shot down and the man in front of him killed on the ramp. He said his Hebrew prayers. His fellows "were being pulled down by those jackets soaked with 100 pounds of weight. Most drowned. . . . Eighty-five percent casualties in the first fifteen minutes." Fourteen American amphibious tanks drowned, most of them with the crews. When Baumgarten landed, one remaining tank was firing. The smell of burning flesh stayed with him. Steven Spielberg later told Dr. Baumgarten that he drew inspiration from the veteran's recorded interviews, using the detailed recollections for the beach combat scenes in the film *Saving Private Ryan*.[23] Seriously wounded five times, the multidecorated Baumgarten became a medical doctor later in life.

A proud Jew, young Bernard Branson (formerly Abramson) of the US Army Air Corps provides another inspiring example.

> We were up at Westover Field, Massachusetts. We'd spend a few days there talking and learning to be together and what about you and what about you? And of course, as soon as I said the name Abramson, they gave me the Abie name—I didn't change my name till later. And we just got along very well. We liked each other. We got along—it was all first name basis. There were no officers, no enlisted men. It was just a bunch of guys who liked each other. We all learned in phase training how to fly the plane, how to do each other's part, because it was important if anybody got hit somebody should have to do what you had to do. . . . This was still in 1943, around the end of 1943. . . . Then one time we went to Cuba and flew for ten days out of Cuba, a ten-day antisubmarine patrol, just to keep the crew knowing how the crew works.[24]

A picture belonging to Branson shows him smiling in the front row with the crew next to their B-24, nicknamed "Flak Happy." After a six-week course of gunnery during which he proved that "Jesus, that fucking Jewboy, he can't miss," Branson was almost ready to fly as a tail gunner on a B-24.

Bernard Branson was most likely a good crew member who knew to respond to slurs with an all too familiar "Oh, fuck you." His looks did not correspond to any Jewish stereotype, and most flight crews got along because they had to in order to work as a team as required by the air force. One thing was clear enough to all, as Branson later emphasized: "If you were hit, you went down as a team.... You'd make friends with a crew, and they were gone the next day. And all you knew was that the next day you would check if you were flying."[25] When life and death are at stake, as for soldiers on the battlefield, each soldier is a buddy and tends to be invisible in the sense that he is totally integrated into a group cemented by existential fears. Branson's words make this argument even more powerful: "Nobody was prepared to fly. You knew you had to do it so you did it. I mean that was all. There was always a fear, a terror inside. When we got there, before we got there, a colonel spoke to us and told us, 'Look to the right of you, look to the left of you. Take a good look because two out of three of you are not coming back.'"[26]

Branson confessed that despite the fear he felt deep inside, he really wanted the enemy to know he was fighting Hitler not only as an American but also as a Jew. That decision was an obvious affirmation of a proud Jewish identity strengthened by war experience: "I wanted those sons of bitches to know that the bombs that are dropping, that there's a Jew up doing it."[27] Yet he had the option to remain totally invisible as a Jew. Within the Air Corps, there was an awareness that the fate of American Jews captured by the Nazis was distinct from the lot of others. This is how Branson accounted for the choice he had to make.

> When we got to the base, they asked all the Jewish flyers to stay behind. And there were quite a few of us, officers, and enlisted men. And this Lieutenant Levine came out, he was the Intelligence officer, and he asked all of us to give him our dog tags so that he can change the *H* on the dog tag from Hebrew to either *P* or *C* for Protestant or Catholic. Because he told us point-blank that if we were shot down and they find the *H* on our dog tags, we will not live, we will not be put in a *Stalag*. We will either be tortured to death or beaten to death or killed right away or sent if we're lucky to a concentration camp. And at that point, none of us would do it, none of us.[28]

The possibility of not dying as a Jew must have loomed in their minds as a betrayal or denial of their mothers and fathers. The Jewish fliers' attitude described by Branson implies that among them, no Jew could be

Fig. 2.2 Dr. Ralph Tomases's dog tags, worn during his service in Europe during World War II. Dog tags were used to identify casualties and secure religious burial. The metal tag has an H for Hebrew on its lower corner—Jewish soldiers could be sent into battle against the Nazis with their religious identity clearly indicated. Dr. Tomases became a prisoner of war (POW) of the Nazis. Courtesy of Ruth Joffe and Faith Tomases.

found who nurtured a fear of being discovered. Every month, wherever they were stationed, chaplains of the three faiths had to prepare a report in which percentages of Protestant, Catholic, and Jewish military personnel were estimated. In a classification made official by the dog tags worn by all the military, a fourth category stamped by the letter O was included: "No religious preference of affiliation." This category must be understood in the context of deep-seated antisemitism accurately delineated by Leonard Dinnerstein. The historian highlights the fact that for the first time in American history, American Jews thought that Jew-haters in the United States might acquire a kind of political influence similar to those in Europe: "American Jews knew of existing antisemitism but before 1933 it had been mainly religious, intellectual, verbal, social, and economic. There had also been sporadic attacks on children and adults in a number of cities in this country. But in the 1930s the intensity of antisemitism, the appeal of hate organizations, and the popularity of demagogues combined with an escalation of serious physical abuse especially in the cities of the northeast and midwest where more than 85 percent of all American Jews dwelled, to have an absolutely chilling effect."²⁹

Let us recall the inflammatory radio speeches of the fiercely antisemitic preacher Father Charles Coughlin, those of Gerald L. K. Smith, and the menacing demonstrations of the Silver Shirts, all threatening the social acceptance of American Jews and stirring feelings of vulnerability.³⁰ In a letter to the editor of the *New York Times*, Paul Lippman of Hoboken, New Jersey, wrote: "Jews have served in America's armed forces in a percentage higher than the percentage of Jews in the American population. As a combat veteran I know that my dog tags and those of many of my Jewish companions were religiously anonymous."³¹ That remark provides one reason why there are fewer Stars of David than there should be in American military cemeteries. Another reason, offered by veteran Victor B. Geller in a letter to the editor of the *New York Times*, is that Jewish parents often had the corpses of their loved ones brought to the United States (June 14, 1994).³² The complete destruction of dog tags in plane crashes, explosions, or deaths at sea may also be a reason for this form of Jewish invisibility—the underestimation of the participation of Jews in World War II.

Edward T. Sandrow, a Jewish chaplain in a large replacement center in Fort Riley, Kansas, and overseas in the Alaskan and Aleutian theater of operations, reflected on the self-identification of Jews and their adjustment to army life, which for some meant coming into contact with non-Jews for the first time. As one charged with censoring Yiddish and Hebrew letters, he could decipher their expectations and frustrations. While acknowledging a new interest in worship by both Jews and non-Jews in the military, he delineated three main categories of Jewish servicemen that bear relevance to our emphasis on the dialectics of visibility and invisibility of Jews in the military. This is his analysis of the "observant type": "While readjustments in the mitzvot, folk habits or religious rites have to be made, this type has an emotional attachment to them and is concerned about clinging to them. . . . Even those from Orthodox or Conservative homes accustom themselves to eating anything and everything, to breaking the sanctity of the Sabbath, etc. If questioned on the subject, they feel badly about having to abrogate these customs due to the stress of military life."³³

SELF-IDENTIFICATION AND EMOTIONAL ATTACHMENT

Harold Ribalow's religious experience in North Africa in December 1943 illustrates the emotional attachment described above by Chaplain Sandrow.

The first Sabbath service he attended since leaving the United States, in Casablanca, reminded him of the atmosphere of home. He was accompanied by an Italian American buddy. Later, on a ship to India, Ribalow described his experience in a literary fashion: "And it was the Sabbath. Sabbath on the Red Sea, the body of water so prominent in Biblical lore." The soldier described his "adjustment" to the existing conditions. The group of Jewish GIs was greeted by two chaplains, a Protestant and a Catholic, since there was no Jewish chaplain on board. Nevertheless, Jewish servicemen volunteered to help the chaplains: "To my ears praying in English was a false note, for I had been reared to serve God in Hebrew. But the voices were young and bold; the words were sharply uttered. Sincerity triumphed over whatever off-color note the English-speaking prayers evoked."[34] It is as if the soldier discovered another type of psycho-religious experience, enriched by the diversity of non-Jews and Jews from all over the United States: "A boy with a South Carolina drawl uttered the prayers in a loud voice. There was also heard the distinctive New York manner of speech. But no accent predominated. This was a unified gathering of Jews from everywhere."[35]

The visibility of Orthodox and Conservative Jews on board the ship seemed to blur as Jews and non-Jews worshiped together.

> Following a rousing Ain Kelohaynu, which brought smiles to the chaplain's lips, Father Kelly was introduced. The spectacle of a Catholic priest addressing Jewish soldiers in an area so intimate with Jewish history was unusual, and the extraordinary nature of the event was recognized by a large part of the audience. . . . His statements were trite, but he spoke with grace and sincerity; and when he spoke of the meaning of the Sh'ma, the idea of the Oneness of God, he forged a chain of sympathy and respect which tied his listeners to him. . . . He told us that our conception of one God was a great contribution to religion and let it go at that.[36]

By showing respect for the Jewish religion in their sermons, the two non-Jewish chaplains provided an anchor for the Jewish servicemen on board, endowing legitimacy to the celebration of the Sabbath. By voicing a sympathetic attitude to basic Jewish precepts, these chaplains enabled Jews to blend without feeling self-conscious. In the microcosm of a ship, such a show of respect was a meaningful act in accordance with the regulations of the American military. In that light, it is not surprising that soldiers who encountered such sympathetic chaplains found less antisemitism in the military than in civilian life.

The need to conceal one's Jewishness while in a foxhole triggered new, creative ways of observing rites alone in difficult conditions. Jack Scharf was an infantryman who studied at a Jewish educational institution (*Yeshiva*) in the Bronx. He confessed that in spite of his background, he "didn't take to Orthodoxy or anything like that."[37] Sharf served in the Forty-Second "Rainbow" Infantry Division in France. Homesick and lonely, he reconnected to the ritual observed at home.

> So you do crazy things. Like on Friday night, I dig a foxhole, and then I dig a hole into the side, all the way in. So what I do is . . . My mother, she used to send me wine. Now, it was illegal to send wine. So she went to the doctor and got a medicine bottle for cough medicine. And she'd take the cough medicine, spill it out, put in the wine, mail it to me and also mail me a salami. And she made me a candle. She told me to light the Sabbath candles. So I kept this in my grenade bag. In other words, let's say you can't fit in four grenades. I threw out two and kept the salami, the wine bottle— the medicine bottle—and a candle. And what I did was, on Friday, I would take my canteen, throw it in the snow over there, and I would take my wine bottle. I just knew the initial blessing. I really didn't know the whole blessing. But I did know the first part of it. It's called "borei pri hagofen." And I'd make that thing, but you're not allowed to light a fire. Because if you light a fire they can see you, and you can get killed. One of my friends got killed that way. So what I did was, I dug in, took a C ration can, put the candle in there, put it like two feet in, and lit the candle. I took my salami and I had my sabbath meal on Friday night.[38]

One day, a military order came for him to leave his freezing foxhole. Without more information, he was put in a jeep heading for Dahn, Germany. He was scared because he knew the Germans stretched wires so that soldiers would be decapitated as they rode through wires. Finally, he was told he was going to attend the first Passover in Germany with all the self-identified Jewish soldiers around. Why? General Eisenhower had made a point of assuring that the approximately fifteen hundred Jewish soldiers would celebrate Passover and that wounded soldiers would receive unleavened bread and wine at the hospitals overseas. Celebrating the first Passover on German soil was particularly meaningful, symbolic of the defeat of Nazi evil and of Allied victory. On March 28, 1945, Chaplain Elie Bohnen, a Conservative rabbi from Rhode Island, pointed out the historic significance of Hitler's defeat and the meaning of freedom after the capture of the town in southwest Germany. Just as Pharaoh's Jewish slaves were freed at last, concentration camp inmates in Dachau would be liberated on April

29, 1945. Sharf and the servicemen of the Forty-Second Infantry also discovered a major Dachau subcamp.[39]

Chaplain Edward Sandrow delineated a second category of Jewish servicemen: the "quasi-observant" Jews, who came from Yiddish-speaking homes but were brought up in a completely American environment. Many Orthodox soldiers belonged to this group, some of them from Jewish working-class families. Drawing on his experience and close contact with soldiers both in a replacement center in Kansas and overseas in Alaska and the Aleutian Islands, Sandrow noticed that among these Jews, there was no "inner urge for prayer." Instead, there existed "a warm attachment to K'lal Israel, the Jewish people." These GIs were generally "sympathetic to the idea of Palestine as a homeland."[40] Morris Rubin, a soldier in the Twenty-Eighth Infantry Regiment of the Eighth Infantry Division, illustrates this case. Born in 1915 in New York to immigrant parents who spoke only Yiddish with him during his youth, the infantryman inherited from his father, a tailor from Lodz, Poland, "his ideas of a Socialist world": "What my parents fought for became part of me and I began to realize my place was with the toiler, the worker, and farmer. I began to dream of that world of peace, of freedom, liberty, and happiness.... I became interested in the Workmen Circle at the age of 18 and devoted all my spare time to [the] English speaking section of the Workmen Circle, ... the only organization that engrossed the broad sphere of Jewish thought. Within the Workmen Circle all, regardless of political affiliation could express themselves."[41]

But in 1941, Morris was "under suspicion for subversive activity" by the military as he freely discussed his views about the world with other soldiers. In his memoir, he complained that he received no help from the Jewish chaplain. In the eyes of the military rabbi, Morris was a communist because he belonged to the Workmen Circle. A Protestant chaplain investigated the matter, and Morris was eventually cleared.[42] In his personal narrative, Morris deplored that the Jewish men who accounted for about 20 to 30 percent of his company (composed of 185 men) showed no interest in Jewish life. He noted that most of them came from New York State and pinpointed the large percentage of Jews among the following divisions: "The 77th, 26th, 27th, and 44th." The soldiers in his company "never denied the fact they were Jewish," and "the great majority were Zionist at heart mainly due to the influence at home." However, they were at a loss to make the case for a Jewish homeland. When their infantry division did not have a chaplain, a soldier would volunteer to lead religious services. This proves that some had a religious background or traditions that linked them to their parents and their homes.⁴³

Chaplain Sandrow noticed that a lot of Jews in the service "did not know where they stood." Those who feared being discovered, he noted, formed "a third type," which included those who declared "no religious affiliation." Thus, the letter O was stamped on their dog tags. The choice of assimilation involved taking on the traits of American culture. It was facilitated by an absence of identification with the Jewish people. Chaplain Sandrow offered his views on this choice: "Officers are the majority in this escapist category. Personal ambition, psychological fear, social aspirations are causes of this attempt at folk suicide."⁴⁴ He voiced his disapproval of those who assimilated to the point of obliterating all traces of their religious or cultural heritage.

Also reflecting on the attempt to assimilate, Rabbi Arthur Hertzberg wrote about the illusion of complete assimilation in his noted autobiography. To him, blotting out one's ethnic belonging is hardly feasible: "The Jew who tries to assimilate is abandoning his own identity in the hope that those who speak for the majority culture will welcome him, or her, and pronounce Jews to be acceptable in their society. But I knew from my own life that this seldom happened."⁴⁵ This was part of the war experiences of some soldiers, as noted in further chapters.

***

Most prejudiced soldiers were more concerned with the negative image of the Jew than with his Jewishness. A decorated infantryman, Marty Silverman endured humiliation in his rifle company: "We caught every lousy detail and all the abuse one could take. But on the other hand, it kind of strengthened us, kept us together—number one and number two—we knew we had to survive this. There was no other way. So we suffered the indignities, we suffered being called a kike, Jew bastard, and all the good things these guys who came up from the South, these redneck, never-saw-a-Jew-before guys called us."⁴⁶ Silverman did not consider himself a religious Jew, although his mother lit the Sabbath candles, and they attended services on Rosh Hashanah (the New Year) and Yom Kippur (the Day of Atonement). Earlier in his testimony, he recounted that in Troy, the Catholic town in which he grew up, "they used to teach the kids in Sunday school that the Jews killed Jesus Christ. Every Monday, we had to either fight or run. . . . I think more than anything else the Catholics made a Jew out of me. If they'd left me alone, I don't know if I'd be so sensitive about being Jewish."[47]

Significantly, no Jew can truly escape his Jewishness. Even if he is tempted to assimilate or convert, he remains a Jew according to Jewish law—and often, too, in the eyes of non-Jews, even if not in his own eyes. This may be called the inescapability of the Jewish condition, a concept developed by French philosopher Emmanuel Lévinas, who was in captivity as a French soldier. For servicemen and women who were victims of antisemitism, being Jewish became, at least momentarily, a source of malaise, distress, or unhappiness within a group that did not accept them. As noted in many essays written by veterans in 1946, the shock of rejection was more important and unexpected for those whose Jewishness was not a meaningful facet of their lives. A service member firmly rooted in his or her Jewishness by family ties or emotional ties to other Jews experienced less of a shock. Therefore, Jews tended to stick together, the better to buffer the shock of rejection.

Jewish servicemen who yearned to be officers, aware of the discrimination practiced against them, understandably hid their Jewishness by changing their name. This was the case of Sergeant Milton Fields, who managed to avoid antisemitism in training but kept attending and even conducting Jewish services. Though soldiers like him were not considered as Jews in the first phase of their military service, they were later identified as Jews by their peers.

Jews negotiated their own identities depending on the environment, the phase of their existence, and their war experiences. Since service members were free to restrict their Jewishness to an island in their personal space, Jewishness could be invisible to others if the serviceman or servicewoman's name did not sound Jewish. The scope of Jewishness was narrowed if the GI suppressed such activities as attendance at collective religious services. Conversely, if Jewishness was linked to certain Jewish activities, the soldier could express religiosity as a Jew in the American military. Religiousness also served as a crutch apt to strengthen the soldier in times of danger. The abridged prayer book published by the Jewish Welfare Board (JWB) offered moral support to service members. Over one million copies were distributed. The small size (thirteen centimeter in length) volume was "designed to be used where the exigencies of life in the army or the navy do not permit attendance at regular synagogue services." Yet when it fell in the hands of the Nazis, it became a dangerous sign of Jewishness.[48]

In view of the high percentage of Jews in the American military during World War II, the scarcity of Stars of David in cemeteries—particularly in D-Day cemeteries—needs to be addressed. In the final draft of a report to the Committee on Army and Navy Religious Activities (CANRA) of the JWB completed at the end of 1945, Rabbi Philip S. Bernstein, who served as Executive Director of CANRA, expanded on this issue, providing historians and sociologists with a precious primary source that is now in the American Jewish Historical Society. In a paragraph entitled "Recording the Dead," Bernstein broached this complex subject with its tragic overtones.

> Despite the detailed regulations, it was early noted that a large percentage of the Jewish dead were not buried under the Star of David. This was due a variety of reasons.... There was undoubtedly some loss through carelessness and incompetence.
>
> These factors combined to present CANRA with a tragic situation: probably no more than half of the Jewish dead were buried under the Star of David. Information possessed by the JWB (The National Jewish Welfare Board) War Records Bureau, based largely on authentic reports from local communities and families was far more complete than that in the possession of the War Department. Sample studies of War Department files thus led to the sad conclusion that nearly 45% of the authenticated Jewish dead were not so recorded in the official records.[49]

Following the steps taken by CANRA, Chief of Staff General George C. Marshall required that every military commander in each theater of war give Jewish chaplains the possibility of visiting the cemeteries in their command. The aim, in cooperation with the War Department, was to provide the opportunity, whenever and wherever possible, to ensure that "a Jewish marker be placed on every grave and Jewish memorial services be conducted."[50] As many soldiers noted in their testimonies, the real heroes were those who did not come back: those who returned to dust with utter humility, embodying the paragon of humanity. When Rabbi Bernstein published his report, first written in 1945, he wrote a preface in December 1970: "Over six hundred thousand Jews served in the U.S. armed forces, the largest number in uniform of all Jewish history."[51]

Heroism may be seen as a selfless response from those who experienced social invisibility as Jews. Jewish soldiers fought on several fronts: for the United States and for Jews all over the world, waging a personal war against anti-Jewish hostility in the American military.[52] Servicemen conducted several Jewish services of worship on German soil after American troops entered Germany on September 11, 1944. But one particular service remains in history. With the sound of artillery guns interfering, the first broadcast of a Jewish religious service from Nazi Germany to the world took place on October 29, 1944, near Aachen, not far from the French line. It exemplified the triumph of Jewish faith over Nazi tyranny, bent on the systematic destruction of the Jewish people and religion. The National Broadcasting Company in cooperation with the American Jewish Committee offered "a special broadcast of historic significance." Under the direction of Chaplain Sydney Lefkowitz of the United States First Army, a choir of over fifty American soldiers evinced their eagerness to pray and demonstrate religious freedom. "May the Lord bless thee and keep thee," they chanted, while artillery fire sounded in the background.[53] The words spoken by Chaplain Edward Waters on behalf of the Catholic faith and those of Lieutenant Colonel Bernard Henry on behalf of the Protestants acknowledged the legitimacy and visibility of the Jewish religion as an American faith.

Jewish servicewomen were visible on two fronts: as courageous American women ahead of their time and as Jews. The next chapter offers an exploration of the challenges faced by the daring "flying women," both as pilots and nurses.[54]

# HEROINES TOOK TO THE SKIES

Sweetwater, Texas, December 7, 1944. The day marked the anniversary of the infamous Japanese attack against the naval base at Pearl Harbor. On that occasion, Commanding General of the Air Force Henry H. Arnold was to deliver a memorable speech. A pioneer airman who had become a four-star general, Arnold addressed the last class of Women Airforce Service Pilots (WASP), class 44–10: "Frankly, I didn't know in 1941 whether a slip of a young girl could fight the controls of a B17 in the heavy weather they would naturally encounter in operational flying. Those of us who had been flying for twenty or thirty years knew that flying an airplane was something that you do not learn overnight. But Miss Cochran said that carefully selected young women could be trained to fly our combat-type planes. So, it was only right that we take advantage of every skill that we, as a nation, possessed."[1] Young American women made aviation history while striving to be accepted in a military framework. Many became pioneers in new fields of wartime service. Too many sacrificed their lives. Only much later did some of them become aware of the outstanding contribution they had made to their country and the world, as is perhaps best expressed by Jewish flight nurse Yetta Moskowitz: "The world should be made aware of what the flight nurses did. We started air evacuation medicine, which helped save thousands of lives."[2]

When the war broke out, all branches of the armed forces launched publicity campaigns to encourage women to enlist to "free a man to fight."[3] This chapter explores the challenges, assignments, and achievements of Jewish women pilots among the WASP and of flight nurses. It sheds light on the difficulties encountered because of gender and sometimes religion, drawing on the testimonies of pilots Bernice Falk Haydu, Selma Kantor Cronan, and Elizabeth Haas Pfister. Unlike the flight nurses, whose itineraries are also examined in this chapter, women pilots were not sent overseas during the war, as they had to replace men in non-combat duties. Some nurses sent to the Pacific, however, were in flight for numerous hours and operated close to combat zones, which is why they had to carry a revolver.[4] Ironically, male combat medics who dodged bullets on the battlefield carried first-aid kits but not weapons. In every unit where Jewish women were accepted, in either the European or Pacific theater of the war, they had to be prepared to confront anti-Jewish attitudes.

## Jewish Women Pilots: A Double Challenge

Bernice Falk Haydu, a woman pilot who fought relentlessly and successfully for congressional recognition of the WASP as military personnel, admitted that she was afraid to encounter anti-Jewish prejudice while training as a pilot. This is how she accounted for this pervasive feeling: "I graduated high school in 1938. The job market was extremely difficult.... It was not unusual to read, 'Jews need not apply.' Usually, when you applied for a job in those days you were asked your religion. In my first job they did not ask but as I was working there I could hear remarks against the Jews. I was only 17 and frankly I did not know how to handle the situation so I would just keep quiet."[5]

By keeping quiet and working hard, the strong-headed woman worked her way to the top, to the "always blue skies" she dreamed of.[6] The letters Bernice Falk wrote to her mother in 1944 and 1945 are a treasure trove. They enable us to understand the exceptional character of war experiences and the challenges faced by a young Jewish woman. On December 15, 1920, Bernice Falk was, in her own words, "born into this industrious family where the women were emancipated and enjoyed the freedom to work and help earn money for their families. They were independent and wanted to succeed. They were not constrained by the Victorian idea that women shouldn't work outside the home or that some occupations were available only to men."[7] Della Blum, her mother, was a role model for the future pilot. She exemplified resourcefulness by opening an employment agency in Montclair, New Jersey, and renting out rooms in the large family house. Bernice knew she would not be able to attend college because of the Depression. There would only be enough money for her brother. One of her high school teachers told her parents that given her school results, she could study accountancy in college. Though very disappointed not to be able to study, she finally decided not to indulge in self-pity. She took courses to become a secretary, "one of the few jobs open to women," she emphasized. In the competitive job market of the Depression, she managed to get jobs as a secretary in two real estate offices. The frustration of not being able to benefit from a higher education prompted her to look for night school courses.[8]

To her surprise, Bernice found courses in aviation. By then, her brother had enlisted in the Army Air Forces, serving in France as a meteorologist during the Allied landings. In 1943, Bernice Falk enrolled in an aviation course at the Newark College of Engineering. Her instructor at the college ran a flight school at Martins Creek, Pennsylvania, some seventy miles away from where she lived in New Jersey. This distance did not alter her zest for flying airplanes, even if she could only find the time to do so on weekends. On Friday nights, she would take a Greyhound bus to Belvedere, where her instructor would pick her and other students up and bring them to Martins Creek. The instructor rented a house on the Delaware River, not far from Martins Creek airport, and Bernice Falk would stay overnight with the other students, mostly young women but also young men. Charlie Grieder, her instructor, only had four planes, but it was in his school that she made her first solo flight on August 1, 1943. It was a milestone for her. Like her brother Lloyd, Bernice Falk was eager to help in the war effort. Together with six other girls who had taken lessons at Martins Creek, she applied for the experimental WASP program and was accepted. One of the requirements was thirty-five hours of flying time. The seven students all qualified to join the WASP class of 44–7. But nothing was easily attained:

> After applying we were interviewed by Mrs. Ethel Sheehy, Jacqueline Cochran's representative. If accepted we had to take and pass the Army Air Force physical for pilots, supply character references and get release forms from our current employers if we had a defense related job. Mine was defense related.
> Once approved and assigned a class we traveled to Sweetwater, Texas, the location of the training school, at our own expense. If we failed any part of the seven-month training program we had to return home, again at our own expense.[9]

Bernice passed the physical examination as well as the other tests.

Her letters from February 1944, her first weeks of army life, depict her impressions of the army and the new environment. As a girl born and raised in Montclair, New Jersey, Bernice was awed when she reached the small Texan cowboy town, where men "wear large hats and talk funny," she pointed out in an interview in 2000.[10] She discovered vast expanses of land she had never seen in New Jersey: "So much sky could be seen all at once."[11]

One letter was intended to reassure her mother about the food she got for meals. Bernice Falk did not follow any Jewish dietary laws and was at first satisfied with the meat they were served. Before ending her letter of February 14, 1944, she added: "I hear we are going to be psychoanalyzed this afternoon."[12] Indeed, being a pilot implied self-control and emotional balance—and this was only the beginning of a training program basically identical to that of male cadets. Marching in a military fashion was one of the drills in this new landscape where girls were transformed into trainees, becoming military material. Unlike the men, they had to wear turbans on their heads to hide their long hair. Indeed, Major Robert Urban, the air force commanding officer at the base, demanded that they cover their heads with what were called "Urban's turbans." The inclusion of female cadets was so new that the rules were pragmatic.

The ample male coveralls or "Zoot suits" worn in the cockpit were another aspect of physical metamorphosis. Tailored for male cadets, such suits were popular in the 1940s: "full-legged, tight-cuffed trousers and a long coat with white lapels and heavily padded wide shoulders."[13] It was no use complaining about their overlarge features because in the military, you wear what is issued. Bernice Falk Haydu added that most of the tall girls—height was a requirement—found a way to tuck the coveralls in with a large belt to adapt them to their size. Female cadets would have worn anything if it allowed them to fly. One piece of evidence of this dedication is a song entitled "Zoot Suits and Parachutes," sung by the girls to familiar tunes as they marched, a large part of ground training together with daily physical training. One of the lines goes: "If you have a daughter, teach her how to fly."[14]

Such details show to what extent the identity of a woman pilot was in the making. All the WASP dreamed of flying, and their emotions and expectations depended on the achievement of a dream of freedom, empowerment, and service to their country. In a letter dated March 9, 1944, Bernice Falk addressed her mother's fear about antisemitism on the base.

> Don't worry about getting on with the girls or liking them. Sure, they are swell, but in a group of over a hundred, you are bound to have one or two who rub you the wrong way. Two of them just happen to be in my bay but there is no outward show of dislike. It is merely that for eating and going out with friends I choose others. Please don't take it seriously. I wrote most of it to give an idea of the partiality of Texans to Texans.
>
> As for antisemitism (which is what I presume you were hinting at), there seems to be very little. I have not seen any and many of the girls already know my religion. *I want them to know.* Besides the kids from Martin

Creeks are swell and I am sure would stick up for me if trouble arose—and I don't think this would ever happen. Don't worry!¹⁵

It is interesting to see how Bernice differentiated between a "dislike" other girls may have nourished for her and antisemitism, which would have led the "kids" (her fellow trainees) of Martin Creeks to defend or "stick up for" her in case of a conflict and hostility. In a postscript to her letter, Bernice Falk added that in her bay of six, "we practiced six different religions and all got along well. Baptist, Christian Science, Jewish, Mormon, Protestant, Seventh Day Adventist. It can be done."[16] Bays were rooms within the barracks that accommodated eight female cadets at Avenger Field. Both inside and outside the bays, cadets were subject to military discipline. In an interview, Falk Haydu mentioned that the barracks were "very primitive": "We slept in cots and had lockers." During the Saturday morning inspection, someone wearing white gloves would come to check if there was any dust in the lockers. If dust was found on top of the lockers and windowsills, cadets could get a demerit; if a female cadet had too many demerits, she could be washed out. But this would more commonly happen when a female cadet did not pass a flight test. Military discipline at Avenger Field implied half a day spent marching, while physical training took place every day. The other half of the day was devoted to flight training.

The next phase of the seven months of training required the use of a device called a Link trainer (now called a flight simulator). Without necessitating leaving the ground, an imitation airplane with illuminated instruments and controls allowed practice of instrument flying, with the pilot in a "black box" simulating the cockpit. In a letter dated April 30, 1944, Bernice detailed to her mother her first impressions and the novel requirements of the new phase of training: "As soon as we finish in the AT-6 we are supposed to go into instrument flying and Link is an aid to that. It is enough to drive you daffy trying to watch all the gadgets at once. We started meteorology in ground school and are still taking navigation and engine maintenance."[17] It was a "big jump" for Bernice and the female cadets. The transition from a PT-17 with 220 horsepower to a 650-horsepower AT-6 with sophisticated gadgets was difficult, as she explained to her supportive mother: "The cockpit procedure is very long and difficult. We use radios in this ship. Every time we take off or land we have to call the tower for permission."[18] Elaborating on the fact that she and the young women experiencing this harsh transition were "guinea-pigs," Falk Haydu emphasized the idea behind the challenge: "if women can do it, then men can do it too."[19] A postscript added to her letter is explicit: "The class of 44-4 (three classes ahead of us) was the first class of trainees to go directly into the AT-6 advanced trainer from PT-17 primary trainer. Jacqueline Cochran visited Sweetwater to explain that this was the first time the Air Force was taking this step and if it proved successful the male cadets would be trained in this manner."[20]

A photograph in Falk Haydu's book captures her looking very focused in what seems to be a serious conversation with her AT-6 instructor. Bernice started flying an AT-6 aircraft with her instructor on April 27 and was able to fly solo after ten and a half hours with him. She wrote to her mother on May 11, 1944.

> Dearest Mom,
>
> With the help of prayers from myself and my five bay mates two nights in a row I managed to at last solo the AT-6 today. Golly, Mom, it sure is hard work to fly this plane. I am going to have to work very hard to get through this phase but if hard work will do, you can be assured I will make it, Mom. This is a picture of the ship. I wish I could take a snapshot of me next to it but we are not allowed to do so.[21]

All this while, she and the other WASP worried about whether or not they would finally be formally militarized after the demanding experimental program, as General H. Arnold hoped.

Thirty-eight young women pilots sacrificed their lives in the service of their country, including Betty Stine in her AT-6. The young woman had to bail out of her aircraft, and her parachute pushed her violently against a cliff in Tucson, causing a fatal head injury.[22] For her well-researched book, Jean Hascall Cole, who was in the same class as Betty Stine, interviewed other WASP of the class (44-W-2) in an effort to understand why Stine's plane failed her. A report mentioned the possibility of sabotaged aircraft. Some mechanics were former cadets who had failed their flying test. Resentment toward women pilots was not unusual. At times, base personnel were lax, and a number of parts could be found loose in a plane. Other instances of sabotage involved repatriated prisoners of war (POWs) from Germany "tested" by the WASP on the base because of the shortage of pilots.

> At one time some of the men who had been prisoners of war in Germany came back. We would take them up and check them out because they hadn't flown for a long time. We rode in the front seat and they rode in the back seat to get the feel of it again. Some of them had been in prison for a long time and they were scary to fly with. They had been instructed by men and they didn't like being checked out by a woman who was going to decide whether or not they could fly. Sometimes they would swear at us.[23]

Another WASP made a relevant comment after Stine's death: "Those AT-6s—when I think they sent us out on those long flights, over mountains with no mountain experience, and very little AT-6 cross-country time, it makes me mad. Also, we didn't have what the FAA requires now—a forty-five-minute gas reserve. I mis-figured my course correction and almost ran out of gas, so there was only a short time of extra flying. There was very little room for error."[24] Commenting on the beautiful AT-6s and their dangers, Falk Haydu made it clear that a number of male pilots had voiced complaints about these aircrafts that the WASP were then entitled to fly. In 2000, her interviewer asked why she felt that women pilots were guinea pigs. With a sad smile, she simply answered: "We were expendable."[25]

A letter to her mother dated April 30, 1944, clearly expresses the worries of the WASP at a time when their resilience was most needed.

> Dear Mom,
>
> We don't know from one day to the next whether we will be kicked out entirely. I fear the latter. Perhaps a letter from you and some of our friends like Sam, Amelia and those guys to our congressman urging him to vote the WASP into the Army Air Force would help. You might say that men are needed in other branches of service, such as the Infantry where women are absolutely useless so why not let the men go into the Infantry and permit the women to do a job that already has been proven they can do and can do well.[26]

Like the other WASP, Bernice Falk learned how to plan cross-country flights by preparing charts and calculations of time, speed, distance, and fuel consumption, checking how wind could affect velocity and cloud coverage could impact visibility with the weather briefer before a flight. On July 31, 1944, she wrote her mother that she would have to undergo pressure chamber tests (up to twenty-eight thousand feet) to evaluate reactions to high altitude.[27] She also experienced two-hour cross-country night trips on Monday and Tuesday nights. After graduation (September 8, 1944), Bernice's first assignment was to Pecos Air Force Base in Pecos, Texas. Bernice explicitly detailed this assignment in a letter dated September 24, somewhat concealing the amount of courage or guts it called for.

> The job the WASP are doing here is test hopping. When an airplane has been repaired, it must be tested. The airplanes are called UC-78, or AT-17s (the same plane). . . . Saturday I went up as copilot with another WASP. You have to fly fifty hours as copilot before you can be checked out as first pilot. . . . Major Rizzo, our immediate superior is a swell guy. He is going to do all he can to get us qualified dual instruction of some sort. He said

he would rather have ten WASP rather than a bunch of lieutenants because the WASP are conscientious, work hard, and try to do all they can instead of doing as little as possible.²⁸

But in a letter to her mother dated October 5, 1944, Bernice recounted the shock she received: the WASP were to be disbanded on December 20. It was a blow, even if they had come to expect it. But instead of indulging in self-pity, she decided to focus on increasing her flying time to get another flying assignment.²⁹

A milestone in Bernice's life was the obtention of the coveted wings and official diploma from the United States Army Air Force with the citation "Bernice Sarah Falk has satisfactorily completed the course of instruction prescribed for women pilots." The noting of the date together with the words "our Lord" reminds us of the religious ethos prevalent in the United States: "Sweetwater, Texas, the eighth day of September in the year of our Lord one thousand nine hundred and forty-four." In her interview for the Museum of Jewish Heritage, the former engineering test pilot and "utility pilot" expanded on the different design of the wings for male and female pilots. She explained that there was a shield on the men's wings, whereas the women's wings had a lozenge representing a diamond. She added humorously that "it is not because diamonds are a girl's best friend, but because diamonds are the Greek symbol of womanhood."³⁰ It is interesting to note that although women pilots did everything the male cadets did, they were reminded of their womanhood and encouraged to wear lipstick. Was it to make them better match gender stereotypes? Or was it because the two prominent pilots who took the initiative to form the WASP, Nancy Love and Jacqueline Cochran, were elegant, feminine, attractive women pilots, as were most of the tall, young WASP? They still faced gender prejudice while on the ground, in restaurants for instance. In several interviews, Falk Haydu deplored that some did not accept women pilots in slacks—their working clothes—because women were expected to wear a skirt or a dress.

Asked why the WASP program ended abruptly and women pilots had to wait until 1977 to be recognized as military personnel with all due honors, Falk Haydu replied: "They needed more men in the infantry, so the male pilots didn't want that, they banded together and got adverse publicity against 'the million dollar glamour girls.'"³¹ Attaining recognition as veterans did not come easily. This recognition came from the resilience of the WASP in the continued struggle to achieve equal status with men and obtain veterans' benefits, a long battle in which Falk Haydu actively took part. On May 26, 1977, the *Stars and Stripes* wittingly summed up the issue at stake: "How 'military' is military? When is a war time military pilot, Not a wartime military pilot? When she is a woman."[32]

Selma Kantor Cronan's itinerary as a WASP has been outlined in the two previous chapters. However, it is worthwhile to mention a sentence that reveals her passion for flying: "From the time my mother took me on a two dollar airplane ride in Asbury Park, New Jersey in the 1920s, I fell in love with flying and I knew I was going to be a pilot someday."[33] Unlike Bernice Falk, Cronan was already a certified pilot in 1943 and had a supportive husband when she enlisted "to do the job," eager to fight the Nazis. Her enlistment as a pilot followed Jacqueline Cochran's invitation in 1943 to join the WASP. It was quite an honor to be spotted by the first female aviator to fly for the United States Air Force. However, she confessed having felt excluded from activities while based at Avenger Field on account of being Jewish, as detailed in the previous chapter. Notwithstanding, Cronan achieved recognition as a pioneering American woman pilot. A few words in her interview by the Museum of Jewish Heritage reveal that she was sent to France immediately after the end of the war in Europe to locate French women pilots who had been part of the underground in France. It is inspiring to know she met with celebrated French aviator Maryse Bastié, and both talked about their war experiences. Bastié, a pioneer woman pilot who obtained her license in 1925, shared with her American counterpart personal stories "too long to retell" in her interview with the Museum of Jewish Heritage in New York.[34]

Selma Cronan, who competed in several all-women transcontinental air races, participated in a meeting with Russian women pilots in 1990.[35] During that conference, she seized the opportunity to visit Kiev, which was the capital of Soviet Ukraine when the German forces invaded the Soviet Union in June 1941. One hundred sixty thousand Jews had lived in Kiev before a large number of Jewish men, women, and children were systematically murdered by Einsatzgruppen detachments. Shootings in Odessa claimed more than fifty thousand victims. Selma Kantor Cronan placed a wreath at the memorial at Babi Yar in remembrance of the 33,771 Jews executed there in two days. Identifying more with the Jewish people and culture than with Jewish religious practice, she admitted: "This experience strengthened my identity as a Jew as nothing had before."[36]

Some thirty former WASP encountered the "Night Witches," many of whom flew bombers on night raids against the enemy. Pilot Jean Hascall Cole cites another Jewish pilot, Elizabeth Haas Pfister, as having met the intrepid Russian World War II women pilots who downed Nazi planes in the dark of the night.³⁷ These encounters emphasize the identity of American women pilots as one having much in common with women pilots of other Allied nations.

In a March 2006 interview published by *Airport Journals*, an online magazine that serves the general aviation community, Elizabeth Haas Pfister, reflected on her life path. She was born in July 1921 to a well-to-do family in Great Neck, Long Island. Her mother, Merle Simon Haas, was a housewife, while her father, Robert Haas, was a vice president of Random House Publishing Company in New York City. She was the middle child between her brother, Robert "Bob" Jr., whom she admired and imitated, and her sister, Priscilla. She developed a love of flying after a first ride that cost her five dollars on "an old Waco biplane with an open cockpit."³⁸ Betty, who studied marine biology at Bennington College in Vermont in 1940, made a deal with her father: if she studied hard and kept her grades up, he would pay for her flying lessons. Motivated by her handsome brother, who attended Yale University and enlisted as a pilot in the navy, she obtained her private license at age twenty: "He was a year older than I was. Really, he was one of the reasons I started flying. I wanted to try everything he did."³⁹ In the context of the severe shortage of both pilots and airplanes, Betty Haas, like all women pilots who had recorded between 170 and 180 hours of flight time with the Civil Aviation Authority, was contacted by telegram by noted pilot Jacqueline Cochran. Betty's immediate response was to accept. "It was a wonderful program; I was so lucky. I was at the right age, at the right place and at the right time," she recalled, adding that she was soon assigned to join class 43-W-4. She "was in the first WASP class held at Sweetwater." This is probably why there were still male cadets on the base whom they did not have time to meet or "say hello [to] because we were so busy with our own program."⁴⁰ While Betty Haas was studying and flying, her gifted twenty-one-year-old brother was a naval aviator aboard a baby flat-top carrier. One day, she received the news that he had died in a maneuver off the coast of North Africa when the ship's catapult had failed.⁴¹ "It was a very traumatic experience for me," she could only say. The following day, she flew home to support her parents. With such a loss, Betty's enlistment as a WASP became questionable. Her flight assignments involved much danger. Knowing that their daughter would be ferrying planes from one coast to the other and testing old repaired planes that had been damaged in their missions was terrifying for her parents. But her brother's tragedy only made Betty more determined to accomplish the missions he could no longer undertake. She identified with him so much that she almost lived through him. Respecting their daughter's will, the family eventually decided that Betty could finish her training. After graduating in September 1943, Betty took on flying duties that included ferrying all types of planes across the country.

In October 1944, she and other WASP were transferred to Williams Field in Mesa, Arizona, where she was to serve as a test pilot along with performing other duties: "The cadets would crack up a plane quite often. Every time they did, a WASP always test-flew it first, before the male cadets. We were considered expendable."[42] The distrust and negative attitudes some male pilots harbored against the WASP are demonstrated in interviews that pilot Jean Hascall Cole gathered for her book. Confirming this stance, Pfister added in her interview for *Airport Journals* that it was "a miracle" if everything went well with the planes they checked. She went so far as to state that some mechanics would sabotage aircraft so as to frighten the WASP out of service for their country.[43] In her research drawing on interviews with the members of her class 44-W-2, former WASP and author Hascall Cole also found that although the stories of sabotage seemed unlikely at first, three women pilots were convinced that damage to their aircraft was deliberate. Cole added that many of the WASP "had some frightening and difficult emergencies."[44] Pfister noted that sabotage was not done on every base to which she was dispatched; however, there were recurring cases in which "they were putting sugar in the tanks, which would plug the engine up very nicely"—it "was enough to scare the heck out of you."[45]

Given the hurdles these young women pilots encountered on the road to gaining their peers' acceptance, one might expect a general feminine solidarity based on the prevailing identity of WASP, acquired through so much effort and pain. Yet the bonds created by the new shared identity depended on military facilities. In Williams Field, Mesa, Elizabeth Haas Pfister and other young WASP found that they were not made to feel unwelcome only by male pilots. She was surprised to find that the other females on the base also received them coldly. Trying to understand this unfriendly attitude, Pfister offered a plausible explanation: "Probably because they had to share their barracks with us."[46]

When the war program ended on December 20, 1944, Pfister shared with other WASP the feeling that "she had done what she had to do" to serve her country. Like most of the women pilots in the ferrying division who had specialized in this demanding type of flying for a period of eighteen months, she had acquired great efficiency. Thanks to her war experiences, she had accumulated some eight hundred hours of flight. But after the WASP disbanded, she found herself with no flying job, although she wrote to every aviation company. Some of them bluntly refused the services of women pilots while others were less direct when formulating a negative response. She had to accept a few odd jobs, including a position as pilot of nonscheduled cargo planes of livestock bound for South Africa and as a flight attendant for Pan American Airways between 1948 and 1952. She married Arthur Pfister, a veteran also of Jewish origin, and they settled in Aspen, Colorado. Both left a mark on the social and physical landscape of Aspen. The deep trauma of the accidental death of Betty Haas Pfister's admired pilot brother during World War II triggered in her a lifelong concern with safety. A rated glider pilot, her achievements were numerous and included founding the Pitkin County Air Rescue Group in 1968, which gathered local pilots to search for overdue aircraft in the Aspen area, and supervising the construction of the Aspen Valley Hospital Heliport with safety in mind, as she explained in a video interview.[47] Serving as an accident prevention specialist, she was a member of the US Nixon's Women's Advisory Committee on Aviation from 1969 to 1972. A founder of the Aspen chapter of the women pilot organization the Ninety-Nines in 1981, Betty was also a 1995 inductee to the Aspen Hall of Fame as a helicopter pilot. Like Selma Kantor Cronan, who engaged in air races, Pfister participated in World Helicopter Championships in England in 1973 and in Russia in 1978. She received a Congressional Gold Medal in 2009 together with other surviving WASP, including Bernice Falk Haydu, who was influential in obtaining recognition of the WASP as veterans. Selma Kantor Cronan died in 2002, too early to receive belated recognition, and was interred at Arlington National Cemetery—a noted military distinction, though one that required her body be cremated. These three former WASP also raised children: Cronan adopted twins, and both Bernice Falk Haydu and Betty Haas Pfister had three children. They all had supportive husbands who were World War II veterans and understood their passion for flying. To mention one, Arthur O. Pfister was a pilot during World War II; first stationed on the Brahmaputra River in the Assam Valley, he flew C-46 planes, delivering gasoline from India to China.

## Jewish "Winged Angels" and Evacuation Medicine

If gasoline was needed to wage the war, medical services were needed to keep the GIs fighting. With the development of air routes, a new program of evacuation medicine turned enlisted flight nurses into pioneering women. The global aspect of World War II led the US Army Air Forces to introduce a revolution in medical care, today called aeromedical evacuation. The urgent need for flight nursing was felt acutely after the Allied invasion of North Africa on November 8, 1942. Operation Torch involved American and British military forces in an amphibious operation against the French-held territories of Algeria and Morocco.[48] Although the nurses at Bowman Field (near Louisville, Kentucky) had not yet completed their four weeks of basic training at that time, they were sent to North Africa on Christmas Day. The first class of flight nurses graduated on February 18, 1943, at Bowman Field.[49]

Nurses had the lives of soldiers in their hands and therefore had to gather equipment and medicines necessary for a long flight, sometimes up to a week. Evacuation by air of wounded and ill military personnel from the various theaters of war required efficiency, professional skill, and intuition—and, of course, the ability to cope with severe sleep deprivation and permanent stress. Flight nurses who slept on GI cots and under GI blankets during training also received dog tags and silver wings.[50] As declared in a 1944 film from the American War Department, "above and beyond duty, the nurse gently guides men to the way of life they fought to protect."[51] The five hundred army flight nurses serving with the Army Air Force as members of more than thirty medical air squadrons in the Pacific and the European theaters evacuated over one million patients by air between January 1943 and May 1945.[52] Prepared for the unexpected, flight nurses did everything a medical doctor does except perform surgery. They guided GIs back to life and health while encouraging them with a reassuring smile.[53]

One of these "winged angels" was young curly-haired and light-eyed Yetta Moskowitz (nicknamed "Mosky"), a Jewish flight nurse who enlisted and was sent overseas immediately after graduation. She was one of three nurses on board an American ship attending to seven thousand troops, including a primary contingent of Women's Army Corps (WAC), and the prime minister of Australia. The courage and resourcefulness of Yetta Moskowitz under fire earned her a promotion to chief nurse of her squadron: the 804th MAES Fifty-Fourth TCC Fifth AF. Yetta (also written Etta) completed her training at the Air Force School of Air Evacuation at Bowman Field in June 1944, where she learned crash procedures and how to prepare for an emergency. This training served her when she faced adversity overseas.[54] The first line of the "Flight Nurse's Creed" must have resonated in her mind while the adrenaline did the rest: "I will summon every resource to prevent the triumph of death over life."[55] The emergency procedures for flight nurses included carrying thirty-eight-caliber revolvers. In a photograph dated June 1943, First Lieutenant Yetta Moskowitz carries a weapon on her shoulder. An emergency could occur if an aircraft was shot down and the crew needed to bail out into enemy territory. Survival training and physical training were helpful when bailing out onto stretches of land inhabited by wild animals, as in New Guinea, where Yetta Moskowitz was sent. The sky became a new home for flight nurses like her. When First Lieutenant Moskowitz was discharged from the Army Air Force in December 1945, she received an air medal for flying more than a hundred hours above combat zones to evacuate wounded GIs in New Guinea and the Philippines.[56] Moskowitz was also among the first Americans to enter Manila after the capture of the Philippines. She later flew to Tachikawa, Japan, to evacuate POWs. On her safe return to the United States in December 1945, she was discharged at Fort Dix, New Jersey. Barely a month later, Moskowitz sailed to England to bring back the first group of war brides.[57]

Moskowitz's best friend died while on a mission. Like sixteen other flight nurses, young Lieutenant Beatrice H. Memler, a Jewish flight nurse nicknamed "Bobby," was killed in action off Mindanao Island in the Philippines on March 12, 1945.[58] She, too, had volunteered to dedicate herself to saving American soldiers' lives. Her aircraft was part of the 804th MAES squadron. Beatrice Memler was declared dead while missing on a medical air evacuation mission from Elmore Airstrip (Mindoro) to Tanuan Airfield (Leyte). No survivors were found; the plane's crew perished together with twenty-eight wounded.[59] Her name is commemorated on the funeral tablets of the missing at the Manila American Cemetery in the Philippines. It is also recorded in the book by I. Kaufmann that lists the names of Jewish servicemen and servicewomen from every state of the United States who served in World War II.[60] Second Lieutenant Beatrice H. Memler, memorialized by the people of New York, was posthumously awarded a Purple Heart.[61] Her husband, Sergeant Julius Memler, enlisted during the war and survived her.

Women who took to the skies included mechanics. A revealing example is Miranda (Randy) Bloch, who defied her parents' firmly grounded notions that military life was not a proper choice for a Jewish girl. The nineteen-year-old waited until her twenty-first birthday to be able to enlist in the United States Marine Corps on September 30, 1943. Her move was not only defiant—it was impressive. She was sworn in on the steps of the imposing Library of Congress in Washington, DC. The event and its implications were life changing: Miranda Bloch, born in Jerusalem in the

Fig. 3.1 First Lieutenant Yetta Moskowitz carrying a weapon on her shoulder, June 1943. Courtesy of the National Museum of American Jewish Military History, Washington, DC.

Jewish homeland of Palestine on June 26, 1922, stood opposite Major Ruth Cheney Streeter, the first commanding officer of the United States Marine Corps Women's Reserve. Did the major know that Miranda Bloch's father had gone to Palestine as an aide to General John J. Pershing in World War I? Patriotism and a feeling of duty toward one's community must have run in the Bloch family. As with other women pilots and flight nurses who grew up during the Depression years, a sense of adventure may have also spurred this young woman to action.

While stationed at Camp LeJeune, North Carolina, for basic training, Miranda Bloch struck her superiors with an unexpected aptitude for mechanics. In the Marine Corps, the need for qualified airplane mechanics had become critical. It was concomitant with the need for women pilots to perform ferrying tasks and for flight nurses as the war progressed. Together with twenty-nine other enlisted servicewomen, Bloch was sent to an experimental aircraft radio class at a base that is today the Marine Corps Air Station at Cherry Point, North Carolina. Once she had successfully completed her training and could repair and install aircraft radio gear, she became one of the few servicewomen authorized to inspect, install, and repair such gear midflight—an admirable achievement. No wonder Miranda Bloch was among the few women Marines considered competent enough to be issued flight orders. At age twenty-one, her accomplishments did not go unnoticed. Could a young Jewish woman encroach on male territory? Over and above gender prejudice, she felt confident enough to fly with pilots bound for combat. Like all flight crew, she wore a standard alpaca-lined flight jacket or Mae West vest. She also carried a parachute in case it became necessary to bail out. Discharged in December 1945, Miranda Bloch, who later served as president of the greater Philadelphia chapter of the Women Marines Association, voiced the meaning of her enlistment: "I am proud that I had the guts and the patriotism to defy my parents and enlist in the service of my country when it needed me."[62] Miranda Bloch's competence and dedication at a time when mechanics were urgently needed could only foster respect on the part of her peers. She challenged prejudice in civil society, the family cell, and the military.

***

Young nurses and women pilots encountered multiple hurdles in carrying out their patriotic duties. They were confronted with the fact that airfields rarely had restrooms for female fliers and flight nurses. Female pilots defied the social hierarchy by accomplishing tasks traditionally left to men. Although they went above and beyond the call of duty, the WASP upset the social hierarchy by entering male territory and excelling in the elitist specialization of flying military aircraft. In doing so, Jewish female pilots—like their fellow non-Jewish women pilots—challenged the social and symbolic order of the 1940s. Flight nurses, unlike pilots in the WASP, were immediately inducted as military personnel. They not only ministered to every need but also symbolized the tenderness of a mother or a girlfriend; their maternal quality conjured up evocations of home. Women pilots may have been considered as competitors in the job market by men fliers toward the end of the war, whereas flight nurses were often called "flying angels" by GIs. Considering women's enlistment, historian William L. O'Neill contends that women who joined the military at the beginning of the war were viewed by some as "sluts" or lesbians. Consequently, if there had been fewer prejudiced Americans, more would have enlisted.[63] Let us recall that many Jewish parents told their children that "nice Jewish girls" do not join the military, and the determination of daughters to defy their loving parents in the name of patriotism is noteworthy.

In his memoirs, General Eisenhower admitted his own reluctance toward women's contributions in Algiers during Operation Torch, launched on November 8, 1942, as well as the skepticism of officers—until servicewomen proved them wrong. The following passage encapsulates both an awareness of "the changing requirements of war" and the evolution of perceptions of women in uniform in the American military.

> In December we received our first consignment of Women's Army corps personnel, then known as Women's Auxiliary Army Corps. Until my experience in London I had been opposed to the use of women in uniform but in Great Britain I had seen them perform so magnificently in various positions including service in active anti-aircraft batteries, that I had been converted. In Africa, many officers were still doubtful of women's usefulness in uniform—the older commanders in particular were filled with misgivings and open skepticism. What these men had failed to note was the changing requirements of war. . . . An army of filing clerks, stenographers, office managers, telephone operators, and chauffeurs had become essential and it was scarcely less than criminal to recruit these from needed manpower when great numbers of highly qualified women were available. From the day they first reached us their reputation as an efficient effective corps continued to grow. Toward the end of the war the most stubborn die-hards had become convinced and demanded them in increasing numbers.[64]

General Eisenhower's last statement apparently applied to WACs, not to women pilots who felt redundant when men came back from war and reclaimed their positions, threatened by the women's abilities. Nurses were a special category among the WACs because no proof was needed of their necessity alongside a fighting force. Eisenhower sharply noted this point: "From the outset of this war our nurses lived up to traditions tracing back to Florence Nightingale; consequently, it was difficult to understand the initial resistance to the employment of women in other activities."[65]

It is no coincidence that both former WASP pilots Bernice Falk Haydu and Elizabeth Haas Pfister expressed in their interviews the frustration that, no matter what accomplishments women pilots made during World War II, "they remained expendable." Selma Kantor Cronan made it clear that she would not have enlisted in the WASP program without the prospect of serving as a military pilot. They stressed the fact that their prevailing identity was that of a woman pilot who could fly military planes. WASP members were not militarized during the war years despite their contribution to the war effort. Some of them, with Bernice Falk Haydu at their lead, fought relentlessly for recognition, which was only obtained in 1977. Immediately after the war, they could not enjoy the military benefits given to their male counterparts. They could not study with funding from the GI Bill. Nevertheless, prejudice against their gender did not tarnish their cherished idea of America. The American values of liberty and justice continued to inspire them. These values instilled in these women, ahead of their time, the desire to continue to make this world a better place through good deeds. That is what Betty Haas Pfister did when she strove to establish a safe airport in Aspen for helicopters to bring patients to the emergency department. In her case, the core of being a Jew was practicing a moral way of life based on decent conduct toward other people. In so doing, she indirectly showed that Jews are not isolated from the rest of humanity by their ancestral faith or cultural belonging. Furthermore, many women who enlisted felt empowered both as women and as American citizens, if not as Jews. Ellen Levitsky Orkin, the daughter of immigrants—who volunteered as a nurse together with her sister Dorothy—confessed: "It strengthened me, there was nothing I was afraid to do."[66]

While in the military, many GIs noted the recurrence of antisemitic slurs directed not necessarily at Jewish ethics or religion but rather at the negative image of the Jew. How did Jewish GIs respond, when they did, to anti-Jewish hostility? This question is addressed in the next chapter.

# CONFRONTING BIASED ATTITUDES

It has been noted that in times of war, Jewish soldiers suffer in double measure: as citizens and as Jews.[1] A GI expressed his frustration thus: "Many of the boys still think of Jews as aliens, that the war is being fought to save 'Jewish kikes.'"[2] Drawing on soldiers' narratives, later writings, and oral history, this chapter aims to show how servicemen—especially those in combat units—confronted anti-Jewish attitudes in the military. It unveils their private struggles against anti-Jewish hostility and reveals how Zionist aspirations resonated with GIs who became aware of the large-scale extermination of the Jews. For some, the concept of a Jewish homeland in Palestine acquired significance—to which the miracle of Israel reborn and immediately threatened on May 14, 1948, lent extra weight. Historian Leonard Dinnerstein analyzes the deep insecurity still felt by American Jews after the Depression years: "Ironically, although the depression led to increased manifestations of antisemitism, the return of prosperity during World War II did not mitigate its effects."[3]

On this unfolding spiritual journey, soldiers' intimate fight for acceptance and recognition challenges the commonly held notion that the Jewish experience during World War II was mostly one of victimization. How did Jewish GIs overcome the stigma of humiliation? There were various responses to antisemitic slurs.

### Being Three Times as Good Just to Be Even

Captain Jerry Yellin's biography on the website Spiritof45.org describes his war achievements and dedication to the United States: "I served in World War II as a P51 fighter pilot flying escort and strafing missions from the island of Iwo Jima over Japan. On August 14, 1945, as celebrations of joy and relief were breaking out all over America at the news that the war was ended, I was flying the last combat mission over the Japanese island of

Honshu."⁴ On one of his last speaking engagements on October 25, 2018, at the National Museum of American Jewish History in Washington, DC, he revealed stories related to his war experiences as a Jew. Jerry Yellin recalled that his mother persuaded him to have a bar mitzvah despite him not wanting one, perhaps to avoid being different from his non-Jewish friends. Around that time, swastikas were painted on his home—and from then on, etched in his mind. He felt isolated from his schoolmates, and the feeling of rejection fueled his desire to become "the best fighter pilot." But just as in civil life, when he enlisted after the attack on Pearl Harbor, he was made to feel his difference, especially when training with the Seventy-Eighth Fighter Squadron: "Twenty-eight guys roomed with other pilots and I was a Jewish guy and they knew that and I roomed with Marvin Kern and Phil Janoski who were the Intelligence Division of the 78th Fighter Squadron. I was separated because of my religion. I was not accepted as a fighter pilot until I flew and like the Tuskegee Airmen, the black guys who had to be three times as good, just to be even, I had to be three times as good."⁵

In his memoirs, Jerry Yellin expressed the same eagerness to fight in the Pacific as his fellow non-Jewish fighters "to repay the Japanese for what they had done to our Navy at Pearl Harbor": "On March 7, 1945, seventy-two years from the very day that I write these words, I sat in the cockpit of a P51-D Mustang fighter plane, flying at ten thousand feet above the western Pacific, cutting a northerly course through the sunny afternoon sky toward the red-hot island of Iwo Jima, where sixty-seven thousand American Marines were still locked in battle with thousands of Japanese troops."⁶ Like other pilots, some of whom were in their teens, he knew their mission was a deadly one. He knew that "they were entrusted alone in the cockpit of a P-51 by their country." As volunteers in the Army Air Forces, they were prepared to sacrifice their lives—in the Army Air Forces, no one was drafted. The spirit of sacrifice, he thought, had to be enough to cement a bond between pilots. Twenty-year-old Jerry could not yet grasp the extent of pain he would feel after losing one of his five squadron buddies flying over Hawaii, training for the missions off Iwo Jima with the Seventy-Eighth Fighter Squadron. It hurt even more than to be reminded he was a Jew, for religion had not mattered much to him so far. He would later come to understand the bond of cultural heritage, though his Jewishness first stamped him with an indelible stigma: "I was also the same Jewish kid who had later experienced my first taste of an unfathomable prejudice sweeping the world called anti-Semitism, from some of those same friends, a bitter pill that I did not understand."⁷

Would he always have to stick with his own kind? He chose to take under his wing a nineteen-year-old pilot, the youngest son of ten children of poor immigrant parents from Poland. For First Lieutenant Philip Schlamberg, his duty was to serve his country. He felt he had to show what sons of Jewish immigrants from the poor section of Coney Island were capable of doing in gratitude to their host country. Five months and eight days after their first flight to Iwo Jima, six days after President Harry Truman ordered the dropping of the second atomic bomb on Nagasaki to stop a war that continued to take the lives of thousands of American soldiers, they flew a mission they hoped would be unnecessary. The Japanese were still refusing to surrender. The Seventy-Eighth Squadron would have to take to Japanese skies again. On the morning of August 15, 1945, Philip confided to Jerry his premonition that he would die on that mission. Jerry knew that pilots' sense of their coming death was often accurate, so he talked to their commanding officer. This is Yellin's version of this significant event, when Major Jim Tapp agreed to "grounding Phil for the flight" and finding a substitute wingman.

> But Phil would have none of it. He was determined to fly the mission, premonition, or no premonition.
>
> It happened shortly after we had attacked an airfield over Tokyo just after noon. We had avoided being hit by antiaircraft fire up to that point, but I was worried about Phil. I told him to stay tight on my wing, and that he would be okay. And he had done just that. We hit the field, and then climbed into a cloud embankment, with Phil flying tight in beside me. When I emerged from the clouds a few minutes later, Phil was gone. I never saw him again.[8]

Philip Schlamberg proved that he would entertain no excuses whatsoever to avoid sacrificing his life for the United States. The Jewish kid repaid his country for its hospitality and died as an American officer. To those who wondered how he had managed to get into the air force at such a young age, some seventy years later Captain Yellin provided an answer—that unarguable excellence was the best road to acceptance for Jews and immigrants: "The valedictorian of Abraham Lincoln High School in Brooklyn, Phil's service-entrance test scores were among the very highest in the history of the Army."[9]

These examples indicate to what extent demonstrating bravery and excellence was a response to pervasive antisemitic slurs in the military. That was also the case in American society at large, yet a wide range of strategies to confront anti-Jewish hostility were adopted.

## From Fists to Silent Tactics

In Algeria, Burton Roberts, a Jewish soldier termed "a replacement" in the infantry, believed fellow soldiers equated Jews with cowards because they had never met any. He admitted that this insult resulted in fights.[10] Noted American columnist Art Buchwald also responded with his fists, as did numerous other Jewish GIs.[11] Buchwald's wry sense of humor considerably helped him deal with hostility, alleviating the frustration others experienced. Some were shocked by the visceral hatred and Christian hostility against Jews and remained silent. At times, they regretted not having talked or fought back to defend their self-respect.[12]

David Macarov, a Jewish serviceman from Georgia, grew up in the shadow of the 1915 lynching of Leo Frank outside Atlanta, the town in which he lived. It was the first lynching of a Jew in the United States. Leo Frank was unjustly accused of having murdered a young girl who worked in the factory he headed. Although a jury influenced by anti-Jewish hostility found him guilty, the judge revised the sentence, having found the evidence not convincing enough. So did the governor of Georgia, who commuted Frank's death sentence to life imprisonment. But citizens—filled with rage and stirred by a newspaper editor—broke into the jail, violently dragged out thirty-year-old Leo Frank, and lynched him. The young girl's murderer was found after his death. This most dramatic antisemitic incident in American history remained etched in David Macarov's mind.[13] Sent to India during World War II, he was convinced of the need for a Jewish homeland. He immigrated to mandatory Palestine with his American wife, Frieda, in 1947 and fought in the War of Independence in 1948 as a major overseeing coded communications for the Israel Air Force.[14] Writing his memoirs as a veteran, Macarov confided that anti-Jewish hostility in the American military during the war was pervasive and nestled within seemingly innocuous jokes—when it was not openly expressed in antisemitic cartoons.[15]

> There was the usual amount of endemic anti-Semitism on the base.... For example, at an entertainment night, one of the soldier-entertainers was telling jokes, and among others he told of Abie coming home from work and telling his son, who was standing on the top step, to jump into his arms. The son was hesitant, but Abie was insistent, and when the son finally jumped Abie stepped aside. As the son looked up from the pavement, broken and bleeding, Abie said, "Let that be a lesson to you. Never trust a Jew." The entertainer waited for the laughter to subside, and then noticed some of us glancing at one another. He stopped and said, "If there are any Jews here, I didn't mean you, of course. It is just a joke." And that was the way he saw it.

> On the other hand, the sergeant in charge of the motor pool had papered his office with crude anti-Semitic cartoons and sayings, and every time we had to get the vehicle for Friday services, he made sure we all had to walk through the office while he sat there grinning. I eventually complained to the chaplain, but nothing happened.[16]

Anti-Jewish cartoons and jokes contributed to a trivialization of anti-Jewish attitudes. Yet, during the war years, a new acceptance of Judaism within the military and legitimation of Jewish religious services gradually transformed Judaism from a suspicious anomaly to one of America's three main faiths. As worshiping together was encouraged, and since Christian chaplains were entitled to deliver sermons for religious services or conduct them in the absence of a Jewish chaplain, Jewish public worship was lent more weight.[17]

## Maintaining a Strong Jewish Identity

Encountering Jews abroad reinforced the Jewish identity of some GIs, as will be seen in the next chapter. A sense of belonging to the Jewish people, later termed "Jewish peoplehood," was emerging. Religious observance springing from a religious background and a sprinkling of knowledge of Jewish culture helped cope with anti-Jewish slurs. It forged a positive Jewish identity endowed with meaning that could act as a shield against anti-Jewish hostility. Sergeant Naurice Rosen, for instance, a proud Jew and the son of one of the founders of the Jewish community in Camden, New Jersey, was interested in Jewish culture. The local Jewish newspaper, the *Voice*, published a column in several issues under the heading "With Our Men in Uniform." Writing from "somewhere in Italy" (to comply with censorship), Sergeant Rosen of the Eighty-Sixth Bombardment Group explained his reaction to several issues of the *Voice*. The following is an excerpt from the letter he sent to the newspaper, published on February 11, 1944, in which he argued that although he and his fellow soldiers were fighting antisemitism abroad, the fight did not yet entail a victory over prejudice.

> No fault of yours but *The Voice* finally caught up with us. It trailed me through North Africa, Sicily, and now Italy. Nevertheless, no matter what dated editions I am now receiving, a certain proudness overcomes me in reading such subjects of my race [sic] both politically and socially.
>
> My international knowledge of the Jew is very limited except for the suffering, torture, and murder of our innocent people in Nazi-occupied countries. I am aware and quite confused by the anti-semitism existing in our United Nations [Allies] today. Aren't we fighting for the FREEDOM OF RELIGION AND FREEDOM FROM FEAR or am I misinterpreting the freedom of our democracy?

A reply to his letter appeared in the *Voice* a month later, on March 10. The author of the column first apologized for not being able to offer "real help" on the issue. He went on to encourage soldiers on the front to continue writing to the newspaper. The columnist tried to instill hope by arguing that "our leaders in the great war are formulating plans for a better world to which he [Sergeant Rosen] and his comrades can return in peace." He acknowledged the absurdity with which Jewish soldiers were faced: they could encounter, back home, the same religious and ethnic intolerance they were risking their lives to uproot. To Rosen's letter, the author of the response offered hope for persecuted Jews in the world: "Jewish leaders have constantly urged the United Nations to recognize that justice to the Jew must be a declared objective of this war. That there is a general awakening to this is witnessed by the Committee Against Anti-Semitism, formed by Justice Murphy, the President's creation of the War Refugee Board, and the Bi-Partisan Resolutions introduced into the Congress for the creation of a Jewish Commonwealth in Palestine."[18]

In the response Sergeant Rosen received, a link was suggested between the nature of his patriotic engagement and the efforts to establish a Jewish homeland in Palestine, while Britain had been entrusted with a mandate over Palestine by the League of Nations. A tree would be planted in the Jewish homeland in honor of Jewish servicemen and servicewomen like him.[19] Zionism was not Rosen's stance or that of his parents, but the answer he received stirred his reflection. Some seventy years later, Sergeant Rosen's son argued that "the ultimate goal" of his father had been "to build strong Jewish communities in the United States" in which Jews would no longer feel like underdogs.[20] Traditions of tolerance in the United States have lessened the impact of anti-Jewish hostility in times of prosperity, although contradictory trends in American society add to the complexity of the bias against Jews. How can we understand the receptivity of a segment of American society to the similitudes between Zionist aspirations and American ideals? The emergence of American Zionism demonstrated the interaction between images of the Land of Israel and images of America among American Jews. These representations embraced cherished ideals of democracy, freedom, social justice, and pluralism. Before its gradual transformation from an ideal espoused mainly by immigrants to a mainstream American Jewish movement, Zionism gave hope to American Jews: "The [Zionist] movement served as a lens through which American Jews viewed nascent Palestinian and American society as many thought it ought to be: full of promise and opportunity, industrious and expansive, and not least of all, capable of elevating the human condition."[21]

An affinity to Zionism could result from experiences during World War II, as case studies show. Confrontation with extermination camps triggered such responses from American Jewish servicemen and servicewomen. The systematic extermination of Jews was the epitome of antisemitism. Maurice Paper, from Baltimore, enlisted in the army in 1942 and, after a high score on the army's IQ test, entered an officer's school. By the age of twenty, he was a second lieutenant and combat engineer in North Africa, Italy, and Germany. He received a Bronze Star for helping members of the French Maquis (guerrilla resistance fighters) in the French Riviera destroy two bridges to prevent the Germans from advancing. The American officer was surprised to discover that all the resistance fighters he met in this part of France were Jews of Polish origin who spoke Yiddish with him. Maurice Paper was promoted to the rank of captain in 1943. General Eisenhower dispatched him to Dachau on April 29, 1945, because of his knowledge of Yiddish. Though the death camps were not military objectives, he was instructed to gain the trust of Jewish survivors. This is how he recounted his encounter with Nazi barbary:

> They found it hard to believe that they lived, at least they lived. . . . I got very sad over all of this. I told them we were going to do what we could, to have faith, and that they would all be set free with identity papers.
>
> I became a Zionist because I realized that there was no other answer for the Jewish people. Because of my war experiences I saw what happened to a people, a whole people.[22]

In fact, Maurice Paper's overwhelming experience strengthened his vision of Zion as a homeland for uprooted Jews. His vision of Zion was first conveyed through his study of Hebrew as a child in a Hebrew school in Baltimore. Although from a different background, another serviceman came to the same conclusion following his encounter with Nazi extermination camps. Born in 1922, Paul Shulman grew up in New York in a Zionist family close to the legendary Henrietta Szold, the founder of Hadassah, a women's Zionist organization. He graduated from the United States Naval Academy in Annapolis during the war. Sent to the Pacific theater, he was the deputy commander of a destroyer. He served on the USS *Hunt*, which faced both a typhoon and kamikaze bombing.[23] At war's end, the naval hero helped smuggle Holocaust survivors from Europe to the Jewish homeland in Palestine. Maurice Paper belonged to a network of volunteers from the United States and Canada called Machal (a Hebrew acronym for "volunteers from abroad"). Paul Shulman exemplified selflessness and bravery in the service of his country, not ignoring the responsibility he had as a Jew to help Jewish displaced persons. All the American servicemen who did not ignore their responsibility, he commented, "gave their time and their will, their strength and their determination . . . without pay, without fanfare, without reward or praise, and were undeterred by the risks of their lives."[24] Their bravery conveyed a sense of responsibility as representatives of the Jewish people.

### Setting an Example of Extreme Bravery

For many survivors of the Nazi genocide of the Jews, the Jewish homeland in Palestine meant the end of humiliation, degradation, and persecution. Although not drawn to Zionism by his background, Colonel David Daniel Marcus understood the necessity for a viable Jewish state in the context of the extermination of European Jews. Born in February 1901 in the Lower East Side of Manhattan, he was the son of immigrant Jewish parents from Romania. The fifth of six children whose father died prematurely, he was impressed by his older brother Michael, whom he admired for his athletic body and as a leader of a self-defense group formed to protect elderly and weak Jews. He promptly understood the necessity of practicing athletics, embracing ideals of American masculinity while excelling as a student. It was no wonder he lived up to the challenge of entering West Point, the prestigious military academy and bastion where anti-Jewish attitudes (exemplified by General Patton) were ingrained among high-ranking officers, reflecting the prejudice omnipresent in wider civil society.[25] Historian Derek Penslar thus interprets Marcus's challenge: "This decision corresponded to Marcus' ambition and determination not merely to Americanize but to penetrate the bastion of the United States' warrior elite, a caste that historically had had few Jewish members."[26]

For those who met him, David Daniel Marcus was a man who provoked admiration.[27] They reported that "they could not keep up with him," that he would "accomplish in five minutes what it would take others a week to do."[28] He would not only quote Shakespeare, Keats, and the Old Testament but would also tap dance, sing in a baritone voice, pray, and never miss physical exercise. A boxer, an energetic man and cheerful fellow who liked to drink, he shared some of the characteristics often attributed to Irish masculinity, according to those who knew him.[29] As legal officer, he became judge advocate of his army national guard unit, the Twenty-Seventh

Infantry Division. Following the Japanese attack on Pearl Harbor, Marcus was sent to Hawaii with the Twenty-Seventh Division, where he organized and commanded a ranger combat training school. The school trained soldiers in techniques of unarmed defense combat—perhaps inspired by his brother's knowledge and command of self-defense. The aim was to fight Japanese infiltration strategies. Instead of continuing in a field command, he was sent to Washington in 1943 and appointed to the Civil Affairs Division. He participated in American delegations to the conferences at Cairo, Teheran, Yalta, and Potsdam. All the while, Marcus sought out physical challenges, perhaps to give an example of what a Jewish son of immigrants whose mother clung to the Yiddish language could do out of patriotism and gratitude for the country that opened its doors to his family.

Although he was not trained as a parachutist, Marcus insisted on participating in the dangerous Operation Overlord and parachuted into Normandy on D-Day with the first wave of General Maxwell Taylor's 101st Airborne Division. He fought for a week, taking informal command of paratroopers after V-E Day. General Lucius Clay invited Marcus to join his staff in the American zone of occupation in Germany, where he was to take care of displaced persons, among them destitute Jewish survivors he instilled with hope. An army colonel, Marcus was one of the main architects of the United States military's World War II civil affairs policies. His task included organizing war crimes trials in Germany and in Japan. Blessed with a phenomenal memory, Marcus could do "the work of five people," as his secretaries reported. Most of all, he lived by the code with which he had been imbued at West Point: "duty, honor, and country."[30] Inspired by American ideals and the moral obligation to provide a home for Holocaust survivors—who could not wait for a visa that would not come to displaced persons camps in Germany, Austria, and Italy—he heroically participated in the 1948 War of Independence as Israel's first general (*Aluf* in Hebrew). The "moral obligation" to establish a "refuge" for displaced persons had been voiced by President Harry S. Truman, who referred to the postwar problem as a "world tragedy." Marcus understood the depth of the problem and immediately grasped the fact that the Jewish displaced persons issue could not be satisfactorily solved without the emergence of a Jewish state. The American serviceman was killed by friendly fire at his post in the hills of Jerusalem on June 10, 1948. He remained the best-known Machal soldier. The commitment to Israel's fight for freedom exemplified by Marcus was recognized by the United States Military Academy. In the West Point Cemetery, the headstone of the only serviceman interred there who fell while fighting for another country proclaims him "A Soldier for All Humanity." Through bravery and dedication to one's country and American values even abroad, the Jewish plight acquired universalistic overtones—with a potential to overrun prejudice.[31]

### The "Good War" and Its Multiple Implications

The notion of World War II as "a good war" began in response to the "day of infamy," when Japan attacked the American base at Pearl Harbor, destroying ships and aircraft. The revelation of the extent of the slaughter in Europe triggered by anti-Jewish hostility and racial discrimination only reinforced the motivation of Jewish American servicemen and women "to do the job" during World War II. The US Army Signal Corps prepared and distributed *This Is Why We Fight*, a news map evincing Nazi atrocities encountered by American troops in Ohrdruf, a subcamp of Buchenwald, on April 4, 1945, where no inmate was found alive. Until this publication, troops did not grasp that "atrocity stories" were not rumors. General Eisenhower, the supreme commander of Allied forces in Europe, visited the camp on April 12 and instructed that a visit would be compulsory for American troops in the area.[32] *This Is Why We Fight* contains the following unequivocal words.

> Now, we've SEEN it. This is what fascism "New Order" brought to millions in Europe—death by torture, starvation, flogging, and every fiendish method the twisted German mind could devise.
>
> Not so long ago, some of us were saying "the Germans are really nice people, pretty much like us—decent, clean, kindly at heart."
>
> These are the sights—photographed by Signal Corps cameramen that greeted our soldiers who over-ran German concentration camps. This is what General Eisenhower wanted our congressmen and newspaper editors to come and see.
>
> Take a good look and remember.[33]

Many non-Jewish soldiers were overwhelmed and traumatized by the extent of Nazi brutality. Others volunteered in the Machal to fight in Israel's War of Independence. None who witnessed these horrors remained indifferent. Morris Eisenstein, who joined the Forty-Second Infantry (Rainbow) Division as a corporal before being promoted a sergeant in charge of a heavy weapons platoon, saw combat in southern France, Germany, and Austria. On entering Dachau with his unit, he and his fellow soldiers were struck by a horrible sight: "The first thing we saw was a railroad siding with 36 box cars loaded with bodies in various stages of decomposition, both living and dying.... How did my comrades feel about what they saw? The truth was they were more upset than I was."[34] Why was Eisenstein able to bear the shock of that brutal revelation better than his non-Jewish fellows? It may be that because he was born in Poland, news of the sordid fate of European Jews—and probably his own family—had already reached him. Thus, his fight against Hitler was more personal; the serviceman knew about murderous pogroms against the Jews in Poland and the extent of Jew-hatred. Sergeant Morris Eisenstein was awarded two Silver Stars and three Bronze Stars for heroism in battle.[35] In his own way, he fought the stereotype of the cowardly Jewish soldier who dodges military service or finds safer units. African American soldiers in the Black Panthers of the 761st Tank Battalion who joined the liberation of Dachau and Buchenwald also fought on two fronts, achieving belated recognition.[36] Sergeant Leon Bass, one of the African American soldiers who liberated Buchenwald, discovered the outcome of racial hatred of the Jews: "I came into that camp an angry black soldier. Angry at my country and justifiably so. Angry because they were treating me as though I was not good enough. But [that day] I came to the realization that human suffering is not relegated to me and mine. I now knew that human suffering could touch us all.... [What I saw] in Buchenwald was the face of evil.... It was racism."[37]

What was at the source of the insult "nigger lover" hurled at Jews? Was it the empathy that some Jews felt for African Americans, who were also being discriminated against? Was it their both being unwanted underdogs? A Jewish servicewoman in the WAC mentioned that each time a sergeant passed her desk he would mumble: "You can't beat the niggers or the Jews."[38] American army veteran Alan Moskin, who took part in the liberation of the Gunskirchen concentration camp in Austria, admitted in an interview that these words pronounced as an insult affected him.[39] Many American chaplains, like Abraham Klausner, saw in the concentration and extermination camps what Jew hatred could lead to. In his memoirs, Klausner insisted on the need to encourage and even force Jews who languished in displaced persons camps to immigrate to the Jewish homeland of Palestine. His stance was firm, although the British drastically limited entrance of Jewish refugees by intercepting their vessels and deporting the displaced persons to other detention camps in Cyprus or Atlit, near Haifa.[40]

Numerous American chaplains encouraged Jewish displaced persons to stand up for their right to start a new life in Palestine and flee from a bloody Europe where their families had been massacred. Although American chaplains risked court-martial, they strove to provide food and supplies to survivors with the help of Jewish soldiers in occupied Germany and Austria.[41] They also collected weapons for the underground Jewish army in Palestine, the Palmah, elite force of the Haganah. Former Jewish GIs and some of their non-Jewish buddies helped smuggle Jewish displaced persons across the Mediterranean Sea.[42] It may be argued that in the war's aftermath, the unofficial collaboration of the American army with helpful Jewish chaplains and soldiers balances the picture of pervasive anti-Jewish attitudes in the military.[43] A strong Jewish identity, whether grounded in Zionist aspirations expressed after the Holocaust, a religious background, spiritual awareness, or a knowledge of Jewish culture, could foster respect.

### Inspiring Respect for Jewishness

Years later, Jewish servicemen expressed perceptions of Zionist aspirations as the hope of a return to Zion that empowered them both as Americans and as Jews. Former naval officer Herman Wouk, who served from 1941 to 1949, inherited Zionism and Orthodoxy from his father, as expressed in his book *Sailor and Fiddler: Reflections of a 100-Year-Old Author*: "Yiddish was not a language I had to learn; rather an ambiance absorbed in infancy. Reading Shalom Aleichem today, I hear in his warm clear prose my father's Friday-night voice—the lover of Jewish characters and traditions, the Zionist, the unshakable optimist, the naive American patriot who freed himself from czarist Russia. 'If you ever get called into the army,' Papa once said, 'I'll come and wash the floor of your barracks.'"[44] American Zionists did not reject "the New World," an act that would imply negation of the American diaspora. This is one reason why the synthesis of Jewish idealism and American progressivism was possible in the United States.

In his nonfiction book *This Is My God*, prize-winning author Herman Wouk wrote a dedication to his grandfather Mendel Leib Levine, "rabbi in Minsk, New York, and Tel Aviv," who ended "his lifetime of ninety-four years" in the "reborn land of Israel."[45] Wouk did not make a similar move, although he visited the land of his forefathers several times, and one of his sons chose to live there.[46] In the United States Naval Reserve, he participated in several invasions of the Pacific Islands aboard a minesweeper. The talented writer grew up in the Bronx and graduated from Columbia University before writing as a "gagman" for comedian Fred Allen's popular radio show. In *This Is My God*, he pointed out that even in the Pacific Islands, he had managed to observe the same ritual that he, his father, and his grandfather practiced on the solemn Day of Atonement, that is, reading a special, meaningful portion of the Scriptures: "To this day my brother and

I read the Book of Jonah at Yom Kippur services wherever we can. We have done so in places as far apart as Chicago, Hawaii, and Okinawa."[47]

This example reminds us that in World War II, the religious cooperation of chaplains fostered by the American military made it possible for observant Jews to reconcile religious tenets with military duty. Military constraints and the various theaters of war entailed new, creative forms of religious expression.[48] In a report about the essays collected by the YIVO Institute of Jewish Research in 1946, Moses Kligsberg, a member of the institute, aptly noted that the GIs who "accept their Jewishness as a positive possession" described antisemitic incidents with more distancing than those who perceived Jewishness as a burden.[49] Zionists who had been members of youth movements as teenagers or whose parents were Zionists, like Herman Wouk, fall into the category of those who accept their Jewishness as a positive possession. Their strong Jewish identity seemed to protect them against anti-Jewish slurs. While interest and hope in Zionism provided a response to anti-Jewish hostility, open confrontation was another response. As noted above, famous American columnist Art Buchwald responded with his fists, as did numerous GIs.[50] This choice inspired respect as an expression of American masculinity.

Zionism included an image of the "muscular Jew," proud, upright, and physically trained, that ran counter to the negative perception of a physically weak Jew. Through the lens of Zionism, the notion of Jewish masculinity evolved. It bore the memory of the heroic image of Jews at the time of the Maccabees and Bar Kokhba. Such inspiring representations were vital at a time when Jewish Americans engaged in combat. When they enlisted, Jewish servicemen and women had fresh in their minds how they were rejected by their schoolmates once the teacher had pointed out their difference. Army nurse Mimi Rivkin explained in an interview that a classmate had refused to play with her once he learned she was Jewish.[51] The perception of the Jew as the "other" continued in the military, a bastion where officers traditionally thought that Jews avoided combat and were poor military material. Researching the topic, historian Joseph Bendersky has found that in the 1920s, American culture did not perceive Jews as soldiers. They were seen as undesirables who did not melt in the melting pot, and these prejudiced views persisted throughout World War II.[52] In the 1940s, the American Jewish community was far from homogeneous. It comprised religious and secular Jews, socialists, communists, Zionists, and a few pacifists, like Reform Rabbi Roland Gittelsohn, who later enlisted and was sent overseas as a chaplain. It is a well-known fact among those versed in World War II history that Gittelsohn was prevented from delivering the sermon he had prepared for the dedication of the Fifth Marine Division Cemetery on Iwo Jima. Was the reason anti-Jewish prejudice? A number of Christian chaplains did not agree with his liberal politics, which included support of African American servicemen. Could such a stance have disrupted a shared white American identity? Professor of Jewish history Marc Saperstein notes that the cemetery Gittelsohn described and fleshed out in his powerful sermon exemplified "the ideal of how American society should be."[53]

Under the stress of rejection or persecution, some Jewish GIs found refuge among other Jews, which also reinforced their faith.[54] The legitimation of Judaism eased this return to the faith of their ancestors. Some soldiers joined services as a response to anti-Jewish prejudice, while others discovered new religious meaning in services.[55]

Reflecting on the three main faiths whose members served in the American military in World War II, Historian Kevin Walters establishes the following distinction: "Uniquely, however, Jewish identity consisted of both strong cultural and religious aspects that were often difficult to differentiate. At the same time, anti-Semitic attitudes often compressed these distinctions. The experience of overt anti-Semitism challenged the self-perceptions of many Jewish soldiers and sailors." He provides the example of medic Melvin Preston, who "became a Jew in faith" after experiencing a battlefield Rosh Hashanah service in France.[56] Beyond spiritual experiences, religious practice empowered Jewish servicemen. Innovative frameworks of legitimized religious observance reduced the sting of religious discrimination tinted with xenophobia. Various other personal attitudes confronting anti-Jewish bias ranged from not advertising one's Jewishness to regretting not having fought back.[57]

## Physical Force as a Deterrent against Anti-Jewish Hostility?

To fathom the range of emotions that touched individual soldiers, their voices need to be heard. Infantry soldier Ernest Stock was reluctant to use his fists when antisemitic slurs became too harsh too bear. One day, a soldier in his unit crossed a line, proclaiming that "once the war ended . . . he would take care of all the Jews in South River." The bigoted serviceman from New Jersey did not "let a day pass without trying to injure my pride and sensitivity," Stock admitted. Although Stock recoiled from physical violence, included in the soldiers' daily practice was "dirty fighting," which they were told was "an indispensable weapon of the infantry man." Not surprisingly, it was in one such setting that their antagonism found full expression and resolution.

> The fight lasted until one of the fighters signified his desire to give up by tapping with his hand on the ground, usually forced to do so because his foe had him by the throat.... For the first time I felt capable of prowess which I had never suspected in me. The rest of the men circled around us, and suddenly I became aware that they were rooting for me. They had known about the undercurrent of personal animosity which made our struggle such a bitter one, they had not expected that I would be a match to my opponent, and when they saw me put a good fight, their sense of sportsmanship and fair play made them cheer for me.
> When it was all over—the sergeant had finally declared the fight a draw—they came to pat me on the shoulder and shake hands with me, not only my friends but even those whom I had thought my enemies.[58]

If the fight won him the camaraderie of his fellow infantrymen, did his show of physical force win the respect of his prejudiced opponent? Ernest Stock said that "he regarded me with a kind of distrustful respect and refrained from making remarks about Jews." To conclude his reflection about the life-changing experience, he added with poise and pride: "I had learned something about the necessity of physical force."[59]

Stock had paid the price to learn more about the American ideal of masculinity. Born in 1924 in Frankfurt-am-Main, Ernest was sixteen when he came to the United States as an immigrant in July 1940, "after a turbulent flight from the Nazis which took me from my native Germany to France and later to Spain and Portugal." He had no idea that he would go back to Europe as an infantryman a couple of years later; his only desire was to settle down after so many tribulations as a German refugee. When learning about the soldier's past, one cannot help but be impressed by his resilience and efforts to shift the emphasis in his identity from German to Jewish, and then from Jewish to American.[60] Such drastic uprooting sounds even more overwhelming with the addition of another piece of information: "In November 1938, my father was hauled off to Buchenwald together with thousands of other male Frankfort Jews. I was not to see him until years later when I, a U.S. soldier, would find him in a newly liberated country."[61]

In a short span of time, this infantryman experienced both the murderous antisemitism of the Nazis in his native land and the anti-Jewish hostility of American servicemen in his new country of residence.[62] By using physical force, he took a first step toward social acceptance, which he expressed as "distrustful respect." The oxymoron used in this essay for the YIVO Institute for Jewish Research in New York in 1946 translates both the ingrained prejudice of his opponent and the new social status the Jewish immigrant acquired through fighting. This story also points to the transformation of identities that occurred during military service.

A passage from an essay submitted to the YIVO Institute that same year by Sergeant Isadore Rosen, who fought with the Tenth Armored Infantry Battalion, is revealing as a reflection on how to do away with biased misconceptions toward Jews. Could behaving as both an American patriot and a representative of the Jewish people help fight prejudice? Not without emotion, the young infantryman voiced ways to combat the venom of prejudice while lucidly stating how "tough and depressing" this fight is bound to be.

> We should conduct ourselves *so that we bring credit upon the countries in which we live.* . . . Each Jew in the world should take cognizance of certain inconsistencies which cast aspersions on entire groups, and take steps to rectify those that have been falsely made . . . and if he can *demonstrate by his behavior that different religions are not barriers to friendship* and understanding, he will be cementing the shaky underpins of a newly erected structure, and he will help cleanse the minds of those who have been infected with these cancerous prejudices against us. The fight to overcome these prejudices will be tough and depressing. But it is worth our entire effort and determination to try.[63]

Daily efforts of Jewish servicemen to gain acceptance as Americans translated into their brave deeds, awards, and citations—the latter of which were often posthumous. A list of these accomplishments was drawn up as early as 1942 for the War Records Bureau of the National Jewish Welfare Board (JWB) by its director, Dr. Samuel C. Kohs.[64] In the *Chicago Daily News*, April 10, 1942, Edwin Lahey published an article titled "Heroic Records of Jews in the Army and Navy to Disprove Vicious Canard," emphasizing those who saw combat and displayed extreme bravery.

### REASSESSING ANTI-JEWISH ATTITUDES AMONG HIGH-RANKING OFFICERS

Some bigoted officers displayed contempt toward Jews and would "rather kill a Jew than a Jap," according to a written testimony by Ernest Stock, whose identity was first and foremost that of an American. Anti-Jewish hostility in the military hurt him all the more as he felt "an American through and through" and that his religion did not matter: "Being an

American, I found it too breath-taking a business to leave time for such old-fashioned, sentimental stuff."[65] It was then that an incident affected him and two other Jewish men in his platoon: an officer claimed publicly that he would rather kill a Jew than a Jap "any day." The three Jewish servicemen resolved to report this slur to the commanding officer. Stock related the settlement of the issue: "It was rumored that the Commanding Officer, a young West Point graduate named Lt. Aycock, who was well liked by everyone, called Cook (the author of the insult) into the orderly room and threatened him with severe disciplinary measures if he continued his actions. From that time on he kept his thoughts to himself."[66] This measure did not prevent other bigoted servicemen from verbally assaulting Jews in the unit. Ernest Stock analyzed this expression of Jew hatred thus: "I formed the conviction that their kind are mostly made up of people who are not intelligent enough to be receptive to argument." This led him to conclude that in such cases, "brute physical force must be met by force, if that is the only language the other one understands."[67] However, other examples in the American military, as in civil society, indicate that visceral anti-Jewish hostility derives partly from the environment in which a person lives in his formative years.

General George S. Patton acquired fame as a gifted strategist. He was also known as an antisemite who held a different perception of Jews around him who enjoyed "the refinement of culture," such as Secretary of the Treasury Henry Morgenthau. He despised other Jews, especially Holocaust survivors in displaced persons camps, whom he considered "lower than animals."[68] In contrast, President Harry Truman, a Christian, was generally considered sympathetic to the Jewish plight. After the murder of six million Jews was revealed, he was determined to help establish for them a refuge in the Jewish homeland. Having a close relationship with longtime Jewish friend and former business partner Eddie Jacobson, he, too, made a distinction between Jews, as confirmed by a passage of his *Memoirs*: "I kept my faith in the rightness of my policy in spite of some of the Jews. When I say 'Jews' I mean, of course, the extreme Zionists. I know that most Americans of Jewish faith, while they hoped for the restoration of a Jewish homeland, are and always have been Americans first and foremost."[69]

Harry Truman, like high-ranking officers who graduated from West Point Military Academy, was also a product of his environment in Missouri. When venting annoyance at Jews, he expressed the anti-Jewish prejudice of deep America, of his native town of Independence. In the above-quoted passage from his memoirs, the stereotype of Jews as dishonest people is conveyed through the idea of a possible dual loyalty among "extreme Zionists."

In bringing nuance to an assessment of anti-Jewish hostility in the American military, it is useful to recall historian David Wyman's point that "anti-semitism ran through the upper ranks as well," not only among ignorant young soldiers who had never met a Jew. In his study of anti-Jewish attitudes and politics in the American army, Bendersky demonstrates the pervasiveness of anti-Jewish and racist thoughts from World War I to World War II. He reveals that negative views of Jews among West Point trainees reflected the values and attitudes of White Anglo-Saxon Americans. Jews were not only characterized as cowardly, weak, and selfish, but their "anatomical characteristics" were also noted as being different. Seen as belonging to "a troublesome minority," any Jew who served in the Roosevelt administration (dubbed "the Jew Deal"), such as Felix Frankfurter, was considered a "dangerous radical." Even Albert Einstein was labeled an "extreme radical." In that context, it comes as no surprise that Jewish organizations were seen as nests for subversive activities. Zionism was synonymous with communism for West Point attendees, who were told that the hoax titled "The Protocols of the Elders of Zion" offered insights about international Jewry.[70] No wonder army personnel were reluctant to save European Jews during the Holocaust, claiming that the best way to end their persecution was to bring an end to the war.

In his seminal work about antisemitism in America, historian Leonard Dinnerstein observes the following, confirming the existence of contradictory trends: "If some officers and GIs were highly antisemitic in practice, in fairness to the armed services it must be acknowledged that lectures and courses on ethnic and religious tolerance were given.... Placing Jews among Christians in the armed forces increased the likelihood of bigotry expressing itself but nothing could be done about that since religious segregation was unconstitutional. Therefore, Secretary of the Navy Frank Knox and Secretary of War Henry Stimson issued orders forbidding the circulation of antisemitic publications at all naval and military posts."[71] Instances of high-ranking officers defending enlisted men are provided through the voices of individuals and the life-story approach of the present volume. Larry Yellin fought a battle for his Jewish identity during World War II when he was sent to the European and Pacific theaters. It began in basic training, which was mostly amphibious training. He spent the time rigorously allotted for breakfast praying inside the army barracks. Some seventy years later, Sergeant Larry Yellin, an Orthodox Jewish veteran born in 1925 who grew up near Chicago, recalled an edifying story that may sound unusual for the military. Once, a general who had watched him pray on entering the barracks asked the second lieutenant in command if Larry was given extra time to get breakfast. The lieutenant replied adamantly: "Absolutely not, it's not in the book." "Well," the general answered promptly, "I want you to give this soldier fifteen minutes every day to pray, and afterward, I want you to see that he gets breakfast."[72] Stunned, the lieutenant had to comply.

Larry Yellin, then a private, had promptly enlisted to fight the Nazis and promised his mother that wherever he was stationed, he would be "a representative of the Jewish people." It is a matter of fact that when a Jewish GI did not behave properly, others in the unit or in society at large tended to condemn all Jews for the improper behavior. This promise led Yellin to make keeping kosher a priority, unlike most Conservative and perhaps also Orthodox soldiers. Eating being a necessity in times of war, Conservative and Orthodox Jews, who were in the majority, were told by Jewish chaplains that they could eat nonkosher food.[73] The choice to avoid meat and eat rice without gravy was not easy to sustain every day, and there were times when Yellin did not have anything to eat. However, this discipline gained him a few friends: "The positive side of my dietary requirements was that soldiers noticed that I did not take the main entrees when there was meat. They would always like to get right behind me because when I went through and I said 'no thank you' they said 'I'll take Yellin's main entree.' So I became quite popular."[74]

Some non-Jewish chaplains—holding officer rank—also displayed a tolerant and even a generous attitude toward Jewish soldiers, sometimes at the risk of their lives. As Yellin's division, the Eighty-Sixth Infantry, was deployed along the west side of the Rhine River in the area of Cologne, Germany, he realized that the first evening of Passover had come without him having anything to commemorate the holy day. He, together with some fifteen thousand troops, knew that German commandos were intent on probing the strength of American fortifications. He and two other soldiers from Company E were manning a strategic point with a heavy machine gun in an abandoned Bayer factory with orders to shoot at moving targets, which they did. He recalled the memorable and unexpected event on the eve of Passover of the year 1945.

> We were surprised to see in the moonlight that the noisy intrusion was one of our jeeps without lights, slowly moving toward our position. It turned out to be a driver with a passenger, a Christian chaplain friend from Wheaton, Illinois. He was a young man recently out of seminary who was

interested in learning about Judaism and would join our unit on hikes and training to talk to me about Shabbat and holy days. He greeted me with, "Larry, I know it's the first night of Passover. I just got hold of a bottle of wine and a box of matza sent over by the Jewish Welfare Board from New York for you and your buddies. They sometimes do things like this a little late."[75]

Nineteen-year-old Larry greeted the Christian chaplain, who had risked his life to come to a dangerous zone, with his Browning automatic rifle. He first thought that Nazi commandos had landed without being detected, before finding out that the visit was nothing short of a "miracle." Larry "sent his two Gentile soldiers to find and replace Jerry Shpall and Jay Singer, the only two Jewish soldiers in the area who were manning positions down the line." They improvised a makeshift igloo with fifty-pound sacks of sugar from the deserted factory and used the flickering light of a candle together with an army-issued flashlight: "To three lone soldiers on the bank of the Rhine, it was an especially meaningful Passover, because it was being held on German soil. Without a Haggada the three of us recited as much as we could recall from memory."[76]

Out of camaraderie, the non-Jewish soldiers complied with Larry's request to be momentarily relieved of his watch together with his two Jewish buddies. It was not uncommon for Jewish soldiers to volunteer to stand in for Christian soldiers on Christmas or other holy days. Another noteworthy illustration of the understanding displayed by high-ranking officers is given in Yellin's oral testimony for the Museum of the Jewish Soldier in Latrun, Israel. While stationed in the Philippines, Yellin was looking for a place to pray on Friday night with at least ten soldiers to form a *minyan*. Although chapels were supposed to be nondenominational, there was a large Christian icon at the chapel on base that was proper to cover during a Jewish service. The first Shabbat went well. But the following week, the Christian chaplain of the base (who was a colonel) burst in during the middle of the service and, visibly angered, sternly forbade covering the icon facing the men in prayer. Yellin thought the only way to find a place to pray properly would be to appeal to higher echelons. He contacted Major General Harris Melasky, a graduate of the West Point Military Academy who served with the Eighty-Sixth Infantry Division.[77] Larry Yellin emphasized in his interview that the Major General was "very gracious" to him. The synagogue in Manila had been destroyed by Japanese bombs, so his request was not irrelevant. To Larry's surprise, Major General Melasky forwarded his request to General Douglas MacArthur himself, who was then stationed in the Philippines. Melasky reported to Yellin that General MacArthur "asked if he would not mind" praying in the general's mansion, "if it would be suitable for a Shabbath service." On that Shabbat, it was not fifteen soldiers who turned up to pray but fifty. Yellin had doubts whether all were Jewish or simply curious to get a look at the general's beautiful home in Manila. Sergeant Yellin also mentioned that General Lucius Clay, who supervised soldiers dealing with displaced persons in the American occupied zone of Germany, displayed understanding of the Jewish plight. He was sympathetic toward the Jewish survivors going illegally to Palestine at the risk of being thrown again into a detention camp. Indeed, British soldiers controlled the ports and arrested ships, crews, and passengers, sometimes very brutally, to the point that some young Holocaust survivors died of the wounds.[78]

It is significant that Yellin began his oral testimony by recalling how antipathy against Jews, combined with negative feelings against Jewish refugees, penetrated all sectors of American society in the troubled 1930s. He explained, with contained emotion, how his mother reacted to his desire to have a sister and a brother by offering to adopt two child refugees from Germany. But the anti-Jewish hatred of the late 1930s, combined with xenophobia and a fear that immigrants would take American jobs, hampered the admission of Jewish refugee children from Germany. The Wagner-Rogers Bill died in Congress in mid-1939, suppressing the hope of "legislation to permit a set number of children under age eighteen to enter the U.S. outside the quota system," as Richard Breitman and Alan Kraut wrote in their seminal study on American refugee policy and European Jewry. "Twenty thousand charming children would all too soon grow into twenty thousand ugly adults," argued the wife of Commissioner of Immigration James Houghteling, "whose main qualification for the job was that his wife was FDR's cousin."[79] Many instances depicted the atmosphere of Jewish hatred, the seeds of which had been "sown and nurtured for years."[80] Jewish soldiers then reaped the fruits; the taste was all the more bitter as Jewish Americans sacrificed their lives in the hope that Jew hatred and discrimination would vanish at home and abroad.

An incident reported by one of the pilots interviewed by Bruce Wolk reveals how the wounds were kept open after the end of World War II. Paul Kaufman, an officer, flew a B-17 with the 388th Bombardment group of the 560th Bomb Squadron. When his plane, *Millie-K*, was shot down over Merseburg, Germany, he was captured after bailing out and imprisoned in a prisoner of war (POW) camp. At war's end, his family arranged to meet him on Pier Sixty, New York, a long-expected and emotional reunion for the soldiers returning from Europe. But the ship on which he came back to the United States was delayed, and his father was not allowed to take another day off work. This is how he depicted his homecoming: "We finally arrived at Pier 60. Nobody was there to meet us. There was a man handing over flyers to select people. One of my buddies got a flyer and I asked to see it. It said something like: 'So and so died in Europe, Colin Kelly died in Guadalcanal, etc.... and Nathan Goldstein, the son-of-a-bitch got four brand new tires.' I said to myself, will it ever end?"[81]

All over the United States, similar lines, with variations, were sung as parodies on military hymns. There are oral and written versions of the hymn "The First American." Yet no version mentions the name of the bombardier who died in the Pacific next to celebrated American hero Colin Kelly, "the First American to sink a Jap ship," as the line goes.[82] Was it because his name was Meyer Levin and "he was just a Brooklyn boy who grew up in a shabby neighborhood with nothing but free air and hope to let him know he was an American"? The 1942 article in the *Jacksonville Journal* that drew attention to Levin contains these powerful lines: "Let his deed be just another reminder that his much-slandered religious group, though making up only three per cent of our population, has received eight per cent of the Distinguished Service Crosses awarded by the American government."[83] Sergeant Meyer Levin's bravery and achievements were purposely hidden by antisemites. A twenty-five-year-old Air Corps bombardier from Brooklyn, he enlisted in the Air Corps on June 6, 1939, and served in the United States before being transferred to Hawaii. A few days after the surprise attack on Pearl Harbor, he flew on a mission against the Japanese navy. With pilot Captain Colin P. Kelly, bombardier Levin launched a shower of bombs in two separate attacks that destroyed and sank the Japanese battleship *Haruna* in the Pacific. Meyer Levin bravely continued to do his duty in the Battle of the Coral Sea, where he sank an enemy vessel, a feat for which he was awarded a Silver Star and a promotion from corporal to sergeant. He was also one of seventy-five men who made the risky flight to Manila in September 1941 with an air flotilla commanded by fellow Brooklynite Major Emmet O'Donnel. A hero of the Pacific aerial war, Levin received three decorations for gallantry in action—the Distinguished Flying Cross, the Silver Star, and the Oak Leaf Cluster—before he was killed in action off New Guinea when his bomber was shot down.[84] He was the first Jewish hero, and when he died at age twenty-six, he had taken part in about sixty combat flights.

The lengthy list of heroic records established by the JWB includes similar feats on various fronts in all the branches of the military; above all, it evinces the readiness of Jewish American servicemen to die for their country.[85] It is also a tribute to the servicemen's devotion and patriotic loyalty. The story of Jewish participation "that has only begun to unfold" is eloquently expressed in the *Congressional Record*, Seventy-Seventh Congress, second session, July 2, 1942: "That story was written in the foxholes of Bataan, in the bomb bays of high flying fighter planes, on the decks of ships where the guns flash." What is more, the statements pronounced in Congress and made eternal by the written word establish a linkage between the selfless dedication of Jewish GIs to their country and their own religious history, from bondage to freedom: "And now, in this new struggle for liberty we find Jews rendering service of the highest quality, and like Private Schleifer, often being among the first to give their lives for their country whose abiding democratic principles stem from the tenets of their own religious history."[86] Undoubtedly, Jewish veterans were later counted among the warriors for freedom in what has been called the Greatest Generation.[87] Demonstrating Jewish patriotism and contributions to the American military sprung from emotional impulses, as expressed by GIs in their writings during or immediately after the war.[88]

\*\*\*

Jewish heroism was defined and perceived in various ways. What did it mean for American soldiers as Jews? On the one hand, most American Jewish soldiers could not easily refer to Jewish heroes in World War I, although there were some. On the other hand, they identified with the heroic Maccabees in the context of the Hanukkah festival. Memoirs sent to the YIVO Institute in 1946 show that many GIs went to Hebrew school or Sunday school. They learned about the Jewish warrior Judah Maccabee, third son of Mattathias, the Hasmonean who led the revolt against the yoke of Antiochus Epiphanes in the land of Israel (Eretz Israel) and vanquished the oppressor—as told in the Books of Maccabees. As Jews, identification with a Jewish hero boosted morale and helped GIs fight the negative stereotype of the weak Jew. The heroic service that Jews performed during the war shielded them from anti-Jewish slurs. The service is seen through the brave deeds of military officers David Daniel Marcus, Paul Shulman, and Sergeant Meyer Levin, the holder of the Distinguished Flying Cross, Silver Star Award for Heroism at Coral Sea, and Oak Leaf for gallantry. A reflection on heroism as a response to anti-Jewish attitudes in the military is therefore an underlying thread in the narrative of this work.

Responses to victimization included extreme bravery and selflessness. Jewish servicemen embraced American ideals of masculinity and heroism in the same ways as their fellow soldiers, equating the military value of fighting with manly characteristics. In reference to their need for acceptance, their efforts to belong in the military and their deeds may be retroactively interpreted as strategies to combat persecution and anti-Jewish attitudes; on the whole, however, these were spontaneous responses. To put it differently, a reinforced Jewish identity on the one hand and a behavior resorting to heroism on the other were an antidote to anti-Jewish hostility and a stamp of loyalty and devotion to the country's values. This sentiment was confirmed by many American servicemen who fought both during World War II and for the fledgling State of Israel. Brooklyn-born Dan Nadel, a proud patriot who enlisted in the American army after the Pearl Harbor attack, became a combat engineer and experienced twenty-five river crossings under fire in the European theater. He recounted: "I felt that we had served America well, saving the Jewish people in the process. . . . To have survived seven decades ago was against all odds; I believe it was only possible by the grace of God."[89] From 1942 to 1945, wearing a Jewish amulet attached to his dog tags, he fought many battles, including the Battle of the Bulge in France, and landed shortly after D-Day at Omaha Beach in Normandy, sustained by his Jewish faith and motivation to fight what "Hitler was doing to the Jews."[90] Discovering concentration camps under the command of General Patton, he comforted the survivors of Nazi concentration camps. Dan Nadel earned five battle stars in the Battle of the Bulge and the liberation of France.[91]

Ironically, many Jewish GIs excelled in a job they did not like but had to do for their country. As comedy icon Mel Brooks, born in Brooklyn as Melvin Kaminsky to Jewish immigrant parents, put it: "I was a combat engineer. Isn't that ridiculous? The two things I hate most in the world are combat and engineering." Reflecting on what triggered his comedy style, the former combat engineer charged with defusing land mines recalled the frustrations of a Jewish kid who enlisted at age seventeen: "I'm sure a lot of my comedy is based on anger and hostility. Growing up in Williamsburg, I learned to clothe it into comedy to spare myself problems—like a punch in the face."[92]

To counter persistent slander targeting Jewish GIs, the JWB and other Jewish organizations drew up lists of Jewish servicemen and servicewomen. They believed doing so would help dispel the myth that Jews were draft dodgers or mostly in the Quartermaster Corps, where they were good suppliers.[93] As a result, they were indirectly led to think in terms of contribution to the war effort rather than participation. The numerous examples of extreme bravery or heroism indicate that excellence was required to make a mark. Excelling, "being the best," was not only congruent with the American ethos—it was a necessity for acceptance into American society well into the 1950s, mid-1960s, and still later to climb the social ladder. In that light, Jewish soldiers' self-imposed discipline met the ideal of the self-made man as exemplified in American society by Benjamin Franklin, Abraham Lincoln, or Andrew Carnegie. Yet the picture is complex because there were contradictory forces at work in those years. In the military, finding refuge among other Jews was an option or response akin to "sticking to one's own kind," a tendency characteristic of minority groups in the United States. This response happened during religious services and celebration of Jewish holy days, which was legitimate, although more difficult for those who saw combat. The encouragement to mesh with comrades also existed in the American military. Some servicemen volunteered to help non-Jewish chaplains to conduct Jewish services, a practice that proved broadmindedness on all parts. At the same, as historian Jonathan Sarna puts it, "cooperation was in the interest of the military" and supported by the Committee on Army and Navy Religious Activities (CANRA) of the JWB.[94] This new attitude of encouraging observance of the Jewish faith—just like the two other main religions—enables a reassessment of antisemitism or, more properly termed, Jew hatred. Even more significant is the fact that some officers in the higher ranks did not share pervasive negative attitudes toward Jews, according to various testimonies noted above. Furthermore, the fact that a few high reserve officers, like Colonel David (Mickey) Marcus, whose immigrant father was a pushcart peddler, were admitted to West Point testifies to a spirit of tolerance displayed when in harmony with American interests. Proof for this statement is that Colonel Marcus is proclaimed "A Soldier for All Humanity" in the West Point Military Cemetery. In terms of respect for American values and in congruence with the American president's support of the establishment of the Jewish state, the awareness of the Jewish plight's universalistic overtones had the potential to counter prejudice. However, negative stereotypes of Jews as service dodgers, for example, remained entrenched in everyday language and were shared in society. World War II functioned in the various theaters as a laboratory of experiments—physical, mental, and social—for Jewish soldiers and their non-Jewish comrades.

The next chapter will expand on the expression of prejudice that servicemen encountered in French North Africa, among other unique and novel war experiences.

# 5

# OPERATION TORCH AND LOCAL JEWS

The First Major Allied Amphibious Invasion of the War

The idea of Allied landings in Morocco and Algeria (French North Africa) in November 1942 came from British prime minister Winston S. Churchill, who convinced the American president to establish a foothold on the Mediterranean shores and check the advance of the German and Italian forces in the Middle East. Churchill was intent on thwarting the troops led by General Erwin Rommel who had served in the Wehrmacht of Nazi Germany. As commander of Afrika Korps, the German Field Marshal reached Tripoli in northwest Libya in February 1941.

French North Africa was part and parcel of the French colonial empire and under the authority of the collaborationist Vichy government, with which the Roosevelt administration maintained diplomatic (yet controversial) relationships.

President Roosevelt hoped that North Africa would become an arena of French anti-German activity where army or partisan units could be secretly recruited. To that end, General Eisenhower was in contact with General Mast of the French army, senior American diplomat in Algiers Robert Murphy, and several American vice-consuls serving as intelligence agents. In November 1942, cooperation between the Allied forces and French generals in North Africa, especially the commander in chief, Admiral Jean François Darlan, was far from clear. Would the French generals oppose the landings and stand with the Vichy forces? The final aim of the Allied operation was to advance to the Tunis area to engage the Germans there. In his memoirs, General Eisenhower explained that it was of the utmost importance that the landings succeed in the capital of Algeria, Algiers. To secure victory, the Allied landings must not meet with any harsh opposition. In his papers, Eisenhower underlined the importance of the French Resistance

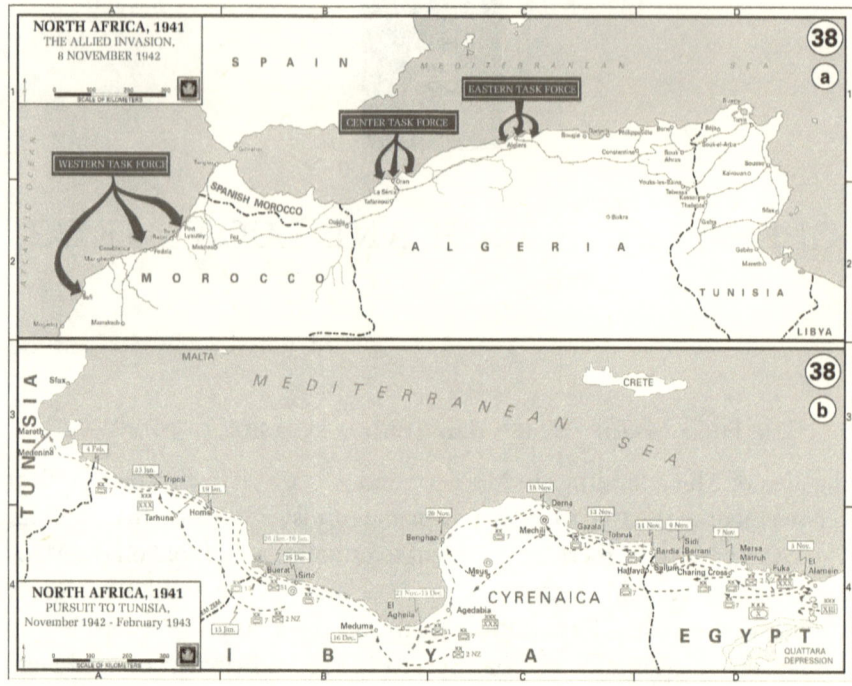

Map 5.1 Operation Torch landings in North Africa, November 8, 1942, and the pursuit to Tunisia (November 1942–February 1943). Courtesy of United States Military Academy Department of History. Public domain.

in standing against the Vichy regime established in French North Africa.¹ Resistance fighters cooperated with the Allied forces in what came to be known as Operation Torch in November 1942, a secret operation that began on the night of November 7 to November 8 under the American general's command. An expeditionary corps of one hundred thousand men landed on the French North African coast at Casablanca, Algiers, and Oran.

General Eisenhower recorded the main goal of the campaign in his memoir: "The minimum objective of the North African invasion was to seize the main ports between Casablanca and Algiers, denying their use to the Axis as bases for submarines, and from them to operate eastward toward the British desert forces."²

As early as autumn 1940, a paramilitary organization was established in Algiers under the guise of a sports club. Led by a twenty-year-old Jewish medical student named José Aboulker, non-Jewish officers joined the group and were involved in establishing contact with Anglo-American military command.[3] To what extent did Jewish members of resistance groups in Algeria participate as Jews? Most Jews in Algeria cherished French patriotic values out of gratitude to France, which had granted their ancestors French citizenship in 1870. They were proud to show that their parents had fought in World War I.

Oral testimonies given later show that several hundred young French Jews from Algeria played a crucial role in the French Resistance and in assisting the Anglo-American landings.[4] Aboulker's unit comprised about four hundred men; more than three-quarters were of Jewish origin. Their operation assumed the character of a seizure of power. In the middle of the night, small detachments of insurgents mounted surprise attacks, seizing the police headquarters, post office, radio station, and—most importantly— the headquarters of the military command of Algiers, the telephone lines of which had been cut. A number of French officers, including Admiral Darlan, the most prominent Vichy leader present in North Africa, were taken prisoner, while throughout the night, Radio Algiers transmitted orders to the French troops not to resist the Allied forces. Though Aboulker's resistance groups suffered two casualties in Algiers, the Allies landed without having to fire a single shot. Shortly afterward, Admiral Darlan joined the Anglo-American forces, followed by the French generals under his command, finally deciding to side with the victors. Because Operation Torch was a secret, it is likely that most members of the French underground were only informed of its launch on the eve of the Allied invasion.[5]

The Jews of Algeria, who had enjoyed French citizenship since the Crémieux Decree of 1870, were the first victims of Vichy legislation. Most had become assimilated Jews—just like Jews in metropolitan France—and were French patriots. But in October 1940, the French government abolished the Crémieux Decree, which had naturalized the Jews of Algeria and given them civil equality with French citizens. With their French citizenship revoked, French-speaking Jews living in Algeria could not fill any public function, and their children could no longer attend public schools. As men were dismissed from the French army, they thought about resistance to express their refusal to submit to injustice.

In the cosmopolitan city of Oran, the landings faced greater difficulties. General Eisenhower reported: "In Oran we got ashore, but the French forces in that region, particularly the naval elements, resisted bitterly. . . . There were casualties. On November 10th, all fighting ceased, but they had been harsh."[6]

For instance, Corporal Bernard J. Kessel, from Brooklyn, was put in the tank unit when the assault against the seaport of Oran was underway. Placed in the driver's seat, he was told to drive on. When he saw a roadblock barring the way, he accelerated and smashed through it. Although there were guns facing him, he "rammed the gun position at full speed and went on," destroying everything on his way, a war correspondent reported. The boys from his crew "opened fire in all directions." The newspaper headline that summarized the story read "Orphan Tank Almost Takes Oran by Itself." When Kessel's mother read the story, she expressed astonishment and relief. How could this have happened to her son, who did not know how to drive and "was just naturally unhandy when it came to mechanics?"[7]

In the newspaper, no mention was made of the Jewish origin of Corporal Kessel, as he was but a soldier in the American army, which did not have a segregated Jewish unit as it did a Black unit. Jews were part of the American nation and, as such, were patriots. As mentioned previously, whether they were drafted or enlisted of their own volition, they often volunteered for the front lines out of patriotism and defiance to prove that they were no cowards. That is precisely what young Kessel did. Numerous Jews served in the infantry and distinguished themselves, such as Private First Class A. Rodman of Ferndale, California, who received the Silver Star for making "a prompt and vital sortie" under enemy fire during the November landings. Others, like Private Milton Gorobetz of Brooklyn, who swam to the beach under heavy fire and helped wounded men, were awarded the Silver Star. Sergeant Robert Arch of Valley Stream, New York, ignored danger when facing heavy enemy machine gun fire from the French Vichy forces. With 254 combat hours over North Africa, Sergeant Schiller Cohen, a New Yorker, was awarded thirteen medals. In Tunisia, Sergeant Herbert Friedwald, another New Yorker, received the Silver Star and the French Croix de Guerre for heroism, as did Sergeant Stanley Lowitz of Jamaica, New York, who distinguished himself during the Oran offensive.[8]

In the 1943 edition of the abridged prayer book, dedicated to "Jews in the Armed Forces of the United States" and published by the National Jewish Welfare Board (JWB), the preface highlights that "this little volume of devotion serves not only the men who use it, but also the highest ideal of America." It stresses the universal character of the Jewish religion. Here is one example: "The prayers here gathered together speak of the eternal aspirations of the Jewish people and, indeed, of all mankind."[9] This pocket-sized volume emphasizes the congruence between American and Jewish values by stressing the need for prayers "to give courage to spurn evil and hold fast to faith in the ultimate triumph of the good."[10]

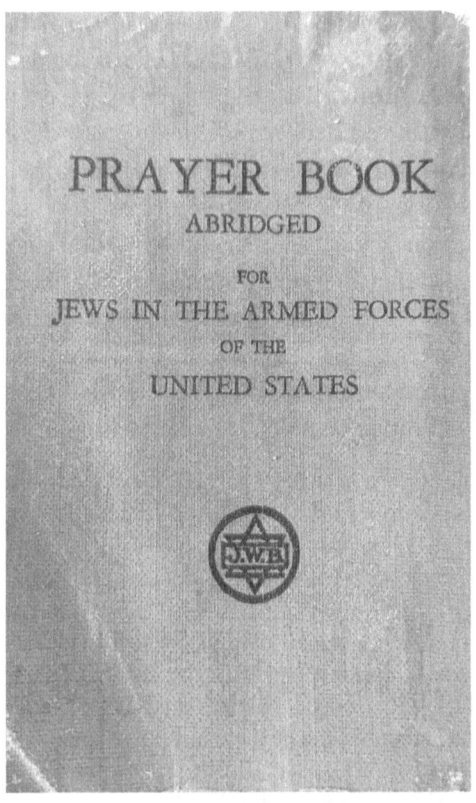

Fig. 5.1 Abridged Jewish prayer book issued by the National Jewish Welfare Board, 1943, used by soldiers, sailors, airmen, and women in the military. Collection of the author.

In stressful moments—before a battle or after a tragic loss—prayer books were a comfort. It is important to note that the JWB agreed to publish a prayer book that would represent Conservative, Orthodox, and Reform Judaism. Among the passages that were often dog-eared by soldiers is "Prayer for Home." It reads, in reference "to those I love" and "far from home": "Keep me under the influence of the ties that bind me to them, so that even in *strange surroundings* I may conduct myself in ways that do them honor."[11] It is probably with that moral obligation in mind that Jewish American soldiers encountered the Jewish families who invited them to their homes and synagogues for the Sabbath and Jewish festivals in North Africa, giving them a break from army life and fighting.

From that perspective, attending a synagogue was akin to finding an anchor. It was also a means to express thankfulness for being alive after the landings; a dozen GIs drowned on the shores of Algiers and Oran during Operation Torch, which resulted in an Allied victory.[12] For the most observant soldiers, prayers powerfully conjured associations of family life at home.

Herbert Cohen, one of the fifty-two veterans who submitted an essay to the YIVO contest on "the experiences and observances of a Jew in World War II," provided a rather literary rendering of what he went through, referring to himself as "GI Joe." His voice deserves to be heard, as it stresses the universal character of his experience as a soldier before evoking the specificity of his encounters as a Jew whose Jewish identity could not be concealed because of his surname.

> Twenty-eight days aboard a British transport hardened his soul, as daily scaling maneuvers up and down the ship in Mid-Atlantic proved of inestimable benefit to him when the gray dawn crept upon the huge convoy as it slipped into Oran harbor, November 8th. His efforts in turning the invasion from doubt into clear-ringing success were confined to unloading supplies, vehicles, ammunition and all the prerequisites for warfare . . . Jews, Protestants, Catholics—all had joined hand in hand in the greatest tasks of Allied force and output in evolving the highest pinnacle of success. Once the battle had subsided in the immediate area of Oran, Joe renewed his stance in the exploration of civilization, strange in outward appearance but human and identical under the skin.[13]

Cohen, previously stationed in London, had met English Jews at Yom Kippur services in Glasgow "just in time for Kol nidre," where he felt "religiously imbued." In Oran, he participated in religious services that led him to build friendships: "Joe maintained most friendly relations, uncovering true feelings and sentiments of a segment of the Jewish race that had felt in all its fury, the fang of hatred and sting of injury and yet, had the courage to hurdle such obstacles with a heavy heart but grinning countenance."[14] In a number of soldiers' accounts of experiences in North Africa, the reader realizes that North African Jews managed—in their broken English, or thanks to soldiers' knowledge of a smattering of the French language—to show how much they suffered from antisemitism.

### Jewish Refugees, Local Jews, and the Sense of Jewish Peoplehood

While non-Jewish soldiers often went off to see various places in North Africa and elsewhere, most Jewish soldiers (whose background was often "skeletonized," to borrow the term from a Jewish GI) rushed to the Jewish sections of the towns they were in. They not only observed closely the lives of local Jews but also described them with deep insight, as did this serviceman near Oran, after battles ended: "To his amazement, he [i.e., the GI] discovered that Jewish families, some of them escaped refugees from German tyranny, were in abundance. However, just as populous as they were, so were they secretive in the revelation of their identities, for the stigma of persecution bore its irreplaceable mark upon minds and souls. Later developments imparted credence to this belief as a meeting with one family determined."[15] Close contact with Jews who had been deprived of status and property often appears in the essays collected for the YIVO competition at the beginning of 1946. The resilience, courage, and dignity of suffering Jews had "raised the prestige of Jews and Judaism in the eyes of those previously estranged," as Moses Kligsberg aptly analyzed. Kligsberg considered "estranged" the American servicemen who felt their Jewishness as a burden.[16]

The presence of refugees fleeing Nazism was also noted by another GI who attended Friday night religious services in Casablanca. Harold Ribalow, a twenty-three-year-old former yeshiva student and Zionist from the Bronx, served as a radio operator with the air force and spent twenty-six months in North Africa, India, and Ceylon. He, too, came to feel that the Jews from North Africa and Europe were more interesting to observe in Casablanca than the mere environment, as shown in this short scene.

> There were fruit stands on the streets, just like the stands at home, in the Bronx, in Brooklyn, or Hester Street. Turbaned natives, sat in Indian fashion before they cried out in loud wailing voices.... I began to bargain with a dealer for the fruit (an orange). Then I saw a baggy European, wearing green American fatigues, a G.I. wool knit cap and an American field jacket.
>
> I did not ask him who he was. His appearance seemed to speak for him. He looked like a refugee from Hitler's Europe. His eyes had worry in them. His hands, thin and bluish, trembled slightly. His fingers were slim. His face was a good one, once handsome.
>
> "You see these people would take what they can from you." He shrugged his shoulders a bit resignedly. "Why not?", he asked of no one in particular. "They are poor and they see in you easy money." ... His French was fluent. He talked to the Arab fruit dealer. "I got you ten of them for five francs," he said.... "When I was in Vienna I thought of your country as a brawling, noisy, ignorant land." His command of English was good. His accent was faintly un-American.... "And then you came to Africa. But I came first. Here I was, a graduate of a British University, an Austrian musician, a Jew, and I came to Casablanca long ago." ... The shadows of night

fell across his face and gave him a gaunt expression. Suddenly I saw his face as if it were a distortion. Before I could speak, he looked at me and said "Goodnight" and disappeared. We never saw him again."[17]

This vivid exchange, fraught with silences and meaning, reveals to what extent the uprooted Jewish serviceman could understand the Jewish refugee with fear in his eyes. Ribalow, who spoke Hebrew and Yiddish with his parents, could identify with Jews from central and eastern Europe. Attending Sabbath services in Casablanca for the first time since his induction into the army, he remarked how much religious services connected him to home as well as to Jews overseas. Barely a year after the end of the war in Europe, he wrote: "The draft was the greatest educational institution in the world."[18]

Other testimonies confirm those of the GIs and show that North Africa was not a safe refuge for persons who fled Nazi persecution in Europe. A few refugees from Germany and Austria who worked as interpreters in Tunisia were deported by the SS when their identities were discovered. In Casablanca, some Jews confessed to Jewish GIs their fear that the Nazis were going to kill them. American servicemen were not only perceived as liberators but also as confidants.[19]

On the eve of WWII, there was a vibrant community of about 120,000 Jews in Algeria. At that time, Algeria was a French territory, while Tunisia and Morocco were French protectorates. Jews in Algeria lived among Europeans who generally fostered anti-Jewish feelings, especially during the Vichy regime.

GIs' observations of the Arab population in North Africa are also interesting. Here and there, a serviceman's observations run counter to the stereotyped vision of animosity between Jews and Arabs. This is what Herbert Cohen noticed: "Wherever one crossed the other's path, friendly greetings were exchanged and the atmosphere was one of complete accord, both in business and in neighborhood."[20] The American soldier justified his observation by providing another explanation: "Especially was this so in peril and mortal danger, for huddled together in common prayer and eager demands for safe deliverance, Jew and Arab sought refuge and moral support from the Almighty as each wave of German planes loosed their missiles of terror and destruction."[21]

Our soldier then provided a lively and meaningful portrait of Passover in Algeria in April 1943: "A mixture of fez hats added that certain native hue unmatched anywhere and the influx of American, British, Free French and Colonial troops enhanced the extraordinary color scheme of the congregation. It was Passover and as the chant rose and fell in crescendo, the sacred teachings of the Torah were expounded in glorified tribute and respect to the holiday."[22] The soldier's flowery description continues with an explanation of how servicemen were invited by Jewish families to celebrate Passover and attend the traditional seder, the special religious ceremony and meal that commemorates Passover, at their homes: "The intervention of the Battalion Chaplain, augmented by a directive from the Theater Commander furthered the grant of pass privileges to all members of Armed Forces of Jewish extraction and so it was that Joe indulged in the ceremonious rites of *Pesach* [Hebrew for Passover], the environment, one of total tranquility and exuberant passion."[23]

A *Haggadah* (booklet containing the Passover Eve ceremony) was hastily printed in Casablanca and "prepared for use of Jewish Personnel of the Army and Navy of the United States in French North Africa during the year 1943." It bore the following words in red on its front page: "Because the Passover is the Feast of the Delivrance [sic]." From the misspelling of "deliverance," one is inclined to think it was printed in a hurry.[24] Like most religious publications for American Jews in the armed forces, "Haggadot" were produced by the JWB, which authored the abridged prayer book published in 1941 and 1943. The *Haggadah* outlines what needs to be told and taught, what is to be eaten as symbolic food, and what passages from relevant sacred texts provide the framework for the narrative of Passover. Since the seder is a family reunion, a religious requirement as well as a recapitulation of the Exodus from Egypt, it is household centered. During and immediately after World War II in North Africa, it was conducted in large rooms adjacent to a synagogue. Eating *matzah* instead of bread for eight days is an important requirement that symbolizes the haste with which the Hebrews departed from Egypt.

When in Algeria, Jewish American GIs were surprised to see that the *matzah* (plural: *matzot*) did not resemble the flattened unleavened bread eaten in America, which looks like a big cracker, but rather artistically baked pretzels, while bitter herbs symbolized the bitterness of slavery both in North Africa and in America. The significance and texture of *haroset* (a mixture of dates, apples, wine, and ground nuts) serve as a reminder of the mortar Jews used to relentlessly build the Pharaohs' pyramids and monuments.

The rituals of Passover, which teach the evils of slavery and celebrate freedom, could not have been more relevant during the war; they reminded soldiers about Nazi enslavement in concentration camps, as news of the death camps started to spread in 1942. The Jewish celebration of the Exodus and liberation from enslavement in Egypt had a positive psychological impact on Jewish soldiers. North African Jewish homes became a substitute for the soldiers' own homes they had left to fight a war overseas. Viewed in that light, Jewish observance, far from being a burden, was an asset that instilled strength and serenity in the soldiers' minds. The testimony quoted above at length is representative of many others that share a sense of belonging inspired by memories of home in connection to rituals—even for nonobservant Jews, who experienced a collective feeling of belonging beyond the boundaries of their own countries. Transferred to Italy "in the harsh winter of 1944," our soldier "bade farewell to a life of ease and embarked upon an adventure that promised unbounded thrills and peril."[25]

While the essay quoted above evinces an effort to express these observations in a literary fashion, another YIVO contestant, focusing on the hospitality of Jews in Tunisia, remarked with humor that "their hearts were bigger than their cupboards." But as a witness of religious services in Le Kef, Tunisia, where Jews had been for some six months under German occupation (November 9, 1942, to May 8, 1943), the GI could not help but be impressed by the warmth and religious fervor of the French-speaking Jews. A young Jew born in Philadelphia in 1921 to a father from Poland and a mother from Russia, our observer considered himself imbued with "average religious inklings," having had a bar mitzvah and gone to Hebrew school. Before enlisting, he attended evening classes in accountancy and law at the University of Pennsylvania. This is how he recalled his encounters barely two years later, with a wealth of picturesque details that describe a close and exotic encounter with another world and another type of Jewry.

> It was all subsequent to the capitulation of all Axis forces that we arrived in Cape Bon. Inasmuch as our unit was in an inactive status at the time and were enjoying the fruits of well-earned victory by resting, we had plenty of time on our hands. Each afternoon, we would make the 20 mile hop to Nabeul, and it was by every conceivable mode of transportation, excepting the swaying, stiff-legged camels.
>
> It was a hot, sticky afternoon that we arrived in Nabeul. By good fortune, the day was Friday. And still better yet we heard that Friday evening services were to be held, the first time since the occupation by German forces. When the local people discovered that we were American Jews, they thronged about us, touched us, plying us with a million of questions, and finally imploring us to attend services that evening.[26]

The "indelible imprint" of these scenes, in the words of that veteran, indicates that warmth coupled with religiosity became associated with emotional memories of home while these soldiers were far away. Deep in their minds, they must have been reminded of the gestures or acts of their parents or grandparents, such as lighting candles on Friday eve to welcome the spirituality of sabbatical rest. That same soldier went on to describe the religious service and the feelings it aroused: "Prayers were recited and hymns sung with such passion and with such fervor that I couldn't but feel humble before these people."

Paradoxically enough, the soldier's feeling of humbleness when faced with these people, fervently praying and thanking their Creator for deliverance, awakened not only his interest in Judaism but also a feeling of pride in his Jewishness that probably helped him rebuff any antisemitic slur to come. This interpretation is confirmed by the enthusiasm felt in the rendering of his war experiences: "Before the service was completed, the Grand Rabbi made a benediction for all the Americans present in the synagogue." At this point, the feeling of empathy with Tunisian Jewry reached a peak, as the GIs received a benediction that gave them a feeling of home. The "boys" sensed that someone other than their parents or next of kin cared for them, and this instilled in them strength to pursue the war in Italy, France, Germany, or in other remote and hostile countries. It is therefore not surprising that the young veteran who authored that essay used the adjective "intimate" at least twice to describe his experience in North Africa. He described a Passover service in a synagogue in Le Kef, Tunisia, recalling "the scarcity of able-bodied men" but also the emotions aroused: "There was a light and a sparkle in the eyes of the small boy singing near me, and I felt a lump in my throat as I noticed the way all the young children sang their prayers entirely by heart and in unison. I was filled with a feeling of ecstasy for, in my heart, I could feel that no matter how desperate the position of these people, no matter how miserable their life, they drank the joy of newly won freedom."[27] Far from home, many observant and nonobservant Jews took comfort in traditional Judaism.

Another sociological aspect is that the presence of Jewish GIs drew attention to the poverty of members of Tunisian Jewry at the time. It is interesting to point out that the soldiers were probably the first Americans to notice the prevalence of couscous in inexpensive Friday evening meals in North Africa among local Jews, the humbleness of which was noted: "The only illumination came from two small candles conveniently placed in the room. We sat down at the table to a very heavy evening meal of koos-koos [sic], green vegetables and wine. The Kooskoos is a grainy food covered with gravy, and acts as the main staple of diet for the North Africans."

These pieces of information are accompanied by a comment on what appeared to the GI as something common in Jewish homes, and probably acted as a reminder of his own home in Pennsylvania: "Their homes were surrounded by fifth and squalor, but here was typical Jewish cleanliness within."[28]

### Mutual Boosting of Morale between Jewish GIs and North African Jews

Meeting with local populations in North Africa strengthened the Jewish identity of many soldiers, while erasing some negative effects of anti-Jewish perceptions. For instance, GIs were proudly shown pictures of French Jewish soldiers from North Africa who had been decorated when fighting in France during World War I.

The reassuring succession of sabbatical meals gave some support and joy to soldiers; proof is found in the letters of a soldier to host families with which he remained in contact for some years. The oral testimonies I collected from Jews whose families invited soldiers from Allied armies mention the gifts for the kids that GIs sent in 1944 and 1945. Archival materials provide a few examples of soldiers who attended synagogue services on Passover 1943 and received a letter of invitation from the rabbi of Algiers. This was the case with Samuel Appel, who wrote many letters to the Jewish friends he met. Letters from French Jews in Oran, written in English between 1944 and 1948, testify to the warm relationships between Jewish soldiers and local Jews.[29] The following is an example of a Jewish American soldier's impressions of a special service in the Grand Synagogue in Oran.

> Religion has had little influence on me. . . . Yet how can I explain the flow of tears, involuntary streaming, when attending services at a synagogue for the first time in twenty years? Was I moved by the spectacle of hundreds of men in uniform, from all the States of the Union? . . . Can I attribute it to the loneliness I often felt here (in Oran), the loneliness which comes not from separation alone (from the family), but that which invariably is sensed when a stranger comes among those who shun him? Prejudice naturally exists here as it does at home.[30]

In Oran, like in other places in North Africa, Jewish homes became a refuge for soldiers who suffered from anti-Jewish hostility from their fellow soldiers. In these homes, a powerful bond was created between Jewish servicemen and local Jews. When French Jews hosted Jewish GIs and their non-Jewish friends, it provided encouragement for the rest of the war. As a matter of fact, GIs were acclaimed and admired as liberators by the Jewish population, fearing the occupation of French North Africa by the Germans. In the case of German occupation, many French non-Jews expected to benefit from the local Jews' assets, as was the case in occupied France.

The arrival of Allied forces boosted the morale of Jews in Oran, who had been stripped of their citizenship in 1940 by Vichy France and suffered from social exclusion. Emile Moatti, a former student of the elite French Ecole Polytechnique, could not forget the anguish he felt at home before the Allied invasion. Yet the landings brought about a "liberating atmosphere." He was then eleven years old, and this metamorphosis was etched in his mind.[31] In the Bedeau labor camp, located south of Oran, French Jewish soldiers enthusiastically shouted "Hello, boys" at American jeeps passing nearby. As inmates of a camp that functioned like a concentration camp, they were severely rebuked. Five or six were beaten up, according to a report about "the mistreatment of French soldiers of Jewish descent."[32] Starting in July 1941, a piece of legislation required the confiscation of all Jewish property except for personal homes. Vichy authorities awarded Jewish-owned businesses to "trustees" who could pay themselves with the profits of the business. A published testimony reveals that a family living on a large estate would have been forced to hand over its farm to trustees had the Allied soldiers not landed in time. The arrival of American GIs to their estate was perceived as a stroke of luck. The writer of a memoir recorded what she felt as a young woman: "An outburst of joy flooded our little town. . . . Each house had its GI, its cigarettes, and chocolate and a feeling of freedom in the heart. After a period of hesitation, the families on the far-right (non-Jewish and pro Vichy) joined the manifestations of joy and of course found soul mates among the liberators."[33]

Huguette Lancry, a teacher born in Oran in 1929, recalled the joy shared by the Jews who saw American troops from their balconies following the Allied landings of November 8. She also remembered the disappointed antisemitic neighbors who dared to shout: "We expected the Germans, not the Americans." She was then a thirteen-year-old girl who had been terribly humiliated when she was expelled from the Lycée Stéphane Gsell for girls in Oran, a secular public school, on account of being Jewish. These are the memories she retained from that November day when so many friendly soldiers were seen in her town: "When the GIs entered the streets of the town of Oran, we stood on our balconies. Trucks crowded with black and white soldiers who lavishly distributed chewing gum and chocolate candies to the Arab children in the streets who now clung to the GIs' vehicles. It was as if America had entered Oran." She made it clear that her family knew that meters of yellow fabric were stored at the prefecture in Oran to make yellow stars for the Jewish population to wear had the Allied forces not arrived just in time to avoid that visible discrimination and degradation.[34]

The daring amphibious invasion of North Africa prevented Jews from being deported and engendered immense gratitude toward the Allied troops. American Jewish GIs joined religious services at the synagogues and made America closer. A French sociologist studying the impact of the Vichy antisemitic laws on the lives of Jews in Algeria confirms the above testimony through interviews. All her interviewees shared painful memories: "Each of them related humiliating experiences: having to stand in separate lines in front of food stores, being dismissed from civil service, their children being banned from their schools, and lawyers' and doctors' practices being forcibly closed." What prevails at this juncture in their life stories is a deep feeling of solitude and exclusion: "The anti-Jews were having a field day, seeing our degradation," said one interviewee, echoing what several other respondents said. An Algiers-born doctor scoffed: "The settlers—well, they were all antisemitic! When Vichy began, they were all ecstatic and rushed to join Marshal Pétain's movement." While a majority of French settlers in Algeria were indeed antisemitic, the picture the sociologist drew from her respondents about the Arabs' attitudes toward the Jews is no better: "The Arabs were wholeheartedly anti-Jewish—they'd call their donkeys '*Yehud ben Yehud*' (Jew, son of a Jew) while kicking them to go faster. They had never stomached the Crémieux Decree because we were natives just as they were, and France had made us superior to them. They relished seeing us stripped of our citizenship."[35]

For the Jews of Algeria, this period, which entailed the temporary loss of citizenship, was most traumatic. After holding French citizenship from 1870 to 1940, they were degraded to the status of "natives" (*indigènes*) until the reinstatement of their citizenship on October 21, 1943. Tunisian or Moroccan Jews, unlike their counterparts in Algeria, had never been endowed collectively with French citizenship. Though they had Tunisian or Moroccan passports, their culture, too, was French.

A question arises: Why did Jews in Algeria not recover their citizenship with the Allied landings? Although the answer is complex, it transpired that in return for Admiral Jean-François Darlan's cooperation with General Eisenhower in neutralizing a coup d'état in Algiers on November 8, the American general recognized Darlan as high commissioner for North Africa. This controversial deal meant that Admiral Darlan, who had been appointed by the Vichy regime, was allowed to remain as head of the French administration in North Africa. Darlan had been regularly pressured by Robert Murphy, the top American diplomat in Algiers, to restore the rights of Algerian Jews.[36]

When exhausted American soldiers approached Oran on Sunday, November 8, Arabs greeted them with stiff-armed fascist salutes, mistaking them for Germans. Indeed, some French fascists and antisemitic French North Africans had hoped for the arrival of Germans. One of the aims of the American army was to convert the town of Oran into a supply depot, but this was no easy task because of the resistance of the Vichy French armed forces. Journalist Rick Atkinson described in detail the eventful capture of the city of Oran: "Before noon, on November 8, Company C of Terry Allen's 18th Infantry had been ambushed, driven off, then driven again when it turned to St. Cloud with the bulk of the 1st Battalion."[37] In a description not devoid of humor, the journalist pictured the lively American encounter with the local population: "Festive crowds filled the sidewalks, flashing Vs with their fingers and flinching at occasional sniper fire. The pretty girls Allen had promised blew kisses from balconies on Boulevard Joffre and dropped hibiscus garlands onto tank turrets. A potbellied burgher with a black felt hat and a white flag rapped on a tank hull, introduced himself as Oran mayor, and offered to surrender his town."[38]

The American military gave code names to Algerian villages near Oran. Those names were drawn from soldiers' hometowns, like Brockton, Syracuse, or Brooklyn.[39] But the strange landscape and the discovery of a poor Arab population, begging, their faces "eaten away by syphilis," was a shock for GIs. Stories of Arabs selling women are reported in the war diary of the 526th Fighter Bomber Squadron, which came to the La Sénia Airfield near Oran in May 1943. With the surrender of the city of Algiers and the capture of Oran in November 1942, the Allies "possessed" Algeria. In this confidential diary, the search for a GI brothel is openly reported. With that goal in mind, many men left the airport to explore the various facets of the city of Oran. The reason put forward for this virile necessity was that soldiers found it difficult to get closer to the "beautiful French girls" they saw because these girls "walked with a chaperon and not on their own."[40] The same war diary also accounts for difficulties linked to a hostile environment, some described by the renowned French author Albert Camus in his novels. American soldiers noted that the water was terrible and deplored the "numerous cases of drunkenness among both the officers and the enlisted men" resulting from the lack of drinkable water. While waiting for planes heading to Tunisia, GIs took showers, but "there are no showers except in salt water, which leaves the hair sticky"—and hordes of "mosquitoes here are so discriminating so as to look at the dog tags before taking a bite to make sure they get the proper blood type."[41] The soldiers' sense of humor under trying conditions was probably one of their best weapons against homesickness and depression.

Considering the efforts to be accepted as Jews in the army and to not be excluded from social activities, meeting other Jews in Algiers or Oran answered both an urge for a social outlet and a desire to feel at home, "home" being a set of references that reminded them of the familiar gestures of relatives and friends, like lighting the Sabbath candles.

### Inspiring Interactions

A handwritten essay authored by a GI in 1946 and sent to the YIVO competition about "my experiences and observations as a Jew in World War II" contains these significant lines about an invitation to a home for Passover 1944 in Tunis (April 7–8): "What warmth, what spontaneous understanding. Shalom Aleichem brother, Aleichem Shalom . . . How they fought to possess a soldier. . . . The services started soon and the *Seder* was interesting. Salomon [the host] chanted Hebrew with Arabic intonation, and as he prayed, passed the *matzots* over our heads in a rotary motion. Many of us had forgotten the prayers and ritual, but Solomon tolerantly forgave our paganism." Not only did the spicy food warm the soldiers' hearts but the author of the essay also admitted that from then on, he understood the universal character of Judaism, which had escaped him. This proud understanding would serve him right against Jew haters: "I saw more in a few days to refute the persistent typology theory of anti-Semites than I had previously read in many formal arguments on the subject. If there was anything universal about us, it is our universal misfortune to unjustly bear the burden of man's depravation upon our shoulders."[42]

Through this encounter with North African Jews, some Jewish GIs learned that Jewishness was not a separate part of their identity and realized the similitudes inherent in Judaism beyond the differences. Most of all, awareness of the universal meaning behind ritual practices empowered Jewish American soldiers, providing them with tools and arguments to defend themselves against antisemitic slurs.

Chaplain Werfel's report to the chaplaincy commission is significant regarding the interactions between American and North African Jews. It especially pinpoints the joy these interactions brought him: "It was an inspiring sight to watch those French-speaking, Sephardic-familied youngsters, about 200 of them, singing the same Palestinian songs that our youngsters sing back in the US."[43]

Chaplain Werfel's name is one of the fourteen inscribed on a monument for fallen Jewish chaplains in Arlington National Cemetery's Chaplains Hill. He was the only Orthodox chaplain killed in action in World War II. Chaplain Werfel's statement that "the war has brought me changes of attitude, the full significance of which I still cannot recognize," could apply to most of the Jewish GIs who went overseas.

Chaplains were morale builders. The exemplary deeds of two who served in North Africa will suffice to demonstrate this point. Chaplain Louis (Eliezer) Werfel was on duty with the Twelfth Air Force Service Command in North Africa. He was nicknamed "The Flying Rabbi" because he wanted to reach as many servicemen as possible, an endeavor only feasible by plane. How else could he serve his soldier congregations both in Algeria and Morocco? On the way back to conduct a Hanukkah service in Casablanca in 1943, he was warned that "ceilings were low and it might be dangerous flying," but he decided he had no choice; he had to visit servicemen in many locations throughout North Africa, since American troops were dispersed over vast expanses. On a foggy day, his plane crashed into an unseen mountain top shortly after takeoff on December 24, 1943. As noted in a national government publication by the United States Air Force, hope sustained chaplains' faith, whether they were Jewish, Protestant, or Catholic: "Perhaps their faith was vindicated in the unexpressed feelings of many servicemen who hoped and dreamt that their efforts would make a better world."[44] This faith can be seen in Werfel's motivation to serve despite his poor eyesight preventing him from serving overseas as a soldier. On his insistence, he was assigned to air force units in North Africa and met his death at age twenty-seven.[45] It is now known that in one of his last requests to the JWB, Werfel asked for ten thousand prayer books in French translation to be sent to the Jewish men serving in the French Free Forces.[46] The presence of about sixty Jewish soldiers accompanying him to his final resting place in the American Military Cemetery in Oran was a last mark of gratitude and fellowship.[47]

Chaplain Irving Tepper of Chicago, who also served in North Africa, was the first Jewish chaplain killed in France. He died at age thirty-one while serving with the Ninth Infantry Division, where he was called "Chaplain Courageous"; he was considered a morale builder by Chaplain W. MacLeod, his non-Jewish roommate in England as they were waiting for D-Day.⁴⁸ It seems that chaplaincy in wartime, and overseas in particular, empowered rabbis, who became physically tougher, if not spiritually stronger, as they understood the need not only to serve Jews but also to provide for the spiritual and religious needs of Christians when there was no Christian chaplain available, as was required by the American military.

In every war, demoralization plays a part, and the encouragement and warmth of encounters between persecuted French Algerian Jews and American servicemen was a transformative experience for both sides. Among the Sephardic French Jews of Algeria, Tunisia, and Morocco, traditional rituals, joyful celebrations, and tasty food played a crucial part in boosting GIs' morale. Lasting relationships between Jewish veterans and North African Jews that began in 1942, together with many interviews and testimonies, document this point. All this is without mentioning the marriages after the war: although the beautiful French girls mentioned in the war diary previously quoted were not easily approached, Jewish soldiers invited for the Sabbath or Jewish festivals could gain direct access to girls in families. This is why war brides were not unusual in North Africa. In other cases, the definite departure of handsome young men in uniform who had promised marriage resulted in inconsolable broken hearts. Max Benhamou, a citizen of Casablanca, reminisced that most of the Jewish families in Morocco extended hospitality to American servicemen, "not necessarily Jewish." He mentioned discovering chewing gum, Campbell Soup, and American literature through the small, lightweight paperbacks intended to reduce stress before an imminent battle or provide comfort.⁴⁹ The American government, along with publishers, dispatched millions of books to servicemen in all branches of the military and in most war theaters. Mobile libraries were created once a place was secured. There, American servicemen could borrow Armed Service Editions (ASEs) to help reconnect with home. ASEs reached wounded soldiers in hospitals in Tunisia through Red Cross volunteers.⁵⁰

Jewish American soldiers in North Africa symbolized both liberation and a world in which Judaism could be legitimately expressed in the public sphere, unlike in the French territories, where secularity remained a requirement. It is also significant that starting with the landing of American soldiers, French Jews in North Africa gave American names to their newborns. Some of the most popular were James or William, while Daisy was a favorite during and after World War II.

***

As we reflect on the far-reaching consequences of the encounters of Jewish GIs with local and Jewish populations in North Africa, four points may be highlighted. These encounters were mutually influential, benefiting both sides. They encouraged lobbying efforts of the leaders of the French Jewish community in Algeria, who appealed to the American Jewish Committee and the World Jewish Congress (WJC).[51]

Another result of these interactions was the boost provided to the morale of Jewish soldiers, reinforcing their courage to continue the war in Italy and in other theaters. A point worthy of note is the fact that war experiences brought a sense of collective responsibility for Jews coreligionists. American Jews realized they had come to North Africa to fight both an American and a Jewish battle against the Third Reich and its allies, especially for those whose parents came from Europe, particularly Germany.

Therefore, this interaction helped bridge Jewish communities overseas and triggered a sense of awareness of the unity of one Jewish world. For young, estranged Jews, there was a sudden realization that Jews are a world diaspora, to use a current term. In-depth testimonies point to a sort of brotherhood expressed in letters exchanged long after the encounter. For some, the meeting aroused an interest not only in the Jewish religion or tradition but also in other cultures at a time when American youngsters might have been somewhat xenophobic. Virulent antisemitism on the part of European settlers during the Vichy regime was perceived in this way by a soldier in his essay: "The first things which struck my eyes when I strolled through the streets of Oran were the vicious slogans painted all over the buildings: 'Vive Pétain, mort à la Juiverie.'"[52]

In the testimonies quoted above, the expression of emotions ranges from anger to compassion and friendship, associated with memories of home. Thus, examining behaviors through this prism enriches the traditional conception of history. It also sheds light on the resilience of soldiers. Captain Max Zera, who fought with the Fighting First Infantry Division in Normandy on D-Day, wrote a significant letter a couple of months after the Tunisian campaign encapsulating a wide range of emotions expressed by combat soldiers. The voice of this twenty-eight-year-old, born in New York, who joined the army as a private in March 1941 and whose parents came from Poland, needs to be heard; it provides a global perspective on the war in North Africa from the viewpoint of a Jewish fighter. In the limited space of his letter, there is no mention of the Jewish communities he might have met.

The last look at Africa. You're not particularly unhappy about leaving the country. You have seen all of it you care to. Many thoughts run through your head. The day you landed at Oran, and your subsequent journeys over the Atlas Mountains. Your visits to Constantine, Algiers, and Tunis. The Arabs. The rain and the mud. The sun and the heat. The frost and the snow (yes, in Africa), the wines and the women. You think of all these.

But above all you think about the war. About the bombs and the shells and the bullets . . . of the destroyed vehicles, tanks and planes. Of the men you knew who are no more. Of the graves with the crosses and the stars . . . And then you realize that you are going forward into just so much more of this. Only you realize this will have to be tougher. You've got to land before you can dig in. And there is no telling who will be waiting to receive you.[53]

The next chapter will also convey the importance of the role of emotions in history, examining Jewish GIs' war experiences in contrasted territories such as India and the Pacific.

# RELIGIOSITY IN THE PACIFIC AND INDIA

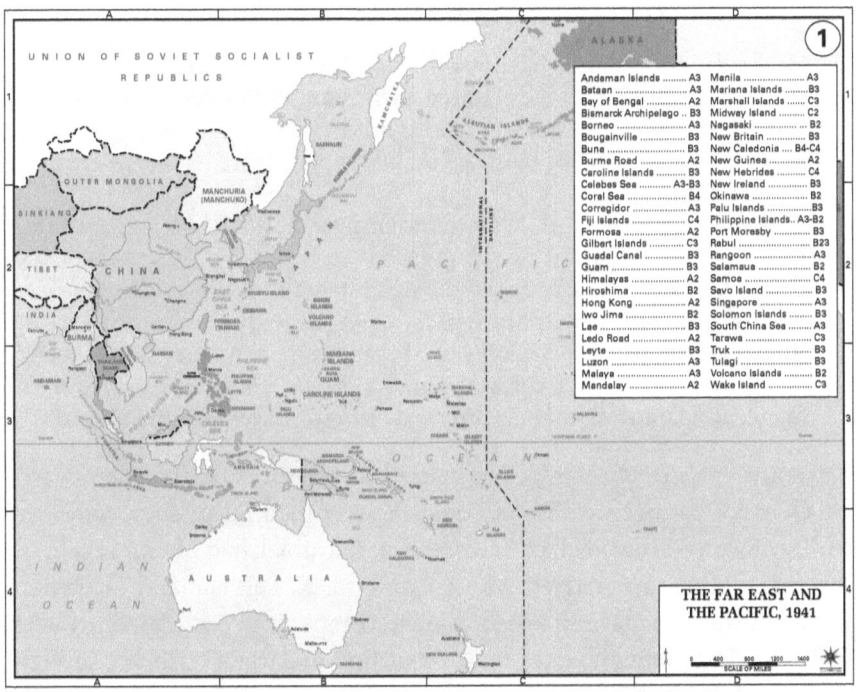

Map 6.1 The Pacific and the Far East, 1941. Courtesy of United States Military Academy Department of History. Public domain.

November 19, 1942. The place was the green, towering, palm jungle of Guadalcanal, not far from the sea. The serviceman—thirty-two years old, quite old for a Marine—was Barney Ross, born in the poor quarters of New York's East Side as Dov-Ber David Rosofsky. Growing up in the dangerous streets of Chicago, Barney used his fists as shields in tricky situations. With fierce determination and many fights, he became the world boxing champion in the lightweight and welterweight divisions. But on that afternoon, crawling through dense vegetation in the deep and tangled jungle, he and the other, younger Marines were on unfamiliar terrain. Not far from his foxhole, he was ready to fire his Browning automatic rifle. One of the men spotted moving shadows some twenty yards ahead, and the word "Japs" passed from mouth to ear. A rain of bullets claimed victims among Barney's buddies. Some were killed instantly; others were wounded and needed the immediate help of medics, who rushed to the battlefield. Leaping into a shell hole, Ross and a few men remained in the dirt all night. When Japanese bullets came closer, Barney Ross, still unhurt, was in position to fire. Isidore Kaufman, a war correspondent in the Pacific, reported what happened.

> He fired eighty rounds of his own rifle ammunition. The soldiers passed their Garands to him and he fired their ammunition, 200 rounds in all. Every time he fired he had to raise his head a little and more than 20 times Jap machine gun bullets bounced off his helmet. These helmets were made of good steel.
>
> Now there was no more ammunition left—nothing but hand grenades. Painfully Heavy passed up his grenades to Ross, so did the others, giving him a total of 21. He tossed them at intervals, one by one, whenever it seemed necessary to keep the Japs away. At last, only one grenade was left. Ross fixed all the men's bayonets and then his own. As they waited for the attack which they were certain would come any time, they prayed. Prize fighter Ross murmured the words of a Hebrew prayer he remembered.[1]

The omnipresence of death on the battlefield and the threat of a new deadly attack called for prayers. Transcendence was called for by the compelling reality of war. At the break of dawn, the feared attack had not materialized. Instead, a relief unit arrived with Captain O. K. LeBlanc and Lieutenant John Murdoch of Barney Ross's Marine company. What happened later, Ross could not remember, as he was battling malaria after being brought back to a safe bivouac area. But the following day, still fighting the disease in the hell of Guadalcanal, Private Ross could distinguish the words of his captain: "Ross, you are now Corporal Barney Ross."[2] Most soldiers' stories are not as uplifting. Bravery was too often recognized by posthumous awards and citations. Sometimes, it went unacknowledged. Yet some Jewish soldiers, sailors, and airmen clung to their Jewish identity in hostile territories. Mosquito-ridden Guadalcanal became the setting for a meaningful Jewish New Year celebration.

The current chapter unveils innovative forms of religious observance in unfamiliar and hostile territories such as the jungle of Guadalcanal, revealing how servicemen volunteered to conduct services when there was no Jewish chaplain in the vicinity. Chaplain Joseph H. Lieb served in Hawaii, while other chaplains in the Pacific included Harry R. Richmond, H. Cerf Strauss, and Norman Siegel, who received a certificate after taking a seventy-hour course in chemical warfare. Marching in the mud with fellow soldiers, Siegel decontaminated gassed areas.[3] In the fall of 1944, the War Department asked the Jewish Welfare Board (JWB) to send a mission to the Pacific zone. There were increasing complaints from military personnel about the lack of chaplains. Two men were selected for the task: Rabbi Philip Bernstein, executive director of the Committee on Army and Navy Religious Activities (CANRA), and Chaplain Arieh Lev. They confirmed the serious shortage of Jewish chaplains in the South Pacific. On the island of Guadalcanal, there had been only one Jewish chaplaincy service since the island's capture by American Marines in a surprise attack in August 1942. The victory secured the control of an airfield under construction, and more than a thousand Jewish GIs remained on that section of the Solomon Islands. Servicemen on islands such as Tinian, Kwajalein, and Tarawa did not receive even one visit by a Jewish chaplain, a role that was then most needed. Chaplains could boost morale, serve the wounded, and bury the dead. Nevertheless, Rabbi Philip Bernstein was impressed by the dedication of chaplains in the Pacific. In a report, he praised their sense of duty, which drove them to visit many adjacent islands. Most were dangerously overworked because of the shortage of chaplains and the fact that troops were scattered. "As a result," Rabbi Bernstein deplored, "a substantial percentage of the Jewish chaplains in the Pacific were broken down in health. All those who had returned to the United States came back via hospitals as medical patients."[4]

To remedy the situation, religious services were led by Christian chaplains along with Jewish military personnel. Laymen volunteered to fill in for chaplains. Two serve as an example: Captain Benjamin Fenichel, a physician from Philadelphia, and Marine Captain Sydney Altman from Brooklyn, both of whom conducted religious services on the Pacific Island for the High Holy Days. In these Days of Awe, Jews practice introspection and pray to be inscribed in the Book of Life. In such surroundings and in wartime, this tradition could not have been more relevant.

### Blowing the Shofar in Guadalcanal

A faded photo offers a good indication of the place and situation: in the jungle, men with unkempt clothing and beards crouch in the vegetation, exhausted but smiling, as if grateful to be alive.[5] The camera memorialized the challenge faced by a medical unit on the battlefront of Guadalcanal in September 1943. The photo includes Captain Benjamin Fenichel, the only Jewish corpsman in the team. Another photo, also miraculously preserved, shows the same Dr. Fenichel, shaved and blowing the shofar (ram's horn) with half-closed eyes, his prayer shawl thrown over his head. The image captures the intensity and fervor of those who linked their destinies with God. In that instant, Captain Fenichel's deeds seemingly stretched him to heaven. As he blew the shofar in that hostile setting, the spirit of transcendence imparted by ancient traditions renewed the chain of transmission. The deep, rousing sound of freedom and liberty attained with the New Year, Rosh Hashanah, tore the silence. The issues every serviceman faced belonged to the reality of the war, now enmeshed with ancient prayers. In the Bible, "the days of blowing the Shofar" (Numbers 29:1) are regarded as the beginning of the year. The rite is observed in synagogues all over the world, a fact servicemen and servicewomen witnessed in the many countries overseas to which they were assigned. Captain Fenichel proved himself capable of improvising the celebration of a universal ritual on a day of divine judgment. This was an achievement. Judgment is passed on the New Year, while one's fate is sealed on the Day of Atonement, known as Yom Kippur. This knowledge was enough to send shivers up his spine. In a state of awe and deep concentration, Captain Benjamin Fenichel was captured in a photograph sounding the shofar. Why did he choose to accept such responsibility? From the testimony of his children, we know that in Newark, Fenichel's observant father had taken him to High Holy Day services as a child.[6] It is possible to recapture the moment when that memory empowered him. As a teenager, he had tried to blow his father's shofar. He knew how much concentration and spirituality had to be put into the simple action. Now, on an improvised cane-thatched *bimah*, or reader's platform, it was the real thing. On this New Year of 5704, he was making the prayers of seventy American soldiers meaningful. The cover picture of the November 1943 issue of the *American Hebrew*, the National Weekly of Jewish Affairs, exposes this spiritual achievement. A Conservative Jew, Fenichel graduated from Jefferson Medical School in Philadelphia, married, and practiced medicine in Newark in the late 1930s. He volunteered after the attack on Pearl Harbor and was sent to Camp Shelby in Mississippi. In mid-1942, he was assigned to the Fiji Islands (where Americans were fighting Japanese troops). His son, Robert, admitted that he and his mother tried "to cope as best as we could." This understatement applied to most families still suffering from the lasting effects of the Depression years. The statement also

## MILITARY RECORD AND REPORT OF SEPARATION
## CERTIFICATE OF SERVICE

| 1. LAST NAME - FIRST NAME - MIDDLE INITIAL | 2. ARMY SERIAL NUMBER | 3. AUS GRADE | 4. ARM OR SERVICE | 5. COMPONENT |
|---|---|---|---|---|
| Fenichel Benjamin | O 326 787 | Maj | MC | AUS |
| 6. ORGANIZATION | 7. DATE OF RELIEF FROM ACTIVE DUTY | 8. PLACE OF SEPARATION | | |
| Watervliet Arsenal Watervliet N Y | 2 Jun 1946 | Thomas M England General Hosp Atlantic City New Jersey | | |
| 9. PERMANENT ADDRESS FOR MAILING PURPOSES | | 10. DATE OF BIRTH | 11. PLACE OF BIRTH | |
| 3020 W Diamond St Phila 21 Phila Co Pa | | 25 May 1908 | Newark N J | |
| 12. ADDRESS FROM WHICH EMPLOYMENT WILL BE SOUGHT | | 13. COLOR EYES | 14. COLOR HAIR | 15. HEIGHT | 16. WEIGHT | 17. NO. OF DEPENDENTS |
| Same as #9 | | Brown | Brown | 5'5 | 160 Lbs. | 3 |

| 18. RACE | 19. MARITAL STATUS | 20. U.S. CITIZEN | 21. CIVILIAN OCCUPATION AND NO. |
|---|---|---|---|
| White X | Married X | Yes X No | Physician O-26.10 |

### MILITARY HISTORY

| | 22. REGISTERED | 23. LOCAL S. S. BOARD NUMBER | 24. COUNTY AND STATE | 25. HOME ADDRESS AT TIME OF ENTRY ON ACTIVE DUTY |
|---|---|---|---|---|
| SELECTIVE SERVICE DATA | YES NO X | None | None | 69 Hillside Ave Newark N J |

| 26. DATE OF ENTRY ON ACTIVE DUTY | 27. MILITARY OCCUPATIONAL SPECIALTY AND NO. |
|---|---|
| 20 Feb 1941 | Medical Officer, General Duty 3100 |

28. BATTLES AND CAMPAIGNS
Northern Solomons GO #33 WD 45

29. DECORATIONS AND CITATIONS  APTO Ribbon   1 Battle Star on APTO Ribbon
Bronze Star Medal 37th Inf Div 45   Medical Badge Ltr O 21-45   *
American Theater Ribbon WD Cir 345-45  World War II Victory Medal WD Cir 326-45

30. WOUNDS RECEIVED IN ACTION
None

31. SERVICE SCHOOLS ATTENDED
None

| 32. SERVICE OUTSIDE CONTINENTAL U. S. AND RETURN | | |
|---|---|---|
| DATE OF DEPARTURE | DESTINATION | DATE OF ARRIVAL |
| 26 May 1942 | APTO | 10 Jun 1942 |
| 26 Mar 1944 | U S | 11 Apr 1944 |

33. REASON AND AUTHORITY FOR SEPARATION
WD Cir 313 45  P #11 SO #48 TMEGH
Atlantic City N J  27 February 1946

| 34. CURRENT TOUR OF ACTIVE DUTY | | | | | | 35. EDUCATION (YEARS) | | |
|---|---|---|---|---|---|---|---|---|
| CONTINENTAL SERVICE | | | FOREIGN SERVICE | | | GRAMMAR SCHOOL | HIGH SCHOOL | COLLEGE |
| YEARS | MONTHS | DAYS | YEARS | MONTHS | DAYS | | | |
| 3 | 4 | 27 | 1 | 10 | 16 | 8 | 4 | 8 |

### INSURANCE NOTICE
IMPORTANT IF PREMIUM IS NOT PAID WHEN DUE OR WITHIN THIRTY-ONE DAYS THEREAFTER, INSURANCE WILL LAPSE. MAKE CHECKS OR MONEY ORDERS PAYABLE TO THE TREASURER OF THE U. S. AND FORWARD TO COLLECTIONS SUBDIVISION, VETERANS ADMINISTRATION, WASHINGTON 25, D. C.

| 36. KIND OF INSURANCE | 37. HOW PAID | 38. Effective Date of Allotment Discontinuance | 39. Date of Next Premium Due (one month after 38) | 40. PREMIUM DUE EACH MONTH | 41. INTENTION OF VETERAN TO |
|---|---|---|---|---|---|
| Nat. Serv. X | U.S. Govt. | None | Allotment X | Direct to V.A. X | | 30 Jun 1946 | 31 Jul 1946 | 7.40 | Continue X | Continue only | Discontinue |

43. REMARKS (This space for completion of above items or entry of other items specified in W. D. Directives)
Lapel Button issued  ASR Score (2 Sept 1945)  112
On Terminal Leave from 2 March 1946 to 2 June 1946 inc.
*American Defense Service Ribbon

44. SIGNATURE OF OFFICER BEING SEPARATED
Benjamin Fenichel

45. PERSONNEL OFFICER (Type name, grade and organization - signature)
J B WEBER Capt MAC
Chief of Mil Pers Br

---

Fig. 6.1 Military Record and Report of Separation Certificate of Service of Dr. Benjamin Fenichel. From New Jersey, Dr. Fenichel volunteered as a medical officer from February 20, 1941, to June 2, 1946, and served in the Solomon Islands. He earned an APTO Ribbon with one Battle Star while in the Asiatic-Pacific theater of operations and a Bronze Star Medal while in battle with the Thirty-Seventh Infantry Division. He also won a Medical Badge, an American Theater Ribbon, and a World War II Victory Medal. He was issued a Lapel Button with the American Defense Service Ribbon. Courtesy of Sandra Fenichel Asher.

Fig. 6.2 Captain Fenichel blowing the shofar at a New Year Service on Guadalcanal, September 1943. Courtesy of Sandy Fenichel Asher.

modestly hides the emotional pain of parting with a father and husband who was not drafted but chose to enlist out of patriotism.

Fenichel trained in the hellish jungles of Guadalcanal after American troops conquered the island. His unit, the Thirty-Seventh Division, participated in the Battle of Munda Point, where he cared for wounded in the battle zone. His daughter, Sandy Asher, stressed that he was awarded a Bronze Star on Munda. His military record and report of separation reveal that he earned a Battle Star, a Medical Badge, an American Theater Ribbon, and a World War II Victory Medal, among other lapel decorations. The captain proved that he could receive respect in the military while displaying his Jewishness. He more than likely healed the souls of many servicemen who thought that Jewish identity would be a burden in the American military.

Records about the enlistment of Jewish American physicians reveal an impressive figure: 60 percent of all Jewish physicians under the age of forty-five served in the armed forces. The study that provides this estimation was carried out between late 1943 and early 1944, covering all of New York State, eastern New Jersey, and twenty-two medium-sized communities throughout the country.[7] The selflessness of Captain Fenichel, shared by many physicians, continued after he returned to Philadelphia. Suffering from a fatal heart attack at the age of fifty-six after many ignored previous alerts, he "died with his boots on at a house call far across town from home," wrote his son Robert.[8]

Captain Sidney J. Altman shared the front page of the *American Hebrew* of November 1943 with Fenichel. Altman was the commanding officer of Company E, Twenty-First Regiment, Third Marine Division. His unit returned to Guadalcanal to recuperate some strength after fighting on the Solomon Islands.

### Vigor of Spirit and High Morale as Military Weapons

The front page of the *American Hebrew* informs the reader that Captain Altman hardly had time to change out of his combat clothes, yet the photo taken on the eve of September 29 captures a man wearing clean white clothes, a prayer shawl, and a pitch helmet. He is in a "tented chapel," as there were no chapels or synagogues on Guadalcanal. Born in Brooklyn in 1917, Altman made the early decision to join the Marines out of patriotism. Although Jews made up only 2 percent of the Marine Corps in World War II, Altman had a good chance of being accepted into this prestigious military bastion. He was an athlete who grew up in the 1930s and became a noted quarterback. His athletic feats earned him a scholarship to New York University, where he played on the football team. Altman joined a fighting unit in 1942 and was sent overseas.

How did he find the stamina and confidence to lead a Rosh Hashanah service on Guadalcanal in the absence of a chaplain? The religious education he had received as a youth in Brooklyn enabled him to do so. He could conduct a religious service. Servicemen who had never prayed before could at least say "Amen"; God's help would be summoned through Altman's dedicated leading of the prayers. His example and that of Captain Fenichel provide evidence that at least two services took place for the Jewish New Year on the island of Guadalcanal.

As was the case with other laymen in the military, Altman immediately volunteered to lead the service when a Protestant chaplain informed him that supplies sent by the JWB had miraculously arrived on those Pacific Islands, the site of not so pacific events. Altman took up the challenge of transforming the surroundings by creating an island within an island, a small ark (maybe with a paper Torah in it) inside a tent. Some forty servicemen participating in the service wore either pitch helmets or Marine Corps caps, covering one's head being a requirement during the religious ceremony. In the article about him from 1943, Altman thanked the GIs for their participation. As customary, he formulated vows so that they might be inscribed in the Book of Life for the New Year.[9] It was an experience of transcendence that released the constant grip of fear. The celebration of Rosh Hashanah with the blowing of the shofar instilled in some servicemen a renewed zest for life and an awareness of the blessing of being alive and healthy. In a way, it combated the mental fatigue that threatens all military units.

A combat soldier who on November 14, 1943, earned a Silver Star for exemplary action on the island of Bougainville in the Solomon Islands, Captain Altman was awarded a second Silver Star for his bravery on the island of Guam as well as two Purple Hearts.[10] Altman's stamina "to do the job," to use military jargon, was remarkable. He might have read a book intended for soldiers in combat entitled *Psychology for the Fighting Man: What You Should Know about Yourself and Others*. A chapter about the importance of morale, "the capacity to stay on the job," might have struck him. The opposite of apathy, morale was defined as the ability to do a long, hard job "with determination and zest."[11] Zest was equated with "vigor of spirit," "love of life coupled with a willingness, an eagerness to risk life itself in a good undertaking."[12] Published contemporaneously with the events, the book *Guadalcanal Diary*, by war correspondent Richard Tregaskis, reveals the fierceness of the first seven weeks of fighting. The movie version of the book, released in 1943, eternalized August 7 as the memorable day of American landings on the island (August 7, 1942). No American could remain unaware of the dangers and horror troops faced on the ground or of the combat experience of young American boys fighting Japanese troops.[13] The military understood that it was important to maintain the morale of soldiers by making it possible for them to observe religious celebrations. The effort on the part of the American military should be emphasized here, as it represents an element that somewhat counters the argument of pervasive antisemitism among the American military. Rabbi Philip Goodman, when describing the aid tended by the military to enable celebration of Passover, noted the details of the enterprise: "New utensils and silverware were provided by the army. In the Hawaiian area, the Army Transport Service delivered two and a half tons of matzot, and other Passover products, 100 gallons of wine, 7,000 Haggadahs for 12 Seders held within this theater of war. Supplies were flown to Midway and other distant islands."[14] It is noteworthy that this impressive endeavor of the American military strengthened the Jewish identity not only of GIs but also of citizens of far-flung countries. Goodman mentioned such interactions in his anthology.

In 1942, thousands of American troops arriving in Australia to fight the Pacific war were stationed in Melbourne, Sydney, and Brisbane: "In the heart of Australia, three Jewish local residents were guests of the Jewish soldiers at their Seder. Said one of these civilians: 'This is the first Seder I have attended in thirty years. Until now I had been worried about the continuity of our people. . . . Suddenly, I see several hundred young vigorous American Jews and now I know that our people are still carrying on. This splendid sight warms my heart, for it is a token that, come what may to you or me, our people will go on forever.'"[15] No doubt the joy of local Jewish inhabitants instilled Jewish American servicemen with vigor and boosted morale. Above all, religious observance in war zones answered two basic needs of servicemen: making sense of one's Jewishness in dire conditions and feeling a sense of belonging while away from home.

### A Religious Service on the Island of Munda

A letter by Captain Elliot Davis of the Eighty-Ninth Field Artillery, published by Philip Bernstein and Philip Goodman in the November 1943 issue of the *Jewish Chaplain* and reprinted in the *Jewish Veteran* in September 1944, provides a rich and moving account of the desire to observe religious requirements together with the patriotic need to pursue the war. It was mid-September, and American soldiers were still engaged in furious fighting against the Japanese Imperial army forces on Arundel, in the New Georgia Islands archipelago of the Solomon Islands. The battle of Arundel Island was fiercely fought from August 27 to September 21, 1943. It was launched after the capture of Munda airfield by American soldiers during the Battle of Munda Point, part of the New Georgia campaign, between July 22 and August 5. Mopping up operations on that island consisted of rooting out remaining enemy forces, whose stubbornness challenged the American troops. With the tension of the war zone so close, the soldier explained in his letter that the perspective of religious services for the Jewish New Year seemed totally remote: "We are fighting a war, the Japs are still around, and in the hearts of all of us there is a conflict, too; War and Prayer."

It was then that, unexpectedly, the Baptist preacher in Davis's unit, Major Evans T. Mosely, approached him and other Jewish boys in his division to inform them that prayer shawls (*talliths*), a shofar, and other religious items were on their way, sent by the JWB! Davis explained that when the GIs had left Guadalcanal, they had been unable to take the "religious equipment" with them, but fortunately one had kept the miniature prayer book printed and distributed by the JWB. They used it to conduct the Rosh

Hashanah service: "We set up an organ in the mess hall and waited for the men. They had to come from the reef studded waters all around the island—from Bairoko Harbor, Piru Plantation, Rendova, Kokorona. We thought 50 would be a crowd. We waited. They came by boat, by truck and jeep and when we started the service there were 125 present."[16] In spite of their physical exhaustion and because of their mental exhaustion and weariness of the war, the Jewish GIs made the effort to find a way to get to the island. They needed the spiritual boost provided by the restarting effect of the Jewish New Year, with its symbols and connotations. To the servicemen suffering from nostalgia, and to Davis in particular, Munda was above all "a place too wild even for the natives to inhabit." Yet the powerful voice of "a cantor singing from the soul" the ancient religious melodies reminded the boys of their beautiful synagogues at home. Soldiers who had been refugees from Nazism were moved to tears at the thought of the burned and desecrated synagogues in Europe, the serviceman commented in his letter, evoking the hope of the new Jewish year of 5704, which began under the auspices of brotherhood and ecumenism: "As the organ softly played on, I looked out of the building and in the distance was that serene blue Pacific separating us from all our loved ones. To my right, I saw the Munda airfield, the object of our recent operation in the South Pacific. Its white, coral runways sparkled in the sun as plane after plane took off from its glasslike smoothness. And as those planes soared into the heavens I could not but compare them with our soaring hopes in this New Year."[17] The captain encapsulated the eternal optimism of the Jew that the next year would be brighter than the previous one. As a Jew serving in the artillery, he mentioned why they were still on the island of Munda, in the dense jungle: the Japanese airfield at Munda Point that American troops had captured needed to be secured. It was a military asset. But on that day, Captain Elliot Davis became aware of other invaluable assets—brotherhood and belonging. He pondered with satisfaction the religious service led by "two Jews who knew no Hebrew but were proud and aware of their Jewishness" with the support of "a Baptist preacher from the hills of Kentucky": "The service we had wasn't Orthodox, it wasn't even Reform; it *was* sincere and Jewish. And the sermon on the New Year by our beloved Chaplain Moseley would have done credit to any of our respected rabbis."[18]

A few photographs in the National Museum of American Jewish Military History reveal that a Passover seder took place on the island of Munda on April 8, 1944. In one photo, three servicemen are busy preparing gefilte fish and fried chicken, as confirmed by the handwritten caption by men from the Signal Corps. *Pre-Seder Scenes at Munda* is the title given, followed by the names of the GIs—from the Bronx, Massachusetts, and New Jersey—while another photo captures three other men, members of the Seabees, making *matzah* balls for the seder. The culinary and gastronomic aspect of Passover is thus recalled. At the same time, Passover symbolizes the liberation of the enslaved Hebrews in Egypt. GIs did not miss the relevance of this religious observance to the war that was being fought to regain freedom. Rumors circulated about the enslavement of prisoners of war (POWs) put to work under dire conditions in camps or cold bloodedly murdered by Japanese guards. By 1943, Allied governments knew for sure that captured airmen in particular were held in inhumane conditions. Jewish airmen also feared being put to death as POWs or enslaved and starved to death in a Nazi labor camp. But Passover boosted morale by turning servicemen's eyes toward a future when Allied forces would be masters of the air and oceans. The defeat of Japanese forces on February 9, 1943, after the battle at Guadalcanal and the Allied victory over Germany in the North African campaign on May 13, 1943, instilled hope among American soldiers.

Noteworthy about Passover on the island of Munda is the presence of many non-Jewish officers. Admiral Kinkaid, a navy legend, was a high-ranking officer. The participation of noted officers in a Jewish religious celebration lent to that ceremony a meaningful American dimension.[19]

This adds weight to our speculation that during the war, a number of high-ranking officers helped with the recognition of Judaism as one of the three main American religions. One may recall that General Douglas MacArthur offered his impressive mansion as a place of worship in Manila for Friday evening religious services, as no other suitable place was found by Sergeant Larry Yellin, who served in the infantry in the Philippines after fighting in Europe.[20] Further interactions between Jewish chaplains and the military were seen especially in the European theater of war, where American generals discovered the "horror camps," as Eisenhower called them in his memoirs. Concentration and extermination camps where millions of Jews were decimated remained etched in his mind as a symbol of evil. In the introduction to a 1946 special edition of the *Haggadah* for American military personnel and displaced persons, Chaplain Klausner referred to General Dwight D. Eisenhower as Moses the Liberator, under whose command American forces restored the moral order of the world. Deborah Dash Moore has aptly noted the transformation that took place in different forms of observance in the military, adapted to each theater of the war and to the conditions imposed by combat zones: "Ecumenical

Fig. 6.3 Seder in Munda, collection of Martin Weiss. Courtesy of the National Museum of American Jewish Military History, Washington, DC.

observance of a Passover seder under military auspices transformed an intimate Jewish home ritual into a public performance."[21]

## Passover in Manila

An unsigned letter from a serviceman to his parents published in the *American Hebrew* provides a detailed account of a historic religious service in the Commonwealth of the Philippines. It was the first Passover service in an American territory that had been liberated from the Japanese enemy: "Last night I became a good Jew for a change and went to Passover Services. However, to you I can confess that if I hadn't heard that they were serving wine and matzohs [sic] there I probably wouldn't have gone. But I am not sorry that I went because it was a very impressive and interesting service. . . . I never thought that there was so many of us in this particular area."[22] He expressed his new awareness of the cultural aspect of Jewishness as well as its ethnic dimension and mentioned how surprised he was to encounter in this ceremony Jewish refugees from Germany and Austria who had fled Hitler. He also encountered Jewish servicewomen (WACs), "Red Cross girls," and nurses. New forms of observance adapted to military life emerged in the process: "We started off by lining up on the chow line for matzohs, herbs, and wine. Incidentally, we had to bring our own mess gear and canteen cups. We were supposed to save the wine, etc . . . for the services, but it was quite a long time getting started so most of us didn't have anything to dip or sip by the time we were supposed to."[23] It was indeed quite a strange situation, not being able to recite the blessing after the corresponding type of symbolic food. But the conviviality and the sense of brotherhood and belonging fostered were enough to make the event unforgettable. The religious services were conducted by two army chaplains with the participation of a German cantor and a German rabbi, both members of the refugee community in Manila.

Ben Magdovitz, an infantryman whose parents were born in Lithuania, was sent to Manila with his unit. His assignment came after his participation in the fighting in France, Germany, Belgium, and Austria. Magdovitz wrote an essay for the YIVO contest in 1946, aware of the fact that "my observations are able to cover two ends of the world."[24] He was on the high seas when the war with Japan finally came to an end; when he reached Manila, "with the initial coming of peace, the Jewish life within the community was again beginning to thrive."[25] The twenty-one-year-old who benefited from extensive Jewish education in the United States was eager to meet other Jews in the Philippines. He was struck by the fact that, unlike in Europe, where Jews were persecuted as such, on that far-flung tropical island "they were treated no different than any other of the whites in the section: Jap [sic] occupied territory spelled doom, in form of privation, hunger, terror, to all white people. . . . Jewish community leaders were among the foremost in the various resistance movements that sprung up."[26] Noting that most of the Jews in Manila were immigrants from Europe and refugees, the infantryman emphasized the warmth of the "well-knit" Jewish community that embraced him: "The hospitality is supreme, and many an American serviceman found a home there that was really *his* home. A Friday evening kiddush, civilian families accompanying GIs to services downtown, parties, and groups in homes—all were common affairs and frequent occurrences in Manila during the stages after the war."[27] The Jewish cemetery on the outskirts of downtown Manila assumed a powerful meaning for him, giving an indication of the dispersion of Jewish communities in the world. The young infantryman was visibly impressed by the story of the "highly educated" head of the family that extended its hospitality to the GI on Friday nights. The man—whose name was Konigsberg—was originally from Russia and came to the Philippines via Shanghai. During the Japanese occupation, he was caught while in hiding. Konigsberg's lengthy imprisonment by the Japanese broke his health. Nevertheless, he displayed a great deal of humor on Friday nights and marked the Sabbath celebration with Talmudic tales "or an occasional proof from Rashi," which made Magdovitz think of the warmth he felt in the home of his Orthodox parents in the United States. The young infantryman perceived the positive interactions between the Jews in Manila and the Jews in the American military: "It was evenings like that, time spent there, that brought my home closer to me, and made my stay in that theatre seem a great deal shorter than what it was. There were often other soldiers there, and with similar get togethers all over the city, it is easy to see the effect the military and civilian populations had on each other."[28]

It struck Magdovitz that the Manila synagogue (erected in 1924) had been used by the Japanese forces as an ammunition dump. It impressed him even more that on the return of American forces in February 1945, the Japanese blew up the synagogue together with its contents. As a healing gesture and a gesture of Jewish brotherhood binding Jews all over the world, a group of American servicewomen and servicemen initiated a fundraising campaign to rebuild the synagogue, of which only the outer walls remained. American GIs expressed comradeship by dedicating it as a memorial not only to their Jewish comrades who fell in that war zone but also to all servicemen and women who sacrificed their lives in the Philippines. A memorial service was conducted in the ruins of the Manila synagogue on Friday November 9, 1945. The memorable date marked the anniversary of the destruction of synagogues in Nazi Germany (Kristallnacht) and a pogrom against German Jews carried out by SA paramilitary forces and civilians, all without the intervention of German authorities. It surprised the infantryman that the Manila synagogue was "the only one under the American flag to be destroyed by enemy action during this war." This is Magdovitz's description of the ceremony barely a month later: "On December 7, 1945, the anniversary of Pearl Harbor day, the formal presentation of the gift to the Manila community was made in an impressive ceremony at the USO-Perez center of Jewish military activities in the community. Lt. Gen. William Styer, Commanding General of Army Forces Western Pacific, made the presentation that evening with a huge crowd in attendance. The project was symbolic of the nearness of the Jewish people to each other and was very touching in its entirety."[29]

The infantryman's account epitomizes the evolution of his Jewish identity, a Jewish American identity shaped by ethnic aspects that characterize a universal Jewish identity. It is striking that the soldier's war experiences led him to analyze aspects affecting diasporic Jews so deeply. He also tried to define the features they share. In his opinion: "they are ambitious, generous and hospitable. . . . We very naturally cling to other brethren in religion, we are willing to sacrifice for them, though they may be strangers past and future."[30] It is interesting that he should point out features of Jewish peoplehood that usually interest scholars but not soldiers. The attitude toward religiosity was much different when servicemen clung together in combat zones. The absence of a Jewish community that offered something reminiscent of home made the difference. However, Jewish pilots' stories provide original accounts of unexpected, last-minute Jewish observance and a link with home.

### Passover in Iwo Jima, 1945

Jerry (Jerome) Yellin, the distinguished pilot of the Seventy-Eighth Fighter Squadron, described the Passover seder in his memoir *Of War and Weddings: A Legacy of Two Fathers*.[31] Etched in his mind was a short ceremony conducted in Hebrew by a Marine chaplain while all were in foxholes. Passover (Pesah) is primarily a festival of the home, which makes foxholes incongruous shelters. It was on March 28, 1945, a couple of days after the Banzai Massacre on the island. Yellin appreciated having "specific foods such as matzos, a flat, unleavened bread, symbolic of the hasty flight from Egypt of the Hebrew slaves." He was grateful to the military, which had arranged for "a shipment of matzos to be brought ashore and an altar to be set up, under heavy guard."[32] The pilot felt that this ceremony created a bond between Dr. Lipshitz, the Jewish dentist of the unit, and himself. He also admitted that although he was not an observant Jew, he was moved by the significance and relevance of the ceremony. In the Jewish liturgy, the festival is described as "the season of our freedom." Yellin interpreted his own mission as one to free the world from the tyranny of the relentless Japanese Imperial forces. Sergeant George Ammerman, who wrote an article about Jerry Yellin, with whom he had spoken, recalled that "as soon as he and the other pilots learned they were the chosen few, they started to joke about the life rafts, and floating alone on the deep blue sea."[33] The twenty-year-old pilot felt blessed to have been chosen for the historic mission to bring an end to a deadly war that had claimed the lives of millions of young American GIs. After the war finally ended, other significant Jewish ceremonies included the New Year of the Trees (Tu B'Shevat) on Okinawa, an island that had been devastated by an eighty-two-day battle from April to June 1945 and violent typhoon Louise on October 9, 1945.

### The New Year of the Trees in Okinawa

Moshe Sachs, an air force chaplain born in Baltimore, Maryland, in 1920, was stationed in Manila before being assigned to Okinawa from 1945 to 1947.

He boosted the morale of soldiers who were bored in Okinawa after the war ended. A man with a dose of humor and a sense of satire, Sachs had them write a *Haggadah* for Passover that included four boys in the military. The boy who did not know how to ask questions would be the one to reenlist in the military for the rest of his life! The chaplain encouraged them to conduct services to empower them. It is interesting that Sachs reinterpreted the religious observance of the New Year of the Trees in 1946 in the universalistic sense of improving the world (*tikkun olam*). In the United States, where he had been a rabbi before being appointed a chaplain, Sachs celebrated Tu B'Shevat by partaking of fruits grown in Palestine and distributing them to school children. The island, which was Japanese territory, had borne the largest amphibious assault in the Pacific theater during the Battle of Okinawa between April 1, 1945, and June 22, 1945. Chaplain Sachs and the American Jewish servicemen on the island adapted Jewish custom to postwar needs. Together with high school children from Okinawa, they planted trees to rehabilitate the land. The ceremony—part of the Jewish calendar—assumed a topical, cathartic value.[34] This move not only met with the approval of the American military but also became part of the rehabilitation program initiated by the American army. Sachs's son confided that his father's perception of Jewishness was ethnic, in line with the notion of Jewish peoplehood. The extermination of more than six million Jews by the Nazis made Sachs interpret the meaning of the New Year of the Trees as requiring the planting of trees in the Jewish homeland of Palestine.[35] His position was congruent with the Zionist vision that had become relevant to numerous servicemen and servicewomen, as seen in chapter 4. In that respect, the Jewish observance of Tu B'Shevat of 5706 in Okinawa added significance to the renewal of life in communities all over the world. Never had Judaism been so universalistic. Rebirth and redemption followed the destruction brought about by the war. The need to rebuild on former enemy territories facilitated the postwar encounter between Americans and natives of Okinawa.

Miles away from Okinawa, American servicemen assigned to India met different people with other customs. Their wartime experience expanded their worldview and lessened their xenophobia.

### Encounters with Jewish Communities in India

"Let me take you on a slow Liberty ship making its way across the beautiful but treacherous Pacific from Los Angeles to Calcutta, India in the summer of 1943." With these lines, serviceman Marshall Wolke opened his memoir. Born in Poland in 1920 as an only son whose mother died when he was twelve years old, Wolke's life depended on the support of relatives in the United States who helped him emigrate in August 1937. Under the guardianship of the relatives who sponsored his admission to the country, he took evening courses to master the English language. He was working in a department store in Chicago when war broke out after the Pearl Harbor attack. He volunteered and joined the armed forces in April 1942 as a private in the air force, serving in the G2 branch of the China-Burma-India theater headquarters until October 1946. Wolke was discharged with the rank of captain.

Why were American troops sent as far as India? General Eisenhower provided an explanation: "As a prerequisite to everything else we had to stop the Jap short of countries that were vital to our successful prosecution of the war—Australia and India."[36]

Wolke recalled that the journey to India took sixty days, with a stop in Australia and through the Indian Ocean and Bay of Bengal toward Calcutta. He was surprised by the presence of Jewish refugees who fled Nazi persecution as far as Indian territories in the hope of finding shelter. In search of a Jewish organization, he finally found Sir David Ezra, a Jew of the upper classes whose wife gave weekly teas and dinners for Jewish Allied soldiers. The native Jews of India with whom he came in contact fascinated him. He observed their customs during his twenty-seven-month tour of duty in the China-Burma-India theater of operations. Like most of the two hundred thousand American soldiers stationed there between 1942 and 1945, he was shocked by the poverty he saw among the general population.[37] He noticed that except for a small number of well-to-do Jews, many were extremely poor, even destitute. An inspiring encounter in Marshall Wolke's account was his meeting with a Jewish chaplain in Karachi. Chaplain Abraham Dubin of New York worked in "cementing relations between Allied white servicemen and their distant dark Jewish brethren in India": "Chaplain Dubin contacted the Karachi Bene Israel leaders when he first arrived, secured their permission to use their synagogue for Jewish services on Thursday evenings (Fridays were for the Native Jews), and generally organized American military-religious-social Jewish activities in coordination and in conjunction with the Bene Israel."[38]

Wolke emphasized the interactions between the American troops and the members of Bene Israel who welcomed them. The community of Jews in India learned a lot from American Jews, he observed. They met for traditional Jewish festivals such as Simhat Torah ("Rejoicing of the Torah"). That day marks the conclusion of the annual cycle of Torah readings in the synagogue and is associated with rejoicing at the beginning of a new cycle. Wolke saw the "little Indian boys" of the Karachi Bene Israel community dance in circles as Torah scrolls were carried by worshippers in seven circuits (*hakafot*) around the reader's platform. They sang Hebrew songs "in an oriental melody" in the "beautifully lit and decorated synagogue." The serviceman, who had taught the Indian children songs, happily joined the ceremonies in Sephardic Hebrew.[39] Although religiously observant, Wolke admitted he "had a hard time following the prayers" because of a chant he did not know and a "weird oriental tune." Yet, he was "flabbergasted and excited by the whole experience," both in Karachi and in Calcutta, where "I learned that American Jewish soldiers attended services during the High Holidays just passed, and that there are weekly gatherings at the Judean club in the city, and that the last names of the Jews are Ezra and Jacob, and Gershon, and Pinchos—just as our first names are."[40]

A glance at the genealogy of serviceman Wolke reveals his original Polish name: Mojsze Haim Wolk from the Volhyn province, where he was educated in Hebrew and gained the knowledge of the Torah expected from boys. In India, he took the initiative to conduct services when there was no chaplain. Wolke confessed that he sometimes found himself "feeling like the other" when he was the only white among Indian Jews. However, the Gershon family in Karachi, in whose residence some religious services took place, made him feel at home. He found there traditional hospitality, a Jewish value he thought crossed all borders.[41]

## Discarding Prejudice

Serviceman David Macarov was assigned to India for two years as a meteorologist. Along with the whims of the weather, he tried to understand the concept of Jewishness and diasporic identity in relation to the Jews he met in India. He, too, was invited by the noted Lady Ezra in Calcutta. Macarov pointed out that Jews who did not speak Yiddish—the language of Ashkenazi Jews of European descent—challenged his understanding of who is a Jew. In his YIVO essay, he went further than Wolke in his analysis of the link between skin color and the feeling of "otherness." He reflected about "prejudice against dark skins" when encountering Jews in Bombay or Calcutta. During his short time in Karachi, David Macarov served as assistant to Chaplain Abraham Dubin, whose work was praised by Wolke.[42] Macarov did his best to get to know Indian Jews through close contact with them: "A short tour of volunteer combat duty won me a furlough to Calcutta, where my acquaintanceship with Indian Jewry really began. Immediately upon return from furlough, I applied for transfer to an airstrip outside Calcutta, which was granted. Here, I spent a bit over a year, and became an actual part of the Indian Jewish community."[43] A native Atlantan brought up in the South, Macarov articulated his own evolution regarding age-old color prejudices. His initial viewpoint, instilled with prejudice shared by white Southerners, was transformed by his experience overseas. His Jewishness was very much linked with Jewish peoplehood, and he emphasized that the bond he felt with the Jews of India helped him overcome the ingrained color prejudice from his Southern environment. But he first thought that his preference for lighter-skinned Indians came from "instinct." He was not yet aware of the fact that his bias was rather a *cultural* outcome of his education and conditioning in the American South. Replying to a letter from his parents in Atlanta, he tried to make them understand his own evolution.

> Yet I know that what you really mean is "Are they dark skinned?" And I find that I get very angry at the question, and I am tempted to answer: "What difference does it make?" Perhaps you don't realize what a remarkable achievement that is for me. Born and bred in the South, it didn't matter what I *thought*, *I felt* an instinctive prejudice against dark skins. Given the choice, I would invariably sit by or talk to a white person, rather than a colored person, even though I knew such an attitude was wrong. I felt that the prejudice had been so deep-rooted by conditioning that I could not overcome it.... And yet [I] don't see how it could have existed.[44]

David Macarov's honesty toward himself and the reproach he addressed to his parents are striking. It is quite unique to read a letter that describes so lucidly a victory over ingrained prejudice with the awareness of prejudice's link to the environment in which one is brought up. Macarov went further by mocking the stance of those who, sometimes unaware, cling to prejudice: "For your information, however, they range from what we would call 'white' to a very dark copper tan, with the majority merely a sunburnt brown." He perceived the concept of tolerance as inherent in Jewishness and therefore felt the incongruity of color prejudice by a religiously educated Jew. Besides, Macarov realized that his encounter with Indian Jews had made him question his own Yiddish-linked American Jewish identity. He was amused to find himself sprinkling his speech with words that replaced the intrusion of Yiddish into the American language: "A little Hindustani has crept into our language, and phrases such as 'Maluum' (Understand?), 'Pucca' (real), and 'Teekhai' (OK) enter in our normal conversations. One of the funniest things happens when Yiddish and Hindustani get mixed up by a speaker and he refers to an unreligious Jew as a 'Pucca Goy.'"[45]

It is not without a touch of humor that the phrase "a real Gentile" is itself not devoid of preconceived views. When considering the encounter of two peoples as different as Americans and Indians, it is not surprising that suspicion works both ways. Macarov, however, deplored that lack of trust. When I talked to his wife, Frieda, in October 2020, she vividly remembered how much her husband was frustrated that American soldiers could not ask for a date with the daughter of a host family. More than that, it was the best way not to be invited back! Yet repaying a dinner invitation by taking the daughter out was common among GIs. Jewish servicemen did so in North Africa, where many war brides later discovered the American dream. A couple of war brides from Calcutta also joined Jewish GIs in the United States and began new lives on American shores.

David Macarov, for his part, became friendly with several Indian Jewish girls, as testified by a photograph he preciously kept. His memoir reveals that he was invited to parties and dances in the Calcutta Jewish community. He met visiting Allied soldiers in the Jewish community of Calcutta and struck up a friendly relationship with a Jewish British soldier who joined the Young Judea club, where his own Jewish identity became intricately bound up with Zionism. Feeling integrated into the Calcutta Jewish community, Macarov seized the opportunity to organize a Zionist meeting for Allied servicemen and local Indian activists who belonged to different Zionist movements. These included leftist youth movements such as Habonim (The Builders, affiliated with Labor Zionism), Hashomer Hatsair (The Young Guard), and Chaluzim (Pioneers). The serviceman rejoiced that the consensus about the importance of Jewish nationhood did away with differences between youth movements. As a Habonim leader, Macarov deepened his own self-understanding and reexamined his views about life in the diaspora versus life in the Jewish homeland of Palestine by bringing these groups together. His introspection and grappling with crucial issues crop up in almost every paragraph of the memoir he intended for his family. His reformulations of life-changing decisions made in Calcutta stand out in his postwar essay about his experiences as a serviceman overseas. After twenty-six months spent in India, his statement is unequivocal: "Seeing how the Jewish people in India live, and knowing what is going on in Europe and Palestine . . . I'm afraid I've finally been forced to the conclusion that I argued with Nat about so many years and miles ago—that only those Jews who go to Palestine are doing all they can for Zionism."[46] Reflecting on the spiritual journey in India presented in Macarov's 1946 essay, Deborah Dash Moore offers a pertinent observation: "Rather than affirming his own Americanness, his contacts generated a Jewish solidarity that gradually dominated his Jewish American identity."[47] An interview I conducted in Jerusalem with Hebe Solomon Benjamin, an Indian woman Macarov met in the Calcutta Jewish community, confirmed his preoccupation with Jewish solidarity. A picture in a peaceful Calcutta garden captures David Macarov with Hebe Solomon standing behind him, together with other girls from the Calcutta Jewish community. Eighteen-year-old Solomon, who immigrated to Israel in the 1970s, can be seen in the middle. She provided information on her encounter with David Macarov, who "was kind of an intellectual and the most serious of all the American boys in uniform" she met.

At my request, ninety-five-year-old Hebe Solomon Benjamin expanded on Jewish solidarity within the Indian Jewish community. A few wealthy Jewish families supported poor Jewish Indians and awarded grants to students. As a serviceman, Macarov observed manifestations of Jewish solidarity. Regularly invited to Mrs. Gubbay's home on Fridays, where meals were organized for scouts, he and his friend Hebe Solomon Benjamin deplored how bad-mannered American servicemen would criticize in Yiddish the food to which they were not accustomed instead of being grateful for hospitality overseas. Asked how she perceived American soldiers, she answered that Jewish GIs were received as Jewish people in Indian homes. However, she remembered her shock at seeing segregated African American troops on army trucks in Calcutta.[48]

Interspersed in Macarov's memoir are testimonies of his patriotism and Americanness. One is the demoralizing effect of a news dispatch on April 12, 1945, announcing the death of President Roosevelt. Macarov was on duty at the weather station in Barrackpore.

> I was greatly affected as FDR had been my hero for years.... VE day in May was also not greeted uproariously, since our war was against the Japanese, and they had already announced that they would fight until the last man. We knew we would have to invade Japan and flush their troops out of caves and hiding places, and even weathermen knew that they wouldn't be able to stay behind in safe India. From May on we followed the war in the Pacific with grim intensity.... As May became June, and July, and August, we realized that our war could go on indefinitely.[49]

*** 

Friday night, September 7, 1945. It was Rosh Hashanah in Guam, in the western Pacific. The small island remained under Japanese control for thirty-one months until July 21, 1944. On the recaptured American territory of the Mariana Islands, the place of celebration and worship was a big B-29 hangar. It was the shelter of the impressive Superfortress B-29, which had played a crucial role in ending the war through ceaseless bombing raids over Japan and, finally, by dropping the atom bomb. At the same place ten days later, on Yom Kippur, the Day of Atonement, "1500 Jewish men in uniform assembled to worship, to give fervent thanks to God for victory and returning peace," noted Isidore Kaufman, a war correspondent in the Pacific.[50] Major David Cedarbaum, the Jewish chaplain of the Twentieth Air Force that operated the B-29s, perceived the unique character of this unit. In addition to his duties, he assembled data on auxiliary units located on the islands of Guam, Tinian, Saipan, and Iwo Jima. Cedarbaum found that in one wing alone, the Seventy-Third, there were 473 Jews, of whom 166 were air crew. There were eleven pilots and sixty-five navigator-bombardiers. A month after the war's end, he found that in the Seventy-Third Wing, thirteen Jewish fighters and fliers had been killed in action, forty-eight were missing, and ten were liberated prisoners. Chaplain Cedarbaum reckoned that General LeMay's command included about three thousand Jewish servicemen, among whom about nine hundred were airmen. "The large number of the missing," commented Kaufman, "gives an indication of how often men and planes were lost on the 1600-mile flight to Japan, and, even more, on the flight back."[51]

The more fortunate GIs encountered Jewish communities overseas. In the Pacific, where the level of Japanese savagery did not match any other theaters of war, new forms of improvised religious observance evoked a sense of home. Soldiers found refuge in Jewish spirituality, which fostered a form of Jewish solidarity and a sense of purpose. The war experience also triggered deep interfaith relations, as shown in a few case studies in this and in earlier chapters. Passover renewed servicemen and servicewomen's willingness to bravely attain victory of freedom over enslavement and tyranny. The efforts of laymen to conduct religious services in hostile territories was an innovation in World War II. There emerged a way to rectify the lack of chaplains in the scattered islands of the Pacific. A *minyan* (a quorum of ten servicemen) was necessary to hold Friday night services in far-flung war zones. When a chaplain was present, he boosted the sense of Jewishness, comforted the wounded, and buried the dead. For Chaplain Joshua Louis Goldberg, a good chaplain was someone with "feet firmly planted on the earth." "You want to reach heaven? Stretch yourself to heaven, but the feet must be on the earth," he advised in an interview.[52] The noted chaplain was in charge of distributing Passover supplies to the navy in the Atlantic and in the Pacific. He had to ascertain the number of Jews who needed supplies. He humorously stated: "I could tell you, quite frankly that I was surprised how many Jews were on some ships for Passover because we used to send wine, and I think that the numbers were a bit padded in some requests. But God bless them all, even in this respect. If a Patrick or a Patterson had a sip of the Passover wine, it's perfectly all right. They took it on their ship, I suppose, in good spirits as we did."

Servicewomen attended Jewish services in New Guinea and other places in the Pacific. Far from home, they sacrificed their lives. Sergeant Belle G. Naimer from the Bronx served as assistant post sergeant major at Kelly Field, Texas. She was one of eighteen servicemen and women listed as American casualties in a far-flung part of Papua, New Guinea, on May 13, 1945. A member of the WAC serving in the Pacific, she was buried in a field grave near the crash site without her remains being recovered by the War Department. Ten years after war's end, her body was reinterred in Jefferson Barracks National Cemetery in St. Louis, Missouri, as part of a group burial, once the other remains were identified. Her name is memorialized in the Manila American Cemetery. Photos account for the war experiences of other servicewomen who served in the Pacific. Some, like Belle Goldman in New Guinea in September 1944, are captured in a photo while attending a Yom Kippur service. When interviewed, she said: "As a conscientious soldier who did whatever assigned, there was a war on, and I tried to do my part." She did not miss the opportunity to observe the Day of Atonement, even on one of the most remote southern Pacific islands.[53]

Religiosity is an important part of the American ethos, as expressed by President Roosevelt on many occasions to strengthen the faith in victory of American GIs and civilians. What is more, it is reflected in the closing lines of the national anthem, "The Star-Spangled Banner," included in the abridged prayer book for Jews in the American forces.

> And this be our motto: "In God is our trust!"
> And the star-spangled banner in triumph shall wave
> O'er the land of the free and the home of the brave![54]

The compelling reality of war, the resilience needed to survive, and the force of religiosity are fathomed in the next chapter on captivity under the Japanese.

# PRISONERS OF WAR OF THE JAPANESE

"In the witch caldron of a Jap prison," Dr. Alfred Weinstein wrote, "G.I. Joe fought for his life with all the breaks against him."[1] On the very day in December 1941 when Japan attacked Pearl Harbor, the Japanese Imperial forces invaded the Philippines. The American commonwealth had been home to a major American military base since the Spanish-American War. American troops surrendered in April of the following year. For troops captured near Manila, the Bataan Death March was a confrontation with horror. Sources indicate that about 80 percent of the American prisoners of war (POWs) in Japanese captivity took part in that death march.[2] The first bombshell to reach Washington was an account about American POWs authored by William Dyess, an officer in the United States Army Air Forces.

Dyess, survived the Bataan Death March in the Philippines on April 9, 1942. The Death March followed the Allied loss at the Battle of Bataan. Unlike the Germans, the Japanese did not separate Jews from other prisoners in most cases. Antisemitism did not exist as it did among the Nazis. What follows in this officer's account is the testimony of a non-Jewish fighter pilot, attempting to describe the unbearable: the brutality of the death march, in which prisoners were forced to walk in the sun without helmets, water, or food. They suffered constant harassment, beatings, terror, murders, and beheadings. Sick soldiers were denied medicine and often water and normal food rations. When the revelations of the airman reached Washington, officials decided not to publish the unsettling information until late January 1944. The War and Navy Departments feared that if published earlier, the information might be detrimental to the war effort and trigger retaliation against prisoners. It would also have worried the parents of servicemen stationed in the Pacific. The report of the fighter pilot William Dyess was therefore classified "secret."

Eager to return to combat duty in the Army Air Forces after returning to the United States, Dyess, who had been promoted to lieutenant colonel, died tragically while flight-testing a P-38 with a mechanical problem. In January 1944, roughly a month after his deadly accident, the *Chicago Tribune* received permission from government censorship to release the account of his war experiences. The lines authored by the pilot are eloquent. They are an understatement of the barbaric deeds of some of the Japanese guards, but they provide a sense of what the captives, Jews and non-Jews alike, endured: "I have tried to put into words some of the things that I have experienced and observed during all these past months, but I fail to find words adequate to an accurate portrayal. If any American could sit down and conjure before his mind the most diabolical of nightmares, he might perhaps come close to it, but none who have not gone [through] could possibly have any idea of the tortures and the horror that these men are going through."[3] Dyess's observations as a POW were later confirmed by the memoirs of two American prisoners who successfully escaped with him from Davao.[4] Their experiences of resilience under barbarity provide context through which the expression of Jewish identity, when it occurred, can be fathomed. Sharing the same urge as Dyess to write a testimony, Alfred Abraham Weinstein, a Jewish surgeon who served in the Philippines, accounted for his war experiences in a memoir published in 1948: "I wrote a story. I had to write it. Every fiber of my brain and body which had survived forty months in prison camps cried out for it. It had to be written from memory. I had written four diaries. They were all destroyed. The first I buried under the lonesome pine towering Little Baguio, Bataan, in the Philippines, the night before we surrendered to the Japs, in April 1942. I returned to the encampment, overgrown by jungle, three and a half years later. Tropical rains had mildewed the diary and red ants had eaten it."[5]

The physician gave the second diary to a prisoner operating a secret radio at Cabanatuan prison, located north of Manila, but never heard from him after the war's end. Weinstein had to destroy his third diary when the Japanese secret police, the Kepei Tai, burst into the Shinagawa POW hospital in Tokyo looking for a clandestine short-wave radio set operated by the prisoners. Weinstein tore up the last diary when he was transferred to the Omori punishment camp in Tokyo in the summer of 1944 after being accused of not cooperating with the Japanese. It was there that he faced the notoriously sadistic disciplinarian Watanabi, nicknamed "the Bird" or "the Animal." Such nicknames were given to guards to avoid punishment when they thought the prisoners were saying their names. "The Bird," infamous for being a psychopath, relished in inflicting harsh daily beatings.[6] In Omori, POWs used coded phrases to inquire about the level of danger they would have to cope with each day. "What's the position?" they would ask. The prisoners knew they would have a few moments to breathe when the reply that followed was "the Animal is in his cage."[7]

Before being transferred to Japan, Weinstein and his fellow prisoners painfully adjusted to life in captivity in the Cabanatuan prison camp. In that place of confinement, personal statements of Jewish identity stood out like a stifled flame unexpectedly rekindled, interwoven with deep reflections on "mankind with his veneer of civilization stripped away." Weinstein's memoir is a document illustrating how American prisoners coped with the threat of mental and physical disintegration. Twenty-two thousand American soldiers were captured by the Japanese Imperial forces after the fall of Bataan and Corregidor. The surgeon was one of four thousand to survive.

Who was that resilient American serviceman? Born in Boston in 1908, Weinstein moved to Atlanta in 1938 after the successful completion of five years of postgraduate research work in surgery and cardiology. In addition to his private practice, he taught surgery at Emory University in Atlanta. He interrupted both his teaching and practice to enlist in the United States Army in 1940 and volunteer for service in the Philippines. He was a chief surgeon of General Hospital Number 1 in Bataan when the Americans surrendered to Japanese forces. A POW for three and a half years, he provided medical treatment to his fellow prisoners, although he himself was underfed and weighed about a hundred pounds. His heroism and resourcefulness when medical equipment was lacking earned him five battle stars, three Presidential Citations, two Purple Hearts, and a Bronze Star. He was awarded the latter decoration for preventing "what might have become a wholesale decimation of American Prisoners of War" by "saving the lives of many comrades" during a diphtheria epidemic in the POW camp. He left service with the rank of lieutenant colonel in the Medical Corps.[8]

Back in Atlanta, the then thirty-eight-year-old physician—whose mental and physical injuries took many years to heal—asked crucial questions: "Does man continue to love his brother when steeped in disease, chronic starvation, and death? Why did the Japs behave like Japs? How much punishment can man take before he loses his divine spark of humanness? What role did the minister and the priest play in keeping that spark flickering? How low in animal like behavior can a man sink and still revert to manliness?"[9]

This chapter attempts to shed light on these issues, emphasizing the Jewish perspective as expressed in the physician's memoir and in archival material. It also aims to show the patriotic aspects of the Jewish experience of servicemen in World War II. It is a fact that as far as the Japanese were concerned, Jewish GIs were first and foremost American nationals. This aspect emerges in Weinstein's memoir, whose provocative questions pave the path of our research.

## Why Did the Japs Behave Like Japs?

Although living conditions in Japanese prison camps were dire, there was no separation of Jews from others, as was often the case for American and Allied soldiers in Nazi slave labor camps, where Jews were starved and worked to death—if not murdered.[10] Jew hatred was largely nonexistent among the Japanese Imperial forces. They considered white people as a group that could be submitted to the worst conditions, as they became deprived of their humanity after surrendering. It is significant to recall that in the Japanese military, it was honorable to kill oneself instead of being captured. In that light, prisoners could be subjected to various atrocities including arbitrary murder, mutilations, and forced labor coupled with malnutrition and chronic disease. The archival film *Know Your Enemy: Japan* introduced a tenet of Japanese ideology from an early period through to World War II. This recurrent motto read: "The Sword Is Our Steel Bible." It endowed Japanese soldiers with a quasi-divine mission focusing on the absolute dedication of their lives to their emperor and on obedience to their superiors.[11]

While in POW camps of Bilibid, O'Donnell, and Cabanatuan in the Philippines, Weinstein and his fellow prisoners received helped from Hanna Kaunitz, an Austrian Jewish refugee in Manila. She benefited from the fact that, being Austrian, the Japanese occupiers did not consider her a Jewess but the national of an ally. The Japanese did not pay much attention to the fact that she and her family had fled Nazi-dominated Austria. Together with her physician brother Fred Kaunitz and other Jewish refugees mentioned in Weinstein's memoir, Hanna joined the "Blue Eagle," an underground resistance movement, and contributed to the survival of many prisoners. The group smuggled medicine, food, and money into POW camps, often with the help of altruistic men and women from the Philippines.[12] No wonder Weinstein dedicated his 1948 memoir to Hanna Kaunitz, who became his wife and "whose love kept a spark of life flickering in a dying body." The American surgeon had met her in Manila before the attack on Pearl Harbor. No incentive to cling to life could have been stronger. Weinstein's strategy of survival included observing the Japanese guards' psychology and picking up their language as fast as he could. Sensing that his Japanese captors would not provide prison camp clothes, the surgeon preciously kept "a complete civilian outfit that Hanna had smuggled into Camp O'Donnell."[13] Resourcefulness coupled with an acute understanding of psychology were key assets for survival. Weinstein focused on signs of humanity around him instead of succumbing to the drudgery of meaningless prolonged confinement and the pangs of hunger. This focus helped him retain his identity.

He admired the role and efforts of chaplains in comforting dying servicemen, even when he had doubts about "the morality" of telling dying soldiers they would live: "If a patient looked as if he might kick the bucket, we called in the chaplain to give him the last rites, collect personal mementos, and write last messages. These men were trained to give religious consolation and comfort in a calm, tender manner. Their appearance meant to the wounded that they were seriously ill, yet, it did not have the same disastrous effect of a flat, 'Yes, you're gonna die' coming from a medical officer."[14] In other cases, chaplains strengthened the faint hope still held by enslaved POWs. As noted, Jewish laymen took it on themselves to perform this role when there was no chaplain of their faith.[15]

### The Layman's Effort to Keep a Humane Spark Flickering

Weinstein related a striking expression of Jewish identity in this place of confinement. His rendering of Yom Kippur, the Day of Atonement, in the Cabanatuan prison camp reveals to what extent the observance of such a day conjured memories of his Jewish heritage. On many occasions, the medical corpsman praised the initiatives of Christian chaplains in the POW camp, who sometimes denied themselves food—as did Chaplain Tiffany—so that weaker men could eat. At a time when people were reduced to animal-like behavior in the sense that their minds could only think of food, such conduct instilled hope in humanity. In the absence of a Jewish chaplain, Lieutenant Jack Goldberg, an "ex-amateur pugilist from New York City," assembled the Jewish prisoners on Friday nights in his galley. This, too, instilled men with faith in humanity and revived a sense of Jewish belonging. On Yom Kippur, a religious service was improvised under the open sky.

> On Yom Kippur, we met near the little entertainment stage in the open field before the sun went down. . . . Of the several hundreds of Jews who started

prison life in Cabanatuan, there was less than eighty alive in the closing days of 1943. We straggled toward our house of worship under heaven's roof from all parts of camp: Americans from New York and San Francisco, refugees from Vienna and Berlin who had volunteered for service at the outbreak of the war. Old Kliatchko appeared before us as the broiling-hot sun dipped toward the serrated edge of the Sierra Madre Range which overlooked the camp.[16]

Yom Kippur became a time of encounters in the unlikely space of a POW camp. American servicemen from different corners of the United States met on that meaningful day of the Jewish calendar and encountered European Jewish refugees fleeing Nazi persecution and extermination. Kliatchko was an American Jew of Polish descent who had married a Filipino woman; they had raised thirteen children together while growing rice peacefully in the plain of Luzon. Kliatchko had learned enough liturgy in a Warsaw rabbinical seminary in his teens to make this day of awe matter for all. He, too, had fled eastern Europe to the United States after a bloody pogrom. After becoming American, he volunteered in War World I and was sent to the Argonne Forest, where he fought during a murderous campaign. He stayed in the American military for years, ended up and retired in the Philippines where he raised a family. At the age of sixty-two, the man volunteered again to fight for America in an engineering outfit. He served through the Bataan campaign, then was captured and interned in the Cabanatuan prison. There, he was responsible for the carabao herd, which he took out to graze. On Yom Kippur, he recited Hebrew prayers he never thought he would remember, leading the High Holy Day service.

> He wore his old-type campaign hat with its wide floppy brim, a sun-bleached kaki shirt with its tails hanging free over neatly patched shorts, and a pair of wooden skivvies. He threw a shredded white-silk tallith (praying shawl) with its fringe of tassels over his bowed shoulders. The deep bronze of his cheek bones, separated by a powerful nose, was heightened by the massive curly white beard that flowed over his chest. He raised his sunken brown eyes heavenward and began the haunting Hebrew melody and prayer of Kol Nidre.
> "Bless the Lord, O my soul, and forget not all his benefits; Who forgiveth all my iniquity; who healeth all my disease; Who redeemeth my life from destruction."[17]

That evening remained etched in the mind of Alfred Weinstein. The precision of his description of Kliatchko, reminiscent of Moses leading his people, proves it. Weinstein's elaborate prose and literary treatment of the event reveals the transcendence achieved in a place of captivity where nothing spiritual or uplifting was meant to happen. Praying to be saved from destruction, praying not to be broken in spirit, and imploring to be forgiven for sins assumed a particular significance in the Japanese prison camp and led to introspection capable of spiritual regeneration. The anxiety of the moment could foster a personal dialogue with the Creator. During the most solemn moment of the holiest day in the year, Yom Kippur, past vows can be annulled while reciting a prayer called "Kol Nidre" (all vows) in Aramaic. For American servicemen, the miniature prayer book for New Year and the Day of Atonement provided explanations of the importance of "the broken word" at a time of repentance for the past year's transgressions: "It is certain that the source of the prayer may be traced to this fundamental principle in the Torah, the sacredness of the plighted word; for as the touch of the dead defiles the body, so does the broken word profane the soul. 'He shall not profane his word; he shall do all that proceedeth from his mouth' (Num. 30.3)."[18]

On that evening, while attending the improvised religious service, surgeon Weinstein and the Jewish American prisoners did not behave like the impersonal beings their Japanese tormentors forced them to be. Through its values and exigencies, Jewishness prevented the dissolution of the prisoners' identity, providing a rare instance of spiritual elevation from the place of confinement. In that light, prayers were regenerative. Weinstein recalled that during the incantation of prayers, the Japanese guard looked at the assembled men with curiosity. "Ragged GIs" walking along the alley on the way to their barracks cast glances at this uncanny gathering. The Jewish prisoners gathered for the Day of Atonement expressed or renewed their relation to God. Apart from God's unity, the Creator's relation to man is the most important doctrine of Judaism.[19] "Inspire with courage all who wait for Thee"—these words struck Weinstein as he focused on the flight of birds in the reddening sky.

> The red ball of the sun dropped behind the purple mountain. In the fast-falling twilight, little white ricebirds wheeled and turned.... Eyes blurred with mist, the scene before me faded. I saw the synagogue in which my family were gathered in prayer and supplication; its high vaulted ceiling with doves of peace flirting about the painted billowing clouds; the colonnaded ark of the covenant with its red-velvet drapery and Ten Commandments of Moses embroidered in white silk; the golden eagle with its outspread wings surmounting it; the painting of the Wailing Wall of the Temple on the wall behind it; the crouching, snarling lions of Judah, tails lashing, hovering protectively over it; the silk flags flanking it; on the right, the American,

on the left, the flag of Zion with its two horizontal sky-blue stripes and its three broader white ones, the blue six-pointed star of David, flaming in the center. I saw my father standing at the tabernacle, his blue eyes fixed on the Bible. I saw a little old gray-haired woman in the balcony turning the pages of her prayer book salted down with the tears that dropped from her cheeks while she dreamt of her son ten thousand miles away.[20]

Weinstein's well-crafted literary rendering conjures up symbols of Judaism. In the richly decorated synagogue whose setting he reminisced, the American flag and eagle were enmeshed with Jewish elements; his identity as an American rose as a major component of his Jewish identity. A Reform Jew, Weinstein conveyed the importance that Jewishness assumed in relation to the family circle and the congregation. His moving text culminates with an image bridging the gap between a son imprisoned in the Pacific and his mother, praying for his return, her eyes blurred by tears. All mothers of servicemen sent overseas must have felt the same way when opening a prayer book, no matter what their religion.

Weinstein reiterated his admiration for chaplains of the three main American faiths: "They built chapels out of scrap wood and transformed them by the magic of their words into places of worship."[21] But on that memorable Yom Kippur, there was no chapel available, no Jewish chaplain, and yet magic was induced under the "heavenly sky" at sunset. Supplications on the Day of Atonement bridged two worlds miles away. The barbed wires of the prison camp were trespassed. The transcendence of the prayers together with man's power to remember was instrumental in bringing about a quasi-magical transformation. One of the questions raised in the medical corpsman's memoir found an answer: yes, man can "revert to manliness" no matter how "low in animal like behavior" he sinks under the pressure of his captors.[22] He needs the right environment that he can transcend with prayers. At least, this was possible in Cabanatuan. In that respect, Kliatchko, like each POW, was a "product of his environment," as suggested by Dutch Chaplain Chaim Nussbaum, who was a POW of the Japanese on the River Kwai.[23] On that Yom Kippur, the American serviceman from Poland became a symbol of the frailty of the human plight, with its ability to "revert to manliness."

> The sunset sent streamers of orange and purple far-flung into heaven. Kliatchko's deep vibrant voice rose to meet them. Beating his chest with clenched, gnarled fist at the end of each sentence, he prayed for forgiveness:
> "For the sin which we have sinned against Thee under stress or through choice;

> For the sin which we have sinned against Thee openly or in secret...
> For all these sins, O God of Forgiveness, bear with us, pardon us, forgive us."
>
> By the light of the flickering stars and the quarter moon, I looked at the intent faces of my neighbors: stubby Captain Berkelheimer, the medic detachment commander, the razor-faced Lenk brothers, refugees from Czechoslovakia; stalwart Ben Hessenberger, carabao driver, refugee from Germany; sway-backed Captain Bennison. They didn't know it but they were attending their last Yom Kippur service on this earth.[24]

With these lines, the reader understands that these men were not inscribed in the Book of Life—including Ben Hessenberger, a refugee from Europe who had enlisted in the United States Armed Forces of the Far East and fought along with American servicemen.[25] Weinstein ended his retelling of Yom Kippur in the Cabanatuan prison with the sounding of the shofar, an improvised, curved carabao horn that the layman blew symbolically at Kol Nidre, the beginning of Yom Kippur. In normal conditions, the shofar is blown at the end of the Day of Atonement, or Neilah (the closure of that day). The adjustment of religious practices fit the circumstances of captivity, for that evening the prisoners immediately returned to their shacks. In that interval of spiritual freedom, some experienced an uplifting feeling of Jewish belonging. In Cabanatuan, as in most places of drudgery and imprisonment, a sense of Jewish brotherhood arose from sharing the same fate.

### Ensign Jack Gordon, a POW with a Jewish Sense of Destiny

In the Breman Archives in Atlanta, Georgia, there is a copy of the 1948 edition of Alfred Weinstein's book, *Barbed-Wire Surgeon: A Prisoner of War in Japan*. Dedicated to Sam Gordon, a friend and colleague, the handwritten lines read: "To my dear friend Sam whose brother Jack was my bunk mate in misery for two years; a misery that was brightened by his smiling face and words of cheer when I was about to crack up."[26]

Who was Jack Gordon, the serviceman capable of soothing others and boosting morale? Born in Atlanta on March 16, 1920, Jack volunteered in the United States Naval Reserve and was promoted to midshipman on February 14, 1941. The handsome, blue-eyed twenty-one-year-old ensign was reassuring, optimistic, and humorous in the letters that eventually reached his mother. Sadie Gordon was divorced. Her life revolved around her sons, both of whom served in the American military. Excruciating letters from

Gordon's tormented mother to naval authorities exemplify the anguish of all parents who strove to locate their missing sons overseas. The documents in the Gordon family archives housed at the Breman Jewish Heritage Museum show that Jack wrote long letters as frequently as possible, requesting his mother write a twenty-five-word letter every day to help him reconnect with home. The sustained link with his beloved mother was essential for his survival; hatred of the Japanese who had enslaved him was not enough to help him cling to life. But it was a well-known and dreaded fact that many letters were thrown away instead of being given to overwhelmed censors. Although Sadie Gordon was desperate, not knowing what had happened to her son, she found the strength to write to Admiral Chester Nimitz of the United States Navy. She received a handwritten letter dated January 14, 1943, from the commander in chief of the Pacific Ocean areas who commanded Allied air, land, and sea forces. Signed by Nimitz himself, it reads in part: "I fully appreciate your anxiety over the fate of your son, and sincerely regret that I cannot help you to communicate with him. . . . There is every chance he will return to you in good shape—a little thinner perhaps, unless he likes rice! Thus far, contact has only been obtained with a very small percentage of American prisoners of war, so your failure to date must not discourage you." The admiral, who served both in World War I and World War II, must have known that Jack had been admitted as a cadet at West Point before joining the Naval Academy. He perhaps knew that Jack was to be promoted to the rank of lieutenant. He also must have known that Mrs. Gordon had two sons in the Pacific. Samuel served as a surgeon in Guam as soon as he qualified at Emory University in Atlanta in 1942. Jack Gordon sent many letters from Cabanatuan to his mother in which he regretted to inform her that he was disease-ridden and "past the hunger stage." He wrote that he knew that "the American forces [were] here and unable to save us."[27]

Prior to his promotion as midshipman in 1941, as mentioned, Jack obtained in 1939 an "appointment and admission as cadet" at the prestigious West Point Military Academy. He sat long hours taking difficult examinations in various subjects, including mathematics, physics, history of the United States, English literature, economics, and government. He finally decided to enroll in the Annapolis Naval Academy.[28] His oath of office is worth recalling because he lived up to it, even while captive under the Japanese: "I, Jack Benjamin Gordon Jr., do solemnly swear (or affirm) that I will support and defend the Constitution of the United States against all enemies, foreign and domestic; that I will bear true faith and allegiance to the same; that I take this obligation freely, without any mental reservation or purpose of evasion; and that I will well and faithfully discharge the duties of the office on which I am about to enter: So help me God."

This document from the Navy Department, Bureau of Naval Personnel, expresses the sacred character of the engagement the ensign took on February 14, 1941. The mention of God's help made the appointment even more solemn for the patriotic Jew, even though in America, the reference to God is customary when taking an oath. His love for the United States of America and willingness to sacrifice his life for his country appeared in most of Gordon's letters, even those whose words were drastically limited by his imprisoners. In one such formulated card, he asked his mother not to forget to buy war bonds. A letter dated January 23, 1942, from Ensign Jack Gordon was sent from Corregidor to his brother, Sam. It sounds like a farewell letter, as if death was the only way out of the prison camp.

> When you tell your kids about the uncle killed in P.I. tell them how I liked to travel, of the many new and different things I did—and I have done more than the average of my age. But also tell them of the hell of war. For it is terrible that we must kill humanity to hope to better it. . . . Bub, do not let mother grieve over my dying. Remember, I've enjoyed life, I have lived, and death holds no fear or punishment. It is only the end. From here on there is no more war, worry or fear. All ends. But do not let it end for mother. See that she travels, meets new people, wears new clothes, and enjoys many more years of happiness. . . . Well, my death will be miserable from the point of conventions—dirty, filthy, stinky. There is nothing honorable about death in war. Regardless of how terrible my conditions, I have no fears. My only regret that I could not give my mother more happiness. My fears, worries, troubles have all ended. I am merely following in the pattern of life laid out for me when I was born. That is something none of us can escape. I have never forgotten the words you gave me of advice just before I saw you last. "Fight hard. Give all you have. Never give up."[29]

Jack was a Reform Jew from Atlanta whose grandfather, an immigrant from Kovno, Lithuania, was a peddler with a pack on his back. Jack Gordon confessed to his brother that his service for the country had made him more mature: "I feel 'mellow' now that I do not think I'll be able to laugh again." He pointed out the main reason for his personal change: "Men are being killed, torn to bits, and cut to pieces." He reiterated in different ways his transformation: "And that has changed me from the carefree college kid to an old man—in just one afternoon. C'est la guerre."[30]

Refusing to indulge in self-pity and only giving out elements permitted by censors, Jack Gordon expressed a notion in Judaism suggesting that the time of death is determined at birth. However, he mentioned that his state of weakness did not enable him to follow his mother's advice to pray to strengthen his faith. A letter dated January 30 was more optimistic, ending with a wishful thought: "When I step down on the good old USA."[31]

Sadie Gordon was notified that her son Jack had been reported missing in action on May 6, 1942, following the capitulation of Corregidor on that day. On March 23, 1943, after sending many distressed letters to the naval authorities, she learned that he was a POW in the Philippines.[32] Formulated letters or postcards with a minimum number of words in which prisoners would underline responses from a set list of words and stamped by censorship enabled Jack to inform his family that he could not receive any letters at the prison camp and that they should write through the Red Cross in Geneva. The heading of his formulated card, rather than a proper letter, bore the French words "Service des prisonniers de guerre" with Japanese characters underneath. Gordon noted his name, nationality, and rank. No mention of religion was included. The navy ensign had to briefly fill in seven points below a heading that read "Imperial Japanese Army." The first three points are worth quoting for their bureaucratic aspect. His place of internment indicated the Philippine Military Prison Camp, Section 1. A second point let him evaluate his health: excellent, good, fair, or poor. Knowing Gordon from his previous letters, it is not surprising he underlined the first choice to reassure his mother. A third point led him to underline (through choices printed on the form) that he was "not under treatment." The link of his prison camp with the Red Cross was a reassuring sign both for prisoners and relatives—there were prison camps unknown to the Red Cross authorities where life was closer to agony than to life itself. In the bulk of the letters sent to his mother, some much longer than fifty words, Gordon thanked her for the vitamins, coffee, and chocolate he asked for and finally received through the Red Cross. In his correspondence to his mother and brother, patriotism is a leitmotif. To the latter, Jack reiterated his willingness to sacrifice his life for his country. As exemplified in his correspondence, he maintained his dignity, an essential element for survival when threatened daily by various humiliations.

### The Prisoner of War Experience as a Stigma

Suggesting that war comprises the genius of killing, General Patton stated in his own dramatic and provocative way: "No poor bastard ever won a war by dying for his country. He won it by making the other poor dumb bastard die for his country."³³ In that respect, Gordon, later depicted as a hero by the Annapolis Institute, would have been defined as a "loser" by Patton. Such a depreciative point of view about unlucky servicemen would be echoed some seventy-five years later with polemics about POWs by President Trump.³⁴

Jack Gordon was finally herded with thousands of fellow prisoners aboard the Japanese *Oryoku Maru*. Reverend John E. Duffy, the chaplain on board the ship, later recounted that he was impressed by Gordon's empathy for fellow servicemen. In a letter to Sam Gordon in 1950, the Christian chaplain, who served as the First Corps chaplain under General Wainwright in the Northern Luzon campaign and in Bataan, mentioned that his brother Jack was "one of the great unselfish who have crossed my pathway." "Bayoneted and left for dead on the death march." Although he was thought dead, Duffy had survived the Bataan March. He first met Jack in the Bilibid prison in Manila in mid-October 1944. There, Jack, like fellow POWs, was forced to do heavy work. The chaplain became better acquainted with him on the *Oryoku Maru*, the ship under attack at Olongapo, Luzon, on December 14–15. Survivors of this harsh transport named the Japanese vessel a "Hell Ship." Such sea transports were justified by the fact that American forces were retaking the Pacific Islands. The Japanese thus moved thousands of POWs to prisons in Japan. In cramped conditions, many POWs suffocated and died. Adding to this hellish experience, the *Oryoku Maru*, on which Jack Gordon was confined, was attacked several times by American bombers in mid-December 1944, a target for American forces who did not know the vessel was packed with American and Allied POWs. The Japanese intentionally did not mark it as such. Records of the Office of the Chief of Naval Operations (RG38) documented the ordeal of another serviceman, John M. Jacobs, who was also in Bilibid prison in Manila and ended up on the *Oryoku Maru*: "The prisoners had been so crowded in these other holds that they couldn't even get air to breathe. They went crazy, cut, and bit each other through arms and legs and sucked their blood. In order to keep from being murdered many had to climb the ladders and were promptly shot by the guards. Between twenty and thirty prisoners had died of suffocation or were murdered during the night."³⁵ Jacobs took off his clothes and shoes, dived into the water, swam ashore, and managed to escape while three American planes were sinking the ship.³⁶ Jack Gordon's ordeal ended differently. Duffy, the Christian chaplain who made his acquaintance, provided an account of Gordon's help to fellow servicemen. They boarded another ship near

Olongapo Naval Station, Subic Bay, Luzon, due to the sinking of the *Oryoku Maru*.

> When the five hundred of us got in this hold we had nothing but squatting room.... Just as we had finished eating our chow we heard air plane motors and then all hell broke loose. Four bombs had been dropped in our hold by the allied fliers.... The naval doctors followed. But we had a mess on our hands; over three hundred dead and most of the rest wounded. I knew we had to clear the mess and make room to make the wounded more comfortable. I called for volunteers among the non-wounded and unseriously [sic] wounded to stack the dead on one side of the hold. Your brother Ensign Jack Gordon was one of those who volunteered and did a wonderful job getting the dead all together on one side of the ship. He was not seriously wounded but had a couple of flesh cuts from bomb fragments. After the dead were cleared and a place was cleared where the legless and the armless and the seriously wounded could be cared for, Jack was quite helpful in trying to comfort the wounded and feed them during the three days and nights we were confined in the hold with no medical care from the Japs. He was a fine outstanding man. I never knew his religion. It never mattered to me. In fact, I knew he believed in God and could care for his fellowman. We were all American and comrades and he was a real comrade to his fellow soldiers in one of our darkest hours.[37]

Stacking the corpses and caring for the wounded demonstrated a single Jew's empathy—part of the spirit of Judaism. Ensign Jack Gordon was among the twenty soldiers the chaplain recommended for a Bronze Star, awarded posthumously, as Duffy wrote to Sam: "Your brother, as I remember it, died early in the morning of January 29th some distance from Japan and was buried at sea the day before the rest of us landed on the island of Kyuchu. You and your family have every reason to be proud of him. He served his country well. He willingly helped his fellow prisoners in their darkest hours and gave unselfishly of himself reflecting great credit on his parents, his family, and his country."[38]

A letter dated August 8, 1945, from the secretary of the navy in Washington stifled the faint hope of a mother. It informed her that her son, "previously reported a prisoner of war, is now known to have lost his life on 15 December 1944."[39]

The official document was signed by James Forrestal, then secretary of the navy and later secretary of defense. The date given for Jack's death does not correspond to that provided by the Christian chaplain in a 1950 letter, but it does match the dates of the American bombings and consequent sinking of a transport ship to Japan. A search for the ensign's name in the National Archives, in the World War II Prisoners of War Data File, yields the following results: "Gordon Jack B. Jr, serial number 097687, in the United States Navy, White (racial group code), a resident of Georgia, in the Southwest Pacific Theatre, Philippine Islands." It is noted that Gordon had been in the POW camp of Cabanatuan. His latest report date, in 1944, was on a POW transport ship in the December sinking (*Oryoku Maru, Brazil Maru, Enoura Maru*); it is noted that he died in transport from Olongapo to San Fernando, Philippine Islands. His "status" indicates "Executed, Died in Ship's sinking or Result of Ship Sinking, Shot While Attempting Escape."[40] No mention is made of his internment in the Bilibid prison, where he was deliberately starved and enslaved like his fellow inmates.[41] One is led to wonder how the young ensign died: was he torn into pieces by a bomb, like many of his buddies, or did he try to dive and escape as is the duty of all American POWs? Chaplain Duffy mentioned that he had dysentery before he died and was "buried at sea." The sea was the final resting place for thousands of POWs under the Japanese, in the company—ironically enough—of the formerly dreaded sharks.[42] The treacherous blue stretches of water were also the final resting place for numerous aircraft pilots, navigators, and bombardiers who were downed, hit by flak, set aflame by kamikaze pilots, or, too often, victims of deadly mechanical failures in training.

When Gordon's mother learned that her younger son was in the hands of the Japanese, she suffered a mental breakdown, though she was comforted by Sam's cards and letters from Guam. In November 1946, a column published in the *Atlanta Journal* announced that Sadie Gordon, a prominent woman in B'nai B'rith, had died "suddenly."[43] This case study suggests that the ordeal of captivity psychologically affected not only POWs but also their parents.

### A Woman Captive of the Japanese: Second Lieutenant Magdalena Eckman

Sixty-eight American army and navy nurses who provided medical aid on the front lines in the Philippines remained in Japanese captivity for three years after the battle of Corregidor. Among them was a Jewish army nurse from Pine Grove, California. Second Lieutenant Magdalena Eckman (Hewlett) was held prisoner in the Santo Tomas internment camp, previously a university campus in Manila. The story of these American women remained untold until the late 1990s.

Two women authors found that "POW army nurses were discouraged from talking about their combat and POW experiences even to their families. At redistribution centers and in reorientation programs, the POW experience was presented to these women as a stigma and they were told that it was time for them to become 'ladies again.'"[44] At the Sonoma County History and Genealogy Library, volunteers discovered documents in a filing cabinet about Magdalena Eckman, born in 1910 in Contra Costa County, who worked as a nurse for a few years on the Hawaiian island of Kauai. On March 1, 1941, she was called to active duty from Palo Alto. The thirty-year-old Army Corps nurse was assigned to the unit defending the harbor of Manila and Subic Bay, on the west coast of the island of Luzon. She became a POW after the Japanese victory. Altogether, over thirty-five hundred prisoners, including civilians, were held in captivity in Santo Tomas. Magdalena Eckman, like the other nurses, continued caring for the wounded for three years. Medical supplies were insufficient; food was scarce. For her, imprisonment under the Japanese implied not only starvation but also degradation, together with the constant need to be resourceful. Santo Tomas was extremely overcrowded, with unwholesome hygienic conditions.[45] And yet, Magdalena continued to treat the wounded, implying an almost constant state of horror, if not terror.

The volunteers of the Sonoma Genealogy Library found that after the war, Second Lieutenant Magdalena Eckman married Thomas H. Hewlett, an army physician captured in the Philippines and taken to a POW camp in Japan. They later divorced. As a retired colonel in the United States Army, Hewlett wrote and published a short memoir about his captivity to inform about the Japanese atrocities and exorcise his war experiences. He expanded on the acute and common diseases during internment under the Japanese, such as bacillary dysentery and respiratory diseases, with which he had to deal as a doctor. Hewlett also described the "psychological problems" endured by prisoners of the Japanese. The following passage, published in 1978, is revealing of the amplitude of the psychiatric casualties of World War II and the underrated nature of the issue.

> I am troubled that the V.A. [Veteran Administration] can recognize a broad range of psychologic and social problems in our current society, and not be cognizant of the fact that some of the patterns they encounter in former P.O.W.'s are long term results in individuals who had no help available when the emotional or psychic traumas occurred during long confinement. The philosophy of the prisoner of war is a strange one, individually developed to make survival possible in the most hostile environment....
>
> The language problem was ever present, interpreters either Japanese or English speaking tended to put themselves in a command position, so they created an atmosphere of distrust. One prisoner of the A detail was

executed for attempting to learn to read Japanese. He was utilized as the target for a bayonet drill by the guard detail. His body when examined showed over 75 stab wounds.⁴⁶

The sharp analysis of a former POW followed by this striking example of cruelty unveil the disastrous effects of psychic trauma that often reappears among the elderly when hyperactivity slows. After the war, it was not unusual for former POWs to resort to verbal or physical aggression and be diagnosed as having "Depressive Neurosis" or an "Anti-Social Personality." But the criteria of post-traumatic stress disorder (PTSD) were not determined until thirty years after the Second World War.⁴⁷

Following her divorce, former servicewoman Magdalena Eckman threw herself into her work, a suitable diversion. Director of nurses in the department of obstetrics of the Jewish Hospital in Louisville, Kentucky, Eckman, under the name Madeline Hewlett, became a nursing superintendent at Sonoma Valley Hospital but died one year later, in 1973, at age sixty-three.⁴⁸ The weight of her trauma and her former husband's trauma as World War II veterans must have been unfathomable.

## War Captivity and PTSD

Another Jewish POW of the Japanese who survived the Bataan Death March, Harry Corre expressed his point of view about the inevitability of PTSD among servicemen in war zones, a pathology only recognized by the American military in the early 1980s: "There is no soldier who has seen any kind of combat action . . . who has witnessed any kind of horrible scenes of bodies being blown apart, or suicide bombings or IEDs [improvised explosive devices], who can come home without having PTSD."⁴⁹

Prolonged confinement and reduction to impersonal beings or victims by the Japanese left open wounds for many years. Alfred Weinstein, for instance, had to write a memoir, the controlled and admirable writing of which was most probably cathartic for him. In the Omori punishment camp, the sadistic Watanabe strove to destroy prisoners' subjectivity and identity by forbidding and severely punishing meaningful relations with other POWs and guards. In an article entitled "I Made My Peace with Japanese War Criminals," published in 1963, Weinstein strove to convey why it took him so long to come to terms with his past as a prisoner of the Japanese. He confessed that "the sharp sound of Japanese speech, heard unexpectedly in Atlanta, terrified me for years after my imprisonment had ended." He further explained his initiative to travel to Japan.

> I wanted to pay homage to the widows of the two prison guards who had befriended me. I wanted to try to forgive Watanabi, a member of the secret police who had tried to beat me to death and had succeeded in breaking my windpipe and arms. I wanted to make my peace with several other Japanese war criminals whom I'd helped put in jail and who had served sentences and had been released.
> Why had I delayed 18 years for this reunion? I'd wanted to see another generation of Japanese young folk grow up so that I could meet them and say "I cannot hate you because of the sins committed by your fathers."[50]

As a human being capable of empathy for others, Weinstein paid tribute to the two guards who had displayed compassion for him. From 1945 onward, he exchanged photographs with the widow, son, and daughter of Nishino-San, one of the guards who had "befriended" him (in his words) at the POW camp at Mitsushima. Nishino-San died in a railroad accident in 1959. Called "the one-armed gentleman" by the prisoners because of his kindness, Nishino-San had lost an arm fighting in China in 1939. Another guard, Nishigaki-San, nicknamed "the Boy Scout," was instrumental in boosting Weinstein's low morale. Eighteen years later, when the surgeon met the two widows in the "crooked streets of Tokyo" with the help of American Ambassador Reischauer and his attaché, he told them stories about their husbands.

> I recalled the great gift of hope that Nishigaki-San gave me when I was a prisoner of the Japanese. He was tiny and walked with his little hands clasped behind his back, his head forward and shoulders hunched. We were climbing a mountain, trudging toward a mining hospital to borrow a few surgical instruments for an emergency operation and some B vitamins. All P.W.'s had beri-beri and death struck the camp daily. I was sick of living and deeply despondent. Nishigaki-San turned to me and said quietly: "Mosukoshi, senso owari." His words translated were: "Don't give up. Soon, the war will be over."[51]

Although he suffered from "tuberculosis of the lungs," Nishigaki-San lived another seven years, thanks to medication Weinstein sent him and passed away in 1952. But the surgeon maintained contact with his widow through gifts and letters. When Weinstein met the twenty-year-old son of Nishino-San, the other trustworthy guard, he told him stories about his father's empathy for the beaten prisoners. When Nishino-San was unable to appease the sadistic guards, he would "physically put his body between their rifle butts and a helpless America P.W." In that moving Tokyo encounter, the two widows "proceeded to load [him] with presents." During his long-planned visit, Weinstein summoned up the courage to meet his former captors: "I looked for others—friends and enemies—in Japan. Watanabi Gunso, the sadist who had tried to kill me was dead; he was executed after his war crimes trial in 1946. Dr. Tokuda, who had used American POWs as guinea pigs was still in in Sugamo Prison. Dr. Fugi, who had sent me to the Omori Punishment Prison for 'failure to cooperate with the Japanese,' was living 60 miles out of the city. He wrote that he 'didn't know what I was up to' and refused to see me unless he was compelled to."[52]

Dr. Fugi's accusation had turned Weinstein's survival under the Japanese into a hell. But he apparently did not feel any guilt about his decision to "punish" Weinstein. The latter, on the contrary, needed to reach out to him to find some sort of peace of mind. Unlike the adamant Fugi, Captain Kubo, former commander of the Mitsushima prisoner camp, met with Weinstein. The surgeon recalled the hard slave labor he did under Kubo's supervision. Like all the POWs, he was ordered to cut and haul timber during the bitter cold winter in the Japanese mountain area while beriberi took its toll in cardiac deaths. Kubo eventually found a way to alleviate some of the prisoners' exhausting labor. It was a spark of humanity.

Eighteen years later, Weinstein and his wife, Hanna, met Kubo at a dinner in Tokyo. In a peaceful atmosphere in which the surgeon used his rusty Japanese, they all listened together to "the plaintive sounds of the string samisen and watched the geisha girls in rice-powder make-up dance." In that setting, the former captor and prisoner talked about their war experiences.[53] With these words, Weinstein concluded the report about his encounters in Tokyo: "I was glad I had returned to Japan—the home of the fanatical military extremists who had bombed Pearl Harbor, broken my body, and destroyed thousands of my friends captured in Japan and Corregidor. Why was I glad? Since my visit I no longer tremble with fear when I hear Japanese spoken. I no longer have desire for revenge."[54]

In his well-wrought article, Weinstein used the word "Japan" almost as a leitmotif, as if to get accustomed to the new representations it evoked. According to neuropsychiatrist Boris Cyrulnik, when the desire for revenge is no longer overpowering, the healing process can begin. Former POWs whose need for revenge is obsessive remain prisoners of their harsh past.[55] A feeling of coming full circle is sensed in the title Weinstein chose for his article: "I Made My Peace with Japanese War Criminals." Significantly, the article appeared in the *Quan*, a publication of the "American Defenders of Bataan and Corregidor, which included any Unit or Force of the Asiatic Fleet, Philippine Archipelago, Wake Island, Mariana Islands, Midway Island, and Dutch East Indies." One may wonder if Weinstein was trying to persuade himself and others that he had found the "closure" expected by patients under therapy. The medical corpsman admitted that his body was "broken" but did not dwell on his mental wounds, knowing that he had no choice but to cope with traumatic memories. He did so until his death in 1964, at the age of fifty-six.

### From Prisoner of War to Survivor and War Hero

During his survival through forty months in several Japanese prison camps, Alfred Weinstein provided medical treatment to his fellow prisoners although he himself weighed only 105 pounds because of severe malnutrition. After the war, he continued to be his brothers' keeper—a Jewish concept—sending medicine to the guards who had shown empathy to him and others. He left military service with the rank of lieutenant colonel in the Medical Corps, decorated several times for saving the lives of many comrades.

The change of perceptions from POW to survivor and hero took several decades. In 2015, ninety-one-year-old Harry Corre was invited to speak in military forums about his path from POW to counselor of veterans. His acquired social status entitled him to be chosen as technical adviser for the film *Unbroken*, directed by Angelina Jolie, about the war experiences of American airman Louis Zamperini.[56] As with Holocaust survivors, a former POW like Corre could share his experience and validate the representation of reality.

Numerous others had to deal with severe PTSD all their lives. Such was the case of radar operator Staff Sergeant Norman Sellz, whose plane was downed while he flew over Tokyo on a mission. His twin brother, Edward, also a radar man, and their family were informed that he was missing in action. When his plane was downed, he was captured by Japanese civilians, who beat him and locked him in a dungeon, where he suffered more torture. When Sellz returned home on August 29, 1945, his father, a Russian soldier who had been captured for four years as a POW of the Germans in World War I, could better understand his lifelong trauma than others.[57]

\*\*\*

In a space of confinement where indifference to others is the norm—the better to dehumanize the POWs—it is striking to uncover occurrences of religious transcendence. Spirituality was a considerable psychological aid for survival.[58] Yom Kippur in the camp of Cabanatuan assumed a special relevance for the prisoners praying to be inscribed in the Book of Life. The regenerative experience of religiosity during improvised religious services temporarily overrode the hierarchy among POWs by bringing prisoners together. Their bond was a feeling of Jewish solidarity and brotherhood. In this context, laymen were social actors able to uplift servicemen's morale. The meaningfulness of prayers is probably best illustrated by letters sent to the wife and son of an infantryman, Aben Caplan, taken prisoner on the German side of the Rhine in January 1945. A technical sergeant who spoke German, he hid his Jewishness from his captors, but some decisions were difficult to take. Burying the miniature prayer book from the National Jewish Welfare Board (JWB) would have been like losing his inner strength: "I had a prayer book in my pocket . . . and there I was tempted to get rid of my prayer book. Yet, I recalled how I had just recently called upon God for the saving of my life and the protection of those I loved." Finding other Jews among the prisoners, the infantryman managed to hold religious services in one of the POW camps where he was interned.[59]

After the war, keeping busy to avoid ruminating about the past was a must for veterans, who could not be understood by those who had not shared their war experiences. Alfred Weinstein chose life and with it, empathy for the few guards he met. Instead of hating the Japanese people, he looked for interactions with his former captors. The Jewish value of empathy liberated him from the obsessive idea of revenge. This positivity helped the physician when he sank into depression. Yet the question he formulated in his memoir remains an existential issue: "How much punishment can a man take before he loses his divine spark?" The two good-hearted Japanese guards gave him lessons of humaneness that resonate today: "Man can remain compassionate, if he wills it, even when surrounded by a mass of evil men."[60]

Ensign Jack Gordon did not survive the transport on a Japanese Hell Ship targeted by American bombers as medical corpsman Weinstein did. The latter was grateful to Gordon for cheering him up when they were both captives in prison camps in the Philippines. Morale-boosting was essential to survival, and camaraderie provided the strength necessary to overcome ordeals.

# 8

# CAMARADERIE BEYOND PREJUDICE

The first American nurse killed in action in the European theater captured the essence and warmth of camaraderie in a letter to the GI newspaper *Stars and Stripes*. Lieutenant Frances Slanger wrote these eloquent lines: "We have learned a great deal about our American boy and the stuff he is made of. The wounded do not cry. Their buddies come first."[1]

Hundreds of stories of mixed crews of American bombers evince the necessary interdependence that led to comradeship in teams of airmen. It was a major element in the high level of performance in the American air force; camaraderie was born of mutual dependence and thus went beyond prejudice.[2] It stemmed from flying missions. Flight officer and former prisoner of war (POW) Harvey Horn, twenty years old when he served, emphasized that this bond was especially strong when the crew of a B-17 had to ditch.[3] This final chapter explores how shared experiences, selflessness, and leadership fostered mutual trust and social acceptance in the military for American Jews.

### Toward Mutual Trust with Japanese Americans

Milton Zaslow, who had just graduated from New York City College in 1941, thought of enlisting in the army as the war broke out. Little did he know that the strange phone call inviting him to start an expensive Japanese language course would shape his life, eventually dedicated to the American military. Nor could he have imagined that deciphering captured Japanese material during the war in the Pacific would lead him to the battleground. In his first assignment in the Mariana Islands, he had to search for Japanese prisoners hiding in caves alongside the US Marines, noted combat units. He was often greeted by a live exploding grenade tossed from within the caves. Leading a team of ten Nisei servicemen, Milton Zaslow, an American Jew who grew up in New York, confessed in an interview conducted in 2004 by Vietnam veteran Bob Nakamura that his unexpected war experience "made him a better person."[4] His example deserves an analysis. His empathy for the Japanese Americans who comprised his team was remarkable—at a time when Japanese people in America were an even less desirable ethnic group after the attack on Pearl Harbor and the outbreak of the Pacific war in 1941. It was then that the exclusionists, groups of men and women active in politics, demanded the evacuation and internment of Japanese Americans in camps.[5]

Milton Zaslow's wartime story evinces that his encounter with Japanese Americans was a life-changing experience. At the time, the young serviceman was perhaps not aware of political debate about the passage of an immigration act in 1924 that would exclude Japanese immigrants from entering the United States and limit the admission of certain Europeans, such as illiterates, Catholics, and Jews. It is ironic to recall that in February 1942, Jews ranked third, after Japanese and Germans, in a poll about the most menacing groups for Americans.[6] Although he had not previously been exposed to Japanese Americans, Zaslow, a patriot, felt it would be useful for the war effort for him to embark on the most intensive course he had ever taken. How else could he have labored over the assigned homework until bedtime after a long day of study?

The intensive course, taught by a Japanese teacher and in complete immersion with other Japanese people, eventually paid off. Zaslow successfully completed the program and was contacted by the army. He enlisted and moved to Camp Savage, outside Minneapolis, in "a very austere bunch of Quonset huts out in the countryside." Camp Savage was a site of the American Military Intelligence Service and a language school that operated in San Francisco before moving to Minnesota. The purpose of the school was to teach Japanese to both military personnel and civilians involved in the war effort. Trainees' acquired skills were to be used to interrogate POWs, interpret, and—most often—translate captured material. It was at Camp Savage in July 1943 that Milton Zaslow met several hundred Japanese American Nisei. Many were "young kids"; a few were older. He recalled that because many had lived in Hawaii, they had never seen snow. They went out stark naked (the way they slept) in the freezing night at the first appearance of the cotton flakes falling from the dark sky. He admitted to feeling like he had encountered "a new kind of person."[7]

The serviceman reacted to several challenges with compassion. He felt empathy for Japanese Americans. Years later, he admitted that as a young man, he had not quite understood to what extent these Japanese Americans were eager to fight for the United States: "I had ten men, and off we went to San Francisco. Before going to Hawaii, we had one night free before embarking. The first special problem occurred. A local law prohibited Japanese Americans to be seen outside, so as a second lieutenant, I told them, tonight you are not Japanese, you are Chinese! Just don't get into trouble and enjoy yourself! And the bond between me and my team became stronger." The Japanese Americans in Zaslow's team traveled with him to Honolulu on a liberty ship "as small as we can get." Another problem cropped up because, although assigned to the navy command, Asian people were forbidden from entering Pearl Harbor. He had to find a place for his Japanese American team to examine material from Guadalcanal and other combat theaters in the Pacific. Zaslow dealt with another major challenge when the team reached the Mariana Islands: "Japanese Americans walking around would be the first to be shot! So we had passwords, it worked very well. The Marines would not take Japanese Americans in uniform. Tinian was an agricultural place. Maybe 8000 Japanese families and Korean families.... We organized a kindergarten. We were kind of successful. It was a new experience for all of us."[8]

Zaslow was cautious and fortunate that no members of his team were killed by American Marines, who could easily have mistaken them for Japanese enemies.[9] Fairly quickly, he adjusted to war zone conditions. He and his team were first attached to a navy command and then to the Marines. In the years 1944–1945, in Okinawa, he was attached to the Army Twenty-Fourth Corps. To land on the Japanese island, he had to swim ashore amid a lot of shooting with a bag full of Japanese dictionaries, a carbine, and a .45 handgun. Asked by the interviewer how his Nisei team felt on August 6, 1945, the day of the bombing of Hiroshima, he answered that although no one knew what it truly was, the news brought relief: "Oh, they were delighted. Of course. Absolutely."[10]

A similar reaction of relief was felt by US Army Corporal David Mandell, a soldier stationed in the Philippines who trained in a unit meant to be the first to hit the beach in the planned invasion of Japan. Corporal Mandell, who had the feeling he would "end among the slain," later told his son how relieved he was at the news that a newly invented atomic weapon would lead the Japanese to accept unconditional surrender.[11]

A chief of staff under Presidents Roosevelt and Truman, General George C. Marshall told the latter that it was the "shock value" of the weapon that would put an end to the war. He explained that dropping the bomb "seemed quite necessary, if we could, to shock them into action.... We had to end the war, to save American lives."[12] Historian David McCullough draws a clear picture of the situation: "Okinawa was on Stimson's mind—Okinawa was on all their minds. An attack on the American armada by hundreds of Japanese suicide planes, the *kamikaze*, had had devastating effect—thirty ships sunk, more than three hundred damaged, including carriers and battleships. Once American troops were ashore on the island, the enemy fought from caves and pillboxes with fanatic ferocity, even after ten days of heavy sea and air bombardment."[13]

And yet, the memories etched in Milton Zaslow's mind were not only of the twelve thousand Americans killed in Okinawa and the thirty-six thousand wounded but also of the Japanese losses, ten times worse: one hundred and ten thousand, while civilian deaths may have reached a third of the population of the island.[14] He recorded a fact that moved him, denoting his empathy and the camaraderie that drew him close to his Nisei team of Japanese Americans.

> If you want to send mail to anyone it has to be censored by your commanding officer for obvious reasons. And so I was in the business of reading the mail of every single one of these young men, mostly young men. And mostly they would write to their families and mostly they were in the relocation camps. And the heart wrenching thing to me was that here—here are these guys not living too well, in danger of being killed at any time, writing letters to their families in the relocation camps and trying to keep their families' spirits up. Whereas normally you would expect the families' letters would be quite the other way. And I felt that—that just was—I was overwhelmed by that. And it was quite common with almost every one of them. They had older parents or grandparents and uncles. They were very attentive. Would talk to them, make sure they mentioned their names and what they were doing. But in every case, they were writing it to try to raise the spirits of the people back in the camps. And that's such an inversion of what you normally would expect coming from people in combat for their country, that it overwhelmed me.[15]

As if Nisei servicemen were not themselves entitled to empathy from relatives, they had to worry about the psychological well-being of their parents. Not surprisingly, the American officer strove to maintain contact with his men and the Japanese community in the United States after the war. He kept in touch with Don Oka, the sergeant of his team, who became a cartoonist for Walt Disney. Invited to a Japanese American Veterans Association (JAVA) meeting in downtown Washington, DC, many years after the end of the war, Zaslow, eager to find people he knew, recognized one of his men among hundreds of Japanese Americans. Asked to recount the striking encounter with a former member of his military team who had become a businessman, Zaslow described recognizing a man of about fifty-five years of age, although the team member was nineteen years old when he was part of his team: "And he had that lovely look in his eyes that you see when somebody who is smart is talking to you, you know? He just radiates. . . . It was the most rewarding experience I can ever recall. So I will never forget them and the service they performed. It made me a better person."[16]

The interviewer did not mention or inquire about Zaslow's Jewish identity. But again, showing empathy for others is a Jewish value that makes one a better person. Once Zaslow had adjusted to life in the Pacific Islands and gotten closer to the ten members of his team, he was basically a white American officer.

Zaslow was not asked to expand on the presence of Japanese American women among those who translated captured Japanese material while serving in the American military. Yet it is worth pointing out that Japanese American women were allowed to enlist in the WACs in March 1943 and later in the Military Intelligence Service Language program, sometimes against the will of a mother who would disown her daughter "for joining the enemy army and help defeat Japan."[17] The importance of deciphering and using foreign languages was recognized throughout the war in many domains, ranging from the use of German by former German Jewish refugees—enlisted in the American military to serve in the Intelligence Service and save thousands of American and Allied lives—to the use of the Navajo code talkers, memorized by young Native Americans. This language, which was originally oral, acted as an unbreakable code; its use saved lives, as enemy Japanese forces never managed to break it unlike other codes.

In 1941, the growing need for airmen spurred a pioneering initiative that eventually broke through the barriers of prejudice. First Lady Eleanor Roosevelt, who also encouraged the Women Air Force Service Pilots (WASP) experiment, convinced her husband, President Roosevelt, to agree to the creation of the first squadron of African American pilots and crewmembers.[18] As seen in earlier chapters, while Jewish pilots—both men and women—were often washed out because of prejudice, African Americans too suffered harshly from rampant discrimination and segregation. No all-Jewish units were created by the American military, but segregated units existed for African Americans, men and women alike. Jewish servicemen and women sent to the American South for military duty often expressed shock at discovering signs reading "no Negroes allowed," which reminded them of panels with "no Jews allowed" at the entrance to some public places in the 1930s and even until the late 1940s. Feelings of empathy and even a sense of fellowship with African Americans pervade the personal narratives of Jewish GIs, especially those from the East Coast.

## Experiencing Fellowship in the Military

Instances of fellowship, friendship, and a sense of brotherhood abounded—and, of course, varied. Psychologically speaking, these interactions not only with Jewish "buddies" but particularly with non-Jewish GIs shared a sustaining function. Small group solidarity was a great help in fighting overwhelming homesickness. But many GIs had never encountered Jews, and some had been exposed to caricatures of Jews with horns on their heads. Time spent together in basic training, battle, or POW camps led to a realization that Jews were first and foremost Americans ready to sacrifice their lives. Infantryman Milton Norman, from Brooklyn, was somewhat upset at his comrades' astonishment that he did not have horns like the Jews they pictured in their minds. He found some comfort in the camaraderie he felt with an Italian immigrant who could not write English and whom he helped write letters.

> And so that there was anti-Semitism, but it wasn't overt, and as a matter of fact, I bonded with a fellow in my Platoon who was from Pennsylvania, of Italian heritage. I think Italian was probably his first language; at least he could write or read English hardly at all. And he had a girlfriend, and I used to help him write letters to his girlfriend. She wrote him in English, and I had to read the letter to him, and we composed an answer, and we became good friends. And he happened to be the Division Lightweight Boxing Champ, which I think was helpful in a sense that here I am, 18 years old, 128 pounds soaking wet, you know, and so we became good friends.[19]

A non-Jewish friend was no doubt a good support, and the proximity of a boxing champion might have deterred Jew haters.

## The Bond of Camaraderie

A lieutenant colonel in the Air Corps, noted filmmaker William Wyler was born in 1902 in Mulhouse, Alsace, which was then a German possession. To produce a morale-building documentary film for the War Department, he took flying lessons to accurately document a bombing mission. The film he produced focuses on the crew of the B-17 Flying Fortress *Memphis Belle* as it prepares to carry out a mission of strategic bombing over Germany. The spectator feels the freezing cold and fear of being hit by flak through the laconic messages exchanged between the flight crew. With empathy, Wyler expressed those boys' feelings and shared their apprehension of bailing out. Each one knew that the loss of a crew member was like the loss of a limb. Wyler wanted to convey the humane side of the war and became attached to this crew, making its twenty-fifth and last mission. As a Jew in uniform flying over Germany, he feared that in case of bailing out, he would be captured and murdered by Germans. While filming a B-17 on a mission, Wyler's Jewish cameraman, First Lieutenant Harold Tannenbaum, a World War I veteran, was killed when the bomber was shot down. Wyler took it on himself to write a letter to inform his wife. The filmmaker never lost contact with the crew of the *Memphis Belle*, whose bravery he played down so that the film footage could speak for itself.[20]

Many Jewish airmen spoke warmly about African Americans in interviews conducted by author Bruce Wolk. Veteran Norman Smeerin of the 332nd Fighter Group found them simply "fantastic." He recalled: "They would pick us up as soon as we got into enemy territory, they would fly cover for us until we got to the target."[21] Technical Sergeant Norman Zalkin, a radio operator with the Ninety-Ninth Bombardment Group, opened up about his flying experiences with African American escorting pilots, who were only allowed to fly P-51s. The interviewee offered moving recollections of fellowship in spite of expected "social distancing": "On several missions we encountered German fighters. . . . We had two engines shot out. Our bomber was a four-engine plane. And we had to turn back and we were by ourselves. We were attacked by German Messerschmitts, and we called for help, and afterwards, we found out that the fighter group that came and shooed them away was the Tuskegee airmen. They took us back to Italy and they were black and we could tell by looking at them that they were the Tuskegee airmen. On that particular mission, the Tuskegee airmen saved our lives."[22] He added that back then, they were not called Tuskegee Airmen: "Black fellows at that time were Negro." He explained that they were college men who had been allowed to enlist and were expected to stick with members of their own squadron.

Technical Sergeant Frederick Bartfield also credited the Tuskegee Airmen for his being alive. In many instances, Jewish fliers felt that close encounters with African Americans were not encouraged. The Jewish veteran reminisced that they escorted his bomber up to the target. He appreciated it all the more as he got hit in the head by flak on a mission once and had to ditch: "I wanted to go over and see them but we had a couple of southerners on our crew who said they weren't particularly anxious to mix with 'coloreds.'"[23] Another Jewish navigator went through similar experiences on dangerous assignments over the Adriatic Sea. First Lieutenant James Ruttenberg was flying a mission to Zagreb, Yugoslavia, when he encountered the Tuskegee Airmen, who escorted his plane back to their airbase. The officer recounted:

> I was on the radio when we were coming into the airbase, and you never heard such wonderful jive talk. Those guys have a very soft place in my heart. . . . I felt very strong kinship to these guys because they were going through the same sort of things because of their race that I went through my whole life because I happen to be born of Jewish parentage. When we stayed there overnight and had dinner with these guys the conversation went along the lines of an apology. I guess I more or less apologized for the rest of my citizens in the United States. I wanted them to know that everybody didn't feel the same way.[24]

Adopting the perspective of the underdog is a Jewish value that overlaps with the spirit of America, a notion formulated by Thomas Jefferson in the Declaration of Independence. The correspondence between these two ideas was particularly striking during World War II, which explains in part why Jewish Americans considered it "a just war" while others cynically viewed it as a "Jewish war." This point has been dealt on in various ways in previous chapters. Considering the numerous common denominators between Jewish and American values, suffice it to mention the safeguarding of freedoms such as religion, speech, and creed guaranteed by law. Let us recall that the preface of the Jewish prayer book issued by the National Jewish Welfare Board (JWB) indicates that "it serves not only the men who use it, but also the highest ideal of America." The prayers instilled both the aspirations of the Jewish people and those of all mankind, as they "quicken loyalty to loved ones and to all one's fellow men."[25]

For Americans of all faiths, camaraderie in wartime was indispensable to maintain high morale under the worst conditions. When Jewish infantrymen were battling their way through the bug-infested Pacific Islands, comrades in arms depended on each other to survive. With no time nor taste for anti-Jewish attitudes, only indispensable words were uttered when conquering the island. Often, each soldier would surpass himself to prove his own worth and sense of purpose to himself and others. A photo captures the courage of three buddies advancing on the Munda trail on New Georgia Island. Among them, erect and tense, ready to open fire, Private First Class Archie Shapiro of the Bronx precedes his two buddies on an uneven and muddy path. Unlike his comrades, he wears no helmet. The year was probably 1943, and Japanese snipers were still around. What mattered was their dangerous mission, conquering Munda and reducing the distance to Tokyo by enabling American bombers to land on airfields in the islands. The same objective in mind and the same spirit of camaraderie are captured in another photo: Major Robert Hirshfield of Chicago and Brigadier General John Arrowsmith of Reno, Nevada, are seen at the window of their bamboo basha office. These two American engineers constructed another road to Tokyo from India—built on the most difficult terrain, it established a connection with the old Burma Road to China. Cutting through the Assam Jungle to send supplies to southern China, it was called a "miracle of a road." Working in cooperation assumed various forms. Another undated photo in the volume published by the JWB shows three people squatting and apparently communicating in a field in China. One identifies Hank Greenberg, former Major League home run champion and now Captain Henry Greenberg, close to two Chinese laborers.[26] The caption indicates that he was "comparing notes" with them. It is probable that those notes accompanied maps or pictures of potential airfields.[27] The champion served for six months in the China-Burma-India theater, spotting locations for B-29 bases. He was also in charge of the physical fitness of the men of the Fifty-Eighth Bomber Wing. This interaction with the Chinese fostered a unique form of fellowship promoted by the necessities of the war.

In this theater of the war, the help and compassion of Chinese people for Allied soldiers saved American lives. A 1944 report, the story of a Jewish airman who later obtained the Distinguished Flying Cross, reads thus: "On his fifty-first bombing mission over Japanese controlled territory, Lieutenant Milton Miller of Brooklyn, New York, was forced to bail out. He landed in Japanese held territory and escaped with the help of Chinese natives."[28]

## Compassion, a Source of Courage

Empathy, a key Jewish value, is perhaps what helped many courageous servicemen become distinguished Jewish officers in both World War I and World War II. Such achievements are illustrated by Vice-Admiral Ben Moreell of St. Louis, Missouri, who arduously and patiently worked his way to the top by selling newspapers in the typical American tradition. As chief of the US Navy's Bureau of Yards and Docks and of the Civil Engineer Corps, he organized the Seabees, who performed engineering feats in the Pacific, and became a four-star admiral and the highest-ranking Jewish officer in naval history.[29] In late 1941, his concern that civilian workers at bases in the Pacific ran the risk of being shot at in case of guerrilla warfare led him to request permission to form "construction battalions" or "CBs," pronounced and named Seabees. The naval officer and engineer thus initiated the idea of training skilled workers to handle weapons as a battalion in case of an attack. Vice-Admiral Ben Moreell (also spelled Moreel) went down in naval history as "King Bee."[30] Although his Jewishness may not have been disclosed, his deeds are in keeping both with the highest American ideals of dedication to the military and the central Jewish value of empathy. The wartime book *Fighting for America: A Record of the Participation of Jewish Men and Women in the Armed Forces during 1944*, which detailed his achievements and contributions to the American military, emphasizes that Jews from all walks of life behaved like American patriots. Brigadier General Julius Klein, another noted officer, also dedicated his life to a larger goal. Recipient of the Soldier's Medal for Heroism, he was decorated for battlefield valor when he saved numerous lives during an explosion in New Caledonia, in the southwest Pacific Ocean.[31]

Yet some service members suspected Jews of cowardice, along with physical weakness, selfishness, and dishonorable behavior. For others, Jews were too bookish or brainy. Such a representation of masculinity seemed at odds with the American ideal of the muscled man and "good left hook." Although the stereotype first created anxiety among Jewish servicemen, such apprehension gave way to assertiveness as they became physically fit. Coping with anti-Jewish slurs eventually strengthened them, as it "happened en route to becoming soldiers," Deborah Dash Moore subtly remarks.[32] Noted counterexamples of these stereotypes include American professional baseball player Hank Greenberg, whose story in the military was detailed in a previous chapter.[33] Let us also recall Colonel David Marcus, a hero and one of the most popular men to graduate from West Point because of his boxing fame. His desire to help "underclass men" made him appear as a compassionate person. With the military help he provided to the fledgling Jewish state in 1948, the story of the American war effort in World War II "touches on the story of Israel," as the authors of *Jews in American Wars* put it.[34] Solidarity with other Jews and American servicemen could entail the sacrifice of one's life.

### Camaraderie through Heroism and Spilled Blood

Jewish servicemen defied the stereotypical idea that Jews were only willing to serve in safe roles as reporters or observers. They were more numerous in the infantry than in any other branch of the army. The final phase of the war in the European theater resulted in many receiving decorations for their courage, often posthumously.[35]

The life and achievements of undefeated world boxing champion Barney Ross powerfully illustrate the transformation of the Orthodox Jew into a muscled Jew. Although Ross broke loose from Orthodoxy, Jewish values of selflessness and empathy guided him when he enlisted. The citation for his Silver Star notes that Ross remained under Japanese fire with two comrades to protect the men of his unit: "He assisted on the following night in dragging the injured and helpless men to comparative safety. Trapped approximately 400 yards in front of the Army's main line of defense, Private First Class Ross and his companions cared for the injured Marines until a rescue party arrived on the morning of the 20th. His great personal courage and sincere devotion to his comrades were in keeping with the highest traditions of the United States Naval Service."[36]

Ross's life was to be an endless fight. After the war, his dedication to helping veterans and people suffering from addiction showed he was not reluctant to go public about his addiction to morphine to alleviate pain as long as it could help others fight addiction. This courageous attitude from the former Talmud student and son of a rabbi—murdered by two robbers in his grocery store—may be construed as a yearning to make the world a better place (*tikkun olam* in Hebrew).[37]

As a war correspondent in the Pacific, Isidor Kaufman noted that in the battle of Guadalcanal, Ross's foot was injured by mortar shells. He also caught malaria and was delirious for ten days. Admirative of "the fighting medics," doctors in uniform and medical aides who left their established practices, the war correspondent observed that they performed the job "often under imminent danger to life and limb from battle raging around them."[38]

### Jews in the Medical Corps: Comrades without Arms?

The story of Captain Ben L. Salomon—serving in the Mariana Islands at Saipan on July 7, 1944, as the surgeon for the Second Battalion, 105th Infantry Regiment, Twenty-Seventh Infantry Division—is emblematic of the dedication of a medic to his fellow soldiers. Salomon's sense of camaraderie led him to infringe the rules of the Geneva Convention according to which a medical officer is not allowed to take up arms against the enemy. His case raises a question: should a medic let his patients be murdered by the enemy if he knows how to handle weapons? Compassion for wounded patients who had been bayoneted by the Japanese and quickness of wit drove him to behave with courage.

Salomon graduated from the University of South California Dental College in 1937. Inducted into the army when the war broke out, he was assigned to the 102nd Infantry Regiment, where his abilities as an infantryman brought him awards. A sergeant in command of a machine gun, he was commissioned an officer in the Dental Corps in 1942. As a first lieutenant, he became the dental officer of the 105th Infantry Regiment, Twenty-Seventh Infantry Division. Promoted to captain, he saw action when he reached the shores of Saipan in June 1944. Realizing that there was little need of a dentist there, he volunteered to replace the Second Battalion's surgeon, who was wounded. On the night of July 6, the Japanese attacked with three to five thousand troops. Ben Salomon realized how desperate the situation was when he saw enemy soldiers inside the aid station tent where he was treating the wounded. The first Japanese soldier bayoneted a wounded American soldier and attempted to kill three others with a knife, which Salomon managed to snatch from him. Soon, about thirty wounded Americans crawled to the tent. Salomon ordered his medical assistants to take the wounded away from the tent; armed with a rifle he grabbed from one of the wounded, he strove to hold off the Japanese from disrupting the evacuation of the wounded and killed several enemy soldiers. Captain Ben Salomon was awarded the Congressional Medal of Honor posthumously on May 1, 2002, by President George W. Bush, some fifty-eight years later.[39] The citation sums up the rest of the action: "After four men were killed while manning a machine gun, Captain Salomon took control of it. When his body was later found, 98 dead enemy soldiers were piled in front of his position. Captain Salomon's extraordinary heroism and devotion to duty are in keeping with the highest traditions of military service and reflect great credit upon himself, his unit, and the United States Army."[40]

An inspiring example of dedication and courage in the European theater of operations, where numerous Jewish GIs served, is provided by an American Jewish servicewoman. Alleviating pain and comforting the wounded was the goal of Lieutenant Frances Slanger. Eager to take part in the war against Hitler, Slanger, who was born in Poland and whose family immigrated to the United States in 1920, was assigned to the Forty-Fifth Field Hospital. She was one of four military nurses who landed in Normandy with American troops after D-Day. A Purple Heart, awarded posthumously, confirms her dedication to healing servicemen at the risk of her life.[41] The lines she wrote in a moving letter to *Stars and Stripes* as a tribute to the American fighting men radiate with her warmth, humor, and sense of sacrifice to heal the wounded and uplift their spirits. A short passage from Slanger's letter reveals her gratitude, love, and understanding for American combat soldiers: "The patience and determination they show, the courage and fortitude they have, is sometimes awesome to behold. It is we who are proud to be here. Rough it? No, it is a privilege to be able to receive you, and a great distinction to see you open your eyes and with that swell American grin say, 'Hi ya, babe?'"[42]

The sense of purpose of this American nurse, who lived in Roxbury, Massachusetts, was in keeping with the Jewish values of *hessed*, doing good things out of generosity, a wish expressed in daily prayers. Her example also evinces that humor helped cope with the dire conditions near the battlefront, showing that "what we can laugh at we can survive"—it does not "hold us captive of fear," as a renowned rabbi put it.[43]

Beyond the dangers they faced in the line of duty, members of the Medical Corps shared a bond with "their" GIs that was not free of emotion. One of the first army nurses to serve in the Pacific theater, Anita Claire "Goldie" Gold, born in 1919 in Brockton, Massachusetts, was commissioned barely two weeks after the attack on Pearl Harbor. She had just graduated from nursing school when she was sent to the Pacific theater. She was transferred to Melbourne, Australia, in April 1942 and to a frontline hospital in New Guinea in January 1943. The hospital suffered daily attacks by enemy bombers and Japanese artillery. Her husband, Fred, later commented on her three-and-a-half-year service: "She took care of all the wounded. It was an awful time, but she saved many lives."[44] Anita Gold also cared for three hundred survivors of Japanese prisoner camps, horrified at the health and mental condition of those who survived inhuman starvation, beatings, torture, and rampant disease.

For some women, military service as nurses encompassed taking care of survivors of the atomic bomb. With the American medical unit sent to Hiroshima, Gertrude Shapiro encountered devastation and strove to comfort and heal those in hospital. She died prematurely in the early 1970s of a cancer likely resulting from exposure to nuclear radiation. Other servicewomen extended compassion and care to former inmates of POW camps and survivors of concentration camps. They included Ruth Karsevar of the 136th Evacuation Hospital's communicable disease unit, stationed near the combat zone of Bad Kreuznach, Germany. Lieutenant Karsevar, from Atlantic City, New Jersey, had previously treated war amputees. She wrote to her parents about "fellow Jews being massacred" in Germany. Working in a hospital and caring for Jewish survivors from concentration camps, she was surrounded by German civilians. She made sure to let them know how "proud she was to be an American Jew."[45] Being an American servicewoman meant she was among the liberating armies. From that perspective, Lieutenant Karsevar thwarted the perception of Jews as victims.

A sense of American fellowship blended with patriotism when young women were courageous enough to oppose their parents and enlist. Proving capabilities to help and care for others in unfamiliar and often dangerous environments demonstrated their capacity for empathy and ability to endure basic training, to follow orders in unfamiliar surroundings. In 1944, Jeanne Zamaloff of the US Women's Army Corps (WAC) was sent to General MacArthur's headquarters in New Guinea, where, she noticed, all the prettiest girls ended up. The friendship of another Jewish servicewoman from Brooklyn was comforting, especially because both of them had boyfriends serving in the army. Her friend was fortunate enough to reunite with her boyfriend in New Guinea, where they were married, while Zamaloff met back with hers after four years of separation. Reflecting on her experiences, she was admirative of the servicewomen she called "politically conscious," who "got in touch with the resistance movement in Manila." While she found that most GIs were respectful and grateful for the presence of women overseas, she added that "there were some rapes in the army."

> I was never subjected to that, but what would happen was the generals would send messages to an office where was somebody they wanted to go out with, and they would ask if that woman would go with them. And they did or they didn't, as they wished. But when I got those invitations, I looked very innocently at my superior officer, the officer in charge of the Department and asked, "Why would I want to go out with him" and he would say "Oh you don't have to, you don't have to." And I would say, well I don't want to, that's it. You know, totally innocent.
>
> But there was another side of the coin—women who did and I don't say that they were a lot. I knew one woman who did, who danced around all the officers and was promoted to warrant officer very quickly so she could consort with them—in a passive sense—not so she could be part of their group. It was very obvious to all the other women that if you wanted to become a warrant officer, you had to do what she did, and nobody wanted to.[46]

Still in New Guinea, in unexpected settings, American servicewomen overseas like Belle Goldman of Milwaukee, Wisconsin, joined religious services in search of fellowship and spirituality. Improvised moments of religiosity were especially needed in the South Pacific, where enemy bombardment, random attacks by Japanese soldiers, and disease took a toll on American troops.

Led by General MacArthur, island warfare in the South Pacific implied "island hopping," a strategy that targeted key islands to establish footholds in the Pacific to get nearer to the enemy homeland. In many places, signs of civilization were scarce, and religious services reconnected GIs to home even if they had not been observant before the war. In New Guinea, where Goldman was stationed, infrastructure boiled down to army tents and barracks. Strips of land served as airfields for aircraft that would be backed by naval and ground forces. In these surroundings, a photo captures Belle Goldman attending Yom Kippur services outdoors in September 1944.[47] For some, such locations implied modifying religious practices such as fasting—refraining from eating and drinking—for twenty-five hours, from sundown to nightfall the following day. Worshiping together not only created cohesiveness between members of a minority but also led to new interpretations of the meaning of the day in light of shared war experiences. Above all, archival photos of Jewish services in war theaters testify to the military's tolerance and even encouragement of Jewish religious practice, although exceptions existed, depending on the convictions of Catholic chaplains. With the three main American faiths represented in the ranks, the American military "promoted the new concept of Judeo-Christianity," as historian Jay Eidelman puts it, and "to express their religion in public was heartening for Jews in service."[48]

### Camaraderie under Exceptional Circumstances

The bond established between Jewish servicemen in the military disregarded hierarchy as well as nationality. As seen in chapter 7, the war experience of Alfred Weinstein, a prisoner of the Japanese who attended the first service of the Day of Atonement in a prison camp in the Philippines, exemplifies this statement. This bond does not apply solely to prisoners of the Japanese but rather to all servicemen and women, including Jewish POWs of the Nazis. Take the case of Ralph Tomases, a twenty-three-year-old Orthodox Jew born in Wilmington, Delaware, to immigrant parents from Romania and Belarus. In the heart of Germany, after a week's march in the snow from the Belgian-German border as a POW, the American officer (who was a dentist) arrived at a prison camp where several hundred soldiers were gathered in a big warehouse. The German officer in charge began calling out names of captured soldiers one by one. Those whose names were called left the warehouse. As the sun set and darkness crept in, Ralph's name had still not been called. Only two American servicemen men were left in the warehouse: he and another GI. Tomases approached the other captured soldier and asked his name. "Kimmelman," a Jewish name, was the reply, confirming his fear that they were being singled out as Jews. Fortunately, the other captive was also a dentist and, like him, would be useful to the

Nazis. The two men bonded because they were the last in the warehouse. They had both been waiting in agony to know if they would be murdered immediately in the dark or sent to die in a slave labor camp. This shared anguish sealed their comradeship.[49]

Ralph Tomases worked in the POW camp as a dentist, physician, and interpreter who knew Yiddish and some German.[50] Toward the end of the war in Europe, the officer wrote from Stalag IV-B to his parents and young wife, reiterating his hope to be freed soon. He secretly attended a religious service on German soil.

> This eve, I went to services. A service which I shan't forget. Here, in the midst of our worst oppressors, in secret, an odd collection of people met in a Catholic French chapel. Serbs, Checks [sic], French, Poles, Yanks, Hollanders, Palestinians, Scotch, English, Greek, and God knows what else. Mixed up uniforms, different tongues, but one thing in common. As I stood there and listened, first to a Hollander and then a Serbian Chazzan, my eyes wandered about. Men, with tear-filled eyes sniffling, lumps in their throats, thinking of other days, and other erevei [eves of] Passover.... With the help of God, I'm sure that we shall be together next Pesach, and that soon the Lord will, with His strong hand, take me out of this bondage like He took out our ancestors. *El Male Neeman. Shma yisrael H' alokeynu H' echad.*[51]

In his letter, Tomases emphasized the relevance he saw in the commemoration of Passover, prefiguring the long-expected liberation from the POW camp.

As observed in earlier examples, many Jewish soldiers attended services to seek Jewish fellowship overseas, in strange surroundings. Participation in religious services also created a bond with Christians, who were sometimes invited to attend by their fellow Jewish GIs. In December 1943, Harold Ribalow was in Morocco. Impatient to visit Casablanca, he seized the opportunity to get "a free pass to town" by joining a group of servicemen to attend a Friday night Jewish religious service and then visit the town. Ribalow was surprised to see that his Italian American buddy, Rogliano, easily passed as a Jew. A first lieutenant in the air force turned to Ribalow's comrade to find the proper page in the prayer book.[52] Rogliano, who had just been guided by his friend, placidly showed the Jewish officer the relevant page of the liturgy.

Although the Jewish serviceman's initial objective was to visit Casablanca, he admitted that he sensed some form of transcendence in the religious service.[53] Now that he was overseas, Jewish prayers reconnected him with home. Many GIs found that religious services and Jewish festivals alleviated homesickness. We may speculate that, better adjusted to their new wartime environment, they could be a better psychological support for their fellow servicemen.

The war experiences of servicemen behind the front lines cannot be compared with those of battlefield soldiers. Those behind the lines in the Pacific were vulnerable to tropical diseases and bombing raids. Although the inhospitable jungles of the Pacific Islands, the burning sands of North Africa, and the hot climate and poverty in India were all unfamiliar, fellow Jews could be found in these areas.

Another type of bond between Jews and Christians arose from challenges. Captain Max E. Zera, who fought in the Tunisian campaign and later with the Fighting First Infantry Division in Normandy on D-Day, wrote about the harsh experiences of infantrymen. There were numerous Jewish servicemen in this corps, despite the misperceptions that Jews shirked harsh combat assignments. Zera recounted in a letter the shared experiences of battle that created a bond between these men.

> Some day, I hope to write a bit about the infantry man. To my mind, he is the Army. . . . He's the plugger that does all the dirty work and gets none of the glory. He is the kid who stays in there pitching, knowing there is no relief in sight. He is the lad who stays in the foxhole all day, blistering in the sun. Then fights his heart out at night . . . chilled in the lull of battle. And all the time he is subjected to gunfire, bombing and strafing. He is the youngster you see in the photos with a mangled body . . . and the soldier, who sits contentedly eating cold hash out of a tin can. He is the expendable doughboy!. . . . Filled with a hate . . . a hatred developed in the realization that it is his life or his enemy's.[54]

This quote demonstrates again the truth behind the statement that there is no antisemitism in foxholes. The fear of death and the need for each soldier in battle leaves little place for subtle anti-Jewish slurs. In the letter to his friend Herman, Captain Zera expressed deep admiration for American infantrymen, his buddies. He thus reiterated this point: "There is no tougher job in the world! And no one can accuse them of shirking out their duties."[55] As a Jewish American infantryman, Zera implied that he did not shirk service in a combat unit either. Born in New York City to parents who had immigrated from Poland, Max Zera joined the army as a private in March 1941. The twenty-three-year-old had graduated from New York University as a physical training teacher. Having previously encountered renowned American war correspondent Ernie Pyle in England, Zera met him again during the North African campaign. Like most American soldiers, Zera was uplifted by the sense of fellowship expressed by the war reporter in his columns. In turn, Ernie Pyle was admirative of the courage and qualities of infantrymen, which he discovered by attending their classroom lectures and basic training. Max Zera wrote to his friend about the journalist from Indiana.

> He was a quiet, unassuming gent. There is a reason for his success as a writer. He lives what he writes, while up at the school he would double time from class to class with us. He doesn't appear to be strong but he subjected himself to the rigors that were ours. He sat through our lectures attended the study periods, went out to the range with us. Ran the obstacle course and took hikes just as the candidates did. He was up at reveille, and was out there at 5:45 doing the calisthenics....
>
> When I got down to Africa, I met him again. He didn't recognize me, so I introduced myself. He was still being thorough in his work, he's the only correspondent that actually went up to the front lines. I mean on the lines.
>
> Pyle spent all his time with us in the Tunisian campaign.[56]

Reciprocal admiration for the war correspondent, who risked his life at their side to inform Americans at home about the sacrifices the boys were making on behalf of their country, could only boost morale. Like some infantrymen, Ernie Pyle cheated death several times in the foxholes of Europe, but he was killed by Japanese bullets near Okinawa.[57]

Unsurprisingly, letters about the death of comrades contain curbed emotion: "For several months I suffered with nightmares. I used to make the landing at Tarawa. They had to fly me from Hilo to Pearl Harbor. There were only six of us in my boat that reached the beach alive. I don't want to tell you these things, but I know there's a war still on and I suffer each day in a way you can't understand while my buddies are still out there."[58] Being able to kill for a buddy—or to die for him—were characteristics shared by comrades in arms, committed to fighting for their country and spurred by the sentiment of living on borrowed time. That made soldiers in combat feel something similar to being part of a big family.[59]

In other instances, friendship grew out of shared respect and empathy. An interesting mention of friendship is found in a letter by infantryman George Bader, addressed to his wife and daughter, from a hospital after being wounded in the leg shortly before the Battle of the Bulge. When a non-Jewish fellow GI told him he was hungry, Bader, an Orthodox Jew, was pleased to take the serviceman with him to a Friday night service where he was the layman conducting the service. There, he invited his hungry buddy to enjoy bread and herring.⁶⁰

## American Spirit, Patriotism, and Brotherhood

The intention of the Jewish War Veterans of the United States of America (JWV) is to encourage and maintain a feeling of fellowship among Jewish GIs. The oldest organization of veterans in the United States, it was founded on March 15, 1896, in New York City. Its first meeting was attended by sixty-three Jewish Civil War veterans, named as "members of the Hebrew Union Veterans." When considering the connected issues of camaraderie and commitment to serving one's country, it is worth recalling the JWV's mission. Still relevant today, the JWV defends the following Jewish values closely intertwined with American moral principles.

> To maintain true allegiance to the United States of America; to foster and perpetuate true Americanism; to combat whatever tends to impair the efficiency and permanency of our free institutions; to uphold the fair name of the Jew and fight his or her battles wherever unjustly assailed; to encourage the doctrine of universal liberty, equal rights, and full justice to all men and women; to combat the powers of bigotry and darkness wherever originating and whatever their target; to preserve the spirit of comradeship by mutual helpfulness to comrades and their families; to cooperate with and support existing educational institutions and establish educational institutions, and to foster the education of ex-servicemen and ex-servicewomen, and our members in the ideals and principles of Americanism; to instill love of country and flag, and to promote sound minds and bodies in our members and our youth; to preserve the memories and records of patriotic service performed by the men and women of our faith; to honor their memory and shield from neglect the graves of our heroic dead.⁶¹

With the world in flames and the war raging in the Pacific, the flag raising on Iwo Jima on February 23, 1945, became an iconic representation of the American spirit as well as an image of comradeship celebrated by Harry Truman in his memoirs: "During the battle for Iwo Jima, Joe Rosenthal, an Associated Press photographer, had taken his inspired photograph of the American flag being raised on Mount Suribachi. Never before, perhaps, had any photograph been so enthusiastically received."⁶² The ineffable, evocative power of the American spirit, uniting diverse ethnic groups and faiths in a commitment to the flag, was captured in a single photograph. In a fraction of a second, amid bullets that whistled around him and killed one of the soldiers holding the flag, Jewish photographer and GI Rosenthal risked his life to convey to the American people the valor, commitment, and comradeship of American GIs. Like many other photographers and reporters, he served as a kind of liaison officer between combat forces and home front. Rosenthal, who was later awarded the Pulitzer Prize for this picture, admitted that of all the photographs he had taken on the front lines, nowhere was the spirit of "GI Joe" so well caught.[63]

It was actually a second flag raising; two hours earlier, a first flag had been raised on Mount Suribachi, but it could not be seen clearly on the other side of the mountain by thousands of Marines fighting to capture the island. Marine Corps commanders decided that another, bigger flag should be flown. It took many years to identify the six soldiers who held the flag, three of whom were later killed in the deadly battle of Iwo Jima. The first day of the invasion of the island took a higher death toll in American lives than D-Day in Normandy.[64] Since Iwo Jima was a small island, close-range fighting was called for, which increased the casualty rate. With over six thousand Americans dying during thirty-six days of combat on Iwo Jima, their number amounted to "five times the number of deaths on either Guadalcanal or Tarawa."[65] This figure provides another indication of the multiple symbolic values of the raising of the flag on Mount Suribachi. In April 1945, Secretary of Treasury Henry Morgenthau Jr. offered the president a painting made from Rosenthal's photograph to be used as a war loan campaign poster. He also presented to the president three of the presumed surviving Marines from the inspiring picture. Among them was Private First Class Ira Hamilton Hayes of the Pima Indian Reservation in Arizona. This encounter highlighted the visibility of minority groups among those who bravely wore the American uniform.[66]

Chaplain Roland Gittelsohn's famous Iwo Jima eulogy for his fallen comrades is also iconic in that perspective. The first chaplain ever appointed to the Marine Corps, he was assigned to the Fifth Army Division. Gittelsohn, a Reform rabbi born in Cleveland, Ohio, in 1910, earned three service ribbons for comforting the wounded of all faiths during the fierce fighting on the island. Division Chaplain Warren Cuthriel, a Protestant minister, asked him to deliver a memorial sermon at an interfaith religious service to dedicate the Marine cemetery, but a few Christian chaplains opposed the decision, arguing that a rabbi could not preach over a majority of Christian graves. It should be emphasized that the division chaplain refused to change his plan. To save him embarrassment from the biased attitude of bigoted chaplains, Gittelsohn suggested that separate services be held for each faith. He thus delivered to Jewish servicemen the speech he had prepared for all the Marines. It included the following excerpt, which honors the sacrifices of all Americans.

> Here there are no quotas of how many from each group are admitted or allowed. Among these men there is no discrimination. No prejudice. No hatred. Theirs is the highest and purest democracy. . . . Whoever of us lifts his hand in hate against a brother, or thinks himself superior to those who happen to be in the minority, makes of this ceremony and of the bloody sacrifice it commemorates, an empty, hollow mockery. To this, then, as our solemn, sacred duty, do we the living now dedicate ourselves: to the right of Protestants, Catholics, and Jews, of white men and Negroes alike, to enjoy the democracy for which all of them have here paid the price.[67]

The chaplain, called to minister to Marines of all faiths and having helped bury the dead on the island, was deeply saddened by the prejudice voiced by a few Christian chaplains—his colleagues. In a gesture of solidarity and objection to bigotry, a few Protestant chaplains attended his service. They listened to his speech entitled "Brothers All?" thus aptly conveying his disillusion. His eulogy became famous because of the rejection it suffered and the moving depiction of those who "have paid the ghastly price of freedom": "Here before us lie the bodies of comrades and friends. Men who until yesterday or last week laughed with us, joked with us, trained with us. Men who were on the same ships with us, and went over the sides with us as we prepared to hit the beaches of this island."[68]

Another Reform rabbi, Alexander Goode of Washington, DC, embodied even more powerfully the ideal of brotherhood beyond prejudice through the sacrifice of his own life. In the faint light of a freezing Atlantic dawn on February 3, 1943, the crowded US Army transport *Dorchester* was torpedoed by a German U-2 submarine. Lieutenant John Mahoney, who was among the two who survived in a lifeboat, admitted that he owed his life to the gloves of the Jewish chaplain who had given his lifebelt to an enlisted man: "My fingers would have frozen stiff had it not been for the gloves." Together with Chaplain Goode, Protestant chaplains George L. Fox and Clark V. Poling and Catholic chaplain John P. Washington—who had all given away their life-preserving equipment—prayed in Latin, Hebrew, and English on the sinking boat for the souls of their comrades. An iconic picture of the four chaplains was eternalized on an American stamp, prefiguring an emerging Judeo-Christian tradition in the military and the development of interfaith memorials. Analyzing this icon of Judeo-Christian

America, historian Jonathan Sarna pinpoints that the sinking of the USS *Dorchester* "symbolized the model of American religion that rapidly gained ground in the postwar era."[69] War reporter Isidor Kaufman indicated that before boarding the USS *Dorchester*, Goode had written a letter to his wife: "We are fighting for the new age of brotherhood, the age of brotherhood that will usher in at the same time the world democracy we all want. . . . Our spirit of tolerance will spread."[70]

In the immediate postwar period, in a society in which manliness was so admired, those affected by what was then called "battle fatigue" were perceived as weak and lacking courage to fight. Even spouses who had longed for the return of their husbands or companions from the war could not understand the mental blockages or deep silences apt to ruin a relationship. Because of a stereotyped American vision of manliness, some veterans would not mention their inability to function normally. A wartime documentary film recounts what some servicemen faced when they returned to the United States in a terrifying though realistic way. *Let There Be Light* (1946) demonstrates how the empathy and expertise of psychologists and doctors could help trace the roots of trauma preventing veterans from even moving their limbs. Former intrepid servicemen seemed like mental wrecks when they came back to America. Former combat soldiers, sailors, and airmen had to adjust to a postwar reality. Directed by American filmmaker John Huston during his military service in the Signal Corps, the documentary was intended to show the traumatic experience of many soldiers. But the presentation Huston and cowriter Charles Kaufman made of mental disability led the American government to suppress the film until the 1980s.[71]

Empathy must have been displayed by American psychiatrists treating "battle fatigue" or "battle shock" (later identified as post-traumatic stress disorder, or PTSD). As indicated in a report published in 1944, Major Harry L. Friedman of New York City "contributed to the successful treatment of men suffering from battle shock." The report mentions that 40 percent of the men treated by this physician of Jewish faith were reassigned to army duty, a great improvement in comparison to the high rate of permanent mental breakdowns that destroyed the lives of thousands of veterans of the First World War.[72]

As recounted in chapter 6, when twenty-one-year-old Captain Jerry Yellin landed back at Iwo Jima, he learned that the war had ended while he had been flying his P-51 over Japan three hours earlier. It was hard to come to terms with the loss of the young Jewish pilot and friend who flew next to him on that last mission and disappeared in a cloud while Yellin and his crew were strafing airfields near Tokyo. The following is how he accounted for his own transformation.

> I hated the Japanese all of my adult life. Then I attended a wedding in Japan on March 6, 1988, between the daughter of a Japanese Imperial Air Force veteran and my youngest son, Robert. This wedding between children of former enemies made me rethink, not only my life as a warrior, but the lives of all of us who served in combat. Today I have three grandchildren living in Japan, aged 19, 17, and 13. They love me, I love them. I can't help feeling that all of Humanity is the same, that the pure purpose of war is to kill and the pure purpose of life is to connect to all of Nature.

Like surgeon and former POW Captain Alfred Weinstein, when Captain Yellin visited Japan, he encountered a new generation. Even after his son and his Japanese wife divorced, Yellin continued his yearly visits to Japan to see his in-laws, with whom he had bonded while sharing war experiences as a pilot (with the indispensable presence of a translator).[73]

### Jewish Veterans Outreach

As a senior patient advocate and member of the Department of Veterans Affairs, Harry Corre—recipient of a Bronze Star and a Purple Heart—helped hundreds of veterans of all faiths and ethnicities. At age ninety-one, Corre continued his welcome visits to VA medical centers four days a week. A former POW, he was sensitive to trauma and inclined to foster positive interactions with fellow veterans. Corre continued a spirit of military fellowship after the war.[74] Providing help to fellow veterans meant seeing reality through their eyes and addressing their emotions. Often, those suffering from traumatic memories kept silent for fear the memories would reemerge and compromise their fragile psychological balance. Corre explained that only veterans can understand each other. That is one reason why veterans are reproached for remaining silent. In his view, most people have forgotten or know little about World War II and what soldiers went through.[75] Robert M. Morgenthau—chairman of the Museum of Jewish Heritage in New York, World War II veteran, and son of Secretary of the Treasury Henry Morgenthau Jr.—emphasized that veterans share characteristics with Holocaust survivors. Given that "thousands and thousands were lost at sea" during attacks that were defeats for the United States, he insisted on the difficulty of putting into words war experiences that involved a tremendous loss of life. Serving as executive officer on the USS *Lansdale* and USS *Harry F. Bauer*, which were attacked by the enemy, he recalled the trauma of those who witnessed the loss of their buddies in simultaneous torpedo attacks and kamikaze raids. He recalled that at Okinawa, 1,900 such suicide attacks occurred.[76] Therefore, veterans often share with Holocaust survivors a sense of guilt for being alive. Numerous were those who remained silent about their traumatic experiences, including discovering the Nazi concentration camps. What GIs in combat zones and POWs went through taught them that the body and spirit can endure a lot and somehow still function. Like survivors of the Nazi enterprise to exterminate the Jews during World War II, they learned the value of resilience and freedom.[77]

Some servicemen whose stories have been shared in this volume exemplified the fact that to contribute to a better world, man must accept to change something in himself. Broadmindedness and a dose of tolerance are the pathway to a form of "repairing of the world." Suffering from PTSD after he returned from the war, Captain Yellin visited Japan in 1983. As seen in chapter 7, Captain Alfred Weinstein attained a similar goal in his postwar visit to Japan.

Stories of Jewish American servicemen that suggest a desire for reconciliation and reconstruction are exemplified by the religious ceremony of the New Year of Trees performed by Chaplain Sachs on Okinawa.[78] Being married in Japan by a navy rabbi in Yokohama was symbolic too. Navigator-Bombardier Stuart R. Reichart saw fierce combat as a member of a B-29 crew conducting bombing raids over Japan, flying at low altitude in daylight.[79] Remaining in the Air Force Reserve after World War II, he was called to active duty and transferred to Japan for a few years. His wedding on Japanese soil with the woman to whom he became engaged before leaving the United States meant embarking on a new life in parallel with the rehabilitation of Japan. The major he became was fresh from the Brooklyn Hebrew Orphan Asylum when he joined the Army Air Corps at age eighteen, enlisting as an aviation cadet in November 1942. The veteran who entered law school at war's end became general counsel of the air force and served for forty years in the air force.[80] In the social landscape of the late forties, remaining in the American military was seen as a factor of integration for Jewish veterans. It also afforded them a long-expected sense of belonging and security.

The narratives of the Jewish American airmen and airwomen, soldiers, sailors, Marines, nurses, and corpsmen offered in the present book—many of whom died too young—testify to their dedication to their country in answering the call of duty and to the dynamics of camaraderie that helped overcome their legitimate fears and homesickness. Camaraderie assumed a sustaining function in the continuous personal fight against prejudice.

# CONCLUSION
## Bridging Worlds Apart

"What is America to me? A name, a map or a flag, a certain word: democracy . . . Especially the people, that's America to me." In November 1945, Frank Sinatra sang these words to a popular melody from the short film *The House I Live In*, which both Jewish and non-Jewish American children would later sing cheerfully in class. Beyond its light tone, the film heralded a change of perception of American Jews in the eyes of Gentiles.[1] This transformation was mostly due to Jews' participation in World War II. Spread throughout every branch of the armed forces and over all fighting fronts, over half a million Jewish men and women contributed to the American military effort in defeating the Nazis, the fascists, and the Japanese Empire. Ironically, while fighting against persecution abroad, Jews faced anti-Jewish hostility in their military ranks. Their interactions with Jews and religious communities in French North Africa, India, and the Philippines reinforced their Jewish identities and empowered them. In 1942, thousands of American troops arrived in Melbourne, Sydney, and Brisbane to fight the Pacific war. In the heart of Australia, GIs invited local residents to join them for Passover celebrations: the sight of several hundred strong soldiers reassured locals about Jewish continuity.[2] In Manila, Jewish service members initiated a fundraising campaign to rebuild the synagogue, which the Japanese had destroyed in February 1945. They dedicated it as a memorial to all GIs who perished there. On December 7, 1945, the anniversary of the attack on Pearl Harbor, Lieutenant General William Styer, commanding general of army forces in the western Pacific, presented it as a gift to the Manila Jewish community. This gesture represented one of many interactions that had an impact on reshaping American Jewish identities.

Servicewomen, too, reinterpreted their sense of Jewishness. They responded to the national emergency by displaying moral and heroic dimensions on the home front and overseas, including the dangerous islands of the Pacific. This book's emphasis on the voices of the young women and men who served sheds light on their soul searching, decision-making processes, and challenges. Its narrative deepens our understanding of the American Jewish military experience. This volume has addressed issues of belonging, drawing on the testimonies, letters, and oral histories of over a hundred service members. Rather than motivate suppression of service members' identification as Jews, anti-Jewish hostility may have led to a reawakening or appearance of religious feelings. The use of testimonies has evinced diverse forms of Jewish identification. As American patriots, young Jews were eager to belong, although they were often made to feel that, as Jews, they did not belong. Nineteen-year-old Harry Zaslow from Philadelphia did not identify himself as a Jew in the military but nevertheless suffered from anti-Jewish hostility during his service in Europe with the 283rd Field Artillery Battalion. Ironically, the most painful instance of this hostility was on the day he and a few American troops stumbled on the gates of the concentration camp at Dachau. Facing railroad boxcars "filled with a mass of dead bodies," one of his fellow soldiers told him, "Zaslow, if you're not careful you're going to be in that boxcar too." Shocked by the Nazi atrocities, the Jewish soldier let it go because he "had a job to do."[3] Despite the strong resolve of enlisted Jewish personnel, anti-Jewish slurs and discriminatory promotion practices occurred frequently. Veterans' memoirs from 1946 reveal that the shock of rejection was more significant among those whose Jewishness was not a meaningful aspect of their lives. Jewish servicemen who yearned to be officers often changed their names or indicated P for Protestant on their dog tags.

In Europe, close to the battleground, the decision to remain identified as a Jew was personal. At the height of heavy bombing during the Battle of the Bulge, when GIs' feet were frozen in snow, it was clear that the Allied soldiers would be captured. Jewish soldiers knew that the situation of European Jews was bad, but the extent of the genocide perpetrated by the Nazis was not fully grasped until the liberation of Hitler's concentration and extermination camps. American soldiers had nevertheless heard rumors that the Nazis shot unlucky Jewish prisoners on the spot. For this reason, many Jewish soldiers threw away their dog tags—some reluctantly—as their religion was noted on the piece of metal that hung from their necks. Captain Ralph Tomases decided otherwise, like many others, although he considered doing the same. He was captured while serving in the Medical Detachment in the 423rd Regiment of the 106th Infantry Division, deployed to the German-Belgium border. Along with him, thousands were made prisoners in the fierce Battle of the Bulge on December 19, 1944. Tomases was imprisoned in Stalag IV-B, one of the largest German prisoner of war (POW) camps near the Elbe River. What could have motivated such a risky decision? His reasoning was that if he died, his family would want him to be identified and to have a Jewish burial.[4]

Why are there so few Jewish Stars of David in the military cemeteries, particularly the D-Day cemeteries? In his 1945 report, Chaplain Bernstein found after examination of sample studies of War Department files "that nearly 45% of the authenticated Jewish dead were not so recorded in the official records." This finding may have led him to estimate that over six hundred thousand Jewish Americans served in World War II. There are several explanations for the relatively small number of Jewish burials. Burial practices may have been careless, and in many cases, the soldiers' dog tags were completely destroyed in plane crashes and combat.[5]

### Fighting Toe to Toe with the Nazis

The large number of decorations awarded, often posthumously, suggest that Jews were more numerous in the infantry than in any other branch of the army, from privates to high-ranking officers like General Rose.[6] Many German-speaking soldiers who immigrated to the United States as young refugees in the late 1930s were eventually drafted into various units of the armed forces, and their naturalization was rapidly handled.[7] In the US military, recent immigrants saw action mainly in Europe and in North Africa. Ironically, toward the end of the war in Europe, GIs from Germany and Austria were sent to serve in their countries of origin. Through their skillful interrogation of German POWs, the soldiers known as "Ritchie Boys" provided intelligence to help defeat the forces of Rommel's Afrika Korps. The information they gathered in intelligence units was crucial and saved thousands of American lives. In the postwar period, they contributed to efforts of denazification—as did Werner T. Angress, who parachuted into France with the Eighty-Second Airborne Division on D-Day. The refugees had experienced years of humiliation in Nazi Germany that continued even after their immigration to the United States. Meeting the challenge of infantry training boosted their self-confidence. This transformation occurred for many Jewish soldiers, immigrants or not—including some two thousand Ritchie Boys. However, the American military encouraged them to hide their Jewish identity for protection when interrogating German POWs. This might explain why some of their graves have no Jewish marking. General Rose's grave does not bear a Jewish Star either, but for different reasons. As an infantry combat soldier in World War I and an officer during World War II, he hid his Jewish identity to avoid anti-Jewish discrimination, as did many other infantrymen. His dog tags were marked with a P for Protestant, and therefore, the American military buried him as such and honored him as an American hero.

Women also met their responsibilities as American citizens. Jewish servicewomen were eager to contribute to the war effort and be fully accepted in the military. This gendered perspective enriches our understanding of the American Jewish experience.

## GENDER AND ANTI-JEWISH DISCRIMINATION

Unlike women pilots in the Women Airforce Service Pilots (WASP), flight nurses were immediately inducted as military personnel. The need for nurses and flight nurses was indisputable. Some servicewomen encroached on male territory even though they were meant to free up male soldiers for the front lines. They strove to be accepted in a military framework. Consequently, their identity was first and foremost shaped by their military roles: an American woman pilot in the WASP, an American aircraft mechanic, an American nurse, or an American woman in the Women's Army Corps (WAC) or Women Accepted for Voluntary Emergency Service (WAVES).[8] Like their Christian counterparts, they crossed gender and social boundaries, especially those who took to the skies. The fact that airfields rarely had women's restrooms remains significant. Air evacuation nurses (who carried a weapon) and airplane mechanics like Miranda Bloch—one of the few female Marines authorized to inspect and repair radio gear midflight—strongly challenged traditional roles. Bloch, whose courage and patriotism led her to defy her parents to enlist, challenged prejudice in the family unit, in civil society, and in the military. In his memoirs, General Eisenhower confessed to his own reluctance to recognize women's contributions in the military at first and described the skeptical attitudes of many officers. He noted that most commanders failed to realize "the changing requirements of the war," which implied a drastic change of attitude toward women. The WACs' efficiency in Algiers during Operation Torch on November 8, 1942, made an impact on him. By the end of the war, General Eisenhower noted that even the "stubborn die-hards had become convinced and demanded them [women] in increasing numbers."[9] Hilda Lehman De Vadetsky, the daughter of Herbert H. Lehman, governor of New York from 1933 to 1942, was on duty in Algiers as a member of the WAC in French North Africa. She lost her pilot brother in 1944.[10] Maneuvers and training flights took a toll among servicemen and servicewomen who took to the skies.

American Jewish women pilots expressed their frustration at being "expendable" as WASP members. To explain the meaning of the adjective they used, Bernice Falk Haydu and Elizabeth Haas Pfister stated in their respective interviews that they were not given military status during the war years despite the remarkable contribution of women pilots to the war effort. General of the air force Henry H. Arnold had made it clear that he intended to officially militarize these women pilots. Some even had the opportunity to fly and test the latest military aircrafts, Superfortress B-29 bombers, in front of the incredulous eyes of male servicemen and envious airplane mechanics. Yet the militarization of WASP members only took place some thirty years after the WASP disbanded. On Capitol Hill, in testimony before the Senate Committee on Veterans' Affairs, Colonel Bruce Arnold, the son of General Hap Arnold, along with women veterans demonstrated that the WASP was not a civilian unit. Their drills, uniforms, secret missions, relentless and arduous training, and flying hours from sunup to sundown attested to the military nature of the unit.

Disbanding the WASP without military status deprived women pilots of military benefits available to their male counterparts. They were not eligible for the support provided by the GI Bill, for example, which funded university tuition. Nevertheless, the discrimination they faced did not tarnish the idea of the America they cherished. The American values of liberty and justice, together with Jewish values of empathy and charity, continued to inspire them. They continued to make the world a better place.

Doubly victims of prejudice, some servicewomen had to confront anti-Jewish hostility as well as sexist attitudes. Selma Kantor Cronan candidly highlighted an important point about the nature of anti-Jewish hostility and prejudice in an in-depth interview conducted by the Museum of Jewish Heritage in New York. She realized that she may have been "excluded" from "some things": "attempts to push me off the base, particularly because I was unidentifiable as Jewish." When Selma's Jewishness was discovered, "it came out as an insult" since she was "very open" about her Jewish origins.[11] It is interesting to point out that some of these attitudes may have stemmed from mythical yet pervasive representations of Jews as conspirators, traitors, and infiltrators. Such accusations against Jews had been made relentlessly throughout the 1940s, culminating in the Sunday night radio broadcasts of Father Coughlin, a Roman Catholic Priest who pictured evil Jews financially "crucifying the whole world." Anti-Jewish propaganda included the publications of the Silver Shirts, which featured "the Jewish minority influence" and blamed Jews for all the ills of the United States.

It is not surprising that many Jewish GIs reacted to insulting remarks with their fists, which often brought results. From interviews, memoirs, and letters, four main strategies for confronting anti-Jewish prejudice emerge: being "three times as good just to be even," as fighter pilot Jerry Yellin observed; setting an example of extreme bravery, as did Colonel David Daniel Marcus; inspiring esteem through physical force, like boxing champion Barney Ross; and fostering respect for Jewishness, as Jewish chaplains and laymen did when conducting religious services. As a reaction to social exclusion, some Jewish GIs sought the company of coreligionists, which was likely to awaken or reinforce their Jewish identification and religious feelings. The examples of excellence or extreme bravery recorded in this book indicate that excelling was not only congruent with the American ethos; it was also a way to achieve recognition in the military. One of the lessons that service in the American military taught many GIs was best expressed by infantryman and German refugee Ernest Stock: "to hide one's being Jewish in a Gentile world was the wrong course. [I] had learned to speak up as a Jew and to be proud of it."[12] The pride that service members took in their Jewishness was reinforced by meeting members of Jewish communities in the different theaters of the war.

### Mutual Impact of Encounters in North Africa

With the simultaneous landing of Allied troops on November 8, 1942, in Oran, Algiers, and Casablanca, a sudden optimism descended on the Jews of North Africa. The daring amphibious invasion of this part of North Africa prevented local Jews from being deported to concentration or extermination camps in Europe. This book's scholarly outlining of meaningful interactions of service members with Jewish families and communities in French North Africa fills a gap in the historiography. A comparison between the testimonies of Jewish American GIs and Jews from French Algeria reveals that a transnational encounter took place during Passover seders. Enacting the story of the Exodus from Egypt, where Jews were enslaved, appeared to some as a harbinger of the restoration of world moral order by

Allied forces. American troops met British and Scottish soldiers, together with French-speaking Jews. These encounters had various effects. Jewish GIs became aware of the existence of a Jewish diaspora in French Algeria and in other parts of North Africa. Furthermore, encounters boosted the morale of both Jews in North Africa and American Jewish GIs, which provided great psychological support on both sides for the rest of the war. Far from being a burden, the GIs' Jewishness helped build bridges with the Jewish diaspora around the world. It became an asset for soldiers, airmen, and sailors, whose nostalgia was alleviated by families eager to receive American liberators in their homes, Jewish or not. For some American GIs, finding a host family to join during furloughs satisfied their longing for home. Even for some non-observant GIs, going to synagogue reawakened nostalgic feelings associated with home. Often, these feelings were intensified as a result of anti-Jewish hostility experienced in the ranks of the American army, an issue that has been overlooked. Attending services in a local synagogue provided refuge and summoned memories from a real or imagined home. Jewish service members also coped with feelings of exclusion within the military by seeking the company of coreligionists—both in the army and with members of the Jewish diaspora. Contrary to widespread belief, many GIs fighting the Pacific experienced war not only as Americans but also as Jews.

## Affirmation of Faith in the Pacific and India

When the guns and cannons fell silent, Jewish service members attended improvised religious services. Servicewomen took part in those services. They were also subjected to deadly diseases like malaria or to random attacks by the Japanese. Belle Goldman, who was awarded an Asiatic-Pacific Theater Ribbon, Bronze Battle Star, and Overseas Ribbon, attended a Yom Kippur service in New Guinea, one of the most remote Pacific islands, in September 1944. Like the members of the WAC, she viewed herself as "a conscientious soldier." Other women who did what they were assigned by the military sacrificed their lives. This was the case of Sergeant Belle G. Naimer, who died in an army transport plane crash in a far-flung part of Papua, New Guinea in May 1945 and was awarded the Army Good Conduct Medal. They, too, were empowered as Americans, female soldiers, and Jews.

In the Pacific, many religious services were led by laymen inspired by a sense of impending death. Improvisations of this kind in hostile territories was a new phenomenon during World War II. Fighting men and military personnel regained moral strength with the prayer to be inscribed in the Book of Life for Rosh Hashanah, the New Year, in 1943. A few striking instances illustrate this Jewish spirit in the military. Captain Benjamin Fenichel was photographed leading a service on Guadalcanal, and Marine Captain Sidney Altman from Brooklyn conducted a service in a chapel on that same island. Captain Fenichel sounded the shofar with a prayer shawl over his head in another photograph. Published in the *American Hebrew* in November 1943, this snapshot not only boosted soldiers' morale but also lifted the spirits of Jewish Americans at home. Religious services released tension before a battle or filled a void afterward. Reflecting on the nature of faith, a noted rabbi has argued that faith does not assume certainty, as it is often thought. On the contrary, he contended that "faith is the courage to live with uncertainty."[13] We may infer that different forms of Jewish observance in the various theaters of the war instilled courage in the fighters. During the celebration of the High Holy Days, faith prompted many Jewish GIs to rejoice as they reconnected with the spiritual or ritual heritage of their ancestors.

Sidney J. Altman, the commanding officer of Company E, Twenty-First Regiment, Third Marine Division, was an inspiring figure. He relentlessly repelled Japanese troops in Guam despite being wounded by a hand grenade. The citation for his Silver Star proves that his devotion to God equaled his "devotion to duty" as he "contributed to the success of his company's mission and upheld the highest traditions of the United States Naval Service."[14]

Other examples evince both the efforts of servicemen to conduct services in makeshift chapels in the Pacific and those of Christian chaplains to encourage these efforts. Captain Elliot Davis of the Eighty-Ninth Field Artillery fought in the Battle of Munda Point, on the island of New Georgia, in July and August 1943. He mustered the strength to organize religious services for the Jewish New Year on September 29, 1943, after a Baptist chaplain informed him that the National Jewish Welfare Board (JWB) had sent prayer shawls and prayer books. The spiritual overtones of Jewish ritual objects could trigger a sense of bonding that some soldiers had not experienced for years. The services were neither Orthodox nor Reform—for soldiers living with insecurity, they still celebrated life. For some GIs, the prayers bridged material and spiritual worlds. Public observance of religious services renewed their Jewish sense of purpose together with their American values.

Could religiosity be expressed in a POW camp in the Philippines? Unexpectedly, religious transcendence could occur during improvised services. The observance of the Day of Atonement, or Yom Kippur, while in captivity provided a double framework for the examination of questions of life and death. Against all odds, the observance of Yom Kippur in the camp of Cabanatuan turned out to be regenerative for some servicemen held by the Japanese.

The triumph of faith is perhaps best sensed in the moving service that took place in Aachen on October 29, 1944, with the sound of artillery in the background. A correspondent for NBC radio introduced the Sabbath prayer service on the battlefield with these powerful words: "The first Jewish religious service broadcast since the advent of Hitler."[15]

Thousands of miles away from home, in the Jewish communities of Bombay and Calcutta, GIs were not received as liberators and heroes as they were by Jews from Algeria or Europe. Indian families perceived them as American Jews in uniform, and members of these communities extended their hospitality. A strong sense of Jewish solidarity emerged from these interactions, which led some to question their own perception of people of color, as did David Macarov from Atlanta, Georgia, who rejected ingrained southern prejudice. He, too, conducted religious services, assisted the chaplain, and met with Zionist Jews in India. Many a service member who had no Zionist inclinations before the war changed his opinions as a result of encounters with Jewish survivors of concentration camps American troops had liberated. This switch also happened after GIs became acquainted with the ordeal of destitute Jewish displaced persons—unwanted in most countries. These wartime experiences were etched in GIs' memory and often silenced for fear the experiences would surge again. Like a number of Holocaust survivors, some World War II veterans chose silence as a way of coping with traumatic memories.[16]

## Wartime Lessons

After World War II, former Jewish servicemen and servicewomen used their wartime experiences to help their fellow Americans. Such contributions were also a way to start a healing process. Aircraft pilot Betty Haas Pfister lost her pilot brother in a maneuver in the Pacific. Her work to improve safety measures for medical helicopters landing at the hospital in Aspen, Colorado, may have helped her cope with her trauma. Army nurses like Gertrude Shapiro took care of Japanese survivors in Hiroshima in an amazing and selfless fashion with the first medical landing group of Americans, which was sent to treat the injured, about a month after the atomic blast.[17] Captain Alfred Weinstein, a surgeon and former Japanese POW, provided support to poor families of deceased Japanese guards who had been good-hearted. His social impact in Atlanta after the war may be read as a response to the discrimination he experienced during the war. Dr. Weinstein was president emeritus of the Spalding Hospital in Atlanta, which served the African American community. It provided training for African American doctors and nurses. Waging a war against segregation, he established the first integrated waiting room in his private practice in Atlanta. He also founded an award program for African American nurses at Emory University's Henry Grady Hospital, where he was a member of the faculty.[18]

Former fighter pilot Jerry Yellin, who flew in the last bombing mission over Japan, managed to create a viable brotherhood after the war with a Japanese pilot. Other examples of unexpected feelings of brotherhood emerge from firsthand accounts.

In interviews, Nisei veterans—Americans of Japanese descent who were declared enemy aliens and not entitled to serve their country after the Pearl Harbor attack—expressed a feeling of being expendable once drafted. Captain Milton Zaslow, who learned Japanese to feel useful in the war and decipher enemy messages, encountered these second-generation Japanese American soldiers in his military duties. His riveting story reveals the empathy of a Jewish serviceman for these young men who felt unwanted and yet were eager to serve their new country. They risked their lives in Hawaii, the Mariana Islands, and Okinawa with their captain. The Jewish officer expressed admiration for their courage, as they could have been shot by friendly fire if mistaken for the Japanese enemy. His identification with the underdog may have stemmed from a personal experience of discrimination. In the postwar period, Milton Zaslow participated in meetings of the Japanese American Veterans Association (JAVA).

An unexpected encounter between GIs and Japanese natives occurred in 1946 on the bombed-out island of Okinawa. There, Chaplain Moshe Sachs reinterpreted the religious observance of the New Year of the Trees in the universalistic sense of improving the world (*tikkun olam*). Together with his fellow servicemen, he planted trees to rehabilitate the island. High school children from the island took part in this initiative, which the American military enthusiastically approved.

Another cathartic experience stemming from the war can be observed in the life story of boxing champion and decorated war hero Barney Ross. Ross suffered from addiction to morphine, and later heroin, administered to soothe the pain from his wartime wounds. After the war, he took on the responsibility of educating high school students about the dangers of drug addiction. The examples of brotherhood, helpfulness, and patriotism in this book make the case for the symbiosis between Jewish and American values, which have a common aspiration to improve the world. When families release more letters and notebooks of American service members to Jewish historical societies, researchers will be able to expand on the insights discussed in the present volume related to the role of gender, anti-Jewish attitudes, and patriotism during World War II.

Anti-fascist artist Arthur Szyk suggested that a transformation of American Jewish self-representation took place during World War II; Jewish service members—wherever they served—had gained new self-confidence. In 1943, several of Arthur Szyk's illustrations of Jewish heroes were exhibited in United Service Organizations (USO) venues for recreational activities put on by the USO for the men and women in the American military. The artist's works capture the wartime transformation that gradually changed servicemen's ideas of themselves as Jews. A lithograph made in New York in 1943 is entitled *If We Don't Destroy That Team We Are Doomed*. The title accounts for the perspective of Joseph Goebels, the German propaganda minister, who is seen sweating at the prospect of facing the combined forces of the Irish and the Jews. The artist dedicated this work "to the immortal team of Kelly's and Levin's, the very might of the nation," epitomizing the powerful and popular story of partnership between the Presbyterian pilot Colin Kelly and the Jewish bombardier Meyer (Mike) Levin.[19]

Significantly, the 1945 film *The House I Live In*—referred to earlier—also made use of the feat of these crewmembers. By telling a wartime story to a group of boys who bullied a schoolmate on account of his Jewish origin, Frank Sinatra conveyed the message that "religion makes no difference." Kelly, the bomber's pilot, and Levin, his Jewish bombardier, were part of the aircraft crew that bombed a Japanese vessel. An American hero, Captain Colin Kelly died while trying to save his crew. Levin became the first American to bomb a Japanese ship, three days after the attack on Pearl Harbor. Sergeant Meyer Levin lost his life after completing sixty combat missions and sinking an enemy ship in the Battle of the Coral Sea. He, too, sacrificed his life to save crewmembers.[20] In *The House I Live In*, the airmen's story remains emblematic of the selflessness and spirit of camaraderie that empowered American Jewish service members. It is significant that the film received a special award for Tolerance Short Subject at the 1945 Oscars and a Golden Globe for Promoting International Tolerance.

Fig. Concl.1 Arthur Szyk, *If We Don't Destroy That Team We Are Doomed*, New York, 1943. Chromolithographic reproduction. This work may have been sponsored by the Jewish War Veterans (JWV). Reproduced with the cooperation of Historicana, Burlingame, CA.

In the dense jungle of the island of Munda, the attendance of high-ranking officers like Admiral Kinkaid, a navy legend, at a Passover celebration on April 8, 1944, proved that Judaism was respected as an American religion.[21] A wartime memoir later captured this mood. The time was Rosh Hashana 1945, the Jewish New Year. A Jewish soldier was on a troopship with over two thousand GIs returning to the United States after the war's end in Europe. Aboard the crowded SS *Sea Robin*, a Protestant chaplain wanted to conduct a Jewish religious service. Once he had found two boys conversant with Jewish rituals, he grabbed the loudspeaker to announce the Jewish services and located a room where service members could observe the High Holy Day with a minimum of disturbance. The non-Jewish soldiers who had to pass through the room made sure they tiptoed their way out. The Protestant chaplain, "wearing a skull cap," delivered a short sermon and read a poem he thought fit for a New Year service. This "thoroughly inspiring religious experience," the serviceman commented, conveyed a "spirit of religious brotherhood." The US military had become a laboratory of religious and social experiments.[22]

Like their male counterparts, young American Jewish women diligently served in the military and earned their place in history. They, too, reclaimed who they already were: Americans at heart. Their accomplishments and sacrifices, both as American service members and as Jews, will remain a source of inspiration for generations to come. War experiences left in their wake the seeds of a brighter new era.

# NOTES

## Introduction

1. Norman Mailer, *The Naked and the Dead* (New York: Rinehart, 1948), 53. The novel is partly based on his war experiences with the 112th Cavalry Regiment during the Philippines campaign.

2. I have closely examined approximately one hundred interviews, testimonies, and memoirs. Of these, fifty-two were essays submitted by GIs to the competition organized by the YIVO Institute for Jewish Research in 1946 on the subject "My Experiences and Observations as a Jew in World War II." These essays are referenced by author along with full details of the Record Group, Box, and Folder numbers. I have compared these personal accounts with interviews I conducted among French-speaking Jews in Algeria, Morocco, and Tunisia who welcomed Jewish GIs into their homes during the North African campaign and with letters from Jewish GIs kept at the National Museum of American Jewish Military History in Washington. These sources have influenced my comparative research method.

3. Primary sources include oral histories and archival material from the Museum of Jewish Heritage in New York, the National Museum of American Jewish Military History, the National World War II Museum in New Orleans, Louisiana, the Library of Congress in Washington, DC (Veterans History Project, American Folklife Center), the William Breman Heritage Museum in Atlanta, Georgia, the United States Holocaust Memorial Museum's Jeff and Toby Herr Oral History Archive in Washington, DC, and the Museum of the Jewish Soldier in Latrun, Israel. The documentary film *GI Jews: Jewish Americans in World War II*, directed by Lisa Ades, 2017, 87 min., also provided interviews.

4. Art Buchwald, *Leaving Home: A Memoir* (New York: G.P. Putnam's Sons, 1993), 174.

5. Ibid.

6. Ibid.

7. Ibid.

8. Deborah Dash Moore, *GI Jews: How World War II Changed a Generation* (Cambridge, MA: Belknap Press of Harvard University Press, 2004).

9. Hasia R. Diner and Beryl Lieff Bendersky, *Her Work Praised Her: A History of Jewish Women in America from Colonial Times to the Present* (New York: Basic Books, 2002).

10. Bebe Koch, for instance, enlisted in the WAVES in 1942 at the age of nineteen. Having heard rumors of Nazi persecution, she was eager to help defeat Germany. Eventually promoted to platoon commander, she became an aide to Rear Admiral Ronald Hopewood. Jewish Women's Archive, https://jwa.org/discover/infocus/military/navy/koch, accessed September 20, 2021. The figure of approximately ten thousand Jewish women enlisted in the US Armed Forces is given in the film *GI Jews*.

11. Martin Sugarman, *Under the Heel of Bushido: Last Voices of the Jewish POWs of the Japanese in the Second World War* (London: Valentine Mitchell, 2014).

12. Jessica Cooperman, *Making Judaism Safe for America: World War I and the Origins of Religious Pluralism* (New York: New York University Press, 2018).

13. Derek J. Penslar, *Jews and the Military: A History* (Princeton, NJ: Princeton University Press, 2013).

14. Ibid., 207.

15. Joseph W. Bendersky, *The "Jewish Threat": Anti-Semitic Politics of the U.S. Army* (New York: Basic Books, 2000). Bendersky's study sheds light on anti-Jewish policies from the turn of the twentieth century to the decades after World War II.

16. Jonathan D. Sarna, *American Judaism: A History* (New Haven, CT: Yale University Press, 2004), 273.

17. Ibid.

18. Conversation with Breuer's daughter, Heddy Abramovitz, Jerusalem, May 28, 2018. Assigned in France to the unit of intelligence reconnaissance, Breuer later participated in the liberation of the Buchenwald concentration camp. See Breuer's interview, Jeff and Toby Herr Oral History Archive, United States Holocaust Memorial Museum, https://collections.ushmm.org/search/catalog/irn513303, accessed September 19, 2021.

19. Atlanta-born Rabbi David Geffen, a friend of David Macarov, kindly gave me the electronic file of the self-published memoir that Macarov intended for his family, "A Small Cog: Tales from My Two Wars" (manuscript in possession of the author, Israel, 2014).

20. Philip Bernstein, *Rabbis at War: The CANRA Story* (Waltham, MA: American Jewish Historical Society, 1971), 33.

21. Ibid., 1.

22. National Jewish Welfare Board-Bureau of War Records, Box 197, Overseas, North Africa, 1942–1943, Folder 14, letter dated November 15, 1942, American Jewish Historical Society, Center for Jewish History, New York.

23. Menachem Butler, "The Flying Rabbi: Chaplain Werfel (1916–1943)," *Commentator*, May 11, 2004, 20.

24. Historian Alex Grobman emphasizes that after the war, no other country permitted their chaplains to assist Jewish displaced persons in camps in the American zones of Germany and Austria. Jewish American chaplains helped Holocaust survivors in their struggle to emigrate and efforts to reclaim their rights as free human beings. However, such activities were considered illegal by the military. See Alex Grobman, *Rekindling the Flame: American Jewish Chaplains and the Survivors of European Jewry, 1944–1948* (Detroit: Wayne State University Press, 1993). On American Jewish chaplains who sought out Jewish survivors and interacted with the French communities they helped to rebuild, see Laura Hobson Faure, *A "Jewish Marshall Plan": The American Presence in Post-Holocaust France* (Bloomington: Indiana University Press, 2022). See also Françoise S. Ouzan, "American Jewish Chaplains and the Survivors' Return to Jewish Communal Life (1945–1952)," in *Postwar Jewish Displacement and Rebirth, 1945–1967*, ed. Françoise S. Ouzan and Manfred Gerstenfeld (Leiden: Brill, 2014), 112–36.

25. The sources and computations for these conclusions are explained in Isidor Kaufman, *American Jews in World War II: The Story of 550,000 Fighters for Freedom*, vol. 2 (New York: Dial Press, 1947), 25, 26. On page 25, table II provides a distribution of Jewish servicemen by branches. The next page offers an estimation of casualties and awards, as reflected by data processed up to July 1, 1946, except for deaths which have been processed up to January 1947. Distinguished Flying Crosses (2,391) and Air Medals (16,068) confirm the significant presence of Jews among fliers. In addition, there are Distinguished Service Crosses (74), Navy Crosses (37), Navy and Corps Medals (30), Distinguished Service Medals (47), Legion of Merit Awards (344), Soldiers' Medals (222), Silver Stars (1,627), and Bronze Stars (6,090). "Of the 80 percent who were in the Army, one sixth were in the Infantry, one twelfth were in other ground forces

units, nearly three out of ten were in the Air Forces, and of these, almost one forth was flying personnel." See Louis Kraft, "Servicemen and Veterans," *American Jewish Year Book* 48 (1946–1947): 166. A study made late in 1943 and early in 1944 covering Jewish communities all over the United States revealed that about sixty percent of all Jewish physicians under the age of forty-five enlisted in the American military. See Samuel Calmin Kohs, "Jewish War Records of World War II," *American Jewish Year Book* 47 (1945–1946), 166. S. C. Kohs, a noted sociologist, was the director of the Bureau of War Records of the National Jewish Welfare Board.

26. Penslar, *Jews and the Military*, 207. As Penslar emphasizes, many continued to serve in the Polish armies in exile under British or Soviet command.

27. On Lidiya Litvyak, see Bill Yenne, *The White Rose of Stalingrad: The Real-Life Adventure of Lidiya Vladimirovna Litvyak, the Highest Scoring Female Ace of All Time* (Long Island City, NY: Osprey, 2013).

28. Leonid Smilovitsky collected letters of Jewish soldiers in the Red Army in the framework of the project on Jewish Soldiers in World War II of the Goldstein-Goren Diaspora Research Center of Tel Aviv University. In a symposium organized by the center in 2017, he noted that the emotions felt by Jews serving in the Red Army were different from those of non-Jewish soldiers. He pinpointed that when one Jew did not behave properly in the military, many Jews were stigmatized. Like American soldiers, numerous Jews in the Red Army concealed the fact they were Jewish. It is generally estimated that at least two hundred thousand of the more than five hundred thousand Jewish soldiers in the Red Army died during World War II. See the number of decorations and statistics provided by the Museum of the Jewish Soldier in Latrun, Israel: http://www.jwmww2.org/USSR_arena, accessed March 23, 2020.

29. Yitzhak Arad, *In the Shadow of the Red Banner: Soviet Jews in the War against Nazi Germany* (Jerusalem: Gefen, 2010), 24.

30. Ibid., 10. See also a synthetic analysis by Gabriel Mayer, whose archival findings illustrate this issue in Gabriel Mayer, "Holocaust and WWII: Jews in the Red Army," *International Journal of Social Science Studies* 3, no. 2 (January 2015): 113. Mayer argues that this aspect of Jewish heroism, which has become part of the mainstream cultural narrative of Jews from the Soviet Union, shaped their Jewish identity.

31. See https://www.ordredelaliberation.fr/fr/compagnons/andre-zirnheld, accessed March 8, 2020. See also https://frblogs.timesofisrael.com/les-parachutistes-juifs-de-la-france-libre/, accessed March 9, 2020, by François Heilbronn, whose uncle was a distinguished paratrooper. The translated text of *The Prayer of the Paratrooper* may be read online: http://airborneassociation.com/e/about/prayer.html, accessed March 8, 2020.

32. Testimony of Woolf Marmot at a workshop initiated by the Goren-Goldstein Diaspora Research Center in Tel Aviv University entitled "Les Combattants Juifs de la Seconde Guerre Mondiale," May 19, 2016. On Jewish participation in the Allied forces in World War II, see Penslar, *Jews and the Military*, 207–14.

## 1. "True to My God, True to My Country"

1. Joseph George Fredman and Louis A. Falk, *Jews in American Wars* (Washington, DC: Jewish Veterans of the United States of America, 1954), 99. The authors are both veterans of World War I. Although estimates of the Jewish participation in World War I may vary, the National Museum of American Jewish Military History, created in 1958 under the auspices of the Jewish War Veterans of the USA, provides the figure of two hundred and twenty-five thousand Jews who served in all the branches of the American military. https://nmajmh.org/stories/over-there-profiles-of-american-jews-in-world-wwi/, accessed June 13, 2023.

2. Moore, *GI Jews*, 263. This is one of the main arguments of Moore's important research.

3. Bernard Branson, "I Wanted These Sons of Bitches to Know," in *Ours to Fight For: American Jewish Voices from the Second World War*, ed. J. M. Eidelman (New York: Museum of Jewish Heritage–Living Memorial to the Holocaust, 2003), 17.

4. Arthur Buchwald Collection (AFC/2001/001/24003), Veterans History Project at the American Folklife Center, Library of Congress.

5. Ibid.

6. Buchwald, *Leaving Home*, 168.

7. Ibid., 177.

8. Ibid., 196.

9. Maximilian Lerner, "I Wanted to Get My Own Back," in Eidelman, *Ours to Fight For*, 68.

10. Ibid., 69.

11. Kathryn Lang-Slattery, *Immigrant Soldier: The Story of a Ritchie Boy*, with a foreword by Guy Stern (Laguna Beach, CA: Pacific Bookworks, 2014), 3. Werner T. Angress, *Witness to the Storm, A Jewish Journey from Nazi Berlin to the 82nd Airborne, 1920–1945* (Bloomington: Indiana University Press, 2019), a posthumous memoir first published in 2012.

12. "Oral History Interview with Manfred Steinfeld," Jeff and Toby Herr Oral History Archive, United States Holocaust Memorial Museum, https://collections.ushmm.org/search/catalog/irn507500, accessed October 10, 2021. An American liberator, Steinfeld found that his mother and sister had been murdered by the Nazis in a concentration camp. He arrested a former concentration camp administrator after the end of the war.

13. Herman J. Obermayer, *Soldiering for Freedom: A GI's Account of World War II* (College Station: Texas A&M University Press, 2005), 63. A large proportion of the over 550,000 Jews who served in the US forces reached the European continent.

14. Fredman and Falk, *Jews in American Wars*, 121.

15. Ibid., 216–17.

16. Ibid., 115.

17. Lee J. Levinger, *A Jewish Chaplain in France* (New York: Macmillan, 1922), 120.

18. Bruce H. Wolk, *Jewish Aviators in World War II: Personal Narratives of American Men and Women* (Jefferson, NC: McFarland, 2016), 203n2.

19. *Jewish Veteran*, 10–12 (December 1942): 11. See also William Starr Myers, *Prominent Families of New Jersey* (Baltimore, MD: Genealogical, 2000), 1:638.

20. Jeanne Zamaloff Dworkin, "I Am Not Going to Stand by and Let Him Do It," in Eidelman, *Ours to Fight For*, 33. Zamaloff Dworkin added that her mother's family in Poland was eventually "wiped out," while most of her father's in Russia was saved.

21. Ibid., 34–35.

22. Bea Abrams Hirshcovici Cohen Collection (AFC/2001/00/86629), Veterans History Project, American Folklife Center, Library of Congress. A short interview with Bea Abrams Cohen also appears in *GI Jews: Jewish Americans in World War II*, documentary film directed by Lisa Ades, 2017, 87 min. Bea Abrams Cohen died in 2015 at the age of 105, the oldest female veteran in California.

23. Ibid.

24. Testimony of Selma Cronan (2000.A.116), oral history, tape one, Museum of Jewish Heritage, New York. The passage in the *mezuzah* begins with "Shema Israel" (Hear O' Israel), which has become a motto of the Jewish people, a sign of belonging as well as an emotional cry. The scroll is traditionally mounted on the doorpost of a Jewish home to symbolize commitment to Jewish ideals and values.

25. Ibid.

26. Material for Annual Report of CG/AAF to Secretary of War. AC/AS, OCR, Requirements Division (Asst. for Air Forces), November 25, 1944, Archives of D. D. Eisenhower, Eisenhower Library, Military Era, World War II, Abilene, Kansas.

27. Ibid. African American women were not allowed to participate in the WASP program. Only two Chinese American women were accepted.

28. Ibid.

29. Diner and Benderly, *Her Works Praise Her*, 331.
30. Sandor B. Cohen, curator, *Women in the Military: A Jewish Perspective*, with an introduction by Harvey S. Friedman and Judith Weiss Cohen (Washington, DC: National Museum of American Jewish Military History, 1999), 24.
31. Ibid., 22.
32. Ibid., 21.
33. Ibid.
34. See "Veterans' Testimonies/Veteran Testimony—Ellan J. Levitsky and Dorothy Levitsky," https://www.med-dept.com/veterans-testimonies/veterans-testimony-ellan-j-levitsky-dorothy-f-levitsky/, accessed February 28, 2020. The Levitsky sisters were sent together to Normandy. See also https://www.defense.gov/observe/photo-gallery/igphoto/2001129317/, accessed February 28, 2020.
35. Cohen, *Women in the Military*, 44–45.
36. Joanne Wallace Orr, "An Oral History, Women, Airforce Service Pilots," interview by Jean Hascall Cole, *The Woman's Collection*, Texas Woman's University, 2004, 46.
37. S. C. Kohs, "Jewish War Records of World War II," *American Jewish Year Book* 47, no. 5706 (1945–46): 165.
38. Benedict Solomon Alper, *Love and Politics in Wartime: Letters to My Wife, 1943–45*, selected and edited by Joan Wallach Scott (Urbana: University of Illinois Press, 1992), 21.
39. Michael Berenbaum, "Arthur Szyk: The Artist as Soldier, the Artist as Messenger," in *Arthur Szyk, Soldier in Art*, ed. David Ungar (Burlingame, CA: Historicana, 2017), 61–81.
40. Ibid., 78.
41. Wolk, *Jewish Aviators in World War II*, 172–73.
42. Ibid., 25. Abe stands for Abraham.

## 2. Invisibility of Jews in the Military?

1. Branson, "I Wanted These Sons of Bitches to Know," 22. The tail gunner on a B-24 provides an example of zeal, as discovered in this chapter.
2. Leonard Dinnerstein, *Antisemitism in America* (New York: Oxford University Press, 1994), 131.
3. Kirk Douglas, *The Ragman's Son: An Autobiography* (New York: Simon and Schuster, 1988), 59.
4. Ibid., 78. A symbol of endurance and a friend of Israel, the Hollywood icon died at the age of 103 on February 5, 2020. A photo in his memoirs captures the moment when he shook hands with Israeli prime minister Golda Meir. His wife, Anne Buydens, converted to Judaism when they renewed their wedding vows in 2004.
5. Ibid., 383.
6. Ibid., 47.
7. Ibid., 383.
8. Testimony of Ruth Cohen (1999.V.50), oral history, tape one, Museum of Jewish Heritage–Living Memorial to the Holocaust.
9. Testimony of Selma Cronan, tape one. She was given a military discharge while at the base of Avenger Field but refused to accept an interruption of her service that was not justified in her eyes and won her appeal.
10. Testimony of Selma Cronan. 2000. A.116, tape one, Museum of Jewish Heritage.
11. Hank Greenberg, *Hank Greenberg: The Story of My Life*, ed. with an introduction by Ira Berkow (New York: Times Books, 1989), 159.
12. John Rosengren, *Hank Greenberg: The Hero of Heroes* (New York: New American Library, 2013), 230.
13. Ibid., 235–50.

14. Greenberg, *Hank Greenberg*, 256. Greenberg noted a link between his secularity and the fact his parents, who both understood Hebrew, did not find the time to teach him the language of the prayers. He died of cancer on September 4, 1986, before he could finish his autobiography, later completed by journalist Ira Berkow. He was the first Jewish ballplayer elected to the Baseball Hall of Fame (1956).

15. Ibid., 257.

16. Ibid.

17. Ibid., 255.

18. Wolk, *Jewish Aviators in World War II*, 23.

19. Ibid., 25–26.

20. Joanne Wallace Orr, interview by Jean Hascall Cole.46. For Jean Hascall Cole's book based on interviews with her fellow WASP, see Jean Hascall Cole, *Women Pilots of World War II* (Salt Lake City: University of Utah Press, 1992).

21. Berenice Falk Haydu, *Letters Home 1944–1945: Women Airforce Service Pilots, World War II*, ed. Rita Cody Casey, foreword by Sally Van Wagenen Keil (Riviera Beach, FL: TopLine, 2003), 27.

22. Baumgarten's interview can be found in the digital collections of the National WWII Museum in New Orleans, https://www.youtube.com/watch?v=UWnPWbx-sXo&ab_channel=TheNationalWWIIMuseum, accessed August 30, 2021.

23. "Farewell to Dr. Harold 'Hal' Baumgarten, D-Day Survivor and Friend of the National WWII Museum," http://www.nww2m.com/2016/12/farewell-to-dr-harold-hal-baumgarten-d-day-survivor-and-friend-of-the-national-wwii-museum/, accessed August 30, 2021. See also Harold Baumgarten, *D-Day Survivor, An Autobiography* (New Orleans: Pelican, 2006).

24. Branson, "I Wanted These Sons of Bitches to Know," 18.

25. Ibid., 18–19.

26. Ibid., 22.

27. Ibid.

28. Ibid.

29. Dinnerstein, *Antisemitism in America*, 126.

30. The popularity of antisemitic demagogues and hate organizations is developed in ibid., 122, 134.

31. In print on June 22, 1994, Section A, page 20 of the National Edition of the *New York Times* with the headline "In World War II, Many Jewish G.I.s Left Religion Off Dog Tags," quoted in Akiva Males, "Jewish GIs and Their Dog Tags," *Hakira: The Flatbush Journal of Jewish Law and Thought* 15 (2003): 275, http://www.hakirah.org/Vol15Males.pdf, accessed April 6, 2020. Males points out the fact that Lippman and many Jewish combat soldiers had no religious preference stamped on their metal identification tag to explain why there are fewer Stars of David in military cemeteries than there should be. Consequently, an estimation of over 600,000 Jewish servicemen and women is likely more accurate than the figure of over 500,000 Jews in World War II usually mentioned.

32. https://www.nytimes.com/1994/06/22/opinion/l-in-world-war-ii-many-jewish-gi-s-left-religion-off-dog-tags-470333.html.

33. Edward T. Sandrow, "Jews in the Army—A Short Social Study," *Reconstructionist*, March 17, 1944, 12.

34. Harold U. Ribalow (pseudonym Meyer Cherniak), Memoirs of American Jewish Soldiers, 1944–1946, YIVO Institute for Jewish Research, RG 110, Box 1, Folder 7, 13.

35. Ibid., 14.

36. Ibid. Often transliterated "Ein Keloheinu," this verse of daily sung prayer means "There is none like our Lord." *Sh'ma* refers to the prayer "Shema Israel" (Hear O' Israel), recited twice a day, morning and night. It is an emotional cry of the Jewish people as well as a commitment to Jewish values and ideals.

37. Jack Scharf, "I Just Couldn't Face It," in Eidelman, *Ours to Fight For*, 90. The complete Hebrew verse is "Baruch Atah A-donay, Eloneinu Melech Ha'Olam borei pri hagofen," uttered to pronounce the blessing on wine and grape, meaning "Blessed are you Lord our God, King of the Universe, Who Creates the fruit of the vine."

38. Ibid., 94.

39. Ibid., 95–96. Over a month before the German surrender, The Rainbow *Haggadah* was printed in Germany by Chaplain Eli Bohnen and his assistant Eli Heimberg for the Passover seder in Dahn. This was the first *Haggadah* printed on German soil since the rise of Hitler. A copy is in the National Museum of American Jewish Military History in Washington. It can be seen here: https://nmajmh.org/2016/04/three-fascinating-world-war-ii-haggadot/, accessed April 12, 2020.

40. Sandrow, "Jews in the Army," 13.

41. Morris Rubin, Memoirs of American Jewish Soldiers, 1944–1946, YIVO Institute for Jewish Research, RG 110, Box 1, Folder 21, 3.

42. Ibid., 4. Jewish chaplains themselves had to be checked for possible subversion, as Jewish GIs were sometimes equated with communism, especially when recent immigrants. Jewish displaced persons seeking admission to the United States after the Nazi genocide of the Jews were often perceived as communists by both public opinion and members of Congress.

43. Ibid.

44. Sandrow, "Jews in the Army," 13.

45. Arthur Hertzberg, *A Jew in America: My Life and a People's Struggle for Identity* (San Francisco: HarperOne, 2002), 260. In the European theater, Major General Maurice Rose, who fought heroically in World War I and World War II, received over fifteen medals and awards, including the Distinguished Service Cross. After his death in March 1945, the Jewishness of General Rose, the son and grandson of Polish rabbis, was questioned. His records indicated P for Protestant, but no record was found of a religious conversion. The American military later replaced the initial Jewish marking on his grave in the Netherlands American Cemetery and Memorial in Margraten, Limburg, by a cross. His example is significant because Jewish officers often concealed their Jewish identity to avoid preventing promotion.

46. Martin Silverman, "The Lord Would Provide," in Eidelman, *Ours to Fight For*, 123.

47. Ibid., 116.

48. Preface to *Prayer Book, Abridged for Jews in the Armed Forces of the United States* (New York: National Jewish Welfare Board, 1941, 1943), iv.

49. Bernstein, *Rabbis at War*, 33. A decade ago, "Operation Benjamin," whose adviser is Rabbi Professor Jacob Schacter, strove to rectify cases of incorrect gravestones in military cemeteries. This nonprofit organization manned by volunteers is working to uncover erroneous headstones and obtain authorization from the American Battle Monuments Commission (ABMC) to rededicate the headstones. The first headstone change occurred on June 20, 2018. So far, more than twenty American soldiers mistakenly buried under Latin crosses have been identified as Jews, and their headstones have been replaced by a Star of David. See https://www.operationbenjamin.org/our-soldiers, accessed July 19, 2023.

50. Ibid., 34.

51. Ibid., preface. Yet the figure of 550,000 is provided by war correspondent I. Kaufman right from the subtitle of his book. His sources were the war records published in Kohs, "Jewish War Records," 153–72. Due to the reasons quoted earlier about the invisibility of Jews in the American military, the figure of 600,000 may be more plausible.

52. *GI Jews* (film).

53. American Jewish Committee Archives, "First Broadcast of Jewish Religious Service from Nazi Germany," under the auspices of the American Jewish Committee (AJC). American forces fought fiercely in Aachen, the first German city to be captured by Allied forces. http://www.ajcarchives.org/AJC_DATA/Files/RD40.pdf, accessed September 27, 2021.

54. It is interesting to mention Eleanor Roosevelt's words about women pilots in 1942: "This is not a time when women should be patient. We are in a war and we need to fight it with all our ability and every weapon possible. Women pilots, in this particular case, are a weapon waiting to be used." Wings across America, http://www.wingsacrossamerica.us/wasp/, accessed April 23, 2020.

### 3. Heroines Took to the Skies

1. Haydu, *Letters Home*, 102.
2. Cohen, *Women in the Military*, Kindle ed., location 406 of 934.
3. The recruiting poster for the Marine Corps Women's Reserve read "Be a Marine, Free a Marine to Fight."
4. Cohen, *Women in the Military*, Kindle ed., location 392 of 934. Ironically, medics on the battlefield did not usually carry weapons.
5. Wolk, *Jewish Aviators in World War II*, 24.
6. My own copy of Haydu, *Letters Home* bears the hand-written dedication "Always blue skies, Bee."
7. Ibid., 4.
8. Ibid., 5.
9. Ibid., 7–8.
10. Testimony of Bernice Falk Haydu (2000.A.197), oral history, tape one, Museum of Jewish Heritage–Living Memorial to the Holocaust, New York.
11. Ibid.
12. Haydu, *Letters Home*, 16.
13. Ibid., 17.
14. Ibid., 18–19.
15. Ibid., 30 (emphasis mine). This quote reveals an assertion of Jewish identity when an attempt to conceal it for smoother integration into the group of trainees could have been expected. However, there may at times have been an ambivalence, manifested in a desire "to keep quiet," as Bernice Falk had in her previous jobs.
16. Ibid., 31. In her interview, she also mentioned that the girls talked about religion but that there was no antisemitism. Testimony of Bernice Falk Haydu, tape one.
17. Haydu, *Letters Home*, 52. Link trainers and simulators are obsolete nowadays.
18. Ibid., 51.
19. Testimony of Bernice Falk Haydu, tape two.
20. Haydu, *Letters Home*, 52.
21. Ibid., 55.
22. Cole, *Women Pilots of World War II*, dedication page. The author, a woman pilot, dedicates her book to the memory of Betty Stine, Mary Mitchell Robinson, and Susan Clarke, who belonged to her class (44-W-2). Some of these tragedies, the author highlights, may have resulted from sabotaged aircrafts. On Betty Stine, see ibid., 1, 67, 70. Her parents had to come to the base and retrieve the body of their only child, at their own expense, without military honors, since only in 1977 were the WASP granted retroactive military status.
23. Ibid., 113, quoting the testimony of another woman pilot, Leona Golbinec. On sabotaged planes, see ibid., 41, 45, 107, 113–14, 115–16.
24. Ibid., 69.
25. Testimony of Bernice Falk Haydu, tape two.
26. Haydu, *Letters Home*, 51.
27. Ibid., 75.
28. Ibid., 86.
29. Ibid., 92.

30. Testimony of Bernice Falk Haydu, tape two. Haydu was asked if WASP were issued dog tags and if hers bore an H for Hebrew. Unlike all her military decorations and gabardine uniform, she did not recall where her dog tags were but assumed they had an H on them. She wore her "good conduct" medal, medals indicating the American theater and victory, and the WASP insignia on her authentic navy-blue uniform with a white shirt and black tie during the video interview.

31. Ibid.

32. Quoted by Haydu, *Letters Home*, 156.

33. Cohen, *Women in the Military*, Kindle ed., location 561 of 934.

34. Testimony of Selma Cronan, end of tape one and tape 2. Maryse Bastié set numerous international records for female aviators during the thirties. Although her husband, a World War I pilot, was killed in a plane crash, she did aerobatics to make ends meet and continued with dangerous maneuvers to purchase her own aircraft. During World War II, she volunteered for the Croix Rouge. After suffering an arm injury during the war, she could no longer fly as a pilot. She died in 1952 when the aircraft on which she was a passenger crashed during takeoff on her way to attend a conference on aviation in Lyon, France.

35. See photo, *Washington Post*, June 8, 1990.

36. Major Marc R. Henderson, CAP, "Flying through the Glass Ceiling," *National Historical Journal* (July–December 2020): 24–25.

37. See chapter 1 of the present volume.

38. Deb Smith, "Love at First Flight: Former WASP Still Living Life at Full Throttle," *Airport Journals*, http://airportjournals.com/love-at-first-flight-former-wasp-still-living-life-at-full-throttle/, accessed May 10, 2020, 2.

39. Ibid.

40. Ibid., 3.

41. Ibid. Another source mentions the waters of the Pacific as the place of the accident.

42. Ibid., 4.

43. Ibid. See also Cole, *Women Pilots of World War II*, 116.

44. Cole, *Women Pilots of World War II*, 116.

45. Smith, "Love at First Flight," 4.

46. Ibid.

47. Ibid., 6. See her interview at the end of the YouTube video about her life and achievements: https://www.youtube.com/watch?v=eZN50SIzNow, accessed May 10, 2020. Rumor has it that records of the WASP were classified for some thirty-five years, but this is difficult to prove.

48. See chapter 5 of this book.

49. "Winged Angels," https://www.nationalmuseum.af.mil/Visit/Museum-Exhibits/Fact-Sheets/Display/Article/196161/winged-angels-usaaf-flight-nurses-in-wwii/, accessed May 30, 2023.

50. *The US Army Nurse in World War II* (1944), War Department, Army Pictorial Service, Signal Corps.

51. Ibid.

52. Judith Barger, *Beyond the Call of Duty: Army Flight Nursing in World War II* (Kent, OH: Kent State University Press, 2013). See blurb of the book for this figure. The author served as a flight nurse in the US Air Force on Clark Air Base in the Philippines in the 1970s.

53. "Winged Angels."

54. Cohen, *Women in the Military*, Kindle ed., location 390 of 934.

55. Ibid.

56. Ibid.

57. See entry for Etta Moskowitz Rosenthal in https://archive.org/stream/TheStoryOfAirEvacuation/TheStoryOfAirEvacuation_djvu.txt, accessed May 18, 2020.

58. On March 12, 1945, apparently in the same attack, Sergeant John E. Brand, a Jewish radio operator on a B-24 Liberator in the Twenty-Third Bomb Squadron, was declared missing before being listed as killed. He, too, received the Purple Heart. His aircraft, *Maiden Montana*, was one of six Twenty-Third Bomb Squadron Liberators given the mission of bombing Japanese positions at Mindanao Island. See "Soldiers from New York: Jewish Soldiers" in the *New York Times*, in "World War II: Sergeant John E. Brand-March 12, 1945," http://theyweresoldiers.com/index.php/2017/05/14/soldiers-from-new-york-jewish-soldiers-in-the-new-york-times-in-world-war-two-john-e-brand/, accessed May 19, 2020.

59. Gary Zaetz, "Pentagon Has Forgotten America's Heroic MIA Women of World War Two," Facebook, November 21, 2017. The author has researched numerous occurrences of air crashes and servicewomen missing in action and details the known circumstances, offering speculations on the possible causes of the crash.

60. Kaufman, *American Jews in World War II*, 1:49.

61. "Beatrice H. Memler," https://www.honorstates.org/index.php?id=351408, accessed May 18, 2020.

62. Cohen, *Women in the Military*, Kindle ed., location 538–44 of 934.

63. William L. O'Neill, "Race, Ethnicity, and Religion in World War II," in Eidelman, *Ours to Fight For*, 114.

64. Dwight D. Eisenhower, *Crusade in Europe* (New York: Doubleday, 1948), 132–33.

65. Ibid., 133. As part of the WAC, the daughter of Governor Herbert R. Lehman, Private Hilda Jane De Vadetzki, was on duty in Algiers. The noted governor lost a son, Lieutenant Peter Lehman, who performed fifty-seven combat missions against occupied Europe.

66. Interview with Ellan Levitsky Orkin, *GI Jews* (film).

## 4. Confronting Biased Attitudes

1. Solomon Grayzel, "A Chronicle of Our Generation," in *Two Generations in Perspective: Notable Events and Trends 1896–1956*, ed. Harry Schneiderman (New York: Monde, 1957), 50.

2. Eliot Blin, Memoirs of American Jewish Soldiers, 1944–1946, YIVO Institute for Jewish Research, RG 110, Box 1, Folder 9, 13.

3. Dinnerstein, *Antisemitism in America*, 127.

4. "Jerry's Message to America," Spiritof45.org, http://www.spiritof45.org/jerry_yellin_message_to_america.aspx, accessed June 29, 2020.

5. Michael Rugel, "Remembering Captain Jerry Yellin," National Museum of American Jewish Military History, January 10, 2018, https://nmajmh.org/2018/01/remembering-captain-jerry-yellin/, accessed July 16, 2020.

6. Don Brown, *The Last Fighter Pilot: The True Story of the Final Combat Mission of World War II*, with forewords by Captain Jerry Yellin and Melanie Stone (Washington, DC: Regnery History, 2017), xvii.

7. Ibid.

8. Ibid., xx–xxi.

9. Ibid., xx.

10. "It was street language, some street language plus some antisemitic remark to me, which resulted, whenever I heard it, into a fight"; Burton Roberts, "Oh, the Great Speckled Bird," in Eidelman, *Ours to Fight For*, 51.

11. Buchwald, *Leaving Home*, 174.

12. Wolk, *Jewish Aviators in World War II*, 19–20.

13. Leonard Dinnerstein, *The Leo Frank Case*, rev. ed. (Athens: University of Georgia Press, 2008); Steve Oney, *And the Dead Shall Rise: The Murder of Mary Phagan and the Lynching of Leo Frank* (New York: Pantheon, 2003).

14. David Macarov, "Small Cog: Tales from My Two Wars," manuscript in possession of the author (Israel, 2014); David Macarov, "Atlantan Led Air Force's Coded Communications,"

*Jewish Times*, April 12, 2018, https://atlantajewishtimes.timesofisrael.com/atlantan-led-air-forces-coded-communications/, accessed July 10, 2020.

15. See, for instance, "It's Your Job to Fight: Antisemitic American Cartoon, 1944," a cartoon aimed at dissuading American soldiers from fighting instead of "the Jews and Wall Street." Tracts américains antisémites et / ou anti-bolcheviques, T9-D-3, Centre de Documentation Juive Contemporaine (CDJC), Paris.

16. Macarov, "Small Cog," 57. Jew hatred was ingrained in the 1920s. A newspaper published by automaker Henry Ford, the *Dearborn Independent*, was bent on describing an international Jewish conspiracy that originated in the notorious anti-Jewish forgery known as "The Protocols of the Elders of Zion." See Neil Baldwin, *Henry Ford and the Jews: The Mass Production of Hate* (New York: PublicAffairs, 2001). On how Ivy League universities drastically limited the number of Jewish students (and also African Americans, women, and minorities) by using quotas, see Jerome Karabel, *The Chosen: The Hidden History of Admission and Exclusion at Harvard, Yale, and Princeton* (Boston: Houghton Mifflin Harcourt, 2005).

17. Moore, *GI Jews*, 134. The author notes the case of two Jewish soldiers who were ordered by their commanding officer to lead the religious ritual of Passover before boarding a troopship heading for the Marianas, as supplies from the National Jewish Welfare Board (JWB) had been received. This experience implemented and legitimized the "Judeo-Christian Tradition," emphasizes Moore. It was forced on the two non-Orthodox servicemen, who were reluctant to be singled out to conduct a Passover seder that "would interfere with nightly poker games."

18. Sergeant Rosen's letter demonstrates that Jews were aware of the murderous persecution in Germany, which no Jew could ignore in February 1944.

19. Ibid. In the Victory Forest in Palestine, Rosen's name is linked with "the greatest constructive effort of our time." An aviation ordnance man, Sergeant Naurice Rosen's name is not listed (like those of many other Jewish GIs) in Louis Dublin and Samuel Kohs, Isidor Kaufman, *American Jews in World War II*, vol. II (New York: Dial Press, 1947).

20. "In that sense, my father was very much a 1950s American Jew." Author's conversation with Howard Rosen, son of Sergeant Naurice Rosen, Jerusalem, May 27, 2020.

21. Mark A. Raider, *The Emergence of American Zionism* (New York: New York University Press, 1998), 4.

22. *GIs Remember: Liberating the Concentration Camps*, exhibition catalog (Washington, DC: National Museum of American Jewish Military History, n.d.), 46. Interview with Maurice Paper by Mort Horwitz, March 18, 1992, kindly sent to me by Pamela Elbe, director of archives and exhibits, National Museum of American Jewish History, Washington, DC. See Françoise S. Ouzan, "From Algiers to Dachau: the Special Assignments of an American Jewish Officer Ordered by General Eisenhower, 1942–1945," *Moreshet, Journal for the Study of the Holocaust and Antisemitism* 103 (2023), Hebrew, Tel Aviv, published by the Mordechai Anielevich Memorial Holocaust Study and Research Center, 125–41. The English edition of this article is forthcoming in Moreshet Journal (vol. 20).

23. For archival pictures of the destroyer, see http://www.navsource.org/archives/05/674.htm, accessed June 28, 2020.

24. See the preface by Paul N. Shulman to Joseph M. Hochstein and Murray S. Greenfield, *The Jews' Secret Fleet*, introduction by Martin Gilbert (Jerusalem: Gefen, 1987), xiii–xiv. After completing his service in the United States Navy, he was asked by Prime Minister David Ben-Gurion to help the fledgling Israeli state. Although he did not speak Hebrew, Shulman laid the groundwork for the modern Israeli navy, of which he became the first commander at the age of twenty-six. See J. Wandres, *The Ablest Navigator: Lieutenant Paul Shulman, USN, Israel's Volunteer Admiral* (Annapolis: Naval Institute Press, 2010).

25. On the so-called international Jewry, a misconception ingrained at West Point, see Joseph W. Bendersky, *The "Jewish Threat": Anti-Semitic Politics of the U.S. Army* (New York: Basic Books, 2000), 157. On polls, see Charles Herbert Stember et al., *Jews in the Mind of America*,

preface by John Slawson (New York: Basic Books, 1966), 52, 92–93, 98; Louis Barish, ed., *Rabbis in Uniform: The Story of the American Jewish Military Chaplain* (New York: Jonathan David, 1962), 279–80. See also George S. Patton, *The Patton Papers*, compiled and edited by Martin Blumenson, vol. 2, *1940-1945* (Boston: Houghton Mifflin Harcourt, 1974).

26. Penslar, *Jews and the Military*, 230.

27. Ibid., 231. Penslar pinpoints the fact that Marcus was already a national celebrity before World War II. As a deputy commissioner, he had led a 1934 police raid on a penitentiary run by gangsters with Tammany Hall connections; he had "wrestled one of them, the 210-pound Joey Rao, off a barber chair and onto the floor."

28. Zipporah Porath, *Col. David (Mickey) Marcus: "A Soldier for All Humanity"* (New York: American Jewish Historical Society, 2010), 19. This booklet, published by the American Veterans of Israel Legacy Corp in cooperation with the American Jewish Historical Society, is based on interviews conducted on the first anniversary of Marcus's death with those who recruited him and the soldiers who fought alongside him. Zipporah Porath was an American student who came to study at the Hebrew University in 1947 on a one-year program and served as a medic during the siege of Jerusalem and in the fledgling Israel air force. For a biography of Marcus, see Ted Berkman, *Cast a Giant Shadow: The Story of Mickey Marcus Who Died to Save Jerusalem* (New York: Pocket Books, 1962), and the film by the same title with Kirk Douglas as Marcus.

29. Porath, *Col. David (Mickey) Marcus*, 19.

30. Ibid., 17.

31. It is significant that American veteran Herman Wouk dedicated his book *Sailor and Fiddler* both "to the memory of David 'Mickey' Marcus, Colonel, United States Army, volunteered and fell in Israel's War of Independence 1948, interred in West Point Military Cemetery" and to "Ilan Ramon, fighter pilot, Colonel, Israel Defense Forces, volunteer astronaut, United States Space Program, killed in crash of space Shuttle *Columbia*, 2003." In this context, it is meaningful to add that Ilan Ramon (born Ilan Wolfermann), whose mother was a Holocaust survivor, was the first Israeli astronaut. He, too, was an example of extreme bravery and a representative of the Jewish people. He is the only non-American citizen to have received (posthumously) the Congressional Space Medal of Honor, which points to the exemplarity and universality of his mission.

32. Dan Stone, *The Liberation of the Camps: The End of the Holocaust and Its Aftermath* (New Haven, CT: Yale University Press, 2015), 66–67.

33. *GIs Remember*, 38. Harry Zaslow, a nineteen-year-old Jewish soldier who served with the 283rd Field Artillery Battalion and participated in the Battle of the Bulge, accounted for his profound shock and confusion on discovering Dachau four hours after the departure of the Germans. Oral history of H. Zaslow, USHMM, Accession Number: 1997.A.0441.125, RG Number: RG-50.462.0125.

34. Morris Eisenstein in ibid., 36. The empathy displayed by non-Jewish soldiers for the plight of Jews during World War II would not last, however. Replacements who had not seen the concentration camps were unaware of what former Jewish inmates had gone through and treated them roughly, sometimes cruelly, as testified in the Harrison Report (July 1945), written by Earl G. Harrison, US representative to the Intergovernmental Committee on Refugees. Investigating the conditions of displaced persons, the American lawyer depicted a grim picture of the deplorable living conditions of Jews in displaced persons camps and of the lack of understanding by soldiers. Another document, *Army Talk*, issued in 1946, explained to soldiers that "displaced persons are human." *Army Talk* 151, War Department, Washington, DC, November 30, 1946, Historical Reference Branch, US Army Military History Institute, Carlisle, Pennsylvania.

35. Morris Eisenstein in *GIs Remember*, 38.

36. Lou Potter, Williams Miles, and Nina Rosenblum, *Liberators: Fighting on Two Fronts in World War II* (New York: Harcourt, Brace, Jovanovich, 1992), esp. 235 and chaps. 9 and 10. In

1978, under the Carter administration, members of the 761st battalion were presented with the highest military honors.

37. *GIs Remember*, 207.
38. Dinnerstein, *Antisemitism in America*, 137–38.
39. *GI Jews* (film).
40. Abraham J. Klausner, *Shārit ha-plātah* (Jerusalem: Gefen Publishing House, 1945). The chaplain published a list of survivors in five volumes. Reprinted in 2021 by Schoen Books, South Deerfield, MA (Five volumes bound in one). See Dalia Ofer, "Holocaust Survivors as Immigrants: The Case of Israel and the Cyprus Detainees," *Modern Judaism* 16, no. 1 (1996): 1–23. Several American Jewish soldiers married concentration camp survivors, as did coast guard Murray S. Greenfield. After the war, he volunteered to fight for the right of uprooted displaced persons to reach a home in the Jewish homeland in Palestine. Together with 250 North American veterans, he volunteered to participate in illegal immigration. Conversation with the author, Tel Aviv, August 26, 2018. See Hochstein and Greenfield, *Jews' Secret Fleet: The Untold Story of North American Volunteers Who Smashed the British Blockade* (Jerusalem: Gefen Publishing House, 1988, revised ed., 2010).
41. Abraham J. Klausner, *A Letter to My Children from the Edge of the Holocaust* (San Francisco: Holocaust Center of Northern California, 2002). In his memoir, the prominent Jewish chaplain argued that the American military failed to realize the survivors' needs promptly enough. His views are in keeping with the findings of the Harrison Report, published in the Department of State Bulletin on September 30, 1945. See also Grobman, *Rekindling the Flame*, which paved the way for research on Jewish chaplains and soldiers who helped Jewish displaced persons.
42. Preface by Paul Shulman in Hochstein and Greenfield, *Jews' Secret Fleet*, xiv.
43. See Ouzan, "American Jewish Chaplains."
44. Herman Wouk, *Sailor and Fiddler: Reflections of a 100-Year-Old Author* (New York: Simon & Schuster, 2016), Kindle ed., 12–13. Sholom Rabinovitch was the real name of Shalom Aleichem, a central figure of Jewish folk humor.
45. Herman Wouk, *This Is My God* (Garden City, NY: Doubleday, 1959), dedication page.
46. Wouk celebrated Israel's seventh year of independence by dedicating a copy of the Liberty Bell installed in a park in Jerusalem; see Wouk, *Sailor and Fiddler*, Kindle ed., 98, location 895.
47. Wouk, *This Is My God*, 123.
48. These will be developed in chapter 6.
49. Moses Kligsberg, "'American Jewish Soldiers on Jews and Judaism': A Report of a Contest," *YIVO Annual of Jewish Social Science* 5 (1950): 256.
50. Ibid., 11n.
51. *GI Jews* (film).
52. Bendersky, *"Jewish Threat,"* 38–39.
53. Moore, *GI Jews*, 152. The author refers on this point to Albert I. Slomovitz, *The Fighting Rabbis: Jewish Military Chaplains and American History* (New York: New York University Press, 1999), 100–101. Marc Saperstein, ed., *Jewish Preaching in Times of War, 1800–2001* (Oxford: Littman Library of Jewish Civilization, 2008), 484.
54. Moore, *GI Jews*, 69.
55. This will be illustrated in the next chapter.
56. Kevin L. Walters, "Beyond the Battle: Religion and American Troops in World War II" (PhD diss., University of Kentucky, 2013), 203.
57. Wolk, *Jewish Aviators in World War II*, 28. One consequence of negative perceptions of Jews was that some fliers were not awarded the Distinguished Flying Cross they were entitled to receive for leading a mission. Although this was frustrating, with much regret, many did not complain. By contrast, Arthur Toppston—a technical sergeant with the Eighth Air Force

(radio operator and gunner on a B24), in which most navigators were Jewish—did complain to his pilot, who was a captain, about his withheld commendation. The captain confronted the anti-Jewish master sergeant who had held up the commendations, and the Distinguished Flying Cross was restored to the Jewish airman; ibid., 27.

58. Ernest Stock (pseudonym Eliezer), Memoirs of American Jewish Soldiers, 1944–1946, YIVO Institute for Jewish Research, RG 110, Box 1, Folder 29, 7. A month after the "Crystal Night" in November 1938, Ernest Stock's mother sent him with his younger sister on a Kindertransport to seek refuge in Alsace, France. In June 1940, the teenagers fled before the invading German army and crossed Spain and Portugal. They eventually reached the United States and joined their mother who had immigrated there.

59. Ibid.

60. His Jewishness reemerged with military service: "There is unquestionably a basis to the oft-heard statement that men in the army find refuge in religion, attend the Post Chapel with more enthusiasm and regularity than they ever pilgrimed to their home-town house of prayer," ibid., 1. Stock, who was drafted into the American Army in May 1943, became an American citizen after basic training.

61. Ibid. Stock was in Frankfort as an American soldier in 1945. The US Army gave him permission to search for his father in Holland.

62. Many Jewish refugees from Germany immigrated in the late 1930s. Eager to enlist in the American military, they saw action in North Africa, Europe, and the Pacific. See, for example, Lerner, "I Wanted to Get My Own Back."

63. Isadore Rosen, Memoirs of American Jewish Soldiers, 1944–1946, YIVO Institute for Jewish Research, RG 110, Box 1, Folder 19, 13 (emphasis mine).

64. Kohs, "Jewish War Records."

65. Ernest Stock (pseudonym Eliezer), Memoirs of American Jewish Soldiers, 1944–1946, YIVO Institute for Jewish Research, RG 110, Box 1, Folder 29, 3.

66. Ernest Stock (pseudonym Eliezer), Memoirs of American Jewish Soldiers, 1944–1946, YIVO Institute for Jewish Research, RG 110, Box 1, Folder 29, 7; Ernest Stock (pseudonym Eliezer), Memoirs of American Jewish Soldiers, 1944–1946, YIVO Institute for Jewish Research, RG 110, Box 1, Folder 29, 3.

67. Ibid., 3, 12.

68. Patton, *Patton Papers*, 2:751, from which I quote this despicable line from General Patton's diary: "Harrison and his ilk believe that the Displaced Person is a human being, which he is not, and this applies particularly to the Jews . . . who are lower than animals." See Françoise S. Ouzan, "Antisemitism in the US at the End of the War and in Its Aftermath: Attitudes toward Displaced Persons," *Antisemitism Worldwide* 2003/2004 (2005): 51–74. During World War II, Patton would not let any Jewish chaplain into his headquarters; see Dinnerstein, *Antisemitism in America*, 139.

69. Harry S. Truman, *Memoirs*, vol. 2, *Years of Trial and Hope* (New York: Doubleday, 1956), 160.

70. Bendersky, "Jewish Threat," 42, 38, 307, 157, respectively.

71. Dinnerstein, *Antisemitism in America*, 137. To illustrate the pervasive antisemitism among officers, we may recall that Captain Eddie Rickenbacker, a World War I ace and American hero, nurtured prejudiced views toward women (whose place he believed was at home) and African Americans (whom he viewed as "good old darkies") and, according to his biographer, had "acquired a reputation in some quarters for holding a low opinion of Jews." See Finis Farr, *Rickenbacker's Luck: An American Life* (Boston: Houghton Mifflin Harcourt, 1979), 247, 296–97.

72. Alum Daniel Gutstein, "A Soldier Fighting for His People," Ida Crown Jewish Academy, 2, https://www.icja.org/2014/05/a-soldier-fighting-for-his-people/, accessed June 23, 2020.

73. Moore, *GI Jews*, has a chapter humorously titled "Eating Ham for Uncle Sam."

74. Gutstein, "A Soldier Fighting for His People." In relation to kosher foods and antisemitic attitudes, Philip Roth's "Defender of the Faith," a short story in his collection *Goodbye Columbus and Five Short Stories*, presents the tale of Private Sheldon Grossbart, who is just the opposite of our real infantryman Larry Yellin. His character is manipulative and repulsive when he connives not to be sent to fight in Japan. Grossbart pretends to be an Orthodox Jew but eats nonkosher. He wants to get a pass to attend his aunt's Passover seder—one month after Passover. In this short and grotesque piece, the noted American Jewish writer both explodes the sacred values of Jewish life and gathers anti-Jewish stereotypes linked to fidelity to the Jewish Law.

75. Larry Yellin, "Passover 1945: A Jewish Soldier's Story," *Jerusalem Post*, April 25, 2016. Yellin was sent to Europe during the Battle of the Bulge in the rugged Ardennes region in southeastern Belgium, the deadliest battle on the western front. The German attack, a massive offensive, took American army units by surprise. After harsh combat in the bitter cold Ardennes Forest—covered with snow in one of the worst winters in decades—from December 16 to December 26, 1944, American forces counterattacked and succeeded in defeating the Wehrmacht. To undermine Allied morale, a German armored unit slaughtered eighty-four American prisoners of war (POWs) at a crossroads near Malmedy, Belgium, on December 17. On both sides, losses were enormous. On January 16, 1945, General Eisenhower estimated that the enemy suffered 120,000 casualties and had "committed all of his remaining reserves." Eisenhower, *Crusade in Europe*, 364–65.

76. Ibid. Around four o'clock in the morning on the first day of Passover, amid a thick fog, the shivering GIs crossed the river on small inflated rubber boats, threatened by German artillery fire, "like a gala fourth of July display, only this was deadly."

77. The citation accompanying the award of the Distinguished Service Cross to Major General Harris Melasky reads: "Inspiring leadership, personal bravery and zealous devotion to duty exemplify the highest traditions of the military forces of the United States and reflect great credit upon himself, the 86 Infantry Division, and the United States army," https://valor.militarytimes.com/hero/6151, accessed June 30, 2020.

78. Oral testimony of Larry Yellin, Museum of the Jewish Soldier, Latrun, Israel. General Lucius Clay's compassion for Jewish displaced persons is recorded in his archives at the Harry S. Truman Library and in his oral history, https://www.trumanlibrary.gov/library/oral-histories/clayl, accessed June 30, 2020.

79. Richard Breitman and Alan M. Kraut, *American Refugee Policy and European Jewry, 1933–1945* (Bloomington: Indiana University Press, 1987), 66.

80. David S. Wyman, *Abandonment of the Jews: America and the Holocaust, 1941–1945* (New York: New Press, 1998), 10.

81. Wolk, *Jewish Aviators in World War II*, 32.

82. This fact was pinpointed by the *Jacksonville Journal* in 1942 and reprinted by the JWB in its booklet *In the Nation's Service: A Compilation of Facts Concerning Jewish Men in the Armed Forces during the First Year of the War*, first printing December 1942, second printing February 1943, RG 110, Box 1.

83. Reprinted in *In the Nation's Service*.

84. Ibid., 34–35. "Sgt. Meyer Levin, Hero of Pacific Aerial War, Killed off New Guinea," *Jewish Telegraphic Agency* 10, no. 42 (February 19, 1943), 4. He was born on June 5, 1916, and died on January 7, 1943.

85. *In the Nation's Service*.

86. *Congressional Record*, proceedings and debates of the Seventy-Seventh Congress, second session, July 1942, Ceremonies in Memory of Louis Schleifer, Extension of Remarks of Hon. Charles L. McNary.

87. In his remarks about the Greatest Generation, Tom Brokaw quoted the letter of a Jewish serviceman, Maury Robb, to his mother stating why he would never ask for a transfer to a less

dangerous position than a pilot on combat missions: "It is because of the way Dad brought me up.... Honor the way the Bible means.... Today Honor means Duty." He was a B-17 pilot who flew thirty missions over Germany. See Tom Brokaw, "Afterword," in Eidelman, *Ours to Fight For*, 172.

88. Chapters 1 and 2 offer several instances of this crucial issue from various perspectives, especially in reference to Jewish servicewomen.

89. Interview of Dan Nadel by David Geffen in David Geffen, "The Jewish War Veterans of America—Alive and Well in Israel," *Jerusalem Post Magazine*, July 3, 2015, 20. Dan Nadel, "who had seen a lot of fighting" during the war, did not take part in the Israeli War of Independence as his American wife wanted, but did immigrate to Israel in 1977.

90. See Aron Heller, "Israeli Recognition, at Last, for Jews Who Fought the Nazis," May 29, 2015, https://www.timesofisrael.com/israeli-recognition-at-last-for-jews-who-fought-the-nazis/, accessed July 24, 2020.

91. Ibid. In Israel, too, the contribution of Jewish veterans has been overlooked, as emphasized by former Brigadier General Zvi Kan-Tor, who led the effort to establish the Museum of the Jewish Soldier in World War II in Latrun, Israel: "World War II in our collective memory has been sealed by a single world: Holocaust. We've heard about the victimhood—Let's tell this side too. This is the missing piece. Maybe we can finally tell the full story of the Jewish people." Quoted by Heller, "Israeli Recognition."

92. "Famous Veterans: Mel Brooks," https://www.military.com/veteran-jobs/career-advice/military-transition/famous-veterans-mel-brooks.html, accessed July 8, 2020.

93. This rumor was apparently shared even by Jews. In his oral testimony to the Museum of the Jewish Soldier in Latrun, Israel, Larry Yellin seemed to think that Jews were more numerous in the Quartermaster Corps, although examples of extreme bravery and awards attributed to Jews show that many were heroes in infantry units or as airmen. See Kohs, "Jewish War Records." See also the impressive records of the JWB kept at the YIVO Institute of Jewish Research, New York, RG 119, Box 1.

94. In the film *GI Jews*, Jonathan Sarna pinpoints the fact that interfaith services, like enabling the Jewish minority to perform their own religious ceremonies, were in the interest of the military.

### 5. Operation Torch and Local Jews

1. Eisenhower, *Crusade in Europe*, 103, 115. See also chapter 7, 116–34. By coincidence, Admiral Darlan, a pillar of the collaborationist Vichy France, was in Algiers visiting his son who lay sick in a hospital when Operation Torch started. On how the British and the Roosevelt administration dealt with the Vichy government, see Michael S. Neiberg, *When France Fell: The Vichy Crisis and the Fate of the Anglo-American Alliance* (Cambridge, MA: Harvard University Press, 2021).

2. Ibid., 115. Estimates of the Anglo-American troops vary. Operation Torch included landings and airborne landings from November 8 to November 15. British troops reached lesser-known ports in Algeria like the Bougie Harbor, on November 11, 1942. The invasion ended on November 16, 1942.

3. José Aboulker, *La victoire du 8 novembre 1942: La Résistance et le débarquement des Alliés à Alger* (Paris: Édition du Félin, 2012).

4. See Gitta Amipaz-Zilber, *The Role of the Jewish Underground in the American Landing in Algiers, 1940–1942* (Jerusalem: Gefen, 1992).

5. Eisenhower, *Crusade in Europe*, 104; Haim Saadoun, "Jewish Leadership in North Africa: The Transformative Implications of World War II," in *The End of 1942: A Turning Point in World War II and in the Comprehension of the Final Solution?*, ed. Dina Porat and Dan Michman, with Haim Saadoun (Jerusalem: Yad Vashem, 2017), 170–71.

6. Eisenhower, *Crusade in Europe*, 103.

7. Kaufman, *American Jews in World War II*, 1:44–45.
8. Fredman and Falk, *Jews in American Wars*, 128–29.
9. *Prayer Book, Abridged*, iii.
10. Ibid.
11. Ibid., 320 (emphasis mine).
12. See the film *US Army Operation Torch "At the Front in North Africa,"* John Ford, produced by the US Army Signal Corps in Algeria and Tunisia during November and December 1942.
13. Herbert Cohen, Memoirs of American Jewish Soldiers, 1944–1946, YIVO Institute for Jewish Research, RG 110, Box 1, Folder 13, 9. Many of the four hundred thousand Jews in North Africa lived in poor quarters, but some belonged to the educated middle class, especially in Oran. A minority of well-off Jews in Algeria engaged in agricultural pursuits. See Michel Abitbol, *The Jews of North Africa during the Second World War*, trans. Catherine Tihanyi Zentelis (Detroit: Wayne State University Press, 1989).
14. Herbert Cohen, Memoirs of American Jewish Soldiers, 1944–1946, YIVO Institute for Jewish Research, RG 110, Box 1, Folder 13, 9. In Oran, the serviceman encountered Jewish refugees from Europe fleeing the Nazis. On Jews in North Africa, see Michael M. Laskier, *North African Jewry in the Twentieth Century: The Jews of Morocco, Tunisia, and Algeria* (New York: New York University Press, 1994).
15. Herbert Cohen, Memoirs of American Jewish Soldiers, 1944–1946, YIVO Institute for Jewish Research, RG 110, Box 1, Folder 13, 9.
16. Kligsberg, "'American Jewish Soldiers on Jews and Judaism,'" 261.
17. Harold U. Ribalow (pseudonym Meyer Cherniak), Memoirs of American Jewish Soldiers, 1944–1946, YIVO Institute for Jewish Research, RG 110, Box 1, Folder 7, 6–8. On wartime refugees, see Meredith Hindley, *Destination Casablanca: Exile, Espionage, and the Battle for North Africa in World War II* (New York: PublicAffairs, 2017).
18. Harold U. Ribalow (pseudonym Meyer Cherniak), Memoirs of American Jewish Soldiers, 1944–1946, YIVO Institute for Jewish Research, RG 110, Box 1, Folder 7, 1.
19. Ibid., 10. On refugees from Europe deported by the SS in Tunisia, see *Les Juifs de Tunisie sous le joug nazi, 9 novembre 1942-8 mai 1943*, récits et témoignages rassemblés, présentés, et annotés par Claude Nataf(Paris: Édition le Manuscrit, , 2012), 263n6. *The Jews of Tunisia under the Nazi Yoke*, collected and annotated testimonies by Claude Nataf (Paris: Editions Le Manuscrit, 2012).
20. Herbert Cohen, Memoirs of American Jewish Soldiers, 1944–1946, YIVO Institute for Jewish Research, RG 110, Box 1, Folder 13, 10.
21. Ibid.
22. Ibid., 11.
23. Ibid. Passover began on April 20, 1943.
24. "In North Africa, Chaplain Earl Stone, advancing with the liberating Allied armies across Tunisia, paused at every town, as it was freed from the Axis, to arrange with the local rabbi and leading Jews for community seders for Jewish soldiers, leaving *matzot* and other Passover supplies. Army flour was issued to Jewish bakers who prepared the unleavened bread in the ancient kilns in the manner of our forefathers." See Philip Goodman, *The Passover Anthology* (Philadelphia: Jewish Publication Society, 1961), Kindle ed., location 1428 of 8880.
25. Herbert Cohen, Memoirs of American Jewish Soldiers, 1944–1946, YIVO Institute for Jewish Research, RG 110, Box 1, Folder 13, 11.
26. Ibid.
27. Ibid. The presence of American GIs and in particular the reports of Jewish chaplains stationed in North Africa enhanced Jewish American solidarity with the Jews of North Africa and encouraged postwar aid provided by the American Joint Distribution Committee (JDC).

28. Jack Solomon, Memoirs of American Jewish Soldiers, 1944–1946, YIVO Institute for Jewish Research, RG 110, Box 2, Folder 33, 6.

29. Sam Appel, Correspondence, 1943–1948, Archives of the National Jewish War Veterans Museum, Washington, A998 041010. Denise Zerah, whose family invited several Jewish GIs and British soldiers in Tunisia, confirmed the existence of lasting relationships between her family and veterans. Interview with Denise Zerah (born Saada), July 12, 2018, Jerusalem.

30. Eliot Blin, Memoirs of American Jewish Soldiers, 1944–1946, YIVO Institute for Jewish Research, RG 110, Box 1, Folder 9, 13. The veteran who authored this essay was assigned to postal duties in the American navy. The two parentheses are his. In some instances, what appeared as a new interest in worship corresponded to a desire for a social outlet.

31. Interview with Emile Moatti, Jerusalem, September 25, 2015.

32. "Le traitement infligé aux soldats français d'origine juive: Le camp de Bedeau," CCCL XXXV5, Archives of the Mémorial de la Shoah, Centre de Documentation Juive Contemporaine (CDJC), Paris. On this camp, see Norbert Bel Ange, *Quand Vichy internait ses soldats juifs d'Algérie: Bedeau, Sud oranais, 1941–1943* (Paris: L'Harmattan, 2009).

33. Helyett Ben Amara, *Il était une fois là-bas: Algérie, mon pays, comme un feu tu te gaspilles en étincelles* (Grenoble: Editions Alzieu, 2000), 127–28.

34. Huguette Lancry, testimony about American soldiers in Oran, February 28, 2008, unpublished, in the author's archives.

35. Joëlle Allouche-Benayoun, "Intermittently French: Jews from Algeria during World War II," *Journal of Contemporary Jewry* 37, no. 2 (2017): 221, https://link.springer.com/article/10.1007/s12397-017-9230-9.

36. Rick Atkinson, *An Army at Dawn: The War in North Africa, 1942–1943* (New York: Henry Holt, 2002), 125. On the role of the American Jewish Committee (AJC), see Naomi Cohen, *Not Free to Desist, The American Jewish Committee, 1906–1966*, introduction by Salo Baron (Philadelphia: Jewish Publication Society of America, 1972), 267. The AJC was eager to restore the Crémieux Decree of 1870, which granted French citizenship to the Jews of French Algeria. Cohen explains: "A bare two weeks after American invasion forces landed in North Africa in 1942, Adolph Berle of the State Department informed Jacob Landau, acting for the Committee, that steps to annul the anti-Jewish restrictions imposed by the Vichy government were 'on the agenda.'"

37. Ibid. Admiral Darlan was assassinated by a French monarchist and replaced by General Giraud as high commissioner.

38. Ibid., 128.

39. Ibid., 124.

40. "Our GIs are having difficulty getting these girls to warm up to them, and they keep a respectful distance." War diary (classified as confidential) of the 526th Fighter-Bomber Squadron, Eighty-Sixth Fighter-Bomber Group, February 1942–October 1945, 11. The war diary belonged to Sergeant Naurice Rosen, mentioned in the previous chapter. The author is grateful to Howard Rosen for lending his father's document.

41. Ibid.

42. Eliot Blin, Memoirs of American Jewish Soldiers, 1944–1946, RG 110, YIVO Institute for Jewish Research, Box 1, Folder 9, 17–18.

43. Butler, "Flying Rabbi."

44. Daniel B. Jorgensen, *Air Force Chaplains*, vol. 1, *The Service of Chaplains to Army Air Units, 1917–1946* (Washington, DC: United States Air Force, Office of the Chief of Chaplains, 1961), 291.

45. Ibid.

46. Numerous Jews volunteered for service in the Free Corps (Corps franc), which included civilians and military men whether attached to an army or not. See Jacob Kaplan, "French Jewry under the Occupation," *American Jewish Year Book* 47, no. 5706 (1945–46): 111–18. On the

Free Corps and heroism of French Jews fighting in Tunisia, see ibid., 113. Following Chaplain Werfel's death, the Jewish Telegraphic Agency informed Jewish communities around the world that the chaplain's request of ten thousand prayer books in French translation had been granted. See "Jewish Chaplain Killed in Line of Duty: Fourth American Rabbi to Lose Life in War," Jewish Telegraphic Agency, January 9, 1944, https://www.jta.org/1944/01/09/archive/jewish-chaplain-killed-in-line-of-duty-fourth-american-rabbi-to-lose-life-in-war, accessed November 29, 2020.

47. Archives of the National Museum of American Jewish Military History, undated, A 993.047.008, collection: Werfel Louis, accession number: 1993.047.

48. Kaufman, *American Jews in World War II*, 1:310.

49. Conversation with Max Benhamou, born in 1930, Tel Aviv, May 17, 2018. Benhamou's sister dated an American GI in Casablanca for a year. He promised to marry her. When marriage did not materialize, his sister suffered from a lengthy state of depression.

50. Molly Guptill Manning, *When Books Went to War: The Stories That Helped Us Win World War II* (Boston: Houghton Mifflin Harcourt, 2014). The file of wartime photographs and illustrations captures the power of the written word.

51. Henry Torres, Paul Jacob, and Edouard de Rothschild, "Resolution of the French Jewish Representative Committee of the World Jewish Congress," October 23, 1943, United States Holocaust Memorial Museum, USHMM, RG 43.144M (1943–47) contains records about the activities of the WJC in North Africa, antisemitism in the French army, and the Crémieux Decree. On the long history of institutional antisemitism in colonial Algeria and the use of antisemitism by European settlers to gain political influence, see Sophie Beth Roberts, *Citizenship and Antisemitism in French Colonial Algeria, 1870–1962* (Cambridge: Cambridge University Press, 2017).

52. Eliot Blin, Memoirs of American Jewish Soldiers, 1944–1946, YIVO Institute for Jewish Research, RG 110, Box 1, Folder 9, 7. The veteran wrote "Vive Pétain, mort à la Juive [sic]," instead of the pejorative noun "Juiverie," referring to Jews as a collective. However, his perception of the omnipresent and virulent antisemitism in Oran is surprisingly accurate.

53. Letter of Captain Max E. Zera to Herman, in Israel E. Rontch, ed., *Jewish Youth at War* (New York: Martin Press, 1945), 265. In the same book, the letter of Sargent Alex Lang, age twenty-three, born in New York City to Austrian parents, is worth mentioning. Decorated with the Silver Star and the recipient of a Presidential Citation, he saw combat in North Africa and slept in a foxhole for more than four months. He went without water for two days and admitted he had forgotten "the taste of a good big glass of milk." His unit was the one that invaded Algiers and took Bizerte before pursuing the war with the Italian campaign; ibid., 281.

### 6. Religiosity in the Pacific and India

1. Kaufman, *American Jews in World War II*, 1:39.
2. Ibid., 40.
3. *Jewish Chaplain*, February 1943.
4. Bernstein, *Rabbis at War*, 25.
5. Courtesy of Sandra Fenichel Asher; the photo is too faded for reproduction.
6. Electronic correspondence with Dr. Fenichel's daughter, Sandra Fenichel Asher, February 27, 2020.
7. Kohs, "Jewish War Records," 166.
8. David Geffen, "Days of Awe in the Pacific," *Jerusalem Post*, September 8, 2010.
9. Newspaper clipping with photo and article about Marine Captain Sidney J. Altman conducting services; Altman, Sidney J. Archival number: A 994.087.001, National Museum of Jewish Military History, Washington, DC. Altman remained in the Marines all his life. He became a full colonel, fought in the Korean War, where he led a counterattack against the Chinese, and retired after the Vietnam War.

10. Geffen, "Days of Awe in the Pacific."

11. *Psychology for the Fighting Man: What You Should Know about Yourself and Others* (Washington, DC: Infantry Journal, 1943), 289–300.

12. Ibid., 292.

13. Richard Tregaskis, *Guadalcanal Diary* (New York: Random House, 1943), Kindle ed. The war reporter recounted with emotion the stories of the men he lived with and conveyed the human meaning of the battle. He expressed his gratefulness at being alive.

14. Goodman, *Passover Anthology*, Kindle ed., location 1458 of 8880.

15. Ibid., locations 1459, 1465.

16. Isaac Toubin, "D-Day for the Soul," *Jewish Veteran* 13–14 (September 1944): 4–5. Toubin quotes large passages from the letter written by Captain Elliot Davis after the Jewish New Year service.

17. "From the Island of Munda," *Jewish Chaplain*, November 1943.

18. Ibid.

19. Photo Archives of the Museum of American Jewish Military History, Washington, DC; see in particular *Officers at Seder at Munda Including Admiral Kinkaid*, accession number: 1986.001, catalog number: P986.001.062.

20. See chapter 4.

21. Moore, *GI Jews*, 135.

22. "Passover in the Philippines," The Letter Box, *American Hebrew*, May 11, 1945. In 1945, Rabbi David I. Cedarbaum helped conduct the seder in Guam. It was held for 2,700 servicemen. Photos of that event were taken by combat photographer Emmanuel Weinstock and found recently by his grandson.

23. Ibid.

24. Ben Magdovitz (pseudonym Cook), Memoirs of American Jewish Soldiers, 1944–1946, YIVO Institute for Jewish Research, RG 110, Box 1, Folder 4, 2.

25. Ibid., 13.

26. Ibid.

27. Ibid., 14–15.

28. Ibid., 16.

29. Ibid., 17. See also American Jewish Distribution Committee, New York, Philippines General, II-VIII. 1945, 706630; NY AR 194554, 4/60/1/726. February–August 1945. Correspondence on conditions of local Jewish community. Cables regarding fundraising by US Service members to rebuild the Manila synagogue.

30. Ibid., 18.

31. Jerry Yellin, *Of War and Weddings: A Legacy of Two Fathers* (Fairfield, IA: Sunstar, 1995), 130–31.

32. Ibid., 130.

33. George Ammerman, *American Hebrew*, May 11, 1945, 4.

34. Conversation with Noam Zion, son of Chaplain Moshe Sachs, Jerusalem, May 26, 2020.

35. *Jewish Oiy Kinawan*, no. 4 (24 Tammuz 5706), a document kindly handed to me by his son, Noam Sachs Zion, contains the following: "The holiday must teach us to respond constructively, even militantly to the Jewish tragedy.... Not only to mourn but to determine to build a secure homeland for the 'remnant.'" In 1947, a few months after termination of his military service, Sachs and his wife joined the Haganah, the underground Jewish defense force in Palestine. Another example of renewal is captured in a photograph showing "the first Jewish wedding on Okinawa" in September 1945 in the Chapel of Peace. General Joseph Stilwell gave away the bride. The groom was Captain Edward Siegel. The bride was Captain Gretchen Ruth Boody, a Methodist nurse whose wedding dress was made from a parachute. The chaplain was Hershel Lyman. *American Hebrew*, November 1945, 25.

36. Marshall Wolke, Memoirs of American Jewish Soldiers, 1944–1946, YIVO Institute for Jewish Research, RG 110, Box 1, Folder 28; Eisenhower, *Crusade in Europe*, 24.

37. Srinath Raghavan, *The Most Dangerous Place: A History of the United States in South Asia* (Haryana: Penguin Random House, 2018).

38. Marshall Wolke, Memoirs of American Jewish Soldiers, 1944–1946, YIVO Institute for Jewish Research, RG 110, Box 1, Folder 28, 19–20.

39. Ibid., 27, 29–30.

40. Ibid., 6.

41. Ibid., 19–20.

42. David Macarov (pseudonym Ben Zion), Memoirs of American Jewish Soldiers, 1944–1946, YIVO Institute for Jewish Research, RG 110, Box 1, Folder 11, 5. An interview with his widow, Frieda, in Jerusalem in 2020 made it clear that he was openly Jewish in the military and often offered to assist chaplains.

43. Ibid., 9.

44. Letters of David Macarov to his parents excerpted in ibid., 19–23.

45. Ibid., 19.

46. David Macarov, Memoirs of American Jewish Soldiers, 1944–1946, YIVO Institute for Jewish Research, RG 110, Box 1, Folder 11, 23. Macarov went to study at the Hebrew University in Jerusalem after the war on the GI Bill. He settled in Palestine/Israel and became a noted scholar. Involved in the underground, Macarov employed various methods to acquire ships that brought Jewish displaced persons from camps to Palestine in the years 1946–1947 and was instrumental in helping the *President Warfield*, renamed *Exodus 1947*, get official documents to sail.

47. Moore, *GI Jews*, 114.

48. Conversation with Hebe Solomon Benjamin, December 12, 2020.

49. Macarov, "A Small Cog," 72–73. These lines placed as a foreword to this memoir sum up his commitments: "I have had the infinite honor, great pleasure, and good luck to be a very small cog in two major historical events—the Allies' victory in WWII, and the emergence of the State of Israel. These are some unpublished episodes of the first—which saved the world from slavery; and the second—which changed the Jewish people and the world at large."

50. Kaufman, *American Jews in World War II*, 1:345.

51. Ibid., 1:325.

52. Joshua Louis Goldberg, interview, From Centuries of Service: Military Chaplains—UNCW, William Randall Library Digital collections, 1980.

53. Cohen, *Women in the Military*, Kindle ed., location 641–43.

54. Franklin Roosevelt ensured that every serviceman and servicewoman received a text in which these lines reinforce the faith of every American in God, and therefore in the belief that good will triumph over evil: "Yours is a God Fearing, proud, courageous people, which, throughout its history, has put its freedom under God before all purposes." "The Star-Spangled Banner" is reproduced in *Prayer Book, Abridged*, 331 in the 1943 edition, published in one hundred thousand copies in its fifth impression.

## 7. Prisoners of War of the Japanese

1. Alfred A. Weinstein, *Barbed-Wire Surgeon: A Prisoner of War in Japan* (Atlanta: Deeds, 1975; first edition, 1948), 14.

2. Clifford G. Holderness and Jeffrey Pontiff, "Hierarchies and the Survival of Prisoners of War during World War II," *Management Science* 58 (2012): 1875.

3. William E. Dyess, "Statement of Major William E. Dyess, Air Corps, Concerning Experiences and Observations as Prisoner of War in the Philippines—9 April 1942 to 4 April 1943," RG 18, National Archives, quoted by Stanley L. Falk, "Introduction," in William E. Dyess, *Bataan Death March: A Survivor's Account*, ed. with a biographical introduction by Charles

Leavelle (Lincoln: University of Nebraska Press, 2002; first edition by Marajen Stevick Dyess, 1944).

4. Ibid. See, for example, Stephen M. Mellnik, *Philippine Diary, 1939–1945* (New York: Van Nostrand Reinhold, 1969).

5. Weinstein, *Barbed-Wire Surgeon*, 13.

6. Ibid., 18; Alfred A. Weinstein, "I Made My Peace with Japanese War Criminals," *Quan*, September 18, 1963.

7. Weinstein, *Barbed-Wire Surgeon*, 18.

8. Weinstein's papers are kept by Emory University, Stuart A. Rose Manuscript Archives and Rare Book Library, Atlanta, Georgia. See also Alfred A. Weinstein, "Yom Kippur in Cabanatuan," *B'nai B'rith National Jewish Monthly*, September 1947.

9. Ibid., 9; Weinstein, *Barbed-Wire Surgeon*, 15.

10. Roger Cohen, *Soldiers and Slaves: American POWs Trapped by the Nazis' Final Gamble* (New York: Knopf, 2005), chap. 4, esp. 88–89. The author quotes the testimony of Edward Charles Mayer of the 106th Infantry Division given to war crime investigators in relation to the segregation of Jewish POWs, in violation of the Third Geneva Convention of 1929: "About January 15th, 1945, at Stalag IX-B, the Germans told us that all Jewish prisoners of war had to go to special barracks, which had a fence around." Cohen makes it clear that the investigation of that segregation did not lead to prosecution of those responsible among the Germans (89).

11. Archival film footage *"Know Your Enemy: Japan" (1945)*, War Department Orientation film, produced by Army Pictorial Service, Signal Corps. Some parts included film captured from the Japanese. In his important book about Jewish POWs and internees from Commonwealth and Dutch forces, Martin Sugarman discerns a few cases in which Jews—both refugees and Allied military personnel—were singled out as Jews. He indicates that in 1944, an interpreter was asked by the Japanese to identify Jewish officers; see Sugarman, *Under the Heels of Bushido*, 6.

12. Weinstein, *Barbed-Wire Surgeon*, 139. GIs who were caught trading belongings for food with Filipinos through barbed wire were tied to stakes and left for forty-eight hours without water or food. Then they were executed. Other prisoners were left with the painful task of burying them; ibid., 147.

13. Ibid., 142.

14. Ibid., 59.

15. See previous chapter.

16. Weinstein, *Barbed-Wire Surgeon*, 200–201.

17. Ibid., 201.

18. *Prayer Book: New Year and Day of Atonement, Abridged for Jews in the Armed Forces of the United States* (New York: National Jewish Welfare Board, 1943), 146.

19. "The Soul Thou Hast Given Me Is Pure," excerpt from K. Kohler, 1904, in *A Book of Jewish Thoughts*, Selected and Arranged by Dr. J. H. Hertz, Office of the Chief Rabbi (London: Henderson and Spalding, 1942), 178. This revised edition for Jewish sailors, soldiers, and airmen, distributed to military chaplains and servicemen, contains reflections on Judaism by noted Jews and non-Jews such as Einstein, Pope Pius XI, General Smuts, Churchill, and President Roosevelt.

20. Weinstein, *Barbed-Wire Surgeon*, 202.

21. Ibid., 200.

22. "The Soul Thou Hast Given Me Is Pure" (note 19 above). In relation to the idea of "reverting to manliness," Kohler notes an important characteristic: "Judaism rejects the idea of an inherent impurity of the flesh or in matter opposed to spirit. Nor does Judaism accept the doctrine of Original Sin." A POW of the Germans for five years, Jewish philosopher Emmanuel Lévinas began his fruitful reflection on Jewish identity in captivity. See Emmanuel Lévinas, "Écrits sur la captivité et Hommage à Bergson," in *Carnets de captivité et autres inédits (1940–1945)*, ed. Rodolphe Calin and Catherine Chalier (Paris: Grasset, 2009), 199–219.

23. Chaim Nussbaum, *Chaplain on the River Kwai: Story of a Prisoner of War* (New York: Shapolsky, 1988), 190. His book comprises letters sent to his wife and is dedicated to "those who perished in resignation and those who survived and remember."

24. Weinstein, *Barbed-Wire Surgeon*, 203.

25. It is interesting to note Weinstein's reiteration of the fact that in every prison in the Philippines, "Filipinos rallied to our cry for help" and "Philippine women took over the job of keeping us alive"; ibid., 139. See also the documentary film *An Open Door, Jewish Rescue in the Philippines*, Noel Izon and Sharon Delmendo, 2012.

26. Box 1, Folder 6, Mss 387, Gordon Family Papers, Cuba Family Archives for Southern Jewish History, William Breman Heritage Museum, Atlanta, Georgia.

27. Ibid., Box 2, Folder 16. It must be emphasized that the Japanese had not signed the Geneva Convention on POWs, and the information they gave the Red Cross was scant and often unreliable. Besides, the Japanese military did its best to hide the number of prisoners who lost their lives in POW camps. It is therefore impossible to know the number of Allied POWs, whether Jews or non-Jews, who died on transport to Japan or were executed, starved, beaten, or worked to death. Lack of prisoner information was meant to impede the task of war crimes investigators; see Sugarman, *Under the Heels of Bushido*, 3.

28. Ibid., Box 4, Folder 11, Gordon Jack, West Point, 1939. See also Box 5, Folder 1, Gordon Jack, West Point, undated.

29. Ibid., Box 2, File 4, Correspondence Samuel Gordon and Jack Gordon, 1941–1942, undated, 17/26.

30. Ibid.

31. Ibid., 18/26.

32. Ibid., Box 4, Folder 6. Gordon Jack, Naval Academy Memorial Chair, 1941–1999, undated, 20/60. On J. Gordon "Hero and Patriot," correspondence of S. Gordon with Captain Seymour, see ibid.

33. Ashley Halsey, "Ancestral Gray Cloud over Patton: General George S. Patton's Time-Tested Military Bloodline," *American History Illustrated* 19 (March 1984): 48. I am thankful to Colonel J. N. Hawthorne for drawing my attention to this article while at the United States West Point Military Academy in March 1992.

34. Jeffrey Goldberg, "Trump: Americans Who Died in War Are 'Losers' and 'Suckers,'" *Atlantic*, September 3, 2020, https://amp.theatlantic.com/amp/article/615997/, accessed October 9, 2020.

35. Lee A. Gladwin, "American POWs on Japanese Ships Take a Voyage into Hell," *Prologue Magazine* 35, no. 4 (Winter 2003), https://www.archives.gov/publications/prologue/2003/winter/hell-ships-1.html, accessed August 31, 2020.

36. Ibid.

37. Box 4, Folder 6, Mss 387, 8–9/60 (PDF). Gordon Family Papers, Cuba Family Archives for Southern Jewish History, William Berman Heritage Museum, Atlanta, Georgia.

38. Ibid.

39. Ibid., Box 1, Folder 11.

40. Access to Archival Databases, National Archives, Records of World War II Prisoners of War, 1942–1947, Record Group 389. https://aad.archives.gov/aad/record-detail.jsp?dt=3159&mtch=4&cat=all&tf=F&q=Gordon+Jack&bc=sd&rpp=10&pg=1&rid=125617&rlst=92544,97982,92543,125617, accessed June 5, 2023.

41. On the plight of POWs under the Japanese, see the report of the International Committee of the Red Cross on activities during the Second World War, I:451; see also https://www.icrc.org/en/doc/resources/documents/misc/57jnwq.htm, accessed June 11, 2023.

42. Some American veterans wrote in their wills that they wished to be cremated and their ashes scattered in the Pacific. Such was the case of renowned film star William Holden, a former first lieutenant in the United States Army Air Forces (First Motion Picture Unit, 1942–1945).

43. Sadie Gordon did hear from Sam in Guam; he sent her a V mail Passover Card together with a letter on March 23, 1945, and a Rosh Hashanah Card at the end of August of the same year. Box 2, Folder 6, Passover Card; Box 2; Folder 7 Rosh Hashanah Card, Mss 387, Gordon Family Papers, Cuba Family Archives for Southern Jewish History, William Breman Jewish Heritage Museum, Atlanta, Georgia.

44. Evelyn Monahan and Rosemary Neidel-Greenlee, *All This Hell: U.S. Nurses Imprisoned by the Japanese* (Lexington: University Press of Kentucky, 2000), ix. Quoted in Joanna Kolosov, "Tribute to World War II POW 2nd Lt. Magdalena Eckmann Hewlett," Sonoma County Library, https://sonomalibrary.org/blogs/history/tribute-to-world-war-ii-pow-2nd-lt-magdalena-eckmann-hewlett-by-joanna-kolosov-mlis-0, accessed September 30, 2020. After the 1980s, the emerging field of women's history gradually began shedding light on the personal stories of women who were not previously part of history. Laura Margolis, sent by the American Joint Distribution Committee (JDC) to Shanghai, where tens of thousands of Jewish refugees fleeing Nazi persecution found refuge, was also held in an internment camp for three years as an enemy alien. The Japanese, who occupied Shanghai after the United States entered the war, released her three years later in a prisoner exchange. As a JDC representative, she managed to convince the Japanese to keep soup kitchens open to feed the refugees. See Sara Kadosh, "Laura Margolis Jarblum," https://jwa.org/encyclopedia/article/jarblum-laura-margolis, accessed October 5, 2021.

45. Emmet F. Pearson, "Morbidity and Mortality in Santo Tomas, 28–29," in *The Japanese Story*, American Ex-POW National Medical Research Committee, Packet 10, https://www.axpow.org/medsearch/packet10converted.pdf, accessed September 30, 2020.

46. Thomas H. Hewlett, "Di Ju Nana Bijnshyo-Nightmare-Revisited," in *The Japanese Story*, December 1978.

47. Ron Langer, "Post-Traumatic Stress Disorder in Former POWs," in *Post-Traumatic Stress Disorder: A Handbook for Clinicians*, ed. T. Williams (Cincinnati: Disabled American Veterans, 1987), 35–50.

48. Kolosov, "Tribute to World War II POW 2nd Lt. Magdalena Eckmann Hewlett."

49. Scott Prater, "Former POW Details Inspiring Survival Story," US Army, https://www.army.mil/article/143124/former_pow_details_inspiring_survival_story, accessed October 2, 2020.

50. Weinstein, "I Made My Peace."

51. Ibid. In Japanese, "San" is a title of respect added to a name, both male and female.

52. Ibid. In a postface to the third edition of *Barbed-Wire Surgeon*, S. Delmendo indicates that Weinstein did not attend war crime trials against Japanese officials; ibid., 378.

53. Ibid.

54. Ibid.

55. Cyrulnik discusses the notion of revenge in a French documentary film about Holocaust survivors entitled *Vivre après la Shoah* by Francis Gillery, 2009.

56. Louis Zamperini, hero of the movie *Unbroken* (adapted from the book of the same title by Laura Hillenbrand), was an American veteran and a former Olympic distance runner of the Catholic faith. His life story and experiences as a POW of the Japanese were related in his memoirs: Louis Zamperini with David Rensin, *Devil at My Heels: A Heroic Olympian's Astonishing Story of Survival as a Japanese POW in World War II* (New York: HarperCollins, 2003).

57. See Kaufman, *American Jews in World War II*, 1:346.

58. For examples of Jewish observance among British POWs, see Sugarman, *Under the Heels of Bushido*.

59. Aben S. Caplan, "Memoir," Experiencing War: Veterans History Project, Library of Congress, 1939–1945, 3. Caplan wrote letters to his wife and son in the last two months of the war.

60. Weinstein, "I Made My Peace."

## 8. Camaraderie beyond Prejudice

1. Cohen, *Women in the Military*, Kindle ed., location 436 of 934. On Lieutenant Slanger, a Jewish servicewoman, see ibid., location 903 of 934.

2. L. Roy Blumenthal et al., *Fighting for America: A Record of the Participation of Jewish Men and Women in the Armed Forces during 1944* (New York: National Jewish Welfare Board, 1945), 57.

3. "I Ran to Enlist and I Ran to Get Out," West Point Center for Oral History, West Point Department of History, https://www.westpointcoh.org/interviews/i-ran-to-enlist-and-i-ran-to-get-out-a-wwii-pow-recounts-his-experience, accessed November 4, 2020. Harvey Horn emphasized the fact that he saw a number of good pilots wash out. He, too, was almost washed out as a pilot bombardier, but the colonel said, "You're fine," confirming what is noted in chapter 4 about anti-Jewish attitudes. Harvey Horn served in the 772nd Bomber Squadron, 463rd Bomber Group, Fifteenth Air Force.

4. Interview with Milton Zaslow, Veterans History Project, Library of Congress, Washington, DC.

5. See Roger Daniels, *Politics of Prejudice: The Anti-Japanese Movement in California and the Struggle for Japanese Exclusion* (Berkeley: University of California Press, 1977). Drawing, among other sources, on George F. Kennan's lectures on "American Diplomacy, 1900–1950," the historian shows that through acts of discrimination against the Japanese over the years, the "progressive movement" in American immigration policy "helped to poison relations between the United States and Japan," ibid., 107.

6. Stember et al., *Jews in the Mind of America*, 128. The survey was about "nationality, religious or racial groups" considered "a menace to America." Jews were identified as a threat to Americans by 15 percent of respondents. In June 1945, 58 percent of the American population agreed that "Jews have too much power in the United States"; see "Polls on Anti-Semitism," *Commentary*, 1 (April 1946): 83, quoted in Dinnerstein, *Antisemitism in America*, 146.

7. Interview with Milton Zaslow, Veterans History Project, Library of Congress, Washington, DC.

8. Ibid. Zaslow recalled working on captured material, examining weather-beaten documents "with scorpions running, walking all over my hands," he added in the interview, noting that it was "part of the job."

9. About six thousand Japanese Americans were involved in the Military Intelligence Service attached to the Allied Translator Interpreter Section, filling noncombatant roles. Some encountered former friends in combat zones, under the risk of dying under friendly fire. See Kelli Y. Nakamura, "Military Intelligence Service," Densho Encyclopedia, http://encyclopedia.densho.org/Military%20Intelligence%20Service/, accessed October 18, 2020.

10. Interview with Milton Zaslow, Veterans History Project, Library of Congress, Washington, DC.

11. Calev Ben-David, "My Father, the Soldier of Occupation," *Jerusalem Post*, August 4, 2016. Corporal David Mandell later joined the American troops in the postwar occupation of Japan.

12. Quoted in David G. McCullough, *Truman* (New York: Simon & Schuster, 1992), 395.

13. Ibid. Henry Lewis Stimson (1867–1950), who served as secretary of war under Presidents Roosevelt and Truman, was one of the chief defenders of the bomb decision.

14. Figures presented in ibid.

15. Interview with Milton Zaslow, Veterans History Project, Library of Congress, Washington, DC.

16. Ibid. On the Nisei Soldier Regiment, see for instance *U.S. Department of Veterans Affairs*, documentary film in cooperation with the National Cemetery Administration and San Francisco University, 2018.

17. Such was the case of Yaiye Furutani's mother as recounted in Evelyn Monahan and Rosemary Neidel-Greenlee, *A Few Good Women: America's Military Women from World War I to the Wars in Iraq and Afghanistan* (New York: Knopf, 2010), Kindle ed., location 213 of 456. It should be added that Furutani's father, on the other hand, was proud of his daughter's service.

18. This conclusive experiment led to desegregation in the military in 1948 during the Truman presidency. Eleanor Roosevelt's empathy for the underdog was expressed several times during the Second World War and in its aftermath, especially in relation to European displaced persons.

19. Milton Norman, "'For You the War Is Over': A Jewish U.S. Army Soldier in a German POW Camp," West Point Center for Oral History, West Point Department of History, August 29, 2015, https://www.westpointcoh.org/interviews/for-you-the-war-is-over-a-jewish-u-s-army-soldier-in-a-german-pow-camp, accessed November 4, 2020.

20. *The Memphis Belle: The Story of a Flying Fortress* (1944), 45 min., War Department, directed by William Wyler, Army Pictorial Service, Signal Corps, distributed by Paramount. See also *Five Came Back*, documentary on five Hollywood filmmakers who enlisted in the armed forces to document World War II, 2017, second episode: S1, E2, "Combat Zones." Their stories are told by five contemporary directors, among them Steven Spielberg, who commented on Wyler's exceptional mastery in documenting this episode in the war and his personal implication as a Jew of a European family and ancestry.

21. Wolk, *Jewish Aviators in World War II*, 157.

22. Ibid., 158.

23. Ibid., 159.

24. Ibid., 159–60.

25. *Prayer Book, Abridged*, iii.

26. Blumenthal et al., *Fighting for America*, "All Roads Lead to Tokyo," photo section in the middle of the book.

27. Ibid.

28. Ibid., 61.

29. Fredman and Falk, *Jews in American Wars*, 183.

30. "Admiral Ben Moreell, CEC, USN," Seabee Museum and Memorial Park, Davisville, Rhode Island.

31. Fredman and Falk, *Jews in American Wars*, 191. See also the exhibition "Major General Julius Klein, His Life and Work." Klein was the recipient of many distinctions, including Citation for Heroism, the Philippine Distinguished Service Star, Legion of Merit with two clusters, Bronze Star, Commendation Ribbon with two Oak Leaf Clusters, and the Ribbon of Honor.

32. See chapter 4 of this book; see also Moore, *GI Jews*, 83–84.

33. See chapter 2.

34. Fredman and Falk, *Jews in American Wars*, 239. To a lesser extent, Brigadier General Julius Klein's life story also touches on that of the Jewish state. On April 4, 1948, as national commander of the Jewish War Veterans (JWV), Klein organized an impressive show of strength in favor of the partition of Palestine and the establishment of the State of Israel. The JWV paraded along New York's Fifth Avenue. Jewish solidarity and compassion were also expressed for Holocaust survivors.

35. Ibid., 129.

36. The Hall of Valor Project, Barney D. Ross, https://valor.militarytimes.com/hero/38497, accessed November 15, 2020.

37. Douglas Century, *Barney Ross: The Life of a Jewish Fighter* (New York: Schocken Books, 2006), Kindle ed., location 250 of 2495. See also Barney Ross and Martin Abramson, *No Man Stands Alone: The True Story of Barney Ross* (Philadelphia: J.B. Lippincott, 1957), 8 and esp. 211. Contrary to the myth of Jewish wealth prevalent in the forties, most Jews, like Ross's parents,

were barely middle class at best. When Ross's father was murdered, his siblings had to find foster homes.

38. Kaufman, *American Jews in World War II*, 1:40, 272.

39. Samantha Dorn, "Captain Ben Salomon," National Museum of the United States Army, Army Historical Foundation, https://armyhistory.org/captain-ben-solomon/, accessed December 6, 2020. Several recommendations had been made from the 1950s to give Salomon the medal, but it was only during the Bush presidency in 1998, when Dr. Robert West of the USC School of Dentistry submitted his recommendation, that Congress waived the time limitation for the award.

40. "Ben L. Salomon," National Museum of American Jewish Military History, https://nmajmh.org/exhibitions/permanent-exhibitions/hall-of-heroes/world-war-ii/866-2/, accessed November 15, 2020.

41. Julie Calohan, "Journalist Brings to Life Story of Jewish-American Army Nurse," US Army, April 12, 2010, https://www.army.mil/article/37256/journalist_brings_to_life_story_of_jewish_american_army_nurse_corps_nurse, accessed November 29, 2020.

42. Blumenthal et al., *Fighting for America*, 53.

43. On Frances Y. Slanger, see Diner and Benderly, *Her Works Praise Her*, 271–75. Lord Rabbi Jonathan Sacks, "A D'var Torah by Rabbi Sacks on Vayikra and the Coronavirus Pandemic," https://www.youtube.com/watch?v=ZNZ_Qcj9rB4&ab_channel=TheOfficeofRabbiSacks, accessed November 11, 2020.

44. Cohen, *Women in the Military*, Kindle ed., location 495 of 934. The recipient of many awards, Anita Gold was buried with full military honors in March 1994.

45. Ibid., location 355 of 934. See also Diner and Benderly, *Her Works Praise Her*, 332–33.

46. Zamaloff Dworkin, "I Am Not Going to Stand By," 39–40. On Jeanne Zamaloff, see chapter 1 in this book.

47. Cohen, *Women in the Military*, Kindle ed., 634–41 of 934.

48. Jay M. Eidelman, "Jewish GIs and the War against the Nazis," in Eidelman, *Ours to Fight For*, 15. See also Moore, *GI Jews*, 134–38; 145–49; 257–58. Moore rightly notes that "ecumenical observance of a Passover seder under military auspices transformed an intimate Jewish home ritual into a public performance," ibid., 135, as exemplified in chapter 6 by a seder on the island of Munda that included high-ranking officers.

49. Letter of Ralph Tomases to his mother and grandparents on Passover 1945. The document was kindly sent electronically to the author by Tomases's daughter, Ruth Joffe, October 16, 2020. Before his capture, Tomases was attached to the 106th division.

50. Examples of camaraderie between Christians and Jews occurred—for instance, when Master Sergeant Roddie Edmonds, the highest-ranking noncommissioned officer in the 422nd Infantry Regiment and a participant in the landings of the American forces in Europe, was taken prisoner by the Germans. He opposed their requirement to separate Jewish prisoners from the rest. Aware of the great risk to their survival, he declared: "We are all Jews."

51. Letter of Ralph Tomases to his wife and parents, Passover 1945. *El Male Neeman* is a Hebrew phrase meaning "Faithful King." The officer's letter thus ends with an affirmation of faith reinforced by the *Shma yisrael* (Hear O' Israel), the emotional cry and sign of belonging of Jews.

52. Harold Ribalow (pseudonym Meyer Cherniak), Memoirs of American Jewish Soldiers, 1944–1946, YIVO Institute for Jewish Research, RG 110, Box 1, Folder 7, 8.

53. Ibid. Commenting on Ribalow's war experiences, Deborah Dash Moore notes that Hollywood preferred to stage Jews joining Christian services, pointing to the film adaptation of *Guadalcanal Diaries* (by the same title) that set the ecumenical mood for wartime cinema. See Moore, *GI Jews*, 143n64, 298.

54. Letter of Captain Max E. Zera to Herman, August 19, 1943, in Rontch, ed., *Jewish Youth at War*, 263.

55. Ibid.

56. Ibid.

57. *Ernie Pyle's War: A Documentary on Ernie Pyle, World War II Correspondent*, DVD, 30 min., produced by Todd Gould, WFYI Productions and the Indiana Historical Society, 2005.

58. Letter of Sam Solomon, in Rontch, ed., *Jewish Youth at War*, 197.

59. For a sense of the camaraderie in Easy Company, 101st Airborne Division, 506th Parachute Infantry Regiment during World War II, see Ian Gardner, *Airborne: The Combat Story of Ed Shames of Easy Company* (Oxford: Osprey, 2015). A first lieutenant when awarded three Purple Hearts, Colonel Edward Shames deplored the anti-Jewish treatment in the portrayal of his character in the miniseries *Band of Brothers*, based on Stephen Ambrose's book by the same title. Born to Orthodox parents in 1922 in Virginia Beach, Colonel Shames's father died when Shames was five years old. He became "tough," as he confessed in an interview conducted by the American Veterans Center, https://www.youtube.com/watch?v=tow46KHDJGs&ab_channel=AmericanVeteransCenter, accessed December 20, 2020.

60. Barbara Feinberg, comp., *Your Loving Husband and Father: A Soldier's Story during World War II from the Letters of George Bader* (Jerusalem: Barbara Feinberg, 2018), 187. Bader added humorously: "He thought I was remarkable in being able to conduct the services." Interestingly, Bader's grandson, who did not know his grandfather, typed the letters.

61. Cindy Mindell, "On Memorial Day . . . Honoring the Jewish War Veterans of the United States of America," *CT Jewish Ledger*, May 22, 2013.

62. Truman, *Memoirs*, 1:67. Rosenthal sensed that it was "an uplifting scene for all Americans." Interview of Joe Rosenthal on August 15, 1997, about the story behind the photo, https://www.youtube.com/watch?v=hT-nVMnr-Fo&ab_channel=NBCNews, accessed December 20, 2020.

63. Fredman and Falk, *Jews in American Wars*, 227. The courage of the American forces on the Japanese volcano island—epitomized by the raising of the flag—is memorialized in the impressive Marine Corps Monument in Washington, DC.

64. McCullough, *Truman*, 395.

65. Murray Williamson and Allan R. Millet, *A War to Be Won: Fighting the Second World War* (Cambridge, MA: Harvard University Press, 2000), 513.

66. Harry S. Truman, *Memoirs*, vol. 1, *Year of Decisions* (New York: Doubleday, 1955); Corporal Harold P. Keller, one of the six soldiers who held the flag in Rosenthal's photograph, was mistaken for seventeen years for Private First Class René Gagnon of Manchester, New Hampshire, who was invited to the president's office.

67. Roland B. Gittelsohn, "Brothers All?," *Reconstructionist* 12 (February 7, 1947): 10; For a detailed commentary on Gittelsohn's eulogy, see Moore, *GI Jews*, 148–53.

68. Gittelsohn, "Brothers All?," 10.

69. Moore, *GI Jews*, 119–23, emphasizes that Goode was upset by the segregation of African Americans in Washington, DC, and championed equality. See also Alex J. Goldman, *Giants of Faith: Great American Rabbis* (New York: Citadel Press, 1964), 313, which stresses that Goode was the "Jewish representative on this rendez-vous with destiny."

70. Jonathan D. Sarna, *American Judaism: A History* (New Haven, CT: Yale University Press, 2004), 267. Kaufman, *American Jews in World War II*, 1:308. Major David I. Cedarbaum, the chaplain of the Twentieth Air Force stationed in Guam between March and October 1945, was also spreading the spirit of tolerance. The chaplain's sense of fellowship extended to non-Jewish members of that unit who helped build a Torah ark for improvised religious services; ibid., 1:326.

71. *Let There Be Light* (1946), War Department, directed by John Huston, Army Pictorial Service, Signal Corps, housed at the Library of Congress. See also the movie *The Best Years of Our Lives*.

72. Blumenthal et al., *Fighting for America*, 52–53.

73. The Official Website of Captain Jerry Yellin, https://captainjerryyellin.com/people-wwii-fighter-pilot-finds-family-with-japanese-kamikaze-pilot-after-their-kids-fall-in-love-we-are-all-human/, accessed November 26, 2020. See Yellin, *Of War and Weddings*. Yellin's memoir is about the process of healing the wounds of war, especially through links between the Yellin and Yamakawa families.

74. It is significant that the memoir of Harvey S. Horn, a former Jewish POW of the Germans, is dedicated "To All POWs of All Wars, To All Veterans of All Wars." See Harvey S. Horn, *Goldfish, Silver Boot: The Story of a World War II Prisoner of War* (Jacksonville, FL: Fortis), 2010.

75. Harry Corre Collection (AFC/2001/001/60510), American Folklife Center, Veterans History Project, Library of Congress. See also US Department of War Affairs, VA Greater Los Angeles Healthcare System, https://www.losangeles.va.gov/LOSANGELES/features/Harry_Corre_Former_POW_and_GLA_Patient_Advocate_Who_Understands.asp, accessed November 20, 2020.

76. Robert M. Morgenthau, "Introduction," in Eidelman, *Ours to Fight For*, 9–10.

77. See Françoise S. Ouzan, *How Young Holocaust Survivors Rebuilt Their Lives: France, the United States, and Israel* (Bloomington: Indiana University Press, 2018), esp. 109, 245, 253, 256.

78. See chapter 6 of this volume.

79. Wolk, *Jewish Aviators in World War II*, 170–71. Seriously wounded, Reichart received a Distinguished Flying Cross and a Purple Heart.

80. Ibid. After his retirement, a prestigious award, funded in perpetuity, was founded and named after him: the Stuart Reichart Award for the air force's outstanding attorney.

*Conclusion*

1. *The House I Live In* (1945), 11 min. RKO Radio Pictures, Library of Congress, Washington, DC.

2. Goodman, *Passover Anthology*, Kindle ed., location 1458 of 8880.

3. Oral Interview with Harry Zaslow, Accession Number: 1997.A.0441.125, RG Number: RG 50.462.0125, United States Holocaust Memorial Museum Collection, gift of the Gratz College Hebrew Education Society.

4. Electronic correspondence with Ruth Joffe and Faith Tomases about their father, Ralph Tomases, October 5, 2021.

5. See Bernstein, *Rabbis at War*, 33; Preface, 1.

6. Fredman and Falk, *Jews in American Wars*, 239, 129.

7. Walter Laqueur, *Generation Exodus: The Fate of Young Jewish Refugees from Nazi Germany* (London: Tauris, 2004), 151.

8. Women from all over the British Empire also assisted the British war effort. On January 25, 1942, the first group of sixty Jewish women from the Yishuv, the Jewish community in Mandatory Palestine, joined the British military to train as officers for the Auxiliary Territorial Service (ATS), the women's branch of the British army. They were followed by women joining the British Women's Auxiliary Air Force (WAAF) on May 25, 1943. Altogether, 4,350 Jewish women from Mandatory Palestine volunteered to join the British armed forces during World War II. See Esther Herlitz, "ATS and WAAF in World War II," Jewish Women's Archives, The Shalvi/Hyman Encyclopedia of Jewish Women, https://jwa.org/encyclopedia/article/ats-and-waaf-in-world-war-ii, accessed October 6, 2021.

9. Eisenhower, *Crusade in Europe*, 132–33.

10. The governor's eldest son, First Lieutenant Peter Gerald Lehman, enlisted in the Royal Canadian Air Force in September 1941 after being turned down by the United States Air Force because he was married with a child. In 1943, he was transferred to the US Air Force. Assigned to the 306th Fighter Squadron based in England, he performed fifty-seven combat missions flying Thunderbolts and Mustangs over Europe before he was killed in England in 1944.

Lehman was awarded the Air Medal with five clusters and the Distinguished Flying Cross in 1944, http://www.columbia.edu/cu/lweb/digital/collections/rbml/lehman/pdfs/0538/ldpd_leh_0538_0215.pdf, accessed September 22, 2021.

11. Testimony of Selma Cronan, (2000.A.116), oral history, tape one, Museum of Jewish Heritage–Living Memorial to the Holocaust, August 2000. She realized that other Jewish women on the base "were sensible enough to keep their mouths shut" and hide their Jewish origin.

12. Ernest Stock (pseudonym Eliezer), Memoirs of American Jewish Soldiers, 1944–1946, YIVO Institute for Jewish Research, RG 110, Box 1, Folder 29, 12. In August 1945, before the Japanese surrender, the army publication *Yank* asked GIs to state what changes they would like to see in postwar America. Most of the respondents mentioned "the need for wiping out racial and religious discrimination." See Dinnerstein, *Antisemitism in America*, 151.

13. Rabbi Jonathan Sacks, "The Festival of Insecurity—A Message for Sukkot," Rabbi Jonathan Sacks, https://rabbisacks.org/festival-insecurity-message-sukkot/, accessed September 26, 2021.

14. "Sydney J. Altman," The Hall of Valor Project, https://valor.militarytimes.com/hero/35065, accessed December 20, 2020.

15. "First Broadcast of Jewish Religious Service from Nazi Germany under the Auspices of the American Jewish Committee," October 29, 1944, 1. American forces fought fiercely in Aachen, the first German city to be captured by Allied forces.

16. Irving Goldberg, Memoirs of American Jewish Soldiers, 1944–1946, YIVO Institute for Jewish Research, RG 110, Box 1, folder 24, 13. See Françoise S. Ouzan, *How Young Holocaust Survivors Rebuilt Their Lives: France, the United States, and Israel* (Bloomington: Indiana University Press, 2018), esp. 23, 215, 20, 59, 75, 128, 158.

17. "Gertrude Shapiro in Hiroshima Circa 1945," Jewish Women's Archive, https://jwa.org/discover/infocus/military/nurses/shapiro, accessed June 8, 2023.

18. In the aftermath of World War II, veterans—men and women—continued to assert their rights as American Jewish citizens in the country that shaped them and that they, in turn, helped transform.

19. See Irving Ungar, ed., *Arthur Szyk, Soldier in Art* (Burlingame, California: Historicana, 2017), especially "World War II Non-Aryan Supermen," 154–55. The differences of Jewish self-representation in Szyk's drawings before and after the United States entered the war are striking. For a discussion of Jewish servicemen and servicewomen from Mandatory Palestine and the creation of an independent Jewish Brigade within the British forces in September 1944, see Penslar, *Jews and the Military*, 217–24. "Jewish War Heroes," a comic booklet from 1944 published by the Canadian Jewish Congress, also highlights the mighty contribution of Allied soldiers to the war effort.

20. *The House I Live In*. The eleven-minute American film released by RKO Radio Pictures was intended to combat anti-Jewish prejudice and discrimination.

21. Photo Archives of the Museum of American Jewish Military History, Washington, DC; see *Officers at Seder at Munda Including Admiral Kinkaid*, accession number: 1986.001, catalog number: P986.001.062.

22. Irving Goldberg, Memoirs of American Jewish Soldiers, 1944–1946, YIVO Institute for Jewish Research, RG 110, Box 1, Folder 24, 13. In terms of comradeship, the example of veteran Ralph Tomases is telling: he included the name of Christian fellow POWs in his synagogue's *Yizkor* book in Wilmington, Delaware. Normally, synagogues publish these books annually to record those who died—friends and family members for whom the *Kaddish* is recited on Yom Kippur.

# BIBLIOGRAPHY

## Primary Sources

### Interviews by the Video History Project, Museum of Jewish Heritage—A Living Memorial to the Holocaust

Testimony of Bernice (Bee) Falk Haydu (2000.A.197)
Testimony of Gloria Sosin (2000.V.165)
Testimony of Ruth Cohen (1999.V.50)
Testimony of Selma Cronan (2000.A.116)

### Interviews by the Veterans History Project, American Folklife Center, Library of Congress

Arthur Buchwald Collection (AFC/2001/001/24004)
Bea Abrams Hirshcovici Cohen Collection (AFC/2001/00/86629)
Milton Zaslow Collection (AFC/2001/001/27130)
Tracy A. Sugarman Collection (AFC/2001/001/05440)

### Interviews

### Interviews by the Jeff and Toby Herr Oral History Archive, United States Holocaust Memorial Museum, Washington, DC

Oral History Interview with Alexander Breuer, Accession Number: 1991.264.3 | RG Number: RG-50.234.0003
Oral History Interview with Guy Stern, Accession Number: 1990.379.1 | RG Number: RG-50.030.0223
Oral History Interview with Harry Zaslow, Accession Number: 1997.A.0441.125 | RG Number: RG-50.462.0125
Oral History Interview with Manfred Steinfeld, Accession Number: 1989.346.70 | RG Number: RG-50.031.0070
On North Africa: Activities of the WJC, Antisemitism in the French Army and the Crémieux Decree: USHMM, RG 43.144M (1943–47)

### Interviews by the National World War II Museum, New Orleans

Oral History Interview with Dr. Hal Baumgarten, D-Day Survivor. https://www.youtube.com/watch?v=UWnPWbx-sXo&ab_channel=TheNationalWWIIMuseum.
Farewell to Dr. Harold 'Hal' Baumgarten, D-Day Survivor and Friend of the National WWII Museum.

### Interviews Collected by *Texas Woman's University*

Interview with Joanne Wallace Orr, "An Oral History, Women, Airforce Service Pilots," by Jean Hascall Cole, *The Woman's Collection*.

### US Department of Veterans Affairs

*Nisei Soldier Regiment.* Documentary Film in Cooperation with the National Cemetery Administration and San Francisco University, 2018. YouTube.

### Interviews by the Author

Max Benhamou, May 17, 2018
Murray Greenfield, August 26, 2018
Robb K. Haberman, May 11, 2017
Fabien Lancry, August 20, 1998
Huguette Lancry, February 28, 2008
Frida Macarov, October 18, 2020
Milton Miller, November 18, 2016
Emile Moatti, September 25, 2015
Howard Rosen, June 23, 2021
Hebe Solomon Benyamin, December 12, 2020
Denise Zerah, July 13, 2018
Noam Sachs Zion, May 26, 2020

### Archives

*American Jewish Distribution Committee (JDC), New York*
Philippines General, II-VIII. 1945, 706630
Correspondence on conditions of local Jewish community. Cables regarding fundraising by US service members to rebuild the Manila synagogue.

*William Breman Heritage Museum, Atlanta, Georgia*
Gordon Family Papers, Cuba Family Archives for Southern Jewish History
Box 1, Folder 6, Mss 387, Gordon Family Papers.
Box 2, File 4, Correspondence Samuel Gordon and Jack Gordon, 1941–1942, undated, 17/26.
Box 4, Folder 6, Gordon Jack, Naval Academy Memorial Chair, 1941–1999, undated, 20/60. On J. Gordon "Hero and Patriot," correspondence of S. Gordon with Captain Seymour.

*YIVO Institute of Jewish Research, Center for Jewish History, New York*

*In the Nation's Service: A Compilation of Facts Concerning Jewish Men in the Armed Forces during the First Year of the War*, first printing December 1942, second printing February 1943, RG 110, Box 1.
Memoirs of American Jewish Soldiers, RG 110, 1945–1946. (See Unpublished Memoirs)

*Archives Nationales d'outre-mer (ANOM), Aix en Provence, France*
Cabinet du Gouverneur Général Peyrouton, 6CAB5, Broadcast Address of Marcel Peyrouton, February 22, 1943.
Fonds des Préfectures; département d'Oran
Fonds du gouvernement général d'Algérie
Jewish Associations: boxes 2539, 2541

*Ben Zvi Institute, Jerusalem, Israel (YBZ)*
Documentation Center on North African Jewry during World War II

Photographs of Allied Troops in French North Africa

*Centre de documentation Juive Contemporaine, (CDJC), Mémorial de la Shoah, North Africa, Bedeau internment camp*, CCCL XXXV-5

*Chaim Herzog Museum of the Jewish Soldier in World War II, Latrun, Israel*
Interview with Sergeant Larry Yellin, Thirty-Sixth Infantry Division, https://www.youtube.com/watch?v=KmwQFKto77g&ab_channel=TheJwmww2.

*Zionist Central Archives (CZA)*
Report on the discriminatory measures against Jews in Algeria (during the Vichy Regime), 525/52/7.

Archival material from Howard Rosen:
War Diary of the 526th Fighter-Bomber Squadron, Eighty-Sixth Fighter-Bomber Group, February 1942–October 1945, 11.

*Periodicals and Newspapers*

*American Hebrew*, 1943–1945
*American Jewish Year Book*, 1943–1947
"From the Island of Munda," *Jewish Chaplain*, November 1943
*Jewish Chaplain*, 1943
*Jewish Oiy Kinawan*, no. 4, 1946 (24 Tammuz 5706)
*Jewish Telegraphic Agency (JTA)*, 1944–1945
*Reconstructionist*, 1944–1945
*Stars and Stripes*, 1944–1945, 1977
*Voice*, Camden, NJ, 1944

*Wartime Films, Library of Congress*

*The House I Live In* (1945), 11 min. RKO Radio Pictures, Library of Congress, Washington, DC.
"*Know Your Enemy: Japan*," War Department Orientation film (1945), produced by Army Pictorial Service, Signal Corps.
*Let There Be Light* (1946). War Department, directed by John Huston, Army Pictorial Service, Signal Corps.
*The Memphis Belle: The Story of a Flying Fortress* (1944), 45 min. War Department, directed by William Wyler, Army Pictorial Service, Signal Corps, distributed by Paramount.
*The US Army Nurse in World War II* (1944). War Department, Army Pictorial Service, Signal Corps.

*Contemporary Documentary Films*

*Five Came Back* (2017). Netflix World War II documentary about five Hollywood filmmakers who enlisted in the armed forces to document World War II, second episode: S1, E2, "Combat Zones."
*GI Jews: Jewish Americans in World War II* (2017), 87 min. Documentary film directed by Lisa Ades.
*An Open Door, Jewish Rescue in the Philippines*, Noel Izon (author) and Sharon Delmendo (co-producer), 2012.

*Published Letters, Diaries, Memoirs, and Wartime Publications*

Alper, Benedict Solomon. *Love and Politics in Wartime: Letters to My Wife, 1943–45*. Selected and edited by Joan Wallach Scott. Urbana: University of Illinois Press, 1992.

Angress, Werner T. *Witness to the Storm: A Jewish Journey from Nazi Berlin to the 82nd Airborne, 1920–1945.* Bloomington: Indiana University Press, 2019; first published in 2012.

Blumenthal, L. Roy, et al. *Fighting for America: A Record of the Participation of Jewish Men and Women in the Armed Forces during 1944.* Foreword by Frank L. Weil. New York: National Jewish Welfare Board, 1944.

Eisenhower, Dwight D. *Crusade in Europe.* New York: Doubleday, 1948.

Feinberg, Barbara, comp. *Your Loving Husband and Father: A Soldier's Story during World War II from the Letters of George Bader.* Jerusalem: Barbara Feinberg, 2018.

Haydu, Bernice Falk. *Letters Home 1944–1945: Women Airforce Service Pilots, World War II.* Edited by Rita Cody Casey. Foreword by Sally Van Wagenen Keil. Riviera Beach, FL: TopLine, 2003.

Klausner, Abraham J. *A Letter to My Children from the Edge of the Holocaust.* San Francisco: Holocaust Center of Northern California, 2002.

———. *Shārit ha-plātah.* 5 vols. Jerusalem: Gefen Publishing House, 1945. Five volumes bound in one. Reprinted in 2021 by Schoen Books, South Deerfield, MA.

Kohs, Samuel Calmin. "Jewish War Records of World War II." *American Jewish Year Book* 47 (1945–1946): 153–72.

Kraft, Louis. "Servicemen and Veterans." *American Jewish Year Book* 48 (1946–1947): 164–72.

Rontch, Israel E., ed. *Jewish Youth at War.* New York: Martin Press, 1945.

Saperstein, Marc, ed. *Jewish Preaching in Times of War, 1800–2001.* Oxford: Littman Library of Jewish Civilization, 2008.

## Prayer Books and Books for Jews in the Military

*A Book of Jewish Thoughts.* New York: National Jewish Welfare Board, 1943.

*A Book of Jewish Thoughts.* Selected and arranged by Dr. J. H. Hertz, Office of the Chief Rabbi. London: Henderson and Spalding, 1942.

*Prayer Book for Jews in the Armed Forces of the United States,* abridged. National Jewish Welfare Board. Philadelphia: Jewish Publication Society, 1941, 1943.

*Prayer Book for Jews in the Armed Forces of the United States,* abridged, *New Year and Day of Atonement.* National Jewish Welfare Board. Philadelphia: Jewish Publication Society, 1941.

*Sayings of the Fathers.* Sailors, Soldiers, and Airmen's Edition. London: Soncino Press, 1942.

## Unpublished Memoirs

Brill, Rabbi Mordecai. "My Experiences and Observations as a Jewish Chaplain in World War II." Jewish Theological Seminary of America, December 1946.

Caplan, Aben S. "Memoir." Collection (AFC/2001/001/5190) Personal narratives; Experiencing War: Veterans History Project, American Folklife Center, Library of Congress, 2001.

YIVO Essay Contest. "My Experiences and Observations as a Jew in World War II." Fifty-two entries. YIVO Institute for Jewish Research, 1946.

## Published Memoirs

Buchwald, Art. *Leaving Home: A Memoir.* New York: G. P. Putman's Sons, 1993.

Eliach, Yaffah, and Gurevitch Brana, eds. *The Liberators: Eyewitness Accounts of the Liberation of Concentration Camps.* Vol. 1, *Liberation Day Oral History Testimonies of American Liberators from the Archives of the Center for Holocaust Studies.* Brooklyn: Center for Holocaust Studies Documentation and Research, 1981.

Frucht, Karl. "We Were a P.W.I. Team." *Commentary,* January 9, 1946, 69–76.

*GIs Remember: Liberating the Concentration Camps.* Washington, DC: National Museum of American Jewish Military History, n.d. Exhibition Catalog.

Gittelsohn, Roland B. "Brothers All?" *Reconstructionist,* February 7, 1947, 8–13.

Stock, Ernest. *Tri-Continental Jew: A 20th Century Journey.* Middleton, DE: Mendele Electronic Books, 2015.

Ribalow, Harold U. "The Failure of Jewish Chaplaincy." *Jewish Frontier*, June 1946, 10–12.

## War Department Publications

*Army Talk* 151, War Department, Washington, DC, November 30, 1946, Historical Reference Branch, US Army Military History Institute, Carlisle, Pennsylvania.

## SELECTED SECONDARY SOURCES

Abitbol, Michel. *The Jews of North Africa during the Second World War.* Translated by Catherine Tihanyi Zentelis. Detroit: Wayne State University Press, 1989.

Aboulker, José. *La victoire du 8 novembre 1942: La Résistance et le débarquement des Alliés à Alger.* Paris: Édition du Félin, 2012.

Abzug, Robert H. *Inside the Vicious Heart: Americans and the Liberation of Nazi Camps.* New York: Oxford University Press, 1987.

Allouche-Benayoun, Joëlle. "Intermittently French: Jews from Algeria during World War II." *Journal of Contemporary Jewry* 37, no. 2 (2017): 219–30. https://link.springer.com/article/10.1007/s12397-017-9230-9.

Amipaz-Zilber, Gitta. *The Role of the Jewish Underground in the American Landing in Algiers, 1940–1942.* Jerusalem: Gefen, 1992.

Arad, Yitzhak. *In the Shadow of the Red Banner: Soviet Jews in the War against Nazi Germany.* Jerusalem: Gefen, 2010.

Atkinson, Rick. *An Army at Dawn: The War in North Africa, 1942–1943.* New York: Henry Holt, 2002.

Baldwin, Neil. *Henry Ford and the Jews: The Mass Production of Hate.* New York: PublicAffairs, 2001.

Barger, Judith. *Beyond the Call of Duty: Army Flight Nursing in World War II.* Kent, OH: Kent State University Press, 2013.

Barish, Louis, ed. *Rabbis in Uniform: The Story of the American Jewish Military Chaplain.* New York: Jonathan David, 1962.

Bel Ange, Norbert. *Quand Vichy internait ses soldats juifs d'Algérie: Bedeau, Sud oranais, 1941–1943.* Paris: L'Harmattan, 2009.

Ben Amara, Helyett. *Il était une fois là bas: Algérie, mon pays, comme un feu tu te gaspilles en étincelles.* Grenoble: Editions Alzieu, 2000.

Ben-David, Calev. "My Father, the Soldier of Occupation." *Jerusalem Post*, August 4, 2016.

Bendersky, Joseph W. *The "Jewish Threat": Anti-Semitic Politics of the U.S. Army.* New York: Basic Books, 2000.

Berenbaum, Michael. "Arthur Szyk: The Artist as Soldier, the Artist as Messenger." In *Arthur Szyk, Soldier in Art*, edited by David Ungar, 61–81. Burlingame, CA: Historicana, 2017.

Berkman, Ted. *Cast a Giant Shadow: The Story of Mickey Marcus Who Died to Save Jerusalem.* New York: Pocket Books, 1962.

Bernstein, Philip S. *Rabbis at War: The CANRA Story.* Waltham, MA: American Jewish Historical Society, 1971.

Branson, Bernard. "I Wanted These Sons of Bitches to Know." In *Ours to Fight For: American Jewish Voices from the Second World War*, edited by J. M. Eidelman, 16–31. New York: Museum of Jewish Heritage–Living Memorial to the Holocaust, 2003.

Breitman, Richard, and Alan M. Kraut. *American Refugee Policy and European Jewry, 1933–1945.* Bloomington: Indiana University Press, 1987.

Brokaw, Tom. "Afterword." In *Ours to Fight For: American Jewish Voices from the Second World War*, edited by J. M. Eidelman, 171–73. New York: Museum of Jewish Heritage–Living Memorial to the Holocaust, 2003.

Brown, Don. *The Last Fighter Pilot: The True Story of the Final Combat Mission of World War II*. Forewords by Captain Jerry Yellin and Melanie Stone. Kindle ed. Washington, DC: Regnery History, 2017.

Butler, Menachem. "The Flying Rabbi: Chaplain Werfel (1916–1943)." *Commentator*, May 11, 2004, 20.

Calohan, Julie. "Journalist Brings to Life Story of Jewish-American Army Nurse." US Army, April 12, 2010. Accessed November 29, 2020. https://www.army.mil/article/37256/journalist_brings_to_life_story_of_jewish_american_army_nurse_corps_nurse.

Caplan, Aben S. "Memoir." Experiencing War: Veterans History Project, Library of Congress.

Century, Douglas. *Barney Ross: The Life of a Jewish Fighter*. Kindle ed. New York: Schocken Books, 2006.

Cohen, Naomi W. *Not Free to Desist, The American Jewish Committee, 1906–1966*. Introduction by Salo W. Baron. Philadelphia: Jewish Publication Society of America, 1972.

Cohen, Roger. *Soldiers and Slaves: American POWs Trapped by the Nazis' Final Gamble*. New York: Knopf, 2005.

Cohen, Sandor B., curator. *Women in the Military: A Jewish Perspective*. Introduction by Harvey S. Friedman and Judith Weiss Cohen. Washington, DC: National Museum of American Jewish Military History, 1999.

Cole, Jean Hascall. *Women Pilots of World War II*. Salt Lake City: University of Utah Press, 1992.

Cooperman, Jessica. *Making Judaism Safe for America: World War I and the Origins of Religious Pluralism*. New York: New York University Press, 2018.

Daniels, Roger. *The Politics of Prejudice: The Anti-Japanese Movement in California and the Struggle for Japanese Exclusion*. Berkeley: University of California Press, 1977.

Dawidowicz, Lucy S. *On Equal Terms: Jews in America, 1881–1981*. New York: Holt, Rinehart and Winston, 1982.

Diner, Hasia. *Hungering for America*. Cambridge, MA: Harvard University Press, 2002.

Diner, Hasia R., and Beryl Lieff Benderly. *Her Works Praise Her: A History of Jewish Women in America from Colonial Times to the Present*. New York: Basic Books, 2002.

Dinnerstein, Leonard. *Antisemitism in America*. New York: Oxford University Press, 1994.

———. *The Leo Frank Case*. Rev. ed. Athens: University of Georgia Press, 2008.

Dorn, Samantha. "Captain Ben Salomon." National Museum of the United States Army. Army Historical Foundation. Accessed December 6, 2020. https://armyhistory.org/captain-ben-solomon/.

Douglas, Kirk. *The Ragman's Son: An Autobiography*. New York: Simon & Schuster, 1988.

Dyess, William E. "Statement of Major William E. Dyess, Air Corps, Concerning Experiences and Observations as Prisoner of War in the Philippines—9 April 1942 to 4 April 1943." RG 18, National Archives. Quoted in Stanley L. Falk, "Introduction." In William E. Dyess, *Bataan Death March: A Survivor's Account*. Edited with a biographical introduction by Charles Leavelle. Kindle ed. Lincoln: University of Nebraska Press, 2002; first edition by Marajen Stevick Dyess, 1944.

Eidelman, Jay M. "Jewish GIs and the War against the Nazis." In *Ours to Fight For: American Jewish Voices from the Second World War*, edited by J. M. Eidelman, 13–15. New York: Museum of Jewish Heritage–Living Memorial to the Holocaust, 2003.

———, ed. *Ours to Fight For: American Jewish Voices from the Second World War*. New York: Museum of Jewish Heritage–Living Memorial to the Holocaust, 2003.

Engel, David. "Demonstrative Desertion of Jewish Soldiers in the Polish Army in Britain in 1944: Relations between British, Poles, and Jews during World War II" (in Hebrew). *Yahadut Zemanenu* 2 (1985): 177–207.

*Ernie Pyle's War: A Documentary on Ernie Pyle, World War II Correspondent*. DVD, 30 min. Produced by Todd Gould. WFYI Productions and the Indiana Historical Society, 2005.

Farr, Finis. *Rickenbacker's Luck: An American Life*. Boston: Houghton Mifflin Harcourt, 1979.

Fredman, Joseph George, and Louis A. Falk. *Jews in American Wars*. Washington, DC: Jewish Veterans of the United States of America, 1954.

Gardner, Ian. *Airborne: The Combat Story of Ed Shames of Easy Company*. Oxford: Osprey, 2015.

Geffen, David. "Days of Awe in the Pacific." *Jerusalem Post*, September 8, 2010.

———. "The Jewish War Veterans of America—Alive and Well in Israel." *Jerusalem Post Magazine*, July 3, 2015, 20.

"Gertrude Shapiro in Hiroshima circa 1945." Jewish Women's Archive. Accessed June 8, 2023. https://jwa.org/discover/infocus/military/nurses/shapiro.

*GIs Remember: Liberating the Concentration Camps*. Acknowledgments by Leslie H. Fruedenheim. Introduction by Morton Horvitz. Essay by Robert H. Abzug. Washington, DC: National Museum of American Jewish Military History, 1994.

Gittelsohn, Roland B. "Brothers All?" *Reconstructionist* 12 (February 7, 1947): 10.

Gladwin, Lee A. "American POWs on Japanese Ships Take a Voyage into Hell." *Prologue Magazine* 35, no. 4 (Winter 2003). Accessed August 31, 2020. https://www.archives.gov/publications/prologue/2003/winter/hell-ships-1.html.

Goldberg, Jeffrey. "Trump: Americans Who Died in War Are 'Losers' and 'Suckers.'" *Atlantic*, September 3, 2020. Accessed October 9, 2020. https://amp.theatlantic.com/amp/article/615997/.

Goldman, Alex J. *Giants of Faith: Great American Rabbis*. New York: Citadel Press, 1964.

Goodman, Philip. *The Passover Anthology*. Kindle ed. Philadelphia: Jewish Publication Society, 1961.

Grayzel, Solomon. "A Chronicle of Our Generation." In *Two Generations in Perspective: Notable Events and Trends 1896–1956*, edited by Harry Schneiderman, 3–109. New York: Monde, 1957.

Greenberg, Hank. *Hank Greenberg: The Story of My Life*. Edited with an introduction by Ira Berkow. New York: Times Books, 1989.

Grobman, Alex. *Rekindling the Flame: American Jewish Chaplains and the Survivors of European Jewry, 1944–1948*. Detroit: Wayne State University Press, 1993.

Grossman, Atina. *Jews, Germans, and Allies: Close Encounters in Occupied Germany*. Princeton, NJ: Princeton University Press, 2007.

Gutstein, Alum Daniel. "A Soldier Fighting for His People." Ida Crown Jewish Academy, 2. Accessed June 23, 2020. https://www.icja.org/2014/05/a-soldier-fighting-for-his-people/.

Halsey, Ashley. "Ancestral Gray Cloud over Patton: General George S. Patton's Time-Tested Military Bloodline." *American History Illustrated* 19 (March 1984): 42–48.

Heller, Aron. "Israeli Recognition, at Last, for Jews Who Fought the Nazis." May 29, 2015. Accessed July 24, 2020. https://www.timesofisrael.com/israeli-recognition-at-last-for-jews-who-fought-the-nazis/.

Henderson, Bruce. *Sons and Soldiers: The Untold Story of the Jews Who Escaped the Nazis and Returned with the U.S. Army to Fight Hitler*. New York: HarperCollins, 2017.

Herlitz, Esther. "ATS and WAAF in World War II." Jewish Women's Archives, The Shalvi/Hyman Encyclopedia of Jewish Women. Accessed October 6, 2021. https://jwa.org/encyclopedia/article/ats-and-waaf-in-world-war-ii.

Hertzberg, Arthur. *A Jew in America: My Life and a People's Struggle for Identity*. San Francisco: HarperOne, 2002.

Hewlett, Thomas H. "Di Ju Nana Bijnshyo-Nightmare-Revisited." In *The Japanese Story*, December 1978.
Hindley, Meredith. *Destination Casablanca: Exile, Espionage, and the Battle for North Africa in World War II*. New York: PublicAffairs, 2017.
Hobson Faure, Laura. *A "Jewish Marshall Plan": The American Presence in Post-Holocaust France*. Bloomington: Indiana University Press, 2022. First published in French in 2013.
Hochstein, Joseph M., and Murray S. Greenfield. *The Jews' Secret Fleet*. Introduction by Martin Gilbert. Jerusalem: Gefen, 1987.
Holderness, Clifford G., and Jeffrey Pontiff. "Hierarchies and the Survival of Prisoners of War during World War II." *Management Science* 58 (2012): 1873–86.
Horn, Harvey S. *Goldfish, Silver Boot: The Story of a World War II Prisoner of War*. Jacksonville, FL: Fortis, 2010.
Hyman, Paula, and Dash Moore Deborah, eds. *Jewish Women in America: An Historical Encyclopedia*. 2 vols. New York: Routledge, 1997.
"Jewish Chaplain Killed in Line of Duty: Fourth American Rabbi to Lose Life in War." Jewish Telegraphic Agency, January 9, 1944. Accessed November 29, 2020. https://www.jta.org/1944/01/09/archive/jewish-chaplain-killed-in-line-of-duty-fourth-american-rabbi-to-lose-life-in-war.
Jorgensen, Daniel B. *Air Force Chaplains*. Vol. 1, *The Service of Chaplains to Army Air Units, 1917–1946*. Washington, DC: United States Air Force, Office of the Chief of Chaplains, 1961.
*Les Juifs de Tunisie sous le joug nazi, 9 novembre 1942–8 mai 1943*. Testimonies collected and annotated by Claude Nataf. Paris: Édition le Manuscrit, Fondation pour la Mémoire de la Shoah, 2012.
Kadosh, Sara. "Laura Margolis Jarblum." The Shalvi/Hyman Encyclopedia of Jewish Women. Accessed October 5, 2021. https://jwa.org/encyclopedia/article/jarblum-laura-margolis.
Kaplan, Jacob. "French Jewry under the Occupation." *American Jewish Year Book* 47, no. 5706 (1945–46): 111–18.
Karabel, Jerome. *The Chosen: The Hidden History of Admission and Exclusion at Harvard, Yale, and Princeton*. Boston: Houghton Mifflin Harcourt, 2005.
Kaufman, Isidor. *American Jews in World War II: The Story of 550,000 Fighters for Freedom*. 2 vols. New York: Dial Press, 1947.
Kligsberg, Moses. "'American Jewish Soldiers on Jews and Judaism': A Report of a Contest." *YIVO Annual of Jewish Social Science* 5 (1950): 256–65.
Kohs, S. C. "Jewish War Records of World War II." *American Jewish Year Book* 47, no. 5706 (1945–46): 153–72.
Kolosov, Joanna. "Tribute to World War II POW 2nd Lt. Magdalena Eckmann Hewlett." Sonoma County Library. Accessed September 30, 2020. https://sonomalibrary.org/blogs/history/tribute-to-world-war-ii-pow-2nd-lt-magdalena-eckmann-hewlett-by-joanna-kolosov-mlis-0.
Landdeck Sharp, Katherine. *The Women with Silver Wings: The Inspiring True Story of the Women Airforce Service Pilots of World War II*. New York: Crown, 2020.
Langer, Ron. "Post-Traumatic Stress Disorder in Former POWs." In *Post-Traumatic Stress Disorder: A Handbook for Clinicians*, edited by T. Williams, 35–50. Cincinnati: Disabled American Veterans, 1987.
Lang-Slattery, Kathryn. *Immigrant Soldier: The Story of a Ritchie Boy*. Foreword by Guy Stern. Laguna Beach, CA: Pacific Bookworks, 2014.
Laqueur, Walter. *Generation Exodus: The Fate of Young Jewish Refugees from Nazi Germany*. London: Tauris, 2004.

Laskier, Michael M. *North African Jewry in the Twentieth Century: The Jews of Morocco, Tunisia, and Algeria.* New York: New York University Press, 1994.

Lerner, Maximilian. "I Wanted to Get My Own Back." In *Ours to Fight For: American Jewish Voices from the Second World War*, edited by J. M. Eidelman, 66–77. New York: Museum of Jewish Heritage–Living Memorial to the Holocaust, 2003.

Lévinas, Emmanuel. "Écrits sur la captivité et Hommage à Bergson." In *Carnets de captivité et autres inédits (1940–1945)*, edited by Rodolphe Calin and Catherine Chalier, 199–219. Paris: Grasset, 2009.

Levinger, Lee J. *A Jewish Chaplain in France.* New York: Macmillan, 1922.

Macarov, David. "Atlantan Led Air Force's Coded Communications." *Jewish Times*, April 12, 2018. Accessed July 10, 2020. https://atlantajewishtimes.timesofisrael.com/atlantan-led-air-forces-coded-communications/.

———. "A Small Cog: Tales from My Two Wars." Manuscript in possession of the author. Israel, 2014.

Mailer, Norman. *The Naked and the Dead.* New York: Rinehart, 1948. Fiftieth Anniversary edition. New York: Henry Holt, 1998.

Males, Akiva. "Jewish GIs and Their Dog Tags." *Hakira: The Flatbush Journal of Jewish Law and Thought* 15 (2003): 271–87.

"Major General Julius Klein: His Life and Work." National Museum of American Jewish Military History. Accessed October 13, 2020. https://nmajmh.org/exhibitions/permanent-exhibitions/major-general-julius-kleinhis-life-and-work/.

Manning, Molly Guptill. *When Books Went to War: The Stories That Helped Us Win World War II.* Boston: Houghton Mifflin Harcourt, 2014.

Mayer, Gabriel. "Holocaust and WWII: Jews in the Red Army." *International Journal of Social Science Studies* 3, no. 2 (January 2015): 113–22.

McCullough, David G. *Truman.* New York: Simon & Schuster, 1992.

Mellnik, Stephen M. *Philippine Diary, 1939–1945.* New York: Van Nostrand Reinhold, 1969.

Mindell, Cindy. "On Memorial Day . . . Honoring the Jewish War Veterans of the United States of America." *CT Jewish Ledger*, May 22, 2013.

Monahan, Evelyn, and Rosemary Neidel-Greenlee. *All This Hell: U.S. Nurses Imprisoned by the Japanese.* Lexington: University Press of Kentucky, 2000.

———. *A Few Good Women: America's Military Women from World War I to the Wars in Iraq and Afghanistan.* New York: Knopf, 2010.

Moore, Deborah Dash. *GI Jews: How World War II Changed a Generation.* Cambridge, MA: Belknap Press of Harvard University Press, 2004.

Morgenthau, Robert M. "Introduction." In *Ours to Fight For: American Jewish Voices from the Second World War*, edited by J. M. Eidelman, 9–11. New York: Museum of Jewish Heritage–Living Memorial to the Holocaust, 2003.

Myers, William Starr. *Prominent Families of New Jersey.* 2 vols. Baltimore: Genealogical, 2000.

Nadell, Pamela S. *America's Jewish Women: A History from Colonial Times to Today.* New York: W. W. Norton, 2019.

Nakamura, Kelli Y. "Military Intelligence Service." Densho Encyclopedia. Accessed October 18, 2020. http://encyclopedia.densho.org/Military%20Intelligence%20Service/.

Neiberg, Michael S. *When France Fell: The Vichy Crisis and the Fate of the Anglo-American Alliance.* Cambridge, MA: Harvard University Press, 2021.

Norman, Milton. "'For You the War Is Over': A Jewish U.S. Army Soldier in a German POW Camp." West Point Center for Oral History. West Point Department of History. August 29, 2015. Accessed November 4, 2020. https://www.westpointcoh.org/interviews/for-you-the-war-is-over-a-jewish-u-s-army-soldier-in-a-german-pow-camp.

Nussbaum, Chaim. *Chaplain on the River Kwai: Story of a Prisoner of War.* New York: Shapolsky, 1988.

Obermayer, Herman J. *Soldiering for Freedom: A GI's Account of World War II.* College Station: Texas A&M University Press, 2005.

Ofer, Dalia. "Holocaust Survivors as Immigrants: The Case of Israel and the Cyprus Detainees." *Modern Judaism* 16, no. 1 (1996): 1–23.

O'Neill, William L. "Race, Ethnicity, and Religion in World War II." In *Ours to Fight For: American Jewish Voices from the Second World War*, edited by J. M. Eidelman, 113–15. New York: Museum of Jewish Heritage–Living Memorial to the Holocaust, 2003.

Oney, Steve. *And the Dead Shall Rise: The Murder of Mary Phagan and the Lynching of Leo Frank.* New York: Pantheon, 2003.

Ouzan, Françoise S. "American Jewish Chaplains and the Survivors' Return to Jewish Communal Life (1945–1952)." In *Postwar Jewish Displacement and Rebirth, 1945–1967*, edited by Françoise S. Ouzan and Manfred Gerstenfeld, 112–36. Leiden: Brill, 2014.

———. "Antisemitism in the US at the End of the War and in Its Aftermath: Attitudes toward Displaced Persons." *Antisemitism Worldwide* 2003/2004 (2005): 51–74.

———. "From Algiers to Dachau: The Special Assignments of an American Jewish Officer Ordered by General Eisenhower, 1942–1945." *Yalkut Moreshet* 103 (2023): 125–41, Hebrew; *Moreshet* 20 (forthcoming), English.

———. *How Young Holocaust Survivors Rebuilt Their Lives: France, the United States, and Israel.* Bloomington: Indiana University Press, 2018.

Paper, Maurice. *My War.* Edited by M. Paper and C. Paper. 2nd ed. N.p.: Lulu Press, 2011, Nook, Self Published.

"Passover in the Philippines." The Letter Box, *American Hebrew*, May 11, 1945.

Patton, George S. *The Patton Papers.* Vol. 2, *1940–1945.* Compiled and edited by Martin Blumenson. Boston: Houghton Mifflin Harcourt, 1974.

Pearson, Emmet F. "Morbidity and Mortality in Santo Tomas Internment Camp, 28–29." In *The Japanese Story.* American Ex-POW National Medical Research Committee, Packet 10. https://www.axpow.org/medsearch/packet10converted.pdf.

Penslar, Derek J. *Jews and the Military: A History.* Princeton, NJ: Princeton University Press, 2013.

Peretz, Pauline. *Une armée noire. Fort Huachuca, Arizona, 1941–1945.* Paris: Seuil, 2022.

Porath, Zipporah. *Col. David (Mickey) Marcus: "A Soldier for All Humanity."* New York: American Jewish Historical Society, 2010.

Potter, Lou, William Miles, and Nina Rosenblum. *Liberators: Fighting on Two Fronts in World War II.* New York: Harcourt, Brace, Jovanovich, 1992.

Prater, Scott. "Former POW Details Inspiring Survival Story." US Army. Accessed October 2, 2020. https://www.army.mil/article/143124/former_pow_details_inspiring_survival_story.

*Prayer Book, Abridged for Jews in the Armed Forces of the United States.* New York: National Jewish Welfare Board, 1941, 1943.

*Prayer Book: New Year and Day of Atonement, Abridged for Jews in the Armed Forces of the United States.* New York: National Jewish Welfare Board, 1943.

*Psychology for the Fighting Man: What You Should Know about Yourself and Others.* Washington, DC: Infantry Journal, 1943.

Raghavan, Srinath. *The Most Dangerous Place: A History of the United States in South Asia.* Haryana: Penguin Random House, 2018.

Raider, Mark A. *The Emergence of American Zionism.* New York: New York University Press, 1998.

Roberts, Burton. "Oh, the Great Speckled Bird." In *Ours to Fight For: American Jewish Voices from the Second World War*, edited by J. M. Eidelman, 50–61. New York: Museum of Jewish Heritage–Living Memorial to the Holocaust, 2003.

Roberts, Sophie Beth. *Citizenship and Antisemitism in French Colonial Algeria, 1870–1962*. Cambridge: Cambridge University Press, 2017.

Rosengren, John. *Hank Greenberg: The Hero of Heroes*. New York: New American Library, 2013.

Ross, Barney, and Martin Abramson. *No Man Stands Alone: The True Story of Barney Ross*. Philadelphia: J.B. Lippincott, 1957.

Rugel, Michael. "Remembering Captain Jerry Yellin." National Museum of American Jewish Military History, January 10, 2018. Accessed July 16, 2020. https://nmajmh.org/2018/01/remembering-captain-jerry-yellin/.

Saadoun, Haim. "Jewish Leadership in North Africa: The Transformative Implications of World War II." In *The End of 1942: A Turning Point in World War II and in the Comprehension of the Final Solution?*, edited by Dina Porat and Dan Michman with Haim Saadoun, 159–87. Jerusalem: Yad Vashem, 2017.

Sandrow, Edward T. "Jews in the Army—A Short Social Study." *Reconstructionist*, March 17, 1944.

Sarna, Jonathan D. *American Judaism: A History*. New Haven, CT: Yale University Press, 2004.

Scharf, Jack. "I Just Couldn't Face It." In *Ours to Fight For: American Jewish Voices from the Second World War*, edited by J. M. Eidelman, 90–101. New York: Museum of Jewish Heritage–Living Memorial to the Holocaust, 2003.

"Sgt. Meyer Levin, Hero of Pacific Aerial War, Killed off New Guinea." *Jewish Telegraphic Agency* 10, no. 42 (1943). Accessed June 2, 2023. https://www.jta.org/archive/sgt-meyer-levin-hero-of-pacific-aerial-war-killed-off-new-guinea.

"The Shalvi/Hyman Encyclopedia of Jewish Women." Jewish Women's Archives. Accessed June 21, 2023. https://jwa.org/encyclopedia.

Silverman, Martin. "The Lord Would Provide." In *Ours to Fight For: American Jewish Voices from the Second World War*, edited by J. M. Eidelman, 116–31. New York: Museum of Jewish Heritage–Living Memorial to the Holocaust, 2003.

Slomovitz, Albert I. *The Fighting Rabbis: Jewish Military Chaplains and American History*. New York: New York University Press, 1999.

Smith, Deb. "Love at First Flight: Former WASP Still Living Life at Full Throttle." *Airport Journals*. Accessed May 10, 2020. http://airportjournals.com/love-at-first-flight-former-wasp-still-living-life-at-full-throttle/.

Stahl, Ronit Yael. *Enlisting Faith: How the Military Chaplaincy Shaped Religion and State in Modern America*. Cambridge, MA: Harvard University Press, 2017.

Steinberg, Ben Zion. "With Our Men in Uniform." *Voice* (Camden, NJ), March 10, 1944.

Stember, Charles Herbert, et al. *Jews in the Mind of America*. New York: Basic Books, 1966.

Stone, Dan. *The Liberation of the Camps: The End of the Holocaust and Its Aftermath*. New Haven, CT: Yale University Press, 2015.

Sugarman, Martin. *Under the Heels of Bushido: Last Voices of Jewish POWs of the Japanese in the Second World War*. London: Valentine Mitchell, 2014.

Toubin, Isaac. "D-Day for the Soul." *Jewish Veteran* 13–14 (September 1944): 4–5.

Tregaskis, Richard. *Guadalcanal Diary*. Kindle ed. New York: Random House, 1943.

Truman, Harry S. *Memoirs*. Vol. 1, *Year of Decisions*. New York: Doubleday, 1955.

———. *Memoirs*. Vol. 2, *Years of Trial and Hope*. New York: Doubleday, 1956.

Ungar, Irvin, ed. *Arthur Szyk, Soldier in Art*. Burlingame, CA: Historicana, 2017.

Walters, Kevin L. "Beyond the Battle: Religion and American Troops in World War II." PhD diss., University of Kentucky, 2013.

Wandres, J. *The Ablest Navigator: Lieutenant Paul Shulman, USN, Israel's Volunteer Admiral.* Annapolis: Naval Institute Press, 2010.

Weinstein, Alfred A. *Barbed-Wire Surgeon: A Prisoner of War in Japan.* Atlanta: Deeds, 1975; first edition, 1948.

———. "I Made My Peace with Japanese War Criminals." *Quan*, September 18, 1963.

———. "Yom Kippur in Cabanatuan." *B'nai B'rith National Jewish Monthly*, September 1947.

Williamson, Murray, and Allan R. Millet. *A War to Be Won: Fighting the Second World War.* Cambridge, MA: Harvard University Press, 2000.

"Winged Angels: USAAF Flight Nurses in WWII." National Museum of the United States Air Force, May 1, 2015. Accessed May 18, 2012. https://www.nationalmuseum.af.mil/Visit/Museum-Exhibits/Fact-Sheets/Display/Article/196161/winged-angels-usaaf-flight-nurses-in-wwii/.

Wolk, Bruce H. *Jewish Aviators in World War II: Personal Narratives of American Men and Women.* Jefferson, NC: McFarland, 2016.

Wouk, Herman. *Sailor and Fiddler: Reflections of a 100-Year-Old Author.* Kindle ed. New York: Simon & Schuster, 2016.

———. *This Is My God.* Garden City, NY: Doubleday, 1959.

Wyman, David S. *The Abandonment of the Jews: America and the Holocaust, 1941–1945.* New York: New Press, 1998.

Yellin, Jerry. *Of War and Weddings: A Legacy of Two Fathers.* Fairfield, IA: Sunstar, 1995.

Yellin, Larry. "Passover 1945: A Jewish Soldier's Story." *Jerusalem Post*, April 25, 2016.

Yenne, Bill. *The White Rose of Stalingrad: The Real-Life Adventure of Lidiya Vladimirovna Litvyak, the Highest Scoring Female Air Ace of All Time.* Long Island City, NY: Osprey, 2013.

Zaetz, Gary. "Pentagon Has Forgotten America's Heroic MIA Women of World War Two." Facebook, November 21, 2017.

Zamaloff Dworkin, Jeanne. "I Am Not Going to Stand by and Let Him Do It." In *Ours to Fight For: American Jewish Voices from the Second World War*, edited by J. M. Eidelman, 32–41. New York: Museum of Jewish Heritage–Living Memorial to the Holocaust, 2003.

Zamperini, Louis, with David Rensin. *Devil at My Heels: A Heroic Olympian's Astonishing Story of Survival as a Japanese POW in World War II.* New York: HarperCollins, 2003.

# INDEX

Aachen, Germany, 12, 50, 191
Aboulker, José, 96–97
Abrams Cohen, Beatrice (Bea), 24–24
Adriatic Sea, 14, 166
African Americans, 32, 79, 163–165, 210n71
   African American nurses, 192
   African American servicemen, 82
   African American women, 200n27
Aircrafts
   AT-6, 55–57
   AT-17, 57
   B-17, 89, 159, 164–165, 212n87
   B-24, 40–41, 206n58
   B-29, 37, 136, 167, 182, 187
   P-51, 31, 70, 165, 180
Alaskan and Aleutian theater, 43
Aleutian Islands, 46
Algeria. *See also* Torch, ix, 5, 8, 63, 72, 95, 97, 103, 109, 212n2, 213n13
   French Algeria, 29, 108, 188–189, 214n36, 215n51
   Jews of Algeria, 13, 97, 102, 107–109, 111, 113, 191
   Algiers, 8, 11, 14, 28, 67, 95–97, 100, 106, 108–110, 114, 186–188, 206n65, 212n1, 215n53
   Bedeau labor camp, 107
   Crémieux Decree, 97, 108, 214n36, 215n51
Allen, Fred, 80
Allied powers
   Allied forces, Allied armies, 10, 28, 78, 95–97, 106–108, 125, 189, 203n53, 226n15
   Allied governments, 125
   Allied Intelligence Service, 11
Alper, Benedict, 28
Altman, Sidney, 117, 121–122, 190, 215n9
American servicemen, soldiers, 6, 76, 82–83, 92, 101–102, 112, 130, 135, 143, 146, 168
   Servicewomen, 128, 172

*American Hebrew* (magazine), 118, 121, 126, 190
American Jewish Committee, 50, 113
American Jewish Historical Society, 49
American Joint Distribution Committee (JDC), 213n27, 220n44
American Theater Ribbon, 27, 119–120
American zone of occupation, 93, 198n24
Ammerman, George, 129
Anglo-American military command, Anglo-American forces, 29, 96–97, 212n2
Angress, Werner, Tom, 19, 185
Annapolis Naval Academy, 147
Antisemitism, ix-x, 1–3, 5–6, 32–34, 37–38, 42, 44, 48, 54–55, 69, 73, 75, 79, 83, 86, 93, 100, 113, 122, 138, 175, 204n15, 215n51
   anti-Jewish jokes, 72–73
   anti-Jewish prejudice, 1–2, 6, 38, 52, 82, 85, 188, 226n20, hostility, 2, 6, 27–28, 33, 49, 68–69, 71–72, 74, 78, 81–86, 92, 106, 183–184, 187–189, attitudes, x, 2, 12, 32, 34, 52, 39, 73, 76, 80, 84, 86, 92, 166, hatred, 89, perceptions, 106, slurs, 38, 73, 81, 91, 168, 175, 184 propaganda, 16, 188
antisemitic incident
   in North Africa, 108–110
   in Europe, 107
   in military, 2, 5–6, 12, 34, 43, 68–69, 71, 81–82, 86
   in America, 72
Anzio, Italy, 11, 14
Appel, Samuel, 106
Arabs, 102, 108–109, 114
Arch, Robert, 98
Ardennes, 15, 211n75
Argonne forest, 143

Arlington National Cemetery, 62, 111
Armed Service Editions (ASEs), 112
Army Air Corps, 17, 32, 37, 40, 182
Army Transport Service, 122
Arnold, Bruce, 187
Arnold, Henry H., 25, 51, 56
Arnold, Hap, 187
Arrowsmith, John, 167
Arundel, 123
Asbury Park, 59
Asher, Sandy, ix, 120
Ashkenazi American Jews, Ashkenazi Jews, 5, 132
Aspen, Colorado, 62
Aspen Valley Hospital Heliport, 68, 192
Assam Jungle, 167
Assam Valley, 62
Atkinson, Rick, 5, 109
Atlantic ocean, 7, 100, 137
Atlas Mountains, 114
Atlit, 79
Attweilnau, Germany, 20
Australia, 23, 63, 123, 131, 171, 183
Austria, 5, 7, 18, 77–80, 101–102, 126–127, 141, 185, 198n24
Avenger Field, 21, 34, 36, 39, 55, 59, 201n9

B'nai B'rith, 152
Babi Yar, 59
Bad Kreuznach, 171
Bader, George, 176
Bairoko Harbor, 124
Baltimore, Maryland, 75, 129
Banzai Massacre, 129
Baptist, 55, 123–124, 190
Bar Kokhba, 81
Bar Mitzvah, 2, 70, 104
Barney Ross's Marine Company, 116
Barrackpore, 135
Bartfield, Frederick, 165
basic training, 4, 7, 17–21, 25–26, 63, 65, 86, 164, 172, 176
Bass, Leon, 79
Bastié, Maryse, 59, 205n34
Bataan, 91, 115, 139–140, 157
  Bataan campaign, 138, 143, 150
  Bataan Death March, 138, 150, 154
Battle of Munda Point, 120, 123, 190
Battle of Sidi Barrani, 11
Battle of the Bulge, 27, 92, 176, 184–185, 208n33, 211n75

Battlefield, 7, 19–20, 22, 26, 41, 52, 82, 116, 168, 171, 195
Baumel, Bernice, 27
Baumgarten, Herold, 39–40
Bay of Bengal, 115, 131
Belarus, 173
Belgian-German border, 173
Belgium, 127, 185, 211n75
Bendersky, Beryl Lieff, 3
Bendersky, Joseph, 6, 81, 86
Bene Israel, 131–132
Benghazi, 11
Benhamou, Max, ix, 112
Benjamin, Hebe Solomon, 135
Berenbaum, Michael, 61
Berlin, Germany, 14, 143
Bernstein, Philip S., 49, 117, 123, 185
Bible, 40, 118, 141, 145, 212n87
Bilibid prison, 150, 152
Bizerte, Tunisia, 8, 215n53
Black Panthers of the 761st Tank Battalion, 79
Black unit, 98
Bloch, Miranda, 64–66, 186
Blue Eagle, 141
Blum, Della, 52
Bohnen, Eli, 45, 203n39
Bombay, India, 13, 132, 191
Bombing, 37, 75, 136, 151, 154, 161, 164, 167, 175, 182, 184, 192
Book of Jonah, 81
Book of Life, 117, 122, 126, 158
Boston, Massachusetts, 36, 140
Bougainville, Papua New Guinea, 115, 122
Bowman Field, 63
Brahmaputra River, 62
Branson, Bernard, 17, 40–41
Breitman, Richard, 89
Breman Jewish Heritage Museum, 147
Breuer, Alexander, 7
Brisbane, 115, 123, 183
British Empire, 9, 22, 29, 67, 225n8
British Mandate in Palestine, 11, 29, 72, 225n8, 226n19
British military, British soldiers, 31, 63, 89, 214n29, 225n8
  British Jewish soldiers, 11
Brokaw, Tom, 211n87
Bronx, 20, 35, 40, 45, 80, 101, 125, 137, 166
Bronze Star, 75, 79, 119–120, 140, 151, 181
Brooklyn, 17, 71, 90, 92, 98, 101, 109, 117, 121, 164, 167, 172, 190
  Brooklyn Hebrew Orphan Asylum, 182

Brooks, Mel, 92
Brotherhood, 113, 124, 127–128, 146, 158, 164, 177, 179–180, 192–194
Bucharest, 15, 23
Buchwald, Art, 2, 17–18, 72, 81
Bureau of War Records, 28
Burials, 7–8, 42, 137, 185
Burma Road, 115, 167
Bush, George W., 170

Cabanatuan POW camp, 139–147, 152, 158, 191
Cairo, 15, 77
Calcutta, 7, 13, 115, 130–135, 191
California, 23, 98, 152, 169
Camp Custer, 35
Camp LeJeune, 65
Camp Pickett, 20
Camp Ritchie, 7, 18
Camps (Nazi camps)
  Concentration camps, 7, 26, 31, 41, 78, 92, 103, 107, 171, 182, 191, 200n12, 208n34
  Buchenwald, 78–79, 83, 198n18
  Berga Wöbbelin, 19
  Dachau, 45–46, 75, 78–79, 184, 208n33
  Gunskirchen, 79
  death camps, 75, 103
  extermination camps, 75, 79, 125, 184, 188
  labor camps, 39, 141
Camus, Albert, 109
Canada, 76
Caplan, Aben, 158
Carnegie, Andrew, 93
Casablanca, 8, 14, 96, 101–103, 111–112, 174, 188, 215n49
Catholics, 32, 47, 100, 160, 179
  Catholic faith, 50
Cedarbaum, David I., 136, 224n70
Cemeteries, 43, 49, 185
Central European campaigns, 19
Ceylon, 101
Chaplains, Catholic, 173, 179
  Jewish, 8, 26, 33, 43–44, 46, 49, 73, 80, 87, 111, 117, 123, 125, 131, 136, 142, 145, 179, 188
  Protestant, 46, 121, 179, 194
Cheney Streeter, Ruth, 65
Cherry Point, 66
Chicago, Illinois, 66
China, 37, 62, 115, 155, 167
China-Burma-India theater, China-Burma theater, 1, 7, 37, 131

CBI (China-India-Burma) Theater Headquarters, 131
Chinese, 161, 167, 200n27, 215n9
Christians, 13, 31, 86, 112, 174–175, 223n50
  Christian chaplains, 73, 82, 87–88, 112, 117, 142, 150–151, 178–179, 190
  Christian hostility, 72
  Christian icon, 88
Christmas, 63, 88
Churchill, Winston, 95
Civil Affairs Division, 77
Civil Aviation Authority, 60
Civil War, 22, 177
Clark Field, 31
Cleveland, 37, 178
Cochran, Jacqueline, 24–25, 51, 53, 56, 58–60
Cohen, Beatrice Abrams, 23–24
Cohen Herbert, 100, 102
Cohen, Ray E, 23
Cohen, Ruth Gottlieb, 25, 34
Cohen, Schiller, 98
*Collier's* magazine, 29–30
Cologne, Germany, 87
Columbia University, 80
Committee Against Anti-Semitism, 74
Committee on Army and Navy Religious Activities (CANRA), 7, 49, 93, 117
Communism, communist, 28, 46, 81, 86, 203n42
Coney Island, Brooklyn, New York, 71
Congressional Space Medal of Honor, 208n31
Conservative Judaism, 43–45, 87, 99, 118
Constantine, Algeria, 114
Cooperman, Jessica, 6
Coral Sea, 115
  Battle of the Coral Sea, 90–91
Corre, Harry, 154, 157, 181
Corregidor, 23, 115, 140, 148–149, 156–157
  Battle of Corregidor, 152
Coughlin, Charles, 43, 188
Cronan, Selma Kantor, 4, 16, 24–25, 27, 34–36, 51, 59, 62, 67, 187
Cronan, Walter, 25
Cuba, 40
Cuthriel, Warren, 178
Cyprus, 15, 79
Cyrulnik, Boris, 156
Czechoslovakia, 146

Dahn, Germany, 45, 203n39
Darlan, Jean-François, 95, 97, 108–109, 212n1

Index 241

Davao prison camp, 139
Davis, Eliot, 123–124, 190
Day of Atonement *see* Yom Kippur
D-Day, 19, 23, 26, 40, 49, 77, 92, 112–113, 170, 175, 178, 185, 188
De Gaulle, Charles, 29
Declaration of Independence, 166
Dental Corps, 170
Department of Veterans Affairs, 181
Detroit, Michigan, 35, 198
Diner, Hasia, 3
Dinnerstein, Leonard, 42, 69, 86
Discrimination, discriminatory, 5–6, 26, 29, 64, 48, 78, 82, 89, 108, 163, 179, 184, 186–187, 192, 221n5, 226n20
Distinguished Flying Cross, 90–91, 167, 209n57, 225n79
Distinguished Service Cross, 90, 203n45, 211n77
Dog tags, 7, 27, 34, 38–43, 47, 63, 92, 110, 184–186, 205n30
Domestic flying missions, 25
Douglas, Kirk, 23, 33–35
DP camps *see* Jewish displaced persons
Duffy, John E., 150–152
Dutch East Indies, 157
Dutch forces, 5, 218n11

Eckman (Hewlett), Magdalena, 152–154
Ecumenism, 124
Egypt, 103–104, 125, 129, 188
Einsatzgruppen, 59
Einstein, Albert, 86
Eisenhower, Dwight D., 9, 45, 67, 75, 78, 95–97, 108, 125, 131, 186, 211n17
Eisenstein, Moris, 78–79
Eisner, Gerald, 22
Eisner Jr., Lester, 21
Eisner, Jacques Rodney, 21
Elbe River, 14, 185
Ellison, Ralph, 32
Elmore Airstrip, 64
Emory University, 140, 147, 192
Emotions, empathy, 3, 8, 27, 57, 79, 82, 105, 113–114, 150–151, 155, 157–164, 167–169, 172, 176, 180–181, 187, 192, 208n34, 222n18
England, 14, 26, 62, 64, 111, 175, 225n10
Epstein, Hyman, 20
Europe, 1, 9–10, 12, 14, 18, 22, 27–28, 30–31, 42, 59, 78, 83, 90, 100–102, 113, 124–125, 127, 134, 143, 146, 174, 176, 184–185, 188, 194, 211n75, 223n50, 225n10
European-African-Middle Eastern Theater Campaign Ribbon, 27
European Jews, 10, 22, 75–76, 79, 86, 89, 143, 184, 191
European theater, 4, 9, 39, 52, 63, 92, 125, 159, 168, 170, 203n45
Evacuation by air, 63
Exodus from Egypt, 103, 188
Ezra, David, 131–132

FAA, Federal Aviation Administration, 57
Falk Haydu, Bernice (Bee), 4, 24–25, 27, 39, 51–52, 54–58, 62, 67–68, 187
Fascists, Fascism, 78, 109, 183
Fellowship, 111, 164–165, 167, 172, 174, 176–177, 181, 224n70
Fenichel, Benjamin, xi, 117–121, 190
Ferndale, 98
Ferrying Division, 61
Field Artillery, 22, 123, 184, 190
Fields, Milton, 48, 98
Fifth Army Division, 178
Fifth Marine Division Cemetery, 82 n
First Infantry Division, 113, 175
First World War *see* World War I
Flag (American), 23, 128, 145, 177–178, 224n63
Flight test, 55
Florida, 24
Flying angels, 66
Foreign Legion, The, 11
Forrestal, James, 151
Fort Dix, 23, 26, 64
Fort Riley, 43
Fox, George L., 179
France, 5, 8–9, 11, 18, 22, 27, 29, 45, 53, 59, 75, 78, 82–83, 92, 97, 105–108, 111, 127, 159, 170, 185, 198n18, 205n34, 210n58, 212n1
Free French military, Free French Forces, 10–11, 29
French Ecole Polytechnique, 107
French empire, 95
French fascists, 109
French Jewish soldiers, 106
French Jews, 4, 10–11, 13, 29, 97, 106, 112
French resistance, French underground, 95, 97
French settlers, 108
French Vichy forces, 98
Frank, Leo, 72

Frankfurt-am-Main, 83
Frankfurter, Felix, 86
Franklin, Benjamin, 93
French Croix de Guerre, 98
French Riviera, 75
Friedlander, Sidney, 21
Friedman, Harry L., 180
Friedwald, Herbert, 98

Geller, Victor B., 43
Gender prejudice, 58, 66
General Hospital Number 1 on Bataan, 140
Geneva Convention, 20, 169, 218n10
Georgia, United States, x, 72, 146, 191
Germany, 2, 5, 8–9, 12–13, 18–19, 22, 24, 26, 31, 45, 50, 56, 75, 77–78, 80, 83, 87, 89, 95, 102, 105, 113, 125, 127–128, 164–165, 171, 173, 185, 197n10, 203n39n, 207n18, 212n87
  German commandos, 87
  German forces, 59, 104
  German language, 7
  German prisoners, 83, 185, 188
  German refugee, 146
  German-Jewish refugees, 18, 126, 163, 210n62
GI Bill, 68, 187, 217n46
Gittelsohn, Roland, 81–82, 178
Glasgow, 100
Goebels, Joseph, 193
Gold, Anita Claire "Goldie", 171
Goldberg, Jack, 142
Goldberg, Joshua Louis, 136
Goldman, Belle, 137, 172–173, 189
Goldstein, Nathan, 90
Goode, Alexander, 179–180, 224n69
Goodman, Philip, 122–123
Gorbachev, Mikhail, 10
Gordon, Jack, 146–152, 158
Gordon, Sadie, 146–147, 149, 152
Gordon, Sam, 146, 150
Gorobetz, Milton, 98
Gottlieb Cohen, Ruth, 25, 34
Gottlieb, Yetta, 26
Great Britain *see British Empire*
Great Depression, The, 17, 22
Great Neck, Long Island, New York, 21, 60
Greenberg, Hank, 35–38, 167–168
Greenfield, Murray S., 207n24, 209n40
Grieder, Charlie, 53

Grobman, Alex, 198n24
Guadalcanal, 90, 115–123, 161, 178, 190
  Battle of Guadalcanal, 21, 125, 169
Guam, 115, 122, 135–136, 147, 152, 190, 216n22, 220n43
Gunso, Watanabi, 156

Haas Pfister, Elizabeth (Betty), 4, 21, 51, 59–62, 67–68, 187, 191
Haas, Merle Simon, 60
Haas, Robert, 60
Habonim, 134
Hadassah, 75
Haganah, 80, 216n35
Haifa, 15, 79
Hakafot, 132
Hamilton Hayes, Ira, 178
Hascall Cole, Jean, 39, 56, 59, 61
Hashomer Hatsair, 134
Hawaii, 70, 77, 81, 90, 115, 117, 122, 153, 160–161, 192
Hebrew, 7–8, 34, 38–44, 75–77, 102–103, 110, 116, 124–125, 129, 132, 143, 169, 179, 182, 202n14, 205n30
Hebrew school, 75, 91, 104
Henry, Bernard, 50
Heroism, 12, 30, 32, 49, 79, 91–93, 98, 140, 168, 170, 199n30
Hertzberg, Arthur, 47
Hessed, 171
Hessenberger, Ben, 146
Hewlett, Madeline, 154
Hewlett, Thomas H, 153
High-ranking Officers, 76, 84–86, 88, 125, 185
Hindustani, 133
Hirshfield, Robert, 167
Hitler, Adolf, 6–7, 12, 16–24, 29, 41, 45, 79, 92, 101, 126, 170, 184, 191
Hoboken, New Jersey, 43
Hobson, Laura Z., 6
Holocaust (Shoah), 80, 86
  Holocaust deniers, 28
  Holocaust survivors, 8, 11, 75, 77, 85, 89, 157, 181–182, 191, 198n24, 208n31, 222n34
Honolulu, 161
Honshu, 70
Horn, Harvey S., 159, 221n3
Houghteling, James, 89
Humiliation, 23, 38, 47, 69, 76, 149, 185
Huston, John, 180

Identity, 10, 19, 24, 33, 35, 37, 42, 47, 54, 60–61, 68, 82–84, 110, 132, 142, 144–145, 154, 186
   American Jewish Identity, ix, 12, 128, 135
   Jewish Identity, 5–7, 11–12, 16–17, 22, 29, 34–35, 41, 59, 73, 80–82, 86, 92, 100, 106, 116, 120, 122, 128, 133–134, 139–140, 142, 145, 163, 185–186, 203n45, 204n15, 218n22
Imperial Japanese Army, Imperial Japanese Navy Air Service *see* Japanese military
India, 13, 33, 44, 62, 72, 101, 114, 130–132, 167, 183, 189, 191
   Indian Jews, Jews of India, Indian Jewish community, 3, 9, 130–135, 191
Indian Ocean, 131
Intelligence Services (Intelligence), 7, 11, 13, 18–19, 41, 70, 95, 163, 185, 195n18, 221n9
   Intelligence Service Language program, 160, 163
Iran, 38
Iraq, 38
Irish, 23, 32, 76, 193
Israel, 69, 74, 77–78, 80, 88, 91–92, 135, 207n24, 208n31, 212n91, 217n20, 217n49, 222n34
   Israeli Air Force, 72, 208n28
   Israeli Defense Forces, 31, 208n31
Italian Americans, 44, 174
Italy, 11, 18, 24, 29, 73, 75, 77, 104–105, 113, 165
Iwo Jima, 69–71, 82, 129, 136, 177–178
   Battle of Iwo Jima, 177–178, 180

Jacobs, John M., 150
Jacobson, Eddie, 85
Jamaica, 98
Janoski, Phil, 70
Japan, Japanese, Japanese Empire, xi, 5, 13, 18, 21, 23–24, 29, 37, 39, 51, 64, 69–71, 77–78, 88, 116, 125–128, 130, 135–163, 167, 169–173, 176, 180–183, 189, 191–193, 211n74, 219n27, 220n44, 221n5
   Japanese ideology, 141
   Japanese immigrants, 160
   Japanese occupation, 127
   Japanese prison camps, 141, 144, 157
   Japanese prisoners, 159, 171
   Japanese survivors, 191
   Japanese war criminals, 154–156

Japanese Americans, Nisei, 13, 159–163, 192
   Japanese American Veterans Association (JAVA), 162, 192
   Japanese American women, 163
   Nisei veterans, 192
Japanese forces, Japanese imperial forces, Japanese military, 24, 125, 128–129, 138, 140–141, 149, 163, 219n27
   Japanese artillery, 171
   Japanese battleship, 90
   Japanese Imperial Air Force, 25, 181
   Japanese Navy, 90
   Japanese troops, 20, 70, 118, 122, 190
Jefferson Barracks National Cemetery, 137
Jefferson, Thomas, 31, 166
Jerusalem, 64, 77, 165
Jew-hatred, Jew-haters *see* Antisemitism
Jewish American prisoners, 144
Jewish communities (overseas), 1, 5, 113, 127, 136, 188, 215n46
Jewishness, 1, 10, 13, 16, 31, 34, 45, 47–48, 70, 80–82, 101, 105, 110, 120, 123–124, 126, 130, 133, 136, 144–145, 158, 168, 183–184, 187–189, 203n45, 210n60
Jewish dietary laws, 54
Jewish Displaced Persons, 76–80, 191, 203n42, 209n41, 217n46
Jewish education, 23, 127
   Jewish educational institution, Yeshiva, 45
Jewish faith, 12, 50, 85, 92–93, 180
Jewish festivals, 13, 99, 112, 131, 175
Jewish holidays, 8
Jewish invisibility, 43
Jewish laymen, 142
Jewish observance, 2, 104, 129–130, 190
Jewish peoplehood, 2, 5, 73, 100, 129–130, 133
Jewish refugees, 7, 18, 79, 89, 100, 126, 131, 141, 143, 163, 210n62, 213n14, 220n44
Jewish solidarity, 135–136, 158, 191, 222n34
Jewish spirituality, 136
Jewish values, 3, 24, 169, 171, 177, 187, 202n36
   public expression of Jewishness, 139, 142
   secular Jews, 37, 81
Jewish officers, 167, 174, 192, 203n45
Jewish prisoners, 5, 142, 144, 184, 218n10n 223n50
Jewish survivors, 75, 77, 89, 171, 191, 198n24
Jewish War Veterans of the United States of America (JWV), 177, 194, 199n1

Jewish Welfare Board, JWB *see* National Jewish Welfare Board
Judeo-Christianity, 173

kamikazes, Kamikaze pilots, 18, 75, 152, 162, 182
Kantor Cronan, Selma, 4, 24–25, 34–35, 51, 59, 62, 67, 187
Kan-Tor, Zvi, 212n91
Karachi, India, 131–132
   Karachi Bene Israel, 131–132
Karsevar, Ruth, 26–171
Katz, Harold, 20
Kaufman, Charles, 180 ה
Kaufman, Isidore, 9, 116, 136, 169, 180
Kaufman, Paul, 89
Kaunitz, Fred, 141
Kaunitz, Hanna, 141
Kelly, Colin, 90, 193
Kepei Tai, 139
Kern, Marvin, 70
Kessel, Bernard J., 98
Kiddush, 127
Kiev, Ukraine, 15, 59
Klausner, Abraham, 79, 125
Klein, Julius, 168, 222n31
Kligsberg, Moses, 81, 101
Koch, Bebe, 197n10
Kohs Samuel C., 84
Kol Nidre, 100, 143–144, 146
Kosher, 9, 18, 26, 87, 211n74
Kovno, 148
Kraut, Alan, 89
Krell, Lilian, 26
Kristallnacht, 128
Kwajalein, 115, 117
Kyuchu, 151

Lahey, Edwin, 84
Lancry, Huguette, 107
land of Israel (Eretz Israel), 74, 80, 91
Latrun, 88
Lebanon, 11
LeBlanc, O.K., 116
Lefkowitz, Sidney, 50
Lehman de Vadetsky, Hilda, Jane, 186
Lehman, Herbert R., 187
Le Kef, Tunisia, 104–105
LeMay, Curtis, 136
Lerner, Maximilian, 18
Lev, Arieh, 117
Levin, Meyer (Mike), 90–91, 193
Lévinas, Emmanuel, 48, 218n22

Levine, Mendel Leib, 80
Levitsky Orkin, Ellan, 27, 68
Levy, Asher, 28
Lewin, Sy, 19
Leyte, Philiipines, 23, 64, 115
Lichtman, Gideon, 31, 38–39
Lieb, Joseph H., 117
Lincoln, Abraham, 71, 93
Lippman, Paul, 43, 202n31
Lithuania, 127, 148
Litvyak, Lidiya Vladimirovna, 10
Lodz, 29, 46
London, England, 23, 29, 67, 100
Los Angeles, 23, 130
Louisville, 63, 154
Love, Nancy, 58
Lowitz, Stanley, 98
Luzon, Philippines, 115, 143, 150–151, 153
   Northern Luzon Campaign, 150

Macarov, David, 7, 72, 132–135, 191
MacArthur, Douglas, 23, 88–89, 125, 172
Maccabees, 30, 81, 91
Machal, 76–78
Magdovitz, Ben, 127–128
Mahoney, John, 179
Mailer, Norman, 1, 6
Mandatory Palestine *see* British mandate
Mandell, David, 161, 221n11
Manhattan, 76
Manila, 23, 64, 89–90, 115, 125–129, 138–139, 141, 150, 152–153, 183
   Manila American cemetery, 64, 137
   Manila Jewish community, 13, 127–128, 183
   Manila synagogue, 88, 128, 216n29
   resistance movement in Manila, 172
Manliness *see* masculinity
Marcus, David Daniel, 76–77, 91, 93, 168, 188, 208n27
Margolis, Abram, 10
Margolis, Laura, 220n44
Mariana Islands, 115, 136, 157, 159, 161, 169, 192
Marines, Marine Corps, 2–3, 17–18, 23, 32, 64–66, 70, 82, 115–117, 121, 129, 159, 161, 169, 178–179, 182, 186, 190
   Marine Corps Air Station, 66
   Marine Corps Women's Reserve, 65
Marmot, Woolf, 11
Marshall, George C., 49, 130–131, 161
Martins Creek, 53
Maryland, 7, 18, 129

masculinity, 17, 37–38, 76, 81, 83, 92, 140, 145, 168, 180, 218n22
Massachusetts, 40, 125, 171
Mast, Charles, 95
McCullough, David, 162
Mechanics, 12, 25, 56, 61, 64–66, 98, 186–187
Medal of Honor, 170, 208n31
Medals, 9, 98, 198n25, 203n45, 205n30
Medical Corps, 23, 140, 142, 145, 157–158, 169, 171
Mediterranean Sea, 153
Melasky, Harris, 88–89, 211n77
Melbourne, 115, 123, 171, 183
Memler, Beatrice H., 64
Memler, Julius, 64
Merseburg, Germany, 89
Mezuzah, 24, 200n24
Midway, Midway Island, 115, 122, 157
Military cemeteries, 43, 93, 111, 185, 202n6, 203n49
Military Intelligence Specialist Unit, 19
Military Intelligence Training Center, 18
Military training, 16
Miller, Milton, 167
Milwaukee, 172
Mindanao Island, Phillipines, 64
Minnesota, 160
Minsk, 15, 80
Minyan, 88, 136
Missouri, 85, 137, 167
Mitsushima prisoner camp, 155–156
Mitzvot, mitzvah, 23–24, 43
Moatti, Emile, ix, 107
Montclair, New Jersey, 52–53
Moore, Deborah Dash, 3, 125, 134, 168
Moreell, Ben, 167–168
Morgenthau Robert M., 181
Morgenthau, Henry, 85, 178, 181
Mormon, 55
Morocco, ix, 8, 13–14, 63, 95, 102, 111–112, 174
  Moroccan Jews, 108
Moscow, 10, 15
Mosely, Evans T., 123
Moskin, Alan, 79
Moskowitz, Yetta, 4, 26, 51, 63–65
Mount Suribachi, 177–178
Munda, New Georgia, Solomon Islands, 120, 123–126, 166–167, 190, 194, 223n48
Murdoch, John, 116
Murphy, Robert, 74, 95, 109
Museum of Jewish Heritage, 58–59, 181, 187
Museum of the Jewish Soldier, 88

Nabeul, 104
Nadel, Dan, 92
Nagasaki, 71, 115
Naimer, Belle G., 137, 189
Nakamura, Bob, 160
National Broadcasting Company, 50
National Jewish Welfare Board, 7, 9, 28, 48–49, 84, 91, 93, 98–99, 103, 111, 117, 121, 123, 158, 166–167, 190, 207n17
National Ladies Auxiliary of the Jewish War Veterans, 24
National Museum of American Jewish History, 70
National Museum of American Jewish Military History, 36, 65, 124, 126, 199n1
Native Americans, 163
Navy, 3, 7, 17, 21–22, 24, 33, 48–49, 60, 70, 84, 86, 93, 103, 117, 125, 137–138, 147–149, 151–152, 161, 167, 182, 194
  Navy Aviation Machinist Mate, 21
  Navy Department, 138, 148
Nazism, Nazis, 5, 7, 12, 19, 28–29, 31, 39, 41–42, 48, 59, 83, 87, 101–102, 124, 130, 138, 173–174, 183–185, 200n12
  Nazi annihilation, 10
  Nazi brutality, 78
  Nazi extermination, Nazi genocide, 31, 75–76, 203n42
  Nazi persecution, 19, 102, 131, 143, 197n10, 220n44
Third Reich, 113
Nebraska, 20
New Caledonia, 115, 168
New Georgia Island, 123, 166
New Guinea, 20, 23 64, 90, 115, 137, 171–173, 189
New Order, 78
New York, 21–22, 25–26, 29, 37, 40, 44, 46, 59, 60, 64, 75, 80, 84, 88, 90, 98, 113, 115, 121, 131, 142–143, 159, 167, 175, 177, 180–181, 187, 193–194
New York City College, 159
New York State, 46, 120
New York Times, 43
New York University, 121, 175
Newark, 53, 118
Night Witches, 10, 59
Nightingale, Florence, 67
Nimitz, Chester, 147
Nisei *see* Japanese Americans
Nishigaki-San, 155
Nishino-San, 155

Non-kosher food, 87, 211n74
Norman, Milton1, 6, 164
Normandy invasion *see* D-Day
North Africa, ix, 1, 3, 8, 12–13, 22, 43, 63, 73, 75, 95–100, 102–103, 105, 108–109, 111–113, 134, 175, 185, 188–189, 213n27, 214n36, 215n51, 215n53
   French North Africa, 3–4, 8–9, 28, 94–96, 103, 107, 109, 183, 187, 188
   invasion of North Africa, 63, 108
   North African campaign, 8, 11, 125, 176, 197n2
   North African Jews, Jews of North Africa, 5, 100–101, 104, 106, 110, 112, 188, 213n27
Nussbaum, Chaim, 145

O'Donnel, Emet, 90
O'Donnell, 141–142
O'Neill, William L, 66
Oak Leaf for gallantry, 90–91
Obermayer, Herman J., 20
Odessa, 15, 59
Office of the Chief of Naval Operations (RG38), 150
Ohrdruf, Germany, 78
Oka, Don, 162
Okinawa, Japan, 13, 18, 37, 81, 115, 129–130, 161–162, 176, 182, 192
   Battle of Okinawa, 130
Olongapo, 150–152
Omaha, Omaha Beach, 20, 40, 92
Omori Punishment Camp, 139–140, 154, 156
Operation Barbarossa, 28
Operation Torch (*see* Torch), ix, 5, 8, 13, 29, 63, 67, 95–97, 100, 186, 212n1–2
Oran, 5, 8, 14, 96–98, 100–101, 106–110, 113–114, 188, 215n52
   Jews in Oran, 106–107
   Oran harbor (battle, port disaster), 100
   Grand Synagogue, 106
   American Military Cemetery in Oran, 111
Orthodox Jews, Orthodox, 34–35, 43–46, 80, 86–87, 99, 111, 124, 128, 169, 173, 176, 190, 211n74
Oryoku Maru, 150–152

Pacific, 2, 5, 7–9, 13, 18, 21, 52, 70, 90, 114–117, 136–138, 145, 147, 159, 167, 169, 172, 175, 177, 184, 189–191
   Pacific Islands, 8–9, 80, 117, 121, 150, 163, 166, 175, 189

South Pacific, 1, 4, 26, 117, 124, 172
southern Pacific islands, 137
western Pacific, 70, 128, 135, 183
Pacific theater, Pacific war, 4, 13, 39, 52, 63, 75, 86, 119, 123, 130, 135, 160–161, 171, 183, 189
Pacifists, 81
Palestine, 11, 29, 46, 65, 69, 72, 74–76, 79–80, 89, 130, 134, 209n40, 216n35, 217n46, 222n34
Palestinian songs, 9, 111
Paper, Maurice, 75
Paris, 10, 14, 18, 29
Patriotism, xi, 9–10, 12, 16–17, 21–24, 28–29, 32, 37, 65–67, 77, 91, 98, 120–121, 135, 149, 172, 177, 186, 193
Patton, George S., 76, 85, 92, 149–150
Pearl Harbor, 7, 16, 21, 23–25, 37, 51, 70, 77–78, 90, 92, 115, 118, 128, 131, 138, 142, 156, 160–161, 171, 176, 183, 192–193
Penslar, Derek, x, 6, 9, 76
Pershing, John J., 16, 65
Persian Gulf Command, 38
Pétain, Marshall Philippe, 108, 113
Pfister, Arthur O., 62
Philippine Military Prison camp, 149
Philippines, 1, 12–13, 22–23, 31, 64, 88–89, 125–128, 138–141, 143, 149, 152–153, 158, 161, 173, 183, 190, 219n25
Pine Grove, 152
Pitkin County Air Rescue Group, 62
Plane crash, 9, 43, 111, 185, 189, 205n34
Poland, 22, 46, 71, 79, 104, 113, 130, 145, 170, 175
   Polish Jews, 10
   Polish immigrant, 29
Poling, Clark V., 179
Portugal, 83
Post-traumatic stress disorder (PTSD) *see* psychiatric casualties
Potsdam, 77
Powder Puff Derbies, 4
Prayer book, 48, 98–99, 103, 111, 123, 137, 144–145, 158, 166, 174, 190, 215n46
Prayer shawl *see* Tallith
Prayer, 11, 40, 44, 46, 56, 88, 98–100, 102, 105, 110, 116, 118, 121, 123, 132, 143–145, 158, 166, 171, 174, 189–191, 202n14, 202n36
   Hebrew prayers, 40, 143
   Kaddish, 226n22
   memorial service, 49, 128

Prejudice, 1, 6, 12–13, 20, 29–30, 35, 38–39, 47, 52, 58, 66–68, 70, 73, 76, 78, 81–85, 93–94, 106, 132–133, 163, 179, 181–182, 186–188, 191, 210n71
Preston, Melvin, 82
Prisoners of war, POW, 34, 56, 125, 140, 149, 150, 152–160, 164, 173, 181–182, 185, 211n75, 219n27, 220n56
   Jewish POWs, 5, 13, 154, 173, 218n10
   Japanese POW camp, 23, 125, 138–143, 145–146, 191
   POW camps, 13, 141, 158, 164, 171, 185
Protocols of the Elders of Zion, 86
Psychiatric casualties, 23, 26, 153–154, 157, 180, 182
Purple Hearts, 122, 140
Pyle, Ernie, 175–176

Rabbis, 8–9, 112, 124
   military rabbis (see Chaplains)
Radio operator, 21, 101, 165
Red Cross, 112, 126, 149, 219n27
Red Sea, 44
Reform, 124, 145, 148, 190
   Reform rabbi, Reform Judaism, 81, 99, 178–179
Refugees, 5, 7, 12, 18–19, 79, 89, 100–102, 124, 126–127, 131, 141, 143, 146, 163, 185, 208n34, 218n11, 220n443
Reichart, Stuart R, 182
Reischauer, Edwin O, 155
Rejoicing of the Torah *see* Simhat Torah
Religiosity, 12, 48, 104, 129, 137, 158, 172, 190
   Religious identity, 24, 33, 42
   Religious observance (practice), 5, 73, 82, 123, 125, 130, 136, 192
   Religious rites, 5, 43
   Religious services, 46, 48, 73, 93, 100–102, 104, 108, 117, 123, 125, 127, 132, 136, 158, 172–175, 188–191, 224n70
      Friday evening services, 104
      Hanukkah, Hanukkah service, 91, 111
      Jewish New Year, Rosh Hashanah, Rosh Hashanah service, 9, 13, 47, 82, 116, 118, 121–124, 135, 190, 194
      New Year of the Trees, Tu B'Shevat, 13, 129–130, 192
      Passover (Pesach), 9, 45, 87–88, 102,–103, 105–106, 110, 122, 124–126, 129–130, 136–137, 174, 183, 188, 194, 203n39, 207n17, 211n74, 211n76, 213n24
         Haggada, 88, 103, 122, 125, 130, 203n39

         Haroset, 103
         Matzah, 103, 125
      Simhat Torah, Rejoicing of the Torah, 131
      Yom Kippur, Day of Atonement, 33, 35, 47, 80–81, 100, 118, 136–137, 142–146, 158, 173, 189–191
Rheims, Maurice, 11
Rhine River, Rhine, 87
Rhode Island, 45
Ribalow, Harold, 43–44, 101–102, 174, 223n53
Richmond, Virginia, 37
Richmond, Harry R., 117
Ritchie boys, 7, 13, 19, 185
River Kwai, 145
Rivkin, Mimi, 81
Roberts, Burton, 72
Rockwell, Norman, 29
Romania, 23, 35, 76, 173
Rommel's Afrika Korps, 185
Roosevelt administration, 86, 95
Roosevelt, Eleanor, 163, 204n54, 222n18
Roosevelt, Franklin D., FDR, 3, 89, 95, 135, 137, 161, 163, 217n54
Rose, Maurice (Major General), 185–186, 203n45
Rosen, Isadore, 84
Rosen, Naurice, 73, 207n19
Rosenthal, Joe, 177–178
Rosie the Riveter, 23
Rosofsky, Dov-Ber David, 115, *see* Ross Barney
Ross, Barney, 115–116, 169, 188, 192
Rubin, Morris, 46
Ruttenberg, James, 166

Sabbath, Sabbath meals, Sabbat services, 8, 13, 43–45, 47, 99, 102, 110, 112, 127, 191
Sachs, Moshe, 13, 129–130, 182, 192, 216n35
Saipan, 136, 169–170
Salomon, Ben L., 169–170, 223n39
San Diego Naval Hospital, 27
Sandrow, Edward T., 43, 46–47
Santa Monica, 23
Santo Tomas internment camp, 152–153
Saperstein, Mark, 82
Sarna, Jonathan, 6, 93, 180
Scharf, Jack, 45
Schlamberg, Philip, 71
Schleifer, Louis, 91
Seabees, 125, 167–168
Secretary of War, 25, 86, 221n13

Sellz, Norman, 157
Sephardic, ix, 9, 111–112, 132
  Sephardic traditions, 5
Shalom Aleichem, 80, 110
Shanghai, China, 115, 127, 220n44
Shapiro, Archie, 166
Shapiro, Gertrude, 171, 191
Shaw, Irwin, 6
Sheehy, Ethel, 53
Shofar, 117–118, 120, 122–123, 146, 190
Shpall, Jerry, 88
Shulman, Paul, 75–76, 91, 207n24
Siegel, Norman, 117
Silver Shirts, 43, 188
Silver Star, 20, 79, 90–91, 98, 122, 169, 190, 215n53
Silverman, Marty, 47
Sinatra, Frank, 183, 193
Singer, Jay, 88
Slanger, Frances, 159, 170
Smith, Gerald L.K., 43
Solidarity, 2, 61, 135–136, 158, 164, 168, 179, 191, 213n27, 222n34
Solomon Islands, xi, 115, 117, 119, 121–123
Soviet Union, USSR, 9, 22, 28, 59
  Hero of the Soviet Union, 10
  Russian Army, Red Army, 10, 63, 199n28
  Russian Jews, Soviet Jews, 10
Spain, 83, 210n58
SPARS, 3
Spielberg, Steven, 40, 222n20
St. Louis, 137, 167
Stalag, 41, 174, 185, 218n10
Stars and Stripes, 58, 159, 170
Stars of David, 43, 49, 185, 202n31
Stege, Juliette Jenner, 4, 39
Stimson, Henry Lewis, 86, 162, 221n13
Stine, Betty, 56–57
Stock, Ernest, 82–85, 188, 210n58–60
Stone, Earl, 8
Strauss, H. Cerf, 117
Strobing, Irving, 21
Styer, William, 128, 183
Sugamo Prison, 156
Sugarman, Martin, 5
Survival training, 64
Sweetwater, Texas, 25, 34, 36, 51, 53, 56, 58, 60
Sydney, Australia, 115, 123, 183
Synagogue, 8, 24, 38, 48, 88, 99–100, 103, 105–106, 108, 118, 121, 124, 128, 131–132, 144–145, 183, 189

Szold, Henrietta, 75
Szyk, Arthur, xi, 13, 29–31, 193–194

Tallith, praying shawl, 118, 121, 123, 143, 190, 226n19
Tanuan Airfield, 64
Tapp, Jim, 71
Tarawa, 115, 117, 176, 178
Taylor, Maxwell, 77
Teheran, 15, 77
Tel Aviv, 80
Tepper, Irving, 8, 111
Texas, 21, 25, 34, 36, 51, 53, 57–58, 137
The Ninety-Nines, 62
The Quan, 157
Tikkun olam, Repairing the world, 27, 130, 169, 192
Tinian, Mariana islands
Tokyo, Japan, 117, 136, 161
Tomases, Ralph, 42, 173–174, 184–185
Torah, readings, 131
  Torah scrolls, Torah ark, 132, 224n70
Torch (code name), *see* Operation Torch
Tregaskis, Richard, 122
Truman, Harry, 71, 77, 85, 161, 177, 222n18
Trump, Donald, 150
Trumpeldor, Joseph, 29, 150
Tu B'Shevat *see* New Year of Trees
Tunisia, 5, 8, 13, 96, 98, 102–105, 108, 110, 112, 213n24, 214n29
  Tunisian campaign, 113, 175–176
  Tunis, 110, 114
  Tunisian Jewry, 104–105, 108
Tuskegee Airmen, 32, 70, 165–166
Twelfth Air Force Service Command, 111

US Army, See also *specific military units*, 6–7, 37, 161, 179
US Army Air Forces (USAAF or AAF), 4, 70, 138–139
  Air Force Reserve, 182
  Air Force School of Air Evacuation, 26, 63
  Air medal, 64, 226n10
US Army Signal Corps, 78
  US Army Special Services School, 37
US Coast Guard, 3
US Navy's Bureau of Yards and Docks, 167
USS. Hunt, 75
U-2 submarine, 179
Underground (France), 59
United Nations, 73–74
United Service Organizations, 193

Index  249

United States Military Academy, 14, 77, 96, 115
United States Naval Academy, 75
United States Naval Reserve, 21, 80
US Nixon's Women's Advisory Committee on Aviation, 62
University of Pennsylvania, 104
University of South California, 169
Urban, Robert, 54
USO-Perez center of Jewish military activities, 128
USS Dorchester, 180
USS Harry F. Bauer, 181
USS Lansdale, 181
USSR *see* Soviet Union

Veteran Administration/ V.A, 153
Vichy legislation, Vichy laws, ix, 97
Vichy Regime, Vichy Government, Vichy France, Vichy authorities, 8, 29, 95–98, 102, 107–109, 113, 212n1, 216n36
Victimization, 16, 69, 92
Vienna, Austria, 14, 18, 101, 143
Virginia, 37
Visibility of Jews, 31–37, 43–44, 49–50, 178
Volunteers, 70, 75–76, 112, 151, 153

WACs (Women's Army Corps), ix, 3, 12, 22, 63, 67, 126, 163, 172, 186
Wagner-Rogers Bill, 89
Wainwright, Jonathan M, 150
Wake Island, 115, 157
War of Independence in 1948, 72, 77–78, 208n31, 212n89
War Records Bureau, 9, 49, 84
Warsaw ghetto, 19
Washington, John P., 179
Waters, Edward, 50
WAVES (Women Accepted for Volunteer Emergency Service), 3, 22, 186, 197n10
Weinstein, Alfred Abraham, 138–146, 154–158, 173, 181–182, 191
Werfel, Louis (Eliezer), 9, 110–111, 215n46
West Point, 76–77, 85–86, 88, 93, 147, 168
    West Point Cemetery, West Point Military cemetery, 77, 93, 208n31
Western Desert, The, 11
Westover Field, 40
Williams Field, 61

Williamsburg, 92
Wolk, Bruce, 39, 165
Wolke, Marshall, 130–132
Women
    mothers, 41, 145
    wives, 26, 72, 89, 131, 134, 141, 156, 158, 165, 174, 176, 180–181, 201n4, 212n89, 216n35, 219n23, 220n59
    nurses, Army Nurse Corps, 3–4, 12, 22, 25–27, 34, 50–52, 62–67, 126, 152–154, 170–171, 182, 186, 191–192
    flight nurses, 12, 51, 62–66, 186
    Jewish nurses, 26–27, 34
    Navy Nurse Corps, 22
    Sabotage, 56, 61
    Servicewomen, 1, 4, 6, 16, 22, 27, 35, 66–67, 128, 171–172, 177, 186–187, 189
        Jewish servicewomen, 3–4, 9, 12–13, 16, 27–28, 32, 35, 50, 64, 74–75, 93, 118, 126, 130, 136–137, 183, 186, 191
    sexist attitudes, 187
    WASP (Women Airforce Service Pilots), 4, 12, 16, 21–25, 33, 36, 39, 51–62, 66–68, 163, 186–187, 200n27, 204n22, 205n30
    WAVES, Women Accepted for Volunteer Emergency Service, 3, 22, 186, 197n10
    winged angels, 62–63
    women's contributions, 67, 186
    women pilots, Jewish women pilots, Jewish woman mechanic, 4, 12, 24–25, 27–28, 51–52, 56–67, 186–187, 204n54
    Women's Transcontinental Air Races, 4, 59
World Jewish Congress (WJC), 113
World War I, First World War, 6, 11, 21–22, 29, 91, 97, 147, 157, 165, 167, 180, 186, 205n34, 210n71
Wouk, Herman, 80–81, 208n31
Wyman, David, 86

Xenophobia, 82, 89, 130

Yale University, 60
Yalta, 15, 77
Yellin, Jerry (Jerome), 69–71, 129, 180–182, 188, 192, 225n73
Yellin, Larry, 86–89, 125, 211n74, 212n93
Yiddish, 23, 43, 46, 75, 77, 80, 102, 132–133, 135, 174

YIVO Institute for Jewish Research, 3, 81, 84, 91, 100–101, 104, 110, 127, 132
Yokohama, Japan, 182

Zagreb, 166
Zalkin, Norman, 165
Zamaloff (Dworkin), Jeanne, 22–23, 172
Zamperini, Louis, 157
Zaslow, Harry, 184, 208n33

Zaslow, Milton, 159–163, 192
Zera, Max E., 113, 175–176
Zerah, Denise, 214n29
Zionist, Zionism, Zionists, 46, 74–76, 80–81, 85–86, 101, 134, 191
   Zionist aspirations, 69, 74, 80
   Zionist views, Zionist vision, 7, 130
   Labor Zionism, 134
Zirnheld, André, 10–11
Zoot suits, 54

**Specific Military Units**

1st Infantry Division, 113, 175
101st Airborne Division, 77
102nd Infantry Regiment, 170
105th Infantry Regiment, 169–170
106th Infantry Division, 184, 218n10
116th Infantry Regiment, 40
136th Evacuation Hospital, 171
20th Air Force, 37, 136
20th Bomber Command, 37
27th Infantry Division, 77–78, 169, 170
28th Infantry Regiment, 8th Infantry Division, 46
32nd Infantry Division, 10
283rd Field Artillery Battalion, 184
297th General Hospital Unit, 26

332nd Fighter Group, 165
388th Bomb group, 89
42nd "Rainbow" Infantry Division, 45, 78
45th Field Hospital, 170
526th Fighter Bomber Squadron, 109
3rd Air Commando group, 31
560th Bomb Squadron, 89
58th Bomber Wing, 167
78th Fighter Squadron, 70
804th MAES squadron, 63–64
82nd Airborne Division, 19, 185
86th Infantry Division, 88
89th Field Artillery Battalion, 123, 190
8th Air Force, 209, n.57
9th Infantry Division, 111

FRANÇOISE S. OUZAN is Senior Research Associate at the Goldstein-Goren Diaspora Research Center of Tel Aviv University. A historian, she is the author or co-editor of 11 books, most recently, *How Young Holocaust Survivors Rebuilt Their Lives*. She has a PhD in history from Sorbonne University (Paris).

FOR INDIANA UNIVERSITY PRESS

Lesley Bolton, *Project Manager/Editor*
Brian Carroll, *Rights Manager*
Gary Dunham, *Acquisitions Editor and Director*
Anna Francis, *Assistant Acquisitions Editor*
Brenna Hosman, *Production Coordinator*
Katie Huggins, *Production Manager*
Dan Pyle, *Online Publishing Manager*
Leyla Salamova, *Book Designer*
Stephen Williams, *Marketing and Publicity Manager*

www.ingramcontent.com/pod-product-compliance
Lightning Source LLC
Chambersburg PA
CBHW030615230426
43661CB00053B/1998